D1441893

WRITERS AND THEIR HOUSES

A window in Dove Cottage

WRITERS AND THEIR HOUSES

A GUIDE TO THE WRITERS' HOUSES OF ENGLAND,
SCOTLAND, WALES AND IRELAND

ESSAYS BY MODERN WRITERS

―――――

EDITED BY

KATE MARSH

WITH PHOTOGRAPHS BY

HARLAND WALSHAW AND PETER BURTON

HAMISH HAMILTON · LONDON

HAMISH HAMILTON LTD

Published by the Penguin Group
Penguin Books Ltd, 27 Wrights Lane, London W8 5TZ, England
Penguin Books USA Inc., 375 Hudson Street, New York, New York 10014, USA
Penguin Books Australia Ltd, Ringwood, Victoria, Australia
Penguin Books Canada Ltd, 10 Alcorn Avenue, Toronto, Ontario, Canada M4V 3B2
Penguin Books (NZ) Ltd, 182–190 Wairau Road, Auckland 10, New Zealand

Penguin Books Ltd, Registered Offices: Harmondsworth, Middlesex, England

First published 1993
1 3 5 7 9 10 8 6 4 2

Individual contributions are held in copyright © by the individual contributors, 1993
Introduction and general editorial matter copyright © Kate Marsh, 1993

The moral right of the authors has been asserted

All rights reserved.
Without limiting the rights under copyright
reserved above, no part of this publication may be
reproduced, stored in or introduced into a retrieval system,
or transmitted, in any form or by any means (electronic, mechanical,
photocopying, recording or otherwise), without the prior
written permission of both the copyright owner and
the above publisher of this book

Every care has been taken to ensure the accuracy of the information contained in this
book. The Arts Council and the Tourist Boards of England, Scotland, Wales and Ireland
cannot accept responsibility for any errors or omissions

Filmset in Monophoto Baskerville by Selwood Systems, Midsomer Norton
Printed in Great Britain by Butler & Tanner Ltd, Frome and London

A CIP catalogue record for this book is available from the British Library
ISBN 0–241–12769–6

CONTENTS

───────

CONTENTS

CONTENTS

CONTENTS

FOREWORD

MELVYN BRAGG

The pleasure of this collection is that it is written by authors whose own work inspires a respect comparable with those they are writing about. It opens with P. D. James, who begins with an incisive essay on Jane Austen and her house at Chawton, but what would we not give for a prowl around the crannies of the home of P. D. James herself? Seamus Heaney concludes with an aspect of his continuing absorption with Yeats; Heaney's hidden cottage, less than an hour's drive from Dublin, gives him as much as the Tower of which he writes gives Yeats.

The book ripples with the energy of love and knowledge felt by contemporary writers for their precursors. There is a deep sense of association and even of camaraderie. Here the addresses are given; the rooms are prepared; the keys are handed over. They are all yours, these homes, as useful a part of our heritage as palaces and manor houses, and often much more interesting because of the presence of someone you already know.

The location of the houses is often of the greatest significance – for inspiration, for subject matter, for the best working out of the balance between the life and the work. Wordsworth's Lake District, Hardy's Dorset, Dickens's London, Yeats's Galway and Sligo, Gilbert White's Selborne, Joyce's Dublin, George Eliot's Warwickshire and of course the land of the Brontës – the Yorkshire moors above Haworth Parsonage – all come into this category. In these places a visitor can still today walk out of a house and into landscapes which have barely changed since the writer drew breath from them and breathed literature into them.

If this book entertains those who love their authors, it will have achieved a lot. If it prompts its readers to set out on one or several journeys, then it makes promises it will keep. For the places you set out for offer clues to some of the richest minds in our history.

ACKNOWLEDGEMENTS

All the photographs are the copyright of Harland Walshaw and Peter Burton with the exception of the following: Byron, p 93, John Murray Publishers Ltd; Carlyle in his garden at Cheyne Row, p 101, National Trust Photographic Library; Thomas Carlyle, 1854, and Jane Carlyle, 1838, p 100, National Portrait Gallery, London; Disraeli, p 177, National Portrait Gallery, London; Max Gate, Dorchester, p 209, and Thomas Hardy, p 210, the trustees of the Thomas Hardy Memorial Collection and Dorset County Museum; James Joyce, 1904, p 245, University College, Dublin Library, and Mrs Elizabeth Solterer; D. H. Lawrence, 1908, p 274, Nottingham County Library Services; T. E. Lawrence, 1935, p 280, Liddell Hart Centre for Military Archives, King's College, London; bust of Alexander Pope, p 309, Mr & Mrs Donald Gadge of Hanworth; Vita Sackville-West, p 343, Nigel Nicolson; Bernard Shaw, p 375, British Library of Political & Economic Science, and the Society of Authors; Dylan Thomas, p 426, the National Museum of Wales and Vivien White; W. B. Yeats, p 483, National Library of Ireland.

The first two quotations in the essay on Charles Dickens are reprinted from the *Pilgrim Edition of the Letters of Charles Dickens* (vols. 1–7, 1982–93) by permission of the Oxford University Press. The third quotation is reprinted from *Dickens: Interviews and Recollections* by Philip Collins (1981) by permission of Macmillan Education Ltd.

Material from Boswell's Letters and Journals is quoted with the permission of Yale University, and information from the Introduction to the forthcoming edition of Boswell's correspondence relating to the estate of Auchinleck has been included with the permission of the editor, Dr John Strawhorn.

Part of the contents of the essay on W. B. Yeats appeared in a slightly different form in *The Place of Writing* (1988) published by Scholars Press, Atlanta, Georgia.

This book is the result of a collaboration between the Arts Council of Great Britain and the National Tourist Boards of England, Scotland, Wales and Ireland. It arose from a recognition that the houses in which great authors once lived are of serious interest to the many readers who cherish their work, and that they may introduce visitors to books they may not have known before. We have sought in the book to create imaginative partnerships between writers of the past and the present.

We hope the houses will attract new friends as a consequence of the book and that its readers will be tempted to explore parts of the British Isles which were previously unknown to them.

INTRODUCTION

This book is about famous writers whose houses are open to the public – their lives, their work and the homes in which they lived. The contributors are in the main themselves well-known writers. Each gives a personal view.

The selection does not of course contain every major writer in the canon of English literature. Nevertheless, the representation is surprisingly broad. It commences in the sixteenth and seventeenth centuries with Sidney, Shakespeare and Milton. It then moves into the eighteenth century with figures as disparate as Robert Burns, the Scots farmer and excise officer; urban dwellers such as Alexander Pope, Samuel Johnson and Horace Walpole; and two country parsons, Laurence Sterne and William Cowper. The novelists Jane Austen, the Brontë sisters and Sir Walter Scott come in the first half of the nineteenth century together with the Romantic poets John Keats, Lord Byron, William Wordsworth and S. T. Coleridge. Shortly afterwards there are four Victorians who shared a concern for social improvement – Charles Dickens, Thomas Carlyle, William Morris and John Ruskin. A group of front-ranking novelists takes us into the twentieth century – Thomas Hardy, Henry James, D. H. Lawrence, James Joyce and Virginia Woolf – all of whom made major contributions to the development of the modern novel. Hardy was also an influential poet; indeed, he was one of the first to introduce a modern tone to English poetry. He is accompanied in the twentieth century by W. B. Yeats and Dylan Thomas, both of whom emerged from Celtic backgrounds on to the international stage. Finally, there is Bernard Shaw, who, despite living into his nineties, remained the *enfant terrible* of twentieth-century theatre. Moreover, there are others, who, although impressive writers, are not necessarily thought of as literary figures, such as Charles Darwin, Gilbert White, Winston Churchill and T. E. Lawrence.

The collection also includes six authors whose houses are not open to the public, namely Rupert Brooke, John Bunyan, William Cobbett, George Eliot, Mrs Gaskell and R. L. Stevenson. They are added to the roll because it is possible to go to places with which they are associated and to visit landmarks, buildings and museums connected with their life and work.

We extend our knowledge of a person when we look at his home. We draw conclusions about his taste, aspirations, money and preoccupations. It is one of the ways in which he expresses himself. We are likely to view the houses occupied by these writers with the same natural curiosity that Jane Austen's characters displayed when they studied their neighbours. If we already know and love their work, we will examine them with intense interest, even with reverence. Our curiosity will be rewarded to the extent that the house we visit successfully shows the kind of life the writer led and the period in which he lived. This success will depend on the scholarship and care with which his home has been conserved or reconstructed, and on the chattels that have been retained – furniture, personal belongings, manuscripts, books. Such sensory markers evoke strong intimations of the writer's personality and life. Some writers' houses have been partially converted into museums with glass cases exhibiting manuscripts, letters and objects, and biographical information provided on panels and displays. Sometimes the reconstructions are rather theatrical, and may even include model figures in contemporary dress. Such presentations anchor our minds on the writer and tell a story. But they can also detract from the atmosphere of the house.

A deeper bond with the writer is established when we realize that we are seeing the same view or garden that the writer saw daily; that we are feeling a similar sense of space or confinement in his study or drawing-room, hall or passageway. Cheyne Row is small and dark, and if it seemed a castle to the Carlyles at first, a sense of confinement must have grown with the years. Like some of the other writers, Carlyle moved his study from room to room, finally creating a sound-proof eyrie at the top of the house, lit only by a skylight and insulated from the noise of his neighbours by a passageway between its walls and the outer walls of the house. Bernard Shaw's house, an ugly late nineteenth-century rectory, has no beauty of proportion inside to compensate for its exterior. Its furnishings, which remain as they were when he died, show an absence of taste: he clearly lacked a developed visual sense. But we can escape as he did to the tiny hut at the bottom of his garden, which was just large enough for a table, chair and bunk, and which he could rotate to catch the sunlight throughout the day. During his many years at Max Gate, Hardy moved his study into three different rooms, each facing a different direction and each affording him a different view. Kipling's study at Bateman's, though oak-panelled like most of the rooms, is sunny and spacious with a fine aspect over the gardens to the Sussex countryside. It speaks of the peace he finally found there. From the windows of his spacious and elegant library, Walter Scott could look out on the River Tweed running parallel to the house beyond his terraced garden, as we can today. Dylan Thomas's 'sea-shaked house' in south

Wales is poised over the Tâf estuary, commanding wide expanses of coastline, sea and sky, where he could wake to sounds

> ... from harbour and neighbour wood
> And the mussel pooled and the heron
> Priested shore.

We walk in our writers' footsteps and see through their eyes when we enter these spaces.

The birthplaces, even where they were not occupied for long, tell us directly about their famous offspring and reveal a great deal about their early lives. We become aware of a mystery when we see the small dwellings, the deprivation and the ugliness into which some of these writers were born. When we first view the cottage at Alloway where Burns was born, the miracle that a poet of his stature should emerge from farm labourers' stock and his talent prosper in such hard conditions immediately strikes us. The cottage at Higher Bockhampton built by Hardy's great-grandfather, just one room downstairs and one above when Hardy was a small child, although later extended, evokes a shock of wonder. The unremarkable, modest terraced house in Portsmouth which was Dickens's birthplace does nothing to signal the event of a novelist of enormous energy and originality. The coal-miners' terraces which were D. H. Lawrence's early homes, set in the undistinguished contours of Eastwood on the borders of Nottinghamshire and Derbyshire, appear positively adverse circumstances in which a poet and novelist of genius could be reared. James Joyce lived the first twenty-two years of his life in a succession of unprepossessing, run-down suburban Dublin houses; not an auspicious beginning, and yet the city furnished him with subject-matter for a lifetime. These early experiences worked deep in the imagination to emerge, transmuted, years later.

The impact of some houses and landscapes on a writer's imagination is more obvious. The Brontë girls' lives and novels were moulded by the bleak, windswept landscape of the North Yorkshire moors, and by the setting of their isolated, hilltop parsonage among the gravestones of the Haworth parishioners. The view from every window reminded them of their mortality. This house has perhaps the most compelling atmosphere of all: dark millstone grit of house and church; flat, wet, gleaming tombstones lying between them, with a choir of tall, upright ones crowded together a little further off. Wordsworth's poetic inspiration was grounded in his childhood experiences in the countryside around Cockermouth and nourished by the grandeur, beauty and terror of the Cumbrian landscapes near his houses at Grasmere and Rydal Mount. When W. B. Yeats bought his tower by its rushing stream, standing sentinel in the empty Galway countryside, he acquired a physical symbol which pre-figured the conceptual symbol that played such a key role in his later poetry.

Sometimes the writers actively set out to acquire houses and surroundings to suit the way they wanted to live. Gad's Hill, near Rochester, which Dickens liked when he saw it as a child and bought when he was forty-five, is a comfortable, roomy villa built in about 1780, which was set in a homely garden with a croquet lawn and some twenty-six acres of farmland adjoining it. It has no aspirations to grandeur, any more than its owner had. Hill Top, the Lake District cottage which Beatrix Potter, like Dickens, bought out of her literary earnings, is unpretentious in the extreme. Max Gate, designed by Hardy himself and built by his brother on the edge of Dorchester and the Dorset country of the novels, is a fairly ugly, commodious town villa. It bears comparison with Shaw's Corner, which is hidden in a surprisingly unspoilt part of Hertfordshire. None shouts of wealth or fame. It is evident that these writers were not interested in acquiring houses which would be emblems of the rise in their fortunes and social position. In the main, they are houses where the occupants settled and put down roots in the years of their maturity.

Neither were the more remarkable houses acquired as symbols of affluence. Strawberry Hill and Abbotsford, which were the wildly extravagant creations of Horace Walpole and Sir Walter Scott, were designed and their contents collected with the love and energy which most writers reserve for their books. They gave their owners tremendous pleasure and satisfied other obsessions. Sissinghurst garden was made by Vita Sackville-West and Harold Nicolson with the same sort of creative intensity. When Byron inherited Newstead Abbey, a grand, monastic building set in sweeping parkland and facing a large lake, it was fast falling into ruin. Its operatic atmosphere is peculiarly appropriate to the author of *Don Juan*; indeed, it provides the backcloth for some of the best scenes in the poem. But he never had the money to restore it and for a short time led an eccentric life in its crumbling rooms and draughty corridors before selling it.

While all these houses afforded protection from prying eyes, some were consciously chosen as retreats from the world. They have a hidden, secretive quality about them. Darwin protected himself from the impact of his revolutionary discoveries by buying a large eighteenth-century house in a quiet village some miles outside London. He continued his experiments behind a smoke-screen of family and local community life. Gilbert White could not settle until he returned to the extended fifteenth-century cottage in the sleepy Hampshire village where he had been brought up. His house, The Wakes, lies unobtrusively at the foot of Hanger Wood, the vast bank of beech trees where he conducted many of his naturalist explorations. Clouds Hill, where T. E. Lawrence sheltered from the barrack room, set in a protective ring of hedges and trees, has every appearance of a deliberate hiding-place.

The grand houses included here are important in their own right as fine pieces of architecture, and are conserved and open to the public for this reason. Penshurst and Knole are visited for their splendour and history, rather than for their connections with Sir Philip Sidney and Vita Sackville-West. Knebworth House, Hughenden Manor, Renishaw Hall and Stanton Harcourt have a historical and architectural value, as well as an association with writers. But the ordinary houses of their period included in this book would probably not have survived intact were it not for their famous occupants. They would certainly not be accessible to the public. It is unusual to be able to see the unspoilt interiors of vernacular buildings of the past, like the eighteenth-century rural cottages of Wordsworth and Burns, Jane Austen's seventeenth-century village house, and Dr Johnson's two eighteenth-century town houses.

The houses associated with Shakespeare in and around Stratford-upon-Avon enable the visitor to experience some classic examples of middle-class Tudor houses. Anne Hathaway's cottage in the village of Shottery, some of which dates from the fifteenth century, and the substantial sixteenth-century farmhouse and farm buildings at Wilmcote which was the home of Mary Arden, Shakespeare's mother, are fine buildings. No major alterations have been made to them, and the simplicity of the interiors allows the original structures to be plainly seen. The rooms have been recreated to show how the families would have lived, and furniture of the period is displayed – in fact Anne Hathaway's cottage has some pieces which it seems have never left the house. Hall's Croft in Stratford itself, which is thought to have belonged to Shakespeare's daughter and son-in-law, is a handsome, detached town house, its elegant rooms enhanced by fine Elizabethan and Jacobean furniture. Shakespeare's birthplace in Henley Street may be less impressive; however, it is fitting that it should be the first house of literary pilgrimage: visits by admirers of Shakespeare began in the early eighteenth century. These houses are partly historical museums, but with their carefully preserved exteriors and reconstructed interiors they provide a richer encounter with the past than could be achieved in an ordinary museum setting.

The houses which have museums attached to them tell us overtly about the writer's career in contrast to those which conserve his life-style and leave us to intuit his world. The most successful museums are the ones located in buildings separate from the writer's house. The Wordsworth Museum in Grasmere has a permanent exhibition devoted to Wordsworth and his contemporaries, and displays new exhibitions featuring figures and themes of the Romantic period. In a modern, purpose-designed setting, books, manuscripts, paintings and objects are linked by instructive commentaries. There is nothing to interfere with the experience of visiting Dove Cottage, which remains almost unchanged since the early nineteenth century. The Burns Museum at Alloway, with its scholarly archive of letters, books and manuscripts, as well as its more obvious didactic portrayals of the history of

Burns's life and career, is a separate building from the cottage. The original structure of the cottage is as it was in 1757, just a byre, kitchen and parlour leading out of each other, and can be seen without any loss to its own peculiar character. The wealth of Dickens material on view at the Dickens House Museum in Doughty Street in London represents an immense work of scholarship which is more informative about the man, his writings and the characters he created than perhaps any other collection. But the glass cases which are crammed into the small rooms inevitably convert the house from a home into a museum. The exceptions are the dining-room and the drawing-room, which are furnished with some of Dickens's own furniture and retain an original atmosphere. At Shandy Hall, Sterne's own library houses a collection of first and early editions of his work, manuscripts, newspapers for which he wrote, works he used for reference in editions he would have known, and early editions of books by his eighteenth-century contemporaries. Here the scholarship, and the careful restoration of the house so that it is now virtually as it was in Sterne's time, perfectly complement each other. They are a tribute to the love and personal commitment of the curators who rescued the house from ruin.

The pursuit of writers' houses also introduces us to unspoilt landscapes which remain the same as they were when the writers knew them and drew inspiration from them. Grasmere Vale and Rydal Water are as impressive now as they were when they formed Wordsworth's daily vision. Magnificent views of Coniston Lake and the Old Man of Coniston are still framed in the windows of Ruskin's Brantwood. They explain how he could have bought the house without seeing it first; he knew the Lakes well, and knowing its position was sufficient.

Likewise, the countryside Burns and Scott saw, and walked over, is still much the same. A journey through the Lowlands of Scotland from Burns's cottage in Alloway on the west coast to Scott's Abbotsford in Melrose takes the visitor through a marvellous, changing landscape. The farms where Burns tried to make a living can be seen in the gently undulating countryside of Ayrshire. (The one open to visitors is Ellisland, which lies north of Dumfries in a fine setting on the banks of the River Nith.) Later the farmland is replaced by mountains, rivers, forests and moorland as the traveller continues eastward. Eventually the Tweed, one of the most beautiful rivers in the country, brings us down to Abbotsford, which stands among fields and trees beside the river and against a backdrop of hills rising steeply behind it. The contrast between the dwellings of Scotland's two most famous writers – Burns's two-roomed cottage and the neo-Gothic, baronial Abbotsford – is extreme.

If we go to the town of Laugharne, to Dylan Thomas's boathouse and to 'the blithe country' with its 'legends of green chapels' about which he wrote, we can share his inspiration. The bare, rocky land near Gort in Galway provides a counterpoint to Yeats's magical lakes and mountains of Sligo. A strong response to these landscapes is inescapable. They send us back to the writers' work with renewed excitement and a fresh vision.

There are numerous historical towns which can be visited on these trails – Cambridge, near Rupert Brooke's Grantchester, Thomas Hardy's Dorchester and Henry James's Rye, Dr Johnson's Lichfield, and York, on the way to Sterne's Coxwold. There is often the surprise of the unexpected, such as the little-known town of Olney, where Cowper's house stands in the centre. With its fine, unspoilt grey-stone façades, it returns us to the elegance of the eighteenth century.

This book differs from other studies of the literary contours of Great Britain in that each chapter is written by a modern writer who has a special knowledge of the period described and an interest in the figure discussed. There are poets on poets; novelists on novelists; biographers and historians on their special subjects; and an actor on Shakespeare. There are personal connections between some of the contributors and the writers they portray. Glyn Jones knew Dylan Thomas; Tim Pigott-Smith was brought up in Stratford-upon-Avon and went to the same school as Shakespeare; Mary Archer lives in the house associated with Rupert Brooke; Philip Mason, who writes on Kipling, spent twenty years in the Indian Civil Service. It also includes many strong black-and-white photographs which present the houses from dramatic as well as intimate angles. The lens of the photographers, Harland Walshaw and Peter Burton, has a special intensity and surprises us into seeing sharply the domestic world the writers knew.

The reader is not burdened with a mass of detailed historical, architectural or literary facts. Each essay has a different voice. In the space of a few pages the contributor gives a lively and informative description of the writer, his work and his home. *Writers and Their Houses* awakens our interest in the writers it includes and encourages us to read or reread their work. It urges us to plan visits to their houses or to make detours from other journeys to see them. Its role is to direct the reader to unfamiliar landscapes and new literary territory. It is a guide to discovery.

WRITERS AND THEIR HOUSES

JANE AUSTEN

CHAWTON, HAMPSHIRE

P. D. JAMES

Not every famous writer has cared particularly about the place where he did his writing, and not every writer's house has had a significant influence on the work produced within its walls. Chawton, the cottage in Hampshire where from 1809 Jane Austen lived for the last eight years of her short life, was a notable exception. It was in this modest brick-built house that her genius reached its fruition, and it was here that she found that mixture of rural peace, ordered domestic routine and mild stimulation which best suited her character and her art. The five years preceding the move to Chawton were unsettled and unproductive with her writing virtually at a stop, and it can be argued that, without this unpretentious final home, Jane Austen's name would be little more than a footnote in literary history.

For the first twenty-five years of her life Jane Austen had been a happy member of the large, cheerful and intelligent family of the Reverend George Austen and his wife, Cassandra, at the rectory at Steventon in Hampshire. There were eight children, and Jane, born in 1775, was the second daughter. In 1801 Mr Austen handed over the living to his eldest son, James, and retired to Bath with his wife and daughters. This move, about which Jane was not consulted, was a great shock to her. Although Bath provided her with her first real experience of city life, she was never happy there, disliking its noise and glare as much as did her gentle heroine, Anne Elliott. After Mr Austen's death in 1805 Jane, her mother and her sister Cassandra moved to Southampton to the home of her brother Frank, later to become an Admiral of the Fleet. She spent a few years there with periodic visits to her brother Henry in London until, in 1809, Mrs Austen and her two daughters were offered a permanent home at Chawton on the estate of her brother Edward. They moved in with their friend Martha Lloyd on 7 July 1809.

Edward Austen's lot in life was peculiarly fortunate. In boyhood he took the fancy of the wife of a wealthy distant kinsman, Thomas Knight of Chawton House

Jane Austen's house at Chawton, from the garden

in Hampshire, and Godmersham Park in Kent. The couple had no children of their own and in due course Mr Knight adopted Edward, gave him his name and made him heir to his property. One wonders what Jane Austen thought of this severance of a child from his natural family and whether she shared the view of the warm-hearted Mrs John Knightly in *Emma*. 'To give up one's child! I really never could think well of anybody who proposed such a thing to anybody else.' But the adoption proved fortunate for Mrs Austen and her two spinster daughters who were, inevitably in that age, dependent on sons and brothers to provide a roof over their heads. They must have been relieved, as was Mrs Dashwood in *Sense and Sensibility*, to have a home of their own, and one can imagine them carefully arranging their books and pictures as did the Dashwood sisters when they took possession of their very similar cottage. In November 1808 Jane wrote to her sister Cassandra: 'There are six bed-chambers at Chawton. Henry wrote to my mother the other day and luckily mentioned the number, which is just what we want to be assured of. He speaks also of garrets with store-places, one of which he immediately planned the fitting-up for Edward's manservant, and now perhaps it must be for our own, for she is quite reconciled to our keeping one.' She wrote too to Frank expressing her delight in verse:

> Our Chawton home, how much we find
> Already in it to our mind;
> And how convinced that when complete
> It will all other houses beat
> That ever have been made or mended
> With rooms concise or rooms distended.

Chawton village lies outside Alton, south of the Winchester–Alton road, now the A31. The road passed through the village until the construction of a by-pass in recent years restored to it a measure of the peace and tranquillity it must have enjoyed before the age of the motor-car, making a visit today easier and more pleasant than it was in my childhood. Cottage is perhaps a slight misnomer. What we see is an unpretentious seventeenth-century house of red brick, sprucely painted, lovingly cared for and, although undoubtedly more prosperous-looking than when the Austens moved in, essentially the same. It is possible to visit the interiors of the houses of some dead celebrities and feel that we are viewing the rooms as they were once lived in, but this is usually possible only with larger family houses handed down through the generations when basic changes may be minimal. Jane Austen's cottage is not, of course, such a house, and it suffered many vicissitudes after the death of Cassandra Austen in 1845. It was then divided into three cottages for farm-workers, and it was a hundred years later that it was bought by Mr T. Edward Carpenter and opened in 1949 as a museum dedicated both to the memory of

Jane Austen and to his son, Philip John Carpenter, killed in Italy in June 1944.

Essentially what we discover at Chawton is not a carefully reconstructed period home but a small museum devoted to Jane Austen and her family, with family portraits, silhouettes and mementoes, costume displays, original letters written by Jane's parents and sister, contemporary pictures of Chawton and early editions of the novels. The arrangement of the rooms is basically unaltered since Jane Austen's day and, although the modern wallpaper strikes one with a small shock of recognition, it is appropriate in style and pattern. Some of the original furniture is there, notably the table in the dining-parlour which Jane Austen used when she

The parlour, showing Jane's writing-table and the tea and coffee cupboard

was writing, and a delicately painted cane chair in what was her bedroom. Of particular interest, too, are the two topaz crosses which Charles, the younger sailor brother, bought with his prize-money as gifts for Jane and Cassandra, reminding one of the cross which William Price gave to his beloved Fanny in *Mansfield Park*. Hanging on the wall of Jane's bedroom is the patchwork quilt designed in the old English medallion pattern on which she and her mother worked together while they lived at Chawton. It is fascinating to speculate which patches of material came from her own dresses, and it is obvious that scraps were also collected from other members of the family. Jane wrote to Cassandra: 'Have you remembered to collect pieces for the patchwork? We are now at a standstill.'

Edward Austen (now Edward Knight) had taken trouble to make the cottage comfortable for the Austen ladies. A large window to the left of the front door was bricked up and the left-hand parlour made to look out on to the garden. The right-hand parlour served as a dining-room, and Mrs Knight received an account of the family 'looking very comfortable at breakfast' there from a gentleman who was travelling by their door in a post-chaise. Although the garden at the back was, and still is, very peaceful, the small household had the stimulus of the road and could watch the passing traffic, including post-chaises taking boys back to Winchester College, among them Jane Austen's nephews. The left-hand parlour was the larger of the two main rooms and it was here that Jane kept her piano, but it was in the right-hand room that she did her writing, and one can imagine her looking up at the occasional passing horseman or watching for visitors. She had no separate study to which she could retire and she was invariably subject to interruptions, her only protection being the creaking hinges of the door which gave her warning that someone was coming, when she would slip her writing under the blotting-pad.

When Mr Knight's numerous family were at Chawton House, interruptions must have been frequent, but no member of the family has ever recorded that his or her visit was unwelcome or resented. But the situation must have been frustrating for a writer. A novelist moves into the life of her characters, and during the process of writing their world becomes more real than her own. Nothing is more frustrating than to be arbitrarily summoned back from it, particularly when the work is going well or the interruption is trivial. Jane Austen may not have betrayed this frustration to her family, but her letters show that she was very far from the gentle, uncomplaining spinster of popular legend, and undoubtedly she suffered psychological trauma from the conditions under which, all too often, she was compelled to work. Every writer of genius needs, for her physical and mental health as well as for her art, a small inviolate cell of mental privacy, and it is precisely this emotional privacy that, for much of her life, Jane Austen was denied. In particular, there is ample evidence in her novels of her dislike of noisy and over-indulged children. One remembers the young Lucases visiting Longbourn in *Pride and Prejudice*, the ill-disciplined children of Mary Musgrove in *Persuasion* and the demanding, pampered darlings of Lady Middleton in *Sense and Sensibility*. There can be no doubt that Jane Austen could echo the words of Elinor Dashwood: 'I never think of tame and quiet children with any abhorrence.' Edward had offered his mother and sisters a home near his Godmersham property as an alternative to the Chawton cottage, and it seems likely that they chose the latter to lessen by distance the demands made on unmarried aunts by Edward's growing and rumbustious family.

But apart from this, the life at Chawton Cottage suited Jane admirably. As it was a household without men and the Austens naturally had some servants, the daily round of domestic duties cannot have been arduous and left Jane time and energy to take up again her creative writing. Cassandra Austen was largely responsible for the housekeeping, and all lovers of Jane Austen are deeply indebted to her for her watchful protection of her sister's talent. As Jane wrote during one of her sister's absences: 'I find composition impossible with my head full of joints of mutton and doses of rhubarb.' But Jane prepared the breakfast which they would have eaten together in the small front-room, and she was in charge of the tea and coffee kept locked in the cupboard next to the fire-grate, which is still there. The garden at the rear of the house was Mrs Austen's responsibility and her great pleasure where, clad in an old smock, she would dig potatoes as happily as she tended her flowers. The garden was considerably larger than it is now, since we know from Jane Austen's letters that there was an orchard, a shrubbery large enough for their daily exercise, a vegetable garden and a field for a couple of donkeys. We can still see her donkey-carriage in the bakehouse.

It can be argued that Edward Austen, despite the claims of his own large family, could have done rather more for his widowed mother and sisters than he did. The Chawton estate account-book for 1808–9 shows, however, that he did spend £45 19s. 0d. on structural alterations and £33 6s. 5d. for plumbing, and that his labourers did various odd-jobs about the cottage, including chopping firewood and trenching the garden for Mrs Austen. There would, too, have been gifts of game while Edward was himself in residence at Chawton House. The income of Mrs Austen and her daughters was small and no doubt they were relieved that the neighbourhood was neither so large nor so prosperous that they were required to entertain frequently. When they moved in, there were only about sixty families in Chawton parish, and most of the four hundred or so inhabitants worked in forestry or as agricultural labourers. The family made friends with a number of people in the village, notably the two unmarried daughters of William Prowting, a magistrate and Deputy Lieutenant of the county, who lived in a larger house set back from the road behind the cottage. Jane would walk from her own garden across the field to call on them and there would, too, be walks in the grounds of Chawton House and trips by donkey-carriage into Alton. The local rector, the Revd John Rawston Papillon, was a bachelor and Mrs Knight Senior

Jane's donkey-carriage in the bakehouse

suggested to Cassandra that he might be a suitable husband for Jane, a proposition which prompted a typical Jane Austen reply: 'I am very much obliged to Mrs Knight for such a proof of the interest she takes in me, and she may depend upon it that I *will* marry Mr Papillon, whatever may be his reluctance or my own – I owe her much more than such a trifling sacrifice.' There was, too, the excitement of periodic visits to London. In September 1813 Jane accompanied Edward and his three eldest daughters when they stayed with Henry Austen at 10 Henrietta Street. Jane wrote to Cassandra describing crowded days of theatre visits, dental appointments for the girls and family commissions at the dressmaker and milliner.

But it was at Chawton Cottage that her creative life was centred and the years following 1809 show a miraculous flowering of her genius. In the winter of 1810 *Sense and Sensibility* was accepted for publication and by February the following year she had begun planning *Mansfield Park*. In 1811 *Sense and Sensibility* was published and probably that winter she began revising 'First Impressions' into the lively and enchanting *Pride and Prejudice*, which was published in 1813. *Emma*, one of the most perfectly constructed novels in the English language, was begun in January 1814 and finished on 29 March 1815, and by August of that year she had started *Persuasion*, which was finished in August 1816. *Sanditon* was begun on 27 January 1817, but she did not live to complete it. The money she gained from the published books was important to her, for she had nothing of her own, although Cassandra had a small income from a thousand pounds left to her by her dead fiancé. In a letter of 3 July 1813 to her sailor brother Frank, Jane wrote: 'You will be glad to know that every copy of *Sense and Sensibility* sold and that it has brought me a hundred and forty pounds beside the copyright ... I have now, therefore, written myself into two hundred and fifty pounds which only makes me long for more.' Jane Austen, the supreme realist, was as unsentimental about money as she was about love and marriage. Referring to the critical reaction to *Mansfield Park*, she wrote: 'Though I like praise as well as anybody I like what Edward calls Pewter too ... Single women have a dreadful propensity for being poor.' If she for a moment forgot what genteel poverty could mean for an unsupported spinster, she had a chilling example to hand in the neighbouring parish of Farringdon, where the middle-aged sister of the poverty-stricken Revd John Benn with his dozen children was reduced to renting a mean, run-down cottage from one of the villagers.

James Austen's younger daughter, Caroline, was a frequent visitor to Chawton Cottage during the years 1809–45, and in the 1860s she recorded her memories of these visits for her brother, James Edward, to use in his memoirs of their Aunt Jane.

> Everything indoors and out was well-kept, the house was well-furnished and it was altogether a comfortable and lady-like establishment, though I believe the means which supported it were but small. My visits to Chawton were very pleasant to me and Aunt Jane was the great charm. As a very little girl I was always creeping up to her and following her whenever I could in the house and out. I might not have remembered this but for the recollection of my mother telling me privately that I must not be troublesome to my aunt. Her charm for children was great sweetness of manner. She loved you and you loved her naturally in return.

Jane Austen's other nieces also record the laughter and fun at Chawton Cottage. Fanny Knight's sister Marianne, who was then eleven, remembered how her aunt and sister had shut themselves in one of the bedrooms to read aloud, probably from *Pride and Prejudice*, and how she heard 'peals of laughter through the door and thought it very hard that we should be shut out from what was so delightful'.

But these settled and happy years at Chawton were not unclouded by anxieties and tragedies. With such a large family it would have been surprising had it been otherwise. In the spring of 1815 the Austens had two serious misfortunes: Charles's ship, the *Phoenix*, was wrecked off the coast of Asia Minor and, although he was acquitted of all blame, 'yet such a misfortune is always a disparagement' and, the war being over, he knew that he was likely to wait a long time for another ship. The other event was even more distressing: Henry Austen's banking business collapsed, with disastrous consequences for investors, including members of the family. But his nature was basically optimistic and he seems to have suffered less than his relations and was soon improving his knowledge of Greek so that he could take holy orders. The next year, too, was not free of anxiety: in particular, there was Henry's serious illness, which brought him close to death, and a lawsuit over the Chawton property which Edward was in danger of losing.

Perhaps as a result of the family misfortunes and anxieties, Jane Austen, early in 1816, began to show symptoms of the illness which a year later was to kill her. It is now almost certain that she was suffering from Addison's disease, a failure of the adrenal cortex first described in 1855, which results in increasing weakness and weight loss, severe gastro-intestinal disturbances and often pain in the back. Jane complained of all these symptoms, together with the brown and black pigmentation of the skin typical of the disease. Her illness progressed inexorably with only the customary short periods of remission to give the family some hope of recovery. Despite increasing weakness she thought more of others than herself, as we know from her niece Caroline's pen-picture of her aunt at this time.

> In my later visits to Chawton Cottage I remember Aunt Jane used often to lie down after dinner. There was only one sofa in the room and Aunt Jane laid upon three chairs which she arranged for herself. I think she had a pillow but it never looked comfortable. I wondered and wondered, for the real sofa was frequently vacant and still she lay in this comfortless manner. I often asked her how she could like the chairs best and I suppose I worried her into telling me the reason for her choice, which was that, if she ever used the sofa, Grandma would be leaving it for her and would not lie down, as she did now, whenever she felt inclined.

There was one final family tragedy which may have precipitated the ultimate decline, as Addison's disease is known to be strongly influenced by mental stress. Jane Austen's uncle, Leigh-Perrot, died on 28 March 1816. He was childless, and Mrs Austen had expected that a legacy would provide some immediate additional security and comfort to the small household at Chawton Cottage. But the money was left elsewhere and the ladies were faced with years of continuing dependency on the charity of sons and brothers, most of whom had large families of their own. From 1816 neither Henry nor Frank continued the payments of fifty pounds apiece to Mrs Austen which they had been making since 1805, and Charles had never been able to contribute anything to his mother's upkeep. Jane Austen's life at Chawton, otherwise so peaceful and so conducive to her art, was never free from financial anxiety.

One of the last people to visit her in the cottage was Caroline.

> She was keeping to her room but said she would see us and so we went up to her. She was in her dressing-gown and was sitting quite like an invalid in her armchair. She got up and kindly greeted us, and then, pointing to seats that had been arranged for us by the fire, she said: 'There's a chair for the married lady and a little stool for you, Caroline.' It is strange that those trifling words are the last of hers that I can remember. I was struck by the alteration in herself. She was very pale and her voice was weak and low and there was about her the general appearance of debility and suffering. She was not equal to the exertion of talking to us and our visit to the sick-room was a very short one. I do not suppose we stayed a quarter of an hour and I never saw Aunt Jane again.

Standing today in that small back room which was Jane Austen's bedroom, beside the original fireplace, one can picture vividly that small family group and share the child's sadness.

On 24 May 1817, a day of heavy rain, Jane and Cassandra set out in James's carriage to cover the sixteen-mile journey to Winchester, where she was to consult Mr Giles Lyford, a surgeon of the county hospital who had already been called in to the case by Mr Curtis of Alton. Rooms had been taken on the first floor of 8 College Street, from which address she wrote:

> We have a neat little drawing-room with a bow-window overlooking Dr Gable's garden ... Mr Lyford says he will cure me and if he fails I shall draw up a memorial and lay it before the Dean and Chapter, and I have no doubt of redress from that pious, learned and disinterested body.

But Mr Lyford's belief that the case was hopeless was soon confirmed, and there is no doubt that Jane Austen herself realized that the temporary improvement which followed her move to Winchester could not last. Caroline Austen later wrote:

> Though she had passed by the hopes and enjoyments of youth, yet its sorrows also were left behind, and Autumn is sometimes so calm an affair that it consoles us for the departure of Spring and Summer. And thus it might have been with her.

There can be little doubt that it would, too, have been an autumn of great literary fruitfulness.

Jane Austen died on the dawn of 18 July in Cassandra's arms and was buried in Winchester Cathedral. Her grave there is a place of pilgrimage but, for me, it is of less relevance and importance than the modest brick-built house at Chawton where she spent some of the happiest years of her life and where she found the inspiration, the peace and the strength for the best of her life's work.

J. M. BARRIE

KIRRIEMUIR, ANGUS

ANN THWAITE

Driving to Kirriemuir from Dundee, I passed Glamis Castle and called in, not so much for the association with *Macbeth* but because in 1933, just four years before his death, Sir James Barrie had attended the third birthday party there of Margaret Rose, granddaughter of the house as well as of the then king. Glamis Castle, huge and magnificent, is just down the road from the four-roomed weaver's cottage in Kirriemuir where James Barrie was born in 1860. Nothing could suggest more vividly the distance he travelled socially in his lifetime than the contrast between the two houses, the castle and the cottage.

'Nothing that happens after we are twelve matters very much,' Barrie once said. The Jesuits apparently consider the important years even fewer: 'Give us a child until he is seven ...' James Matthew Barrie left the Tenements, Brechin Road, Kirriemuir, when he was eight years old to take advantage of schooling in Glasgow, where his much older brother was teaching. There is a photo of him taken that year in a frogged velvet suit, legs crossed, hair smarmed down neatly for the occasion. He gazes very steadfastly at the photographer and one knows just how much has already happened to him. There is no doubt of the importance of those first years in the small town in the foothills of the Grampians, in the county of Angus.

It is, after all, mainly for *Peter Pan* that Barrie, the most popular dramatist of his time, is now remembered. *Peter Pan* – that extraordinary entertainment – is dangerously attractive to adult analysis and uncomplicatedly wonderful to its child audiences. It is simplistic to say that there was a part of Barrie that, like Peter himself, never grew up, but the famous play certainly gives resounding evidence of the importance of his childhood. It was punctuated with the sort of moves – to Glasgow at eight, to Forfar at ten, to Dumfries at thirteen – that help a writer to remember what it felt like to be eight or ten or thirteen. Barrie always knew what it felt like to be a boy. And however much we hate 'Do you believe in fairies?' (even J. A. Hammerton, his 1929 biographer, called it 'meretricious'), there is no

Barrie's birthplace and the wash-house

denying the enormous appeal of *Peter Pan*. Given a brilliant production (such as that by the Royal Shakespeare Company in 1982) it is undoubtedly the most effective children's play ever written. At Kirriemuir they quote the dedication to *Peter Pan* in which Barrie said that the communal wash-house was not only the theatre of his first play but 'the original of the little house the Lost Boys built in the Never Land for Wendy'. The last bit is unconvincing and seems as irrelevant as it is to consider the ridiculous suggestion that the moving light in the exhibition room is the descendant of Tinkerbell. 'Our dreams are nearer to us than our childhood, and it is natural that *Peter Pan* should remind us more instantly of our dreams,' Max Beerbohm wrote in 1905. *Peter Pan* is the stuff of dreams and it is horribly banal to have a crude solid model of Peter flying in through the window in the new exhibition in the cottage next door.

At least it is in the cottage next door, *not* in the birthplace itself. Barrie himself knew that the important thing with birthplaces is to recreate them as they were at the moment they commemorate. In a letter to Sydney Cockerell about a memorial to his old friend Thomas Hardy, Barrie wrote: 'What I should like best myself is the birthplace bought and preserved in as like a state as possible to what it was in TH's youth.' In 1931 Barrie unveiled Eric Kennington's statue of Hardy in Dorchester with the words, 'He was a great man. That was his hard fate. In this matter, you and I are the lucky ones. Our lot to be soon forgotten ...' But this was false modesty. Three years earlier a Major R. D. Lauder had purchased Barrie's own birthplace for the nation. Or so Hammerton wrote in 1929, and evidence for the biographer's industry in trying to get at the facts of Barrie's life, without alarming the man himself, exists in a series of letters in the Kirriemuir public library. The National Trust for Scotland pamphlet records a later acquisition by Duncan Elliot Alves, who gave it to the Trust. Barrie himself had done something to make sure he was never forgotten in the town of his birth when in 1930 he presented it with a cricket pavilion and received the freedom of the borough. His fame at the time is suggested by the crowd of ten thousand who turned up to celebrate that day.

Barrie had become a celebrity in Kirriemuir long before the first production of *Peter Pan* in 1904 – as early as 1889, in fact. At one point, the local newspaper actually gave a list of visitors to the town who had come to try to catch a glimpse of the writer, who was there for a few months at Strath View, a rather larger house where his parents now lived. He was working on *The Little Minister*. As the *Times* obituary said: 'He had discovered that literature could be made out of his own people, the people of Kirriemuir. He called the place Thrums and made it famous.'

Robert Louis Stevenson praised Barrie early in a letter to Henry James: 'Barrie is a beauty, *The Little Minister* and *The Window in Thrums*, eh? Stuff in that young man; but he must see and not be too funny. Genius in him, but there's a journalist at his elbow – there's the risk.' There were risks too for Barrie the man as well as Barrie the writer. In *The Little Minister* Gavin Dishart says: 'You've spoilt me, you see, Mother, for ever caring for another woman. I would compare her to you and then where would she be?' These are words Barrie might have said himself. Indeed, the cynics say that Mary Ansell (the actress to whom he was married by his uncle, David Ogilvy, at Strath View in 1894) married him only because she thought he was dying. He recovered, but the following year his strongest bonds with Kirriemuir were broken with the death of his sister Jane Ann (his mother's nurse, her prop and stay) and then three days later that of his mother, Margaret Ogilvy herself. ('Margaret Ogilvy had been her maiden name, and after the Scotch custom she was still Margaret Ogilvy,' as Barrie put it.)

Barrie had an uneasy relationship for many years with the town of his birth – 'the little red town', he called it, though the sandstone of its making is really a greyish pink and rather bleak on a grey June day. Scots have tended to be severe on him 'partly out of a suspicion that Barrie caricatured his fellow countrymen for

14

the amusement of foreigners', as Leonee Ormond commented. 'Generations arose that knew him not, nor he them,' the *Dundee Courier and Advertiser* wrote at the time of his death, recalling the twenty years when he had not set foot in Kirriemuir. 'Some folks did not quite like the notoriety thrust upon it by an absentee native. To old-fashioned notions "Thrums" as a substitute for Kirrie was as noxious as a modern bathing outfit to a Victorian.' This was an odd thing to say because the Thrums that Barrie depicted was as 'old-fashioned' as anyone could wish. It was the Kirriemuir of his mother's childhood, not of his own.

In his famous rectorial address on Courage, given at St Andrews in 1932, Barrie said that his 'puppets seem more real to me than myself'. To us, sixty years later, he himself has become infinitely more real than his own creations – not least

Interior of the wash-house

15

because of Ian Holm's masterly portrayal of him in the television production *The Lost Boys* and the numerous photographs preserved in Andrew Birkin's book that accompanied the programmes. There have been many biographies and Barrie has made plenty of appearances too in the lives of other men – fussing over the arrangements for Hardy's funeral, for instance, or congratulating A. A. Milne on the birth of Christopher Robin. 'He has spun so many yarns about himself that it is up to him to tell the truth some day and so to separate the fact from the fiction,' J. A. Hammerton wrote. But Barrie never wrote a full-scale autobiography. How much is 'true' of what went into the Thrums stories, and how much is not, is now impossible to say.

Although he called himself 'as Scotch as peat' (at a time when Scotch was allowed to apply to things other than whisky), he does not seem to belong to Scotland in the way that Scott and Burns do. Barrie was seduced by London from the moment he arrived there in 1885 and saw a placard on the station advertising one of his own articles. Denis Mackail, describing that moment, pictures his friend 'hauling his wooden box from the van' and 'lugging it along the platform'. And at Kirriemuir we can see the tiny sturdy box itself, complete with padlock, and marvel that it was said to contain all his possessions for the move to London.

Barrie spent a great deal of his life in Adelphi Terrace, overlooking the Thames. Now at Kirriemuir you can sit on his uncomfortable London settle, the one that appears in the portrait of him by Sir John Lavery, which is also in the cottage, on loan from the National Portrait Gallery of Scotland. The settle stands on the stone-flagged floor downstairs where once David Barrie's looms stood, and where there is still a skein-winder with a bunch of thrums hanging from it – thrums being short threads used for repairing faults in the lines. His huge London desk is in the exhibition next door, with his glasses and his pipe, his tobacco pouch and his passport on it – and, scattered about, some xerox copies of issues of the *British Weekly* and *Pall Mall* and *St James'* gazettes. You can pick them up and read some of his early writing, as 'Anon' or 'Gavin Ogilvy'. In the tea-room you can read copies of the *Kirriemuir Observer and General Advertiser* for 1887, but Barrie was a London writer and a very fashionable one. The exhibition emphasizes this with its murals and theatre sets of *Quality Street*, *The Admirable Crichton* and, inevitably, *Peter Pan*. The image I associate with him is a London one – of the statue of Peter Pan in Kensington Gardens. I had a picture of it in my own nursery in the thirties and often walk past it now and see how the bronze gleams where the fingers of countless children over the years have caressed the ears of the rabbits.

If Kirriemuir perhaps resented that Barrie had made London rather than Edinburgh his home, there were other reasons too why Scotland hesitated to love him. Sixty years ago the Revd John Kennedy, BD, a minister in Forfar, wrote in his book *Thrums and the Barrie Country*:

The stairs outside the bedroom

It is often said that Kirriemuir is not proud of Barrie – that it is dead to his greatness and indifferent to his fame ... It is not in the Scottish nature to reveal the secrets of the heart ... The good Scot does not speak of the deep matters of the soul.

It was Barrie's book about his mother, *Margaret Ogilvy*, that seemed most to embarrass them, though it sold extremely well. My edition (bought some years ago for 30p) is the third one (1897) and each edition was of ten thousand copies. Indeed it was this commercial success that probably caused the problem. Barrie was thought to be exploiting for money his most intimate feelings and the most important relationship of his life. It is from this book that we know the terrible story of the death of his brother, David, killed in a skating accident at the age of thirteen, and of James's six-year-old efforts to replace his dead brother.

Visiting the cottage, no one who has read that book can fail to remember, climbing the stairs, the child sobbing on those very stairs outside the door of the bedroom where his mother lay mourning the death of the older boy:

After a time I heard a listless voice, that had never been listless before, say, 'Is that you?' I think the tone hurt me, for I made no answer, and then the voice said more

The bedroom with one of the hair-bottomed chairs

anxiously, 'Is that you?' again. I thought it was the dead boy she was speaking to, and I said in a little lonely voice, 'No, it's no him, it's just me.'

Turning into the bedroom (the only bedroom; it is a mystery where everyone slept in this cottage) where Margaret Ogilvy lay that day, the visitor can see two of the six handsome, 'hair-bottomed' chairs that had arrived six years earlier, on the very day that James Barrie was born:

The coming of the chairs seems to be something I remember, as if I had jumped out of bed on that first day, and run ben to see how they looked ... Neighbours came in to see the boy and the chairs.

18

We can see only the chairs, of course. But that itself seems remarkable. On the wall above one of them is strong evidence of the fact that the Barries from time to time did have some money to spare. There is a photograph of Margaret Ogilvy and the three eldest children taken, it seems, in 1849 – eleven years before James was born and at a time when photography was beyond the reach of many people. From this same year, too, there is further evidence that James's father was no ordinary working weaver but also a dealer in cloth – indeed, in a small way, a manufacturer. The word is in the address on a crumpled letter written on 25 October 1849. It was found recently among the heather used for insulation in the attic. It accuses David Barrie, in a friendly way, of being 'ether drunk or dottal', because it was 'dark coulard [*sic*] cotton' that was ordered and not the woollen cloth that was delivered to Dundee. Another good discovery in the attic, a hundred and twenty years after the Barries left the cottage, was a stained and crumpled clerical collar, which looks as if it might have been used to plug a small leak in the roof. Neatly inked on the collar is the name D. Ogilvy, Margaret's brother, who officiated at his nephew James's wedding.

It is things like this that make one feel the reality of the cottage and the fact that James Barrie did indeed live here; it is not just a pretty set. It *is* pretty with its fresh flowers and shining brass candlesticks – a little too good to feel true, on the whole. It is difficult to imagine the crowded clattering looms or the dead boy's coffin on the kitchen table. There is no honeysuckle on the wash-house in nineteenth-century photos of the place. How many of the thousands of visitors that come to the cottage each year will realize it was reading that transformed the life of the weaver's son? But undoubtedly there will be some who visit because they love his books and others who, knowing nothing but *Peter Pan*, will go away curious to read more.

BLOOMSBURY GROUP

CHARLESTON FARMHOUSE, FIRLE, E. SUSSEX

———

FRANCES SPALDING

Charleston is a house of outward sobriety. Situated amid fields at the foot of Firle Beacon, which is the highest point in a line of downs that runs from Newhaven to Cuckmere, this substantial, rather austere farmhouse, dating in part back to the seventeenth century, has an air of fast privacy. Its exterior leaves the visitor wholly unprepared for the warm, civilized atmosphere found inside, where books, pictures, pottery, textiles and needlework and the decorative talents of Vanessa Bell and Duncan Grant combine to make a Bloomsbury home of exceptional interest and informal splendour.

When told of this house by her sister Virginia Woolf, Vanessa Bell bicycled out from Lewes to see it in September 1916. By this date her personal life had become a little unorthodox, in that, without losing his affection or trust, she had moved out of marriage with Clive Bell, by whom she had two sons. In addition she had fallen in love with Duncan Grant, who shared her passion for painting but whose homosexuality curtailed their relationship. Vanessa, who knew the wisdom of accepting others as they are, made no attempt to curb his susceptibilities and even accepted his current boyfriend, David Garnett, into her household. Both men had been granted exemption from combat service on the condition they undertook work of 'national importance'. In Sussex Vanessa Bell hoped to find not only a house to shelter herself, her children and these two young men, but also employment for the latter on a nearby farm.

At first sight Charleston, which then belonged to the Firle estate, left her unimpressed. None the less she made a return visit a couple of days later in the company of the tenant farmer who was prepared to sub-let. This time she fell in love with it and agreed to move in. She afterwards wrote to Duncan Grant, telling him of the arrangements. In her description of the house and its surroundings she transformed the pond it overlooks into a 'large lake'.

Charleston Farmhouse

21

It was mainly because of Vanessa Bell that Charleston became a significant Bloomsbury haunt during the years to come. She was a central figure within the group, if also somewhat enigmatic owing to a reserve which to outsiders could appear forbidding. She had a knack for managing domestic matters with the minimum of fuss: the easy hospitableness this allowed is one reason why the disparate individuals who composed Bloomsbury continued to meet and retain a group identity long after the circumstances that initially helped bring them together had passed.

Vanessa was the daughter of Sir Leslie Stephen, a literary historian and critic of great eminence. Immediately after his death in 1904, she had moved herself and her two brothers and younger sister away from Kensington to 46 Gordon Square in Bloomsbury, an area which, though respectably weighted with upper-middle-class families, was thought to be considerably less fashionable and smart. This was the first home over which she had control. In her arrangement of it she was determined to avoid the heavy Victorian atmosphere which had cast its pall over their life in Kensington. Whereas their previous living-room had been coloured predominantly red, gold and black, their new home was to be painted mostly white. When Vanessa flung Indian shawls over the furniture, she was delighted to see how rich their colours were when seen against bare walls. In this way she began to discover those telling juxtapositions and combinations of colour, shape and pattern that can transform a room and make it intensely alive.

At Charleston she and Duncan Grant had ample space in which to develop their decorative talents. Earlier, in 1913, they had become co-directors with Roger Fry of his Omega Workshops, a venture which attempted to introduce into the field of applied arts a Post-Impressionist sense of colour and design. Bell and Grant had been very actively involved with the Workshops at a time when mosaics and stained-glass windows were being made, rugs and fabrics designed and all kinds of furniture and objects given some form of decoration. The Omega encouraged artists to rethink their choice of pattern and motif with each and every new task that came to hand. Roger Fry did not impose any house-style on the artists he employed but instead hoped that by giving free play to their sensibilities something would emerge akin to 'the spontaneous freshness of primitive and peasant work'. This was the quality he admired in contrast to the often dead or pretentious finish found in machine-made products. A similar aesthetic was to characterize the style of interior decoration that flourished at Charleston.

When Vanessa Bell moved in, the house was bare and unfurnished. Its ample size and the relatively cheap cost of living-in help meant that she could employ two or three servants. Even so, life at Charleston under wartime conditions, and without piped water or electricity, was not easy. It was famously cold. Visitors have recollected that before washing in the morning it was sometimes necessary to break

The dining-room

the ice on the basin of water. Even forty years later, by which time the house had acquired bathrooms and central heating, the novelist Francis King had to interrupt a meal, pretending need of the bathroom, simply because the cold was more than he could tolerate. But if certain material needs were always imperfectly satisfied, the house nevertheless cast its spell on many. It did so with Vanessa soon after she arrived. While Grant and Garnett undertook farm labouring, she took stock of her surroundings and was pleased with what she found. The garden, though overgrown and in need of extensive work, was enclosed within a flint and brick wall and still

23

The garden-room

further protected from west winds by the row of elms (since destroyed) that grew round two sides. Nearby was a small orchard and the ample pond, its calm surface adding to the peace of the whole. Its new tenant could not help wondering what the future would bring. 'It will be an odd life,' she concluded, '... but it seems to me it ought to be a good one for painting.'

Not until February 1918 was she able to execute her first major decorative scheme. It was then that she painted the marbled circles and vases of flowers on the doors either side of the fireplace in an upstairs bedroom which later became known as Duncan's room. The circles in the lower panels of both doors are echoed

24

in the three discs ornamenting the fireplace. In order to emphasize the unity of the design she painted the surrounding architraves and connecting skirting-board Indian red, thereby binding doors and fireplace into a decorative whole.

Though Charleston was relegated to the role of holiday home after the return to peace, and did not become a permanent residence again until 1939, its attraction each year grew richer as its decorative style evolved like some vegetable growth. Nothing in the house was immune from some form of ornamentation; even the simple box used for keeping logs for the fire was imprinted by Duncan Grant with an angel on each of its four sides. Over the fireplace in the garden-room (so called because its french windows open on to the garden) he painted two large female figures holding between them a cartouche showing a picture of boats which was later replaced with a basket of flowers. Minor details like the bands of criss-crossed lines down the sides of the wall help to relate the decoration to its architectural setting, while the fireplace below is covered with mottled paint in a manner akin to imitation marbling. The harmonious effect of the whole owes much to the fact that the scale of the design perfectly fits the proportions of the room.

In addition to this decorative work the house slowly accrued a collection of paintings which reflected the interests and tastes of its inhabitants. At a time when such works cost relatively little, Clive Bell acquired a still life by Picasso and another by Gris. He also bought a Jean Marchand from the Second Post-Impressionist Exhibition, held in 1912. For many years an unidentified Poussin hung at Charleston which Duncan Grant had bought in Paris. After Roger Fry's death in 1934, the house also boasted a small Matisse, left to Vanessa by Roger in his will. By this date Charleston had become very obviously an artist's house. As such Vanessa Bell felt able to recommend it to another artist, Patricia Preece:

> It is a very shabby house which we have been to for twenty years now and gradually got more or less furnished – only as soon as one room gets in order another seems to fall to pieces. I have painted lots of walls myself and made all the curtains and covers, and everyone has had a hand in it. So it's pleasant for artists if for no one else, as it has at least very little mechanical quality.

Among those who helped in its making were Duncan Grant's mother, who translated his designs into needlework, and Roger Fry, who not only fashioned the hearth in the garden-room out of firebricks but also took a hammer and chisel to the small niche over the fireplace in the dining-room in order to make its arch a more pleasing shape. Then in the late 1930s Vanessa Bell's son Quentin set up a kiln in an outhouse, and thereafter much of the pottery in use at Charleston was indigenous, made by Quentin and decorated by either him, Grant or Bell.

The creative atmosphere fostered by the house was not confined to the visual arts. The house has its place in the annals of literary history not least because some

The book-case in the library

26

of its most regular visitors were Vanessa's sister and brother-in-law, Virginia and Leonard Woolf. Lytton Strachey wanted to become a permanent lodger, but was refused by Vanessa on the grounds that her household was already too oddly composed to allow for any further additions. Lytton did, however, visit, bringing with him part of his manuscript for *Eminent Victorians*, from which he read aloud. Duncan Grant afterwards claimed that it was not the quality or interest of the writing but the effects of farm labour that caused him to fall asleep. The house did not lack ink-pots and pens, and a certain amount of literary composition went on within it. Roger Fry, for example, composed the greater part of a long essay which became the basis for his book on Cézanne, published by the Hogarth Press. During the 1920s Clive Bell became an accepted part of the ménage and in 1939 moved himself and his books to Charleston on a permanent basis. He never abandoned the scholar's way of life and devoted many hours of the day to reading and writing. He wrote letters, articles and books there, though his most significant contribution to the life of the house was the energy and brio that he brought to conversation and the wines that came up from his cellar.

The house itself seemed to foster creativity. Remote from any town and at a distance even from the nearby village of Firle, it offered a haven from the more usual interruptions of everyday life. One major development, which took place in 1925, was the decision to build a large downstairs studio over a part of the courtyard. This was done according to Roger Fry's specifications. With its north-facing windows and high ceiling, it not only provided an excellent working environment for painters, but with its pither stove, armchairs and painted furniture, its fire-surround ornamented with two caryatids and a bowl with goldfish in the middle, together with the many paintings and objects that gathered there, it offered yet another distinctive example of Bloomsbury interior decoration. Dignified yet shabby, cluttered yet purposeful, the studio at Charleston encouraged a creative settling of thought, its peace broken only by natural sounds, the noise of the wind or the lowing of a cow.

Though Charleston continued to change and evolve each year, it became associated with a way of life and a set of values that did not alter. A visitor entering this rather untidy, informal house, littered with books and magazines, was made immediately aware that nothing had been chosen to display social standing or material wealth. Instead the atmosphere was at once more sensuous and more spiritual in that a concern with painting, literature and music was uppermost. The life-style of the house respected the need of all the individuals to pursue their own interests. It drew the inhabitants together at mealtimes on the assumption that good food and conversation were two essential ingredients in any form of civilized existence.

One who helped to secure the existence of Charleston as a Bloomsbury home was Maynard Keynes. During her first years there Vanessa Bell had turned to him for financial advice. While working in the Treasury, where he was involved in the problem of how to fund the 1914–18 war, Keynes frequently descended on Charleston when in need of rest and relaxation. He was adept at weeding and would work his way along a footpath, methodically removing every weed in sight with the aid of a penknife. After the war he had attended the Versailles peace conference as a representative of the British Treasury and as part of the delegation concerned with German indemnities. The hypocrisy and deceit he witnessed led him to write *The Economic Consequences of the Peace* at Charleston, in the first-floor bedroom facing the top of the stairs. This book outlawed Keynes for some time from official circles, but its brilliant analysis and independent thought reaffirmed his place within Bloomsbury, where honesty was esteemed, feelings were assessed with care, and anything that smacked of cant, snobbery or irrationalism was abhorred.

From the start of Vanessa Bell's occupancy children played an important part in the life of the house. As her two sons, Julian and Quentin, became aware of how unorthodox their upbringing was, they began to chronicle events in *The Charleston Bulletin*, which carried humorous illustrations by Quentin. The arrival of their aunt, Virginia Woolf, produced a drawing of her on a bicycle. She was also on occasion persuaded to contribute to the paper. Gradually Angelica, the daughter of Vanessa Bell and Duncan Grant born in 1918, began to play a part in the life of the place. As she grew up she displayed an array of talents which her elders were always ready to indulge. One visitor aware of this was Frances Marshall, later to become the wife of Ralph Partridge and the author of diaries which have made a significant contribution to the history of Bloomsbury. She recollects plays being performed by Angelica and her schoolfriends in costumes designed by Vanessa and Duncan. She herself readily accompanied Angelica on the piano when she sang or played her violin, and was flattered when Angelica referred to her in *The Charleston Bulletin*:

> And then there's Miss Marshall
> To whom we are partial.

Virginia Woolf never ceased to marvel at what she saw and heard at Charleston. She commented on it in her diary in a way that repeatedly affirms her admiration for her sister. 'How much I admire this handling of life,' she wrote of her sister, 'as if it were a thing one could throw about; this handling of circumstance.'

Many have recalled that meals at Charleston were excellent. They were cooked by Grace Higgens, who had first entered Vanessa Bell's employment in 1920 at the age of sixteen. She undertook a variety of roles – maid, nurse, cook – but after marriage to Walter Higgens in 1934 she lived permanently at Charleston as its resident housekeeper. At this time the house was used by Clive and Vanessa Bell, Duncan Grant and others only during the holiday periods and for occasional weekends. But in 1939 it once again became their permanent home and remained so from then on. When Vanessa Bell died in 1961 and Clive Bell three years later, Duncan Grant was left the sole resident apart from the Higgenses. A few years later they too left, Grace feeling she had no alternative but to retire.

Up to that point Charleston had always been kept in very good order, the paintwork regularly cleaned and cut flowers placed in most rooms. But with Grace's departure both the house and some of its contents began to deteriorate. After Duncan Grant's death in 1978 the Charleston Trust was established. It has succeeded not only in acquiring the house from the Firle estate but has seen through a long and complex programme of preservation and restoration work, with the result that the house today looks as it did at its most settled and harmonious period.

Charleston is unique in that it represents the most complete expression of Duncan Grant and Vanessa Bell's decorative style. It demonstrates an attitude towards interior design which is personal and pragmatic and does not promote theory over individual needs. As a result it offers a vital alternative to the ascetic puritanism that has dominated much architecture and design this century. It also provides an insight into the lives lived in these unorthodox, humane, sensuous surroundings, where some remarkable people gathered, laughed and conversed, were both ribald and serious, and where, as one visitor noticed, arguing was regarded a delightful sport.

JAMES BOSWELL

AUCHINLECK HOUSE, AYRSHIRE; AND EDINBURGH

THOMAS CRAWFORD

Even more than Samuel Johnson, Boswell deserved the nickname 'Mr Oddity'. Indeed, he often thought of himself not as a coherent 'character' but as a bundle of contradictory sensations and drives pulling in opposite directions: and one of his greatest conflicts was between home, in the sense of his birthplace, Edinburgh, and London, next to Dr Johnson the great love of his life. His earliest Edinburgh houses were all in the Old Town, in 'lands' (multiple tenements), many of them from seven to twelve storeys high and each occupied by a different family. The first, where he was born on 29 October 1740, was his father's home on the fourth storey of Blair's Land in Parliament Square, to the east of St Giles' Cathedral. It was here that he was educated by private tutors after two years at a private academy in the West Bow, and from here that he left to attend classes at the University of Edinburgh from his fourteenth to his nineteenth year. And it was within the solid elegance of Blair's Land that his tortured antagonism to his domineering father, Alexander Boswell, surely began to take root. (When Alexander was appointed a Lord of Session in 1754, he became Lord Auchinleck, a legal title which was not hereditary.)

After marrying his cousin Margaret on 25 November 1769 in defiance of his father's wishes, the young advocate (as barristers are called in Scotland) lived for a short time in what seems to have been a rather nondescript flat in the Cowgate before moving early in 1770 to Chessel's Buildings in the Canongate, which still dominate Chessel's Court (entered through the arcades of Nos. 234–40 Canongate). The external appearance of the building is much as it was in Boswell's time and many original interiors still survive there, 'notably on the ground and first floors, with panelling, pulvinated friezes on the chimneypieces, overmantels painted with romantic scenes in the manner of Norie, and doorcases with swags of fruit'. We do

James's Court, Edinburgh

not know which flat Boswell lived in, but the most probable ones are 4/1 or 4/2, both of which are now in private occupation.

But the Edinburgh building with which Boswell will always be associated is James's Court on the north side of the Lawnmarket between the Castle and Parliament Square. In May 1771 he rented the flat 'on the eastern portion of the third floor in the west stair', as the publisher and antiquarian Robert Chambers described it, from the previous occupant, David Hume, and two years later moved to the larger apartment downstairs which was to be his permanent home for all the rest of his time at the Scottish bar. It was a duplex, quite a rare design for its day, for it consisted of two floors connected by an internal stair. Its quality can be gauged from a sale advertisement in the *Edinburgh Evening Courant* for 12 February 1763 for a four-bedroom flat in the court with 'two genteel well-finished public rooms each above 18 feet long, with handsome marble chimneys and hearths ... and one of the rooms ornamented with a Chinese temple, Apollo and the Muses, &c.'. This part of James's Court was destroyed by fire in 1857. It was here that Margaret Boswell served late tea to Dr Johnson on his arrival in Edinburgh on 14 August 1773, insisted on giving up her bedroom to him, and at the end of the Hebridean tour again poured tea on several November mornings for Johnson's 'constant levee of various persons' from ten o'clock till one or two, besides organizing dinner on the two occasions when Johnson did not dine out. In mid-career and as children began to come, Boswell rented what he called 'country houses' for the summer, though today these seem ludicrously close to the centre of the city. The first of these, in 1777, was at the far south of the Meadows, an imposing park to the south of the Old Town; it has been identified with the much-altered 15A Meadow Place, which still exists, tucked in behind the main row of the little street. The second, from 1781 to 1782, was at Drumsheugh, in the region of the present Queensferry Street in the west end of the city.

Boswell had been fascinated by London ever since he ran off there in his twentieth year for a brief initiation into 'the circles of the great, the gay, and the ingenious', as he later called them. For his next stay in the capital of nine months in 1762–3, he lodged first in Downing Street in a house long since demolished, and later in the Inner Temple. It was then that he first met Dr Johnson and wrote his first masterpiece, which lay undiscovered till the present century, when it was published as *Boswell's London Journal 1762–1763*. He was next in London in 1766, on the way back from the Grand Tour. For twenty years after that it was his aim to go to London annually, when the Scottish courts were not sitting, and to stay for several months at a time. During these visits he generally lodged with friends. In 1786 he made London his permanent home in order to embark on a new (and unsuccessful) career at the English bar and to work on what is still widely regarded as the greatest of English biographies, the *Life of Samuel Johnson*. Boswell's first London house, attributed to Inigo Jones or to his pupil, John Webb, and once occupied by Sir Godfrey Kneller, was 56 Great Queen Street, near to the Inns of Court; he found it old-fashioned, dark and shockingly infested with rats. At the end of 1788 he moved to 38 Queen Anne Street West, 'a neat, pretty small house ... quite a genteel neighbourhood', and two years later to 47 Great Portland Street, where he was to live for the rest of his life. His children Jamie and Euphemia liked the new house, though Boswell thought it less comfortable than Queen Anne Street West; he found it noisy when he first moved in and was confined to the front parlour, presumably because the house was being decorated.

Home, in quite a different sense from Edinburgh, was the country mansion (in Scots-English, the 'Place') of Auchinleck in Ayrshire, with its surrounding estate. Boswell the townsman, who found it difficult to respond emotionally to natural scenery and was irked by country gentlemen's talk of crops and herds, paradoxically drew his sense of identity from the county where his family had its roots. One of his abiding ambitions was to represent Ayrshire in parliament, and during his continental tour he gloried in calling himself baron, 'as I have just the same right to it as the good gentry whom I see around me'. Not for nothing did he ask, at the end of the sketch of his early life that he wrote for Jean-Jacques Rousseau: 'Tell me, is it possible for me yet to make myself a man? Tell me if I can be a worthy Scots laird.' 'Old laird and family ideas', as he called them, were at the centre of his being, but they had to be renewed from time to time – sometimes spontaneously, sometimes by an effort of the will.

The Boswell family had been in possession of the lands of Auchinleck, twelve miles to the east of the Burns Cottage at Alloway, for almost 240 years before James's birth. In the eighteenth century the areas totalled over 24,000 acres and the laird could ride for ten miles in a straight line through his property, returning the greetings of his several hundred dependants at their doors, or at their work in the fields. The original dwelling ('the old Castle') had been a keep perched on a sandstone rock overlooking two streams, the Dippol Burn and the Lugar Water; only a few stones and two bits of wall remain. In the early seventeenth century it had been superseded by a tower-house built 200 yards to the east in the Scots Renaissance style, to which additions were made later in the century to form an L-shaped house with the stair turret in the 're-entrant angle'. It was here in the 'Old House', as it was later styled, that the infant and schoolboy James stayed on summer visits in his grandfather's time. At the end of the century the antiquarian Francis Grose noted that 'wood, particularly the fir, seems to thrive here very much, some firs in the garden measuring ninety-six feet in height, and their circumference, taken a yard above the ground, near seven feet and a half, they are besides remarkably straight and elegant.' The walls of the old house were then (1789) still standing, but it was unroofed; today it is only a picturesque ruin.

The east front of Auchinleck House

Alexander Boswell succeeded his father as eighth laird of Auchinleck in 1749. He began to build the present house in 1757, but it was not occupied till 1762. It is not quite the 'exquisite piece of neo-classicism in the Adam style' that Frederick Pottle, greatest of all Boswellians, said it was; indeed, it is more interesting than that. Neo-classical proportion is certainly there in the severe west elevation, but there is a lack of mechanical balance between the east front and the side and west elevations, while the ornament of the pediment may upset some doctrinaire preconceptions by its expressive, almost vernacular exuberance. It certainly disconcerted the Duchess of Northumberland when she saw it almost completed in

1760: '[in] the new House the Pediment is terribly loaded with Ornaments of Trumpets & Maces & the Deuce knows what. It is but a middling house, but justly it is a romantic spot.' But hers was a metropolitan and a high aristocratic sensibility; another observer might feel that the tension between regularity and irregularity makes the house an almost perfect embodiment of the spirit of eighteenth-century Scotland. Across the front was carved this motto from Horace:

> Quod petis, hic est,
> Est Ulubris, animus si te non deficit aequus

which has been paraphrased as 'If you have got a good firm mind, you can be happy at Auchinleck, remote and quiet though it be.'

No sooner was the new house occupied than extensions began. Out-buildings called 'office houses' were completed in 1766, though the present stable block dates from the nineteenth century. Boswell's great friend the Revd W. J. Temple wrote after a visit to the house in 1767:

> Let honest James Bruce [the estate overseer] and you persuade my Lord to cut down the row of trees that spoils the meadow, and not to make the wings to the house little bandboxes, but in proportion to the body of the building; otherwise, tell his Lordship from me that the whole will look like a giant with the arms of a dwarf.

These pink sandstone pavilions today seem out of keeping with the grey stone of the main house to which they are joined by link walls, but they were not always like that, for in 1775 Boswell wrote of the 'new-whitened pavilions'. For the rest of Lord Auchinleck's lifetime work proceeded on improving what in Scotland are known as 'the policies'. A new broad road which Lord Auchinleck (always a classicist) called the 'via sacra' was laid out to make a grander approach, bridges were built across the Dippol, and in 1768 Boswell organized the digging of what he described as 'a superb grotto' near the old castle, similar to several older ones along both the Lugar and the Dippol.

The house itself consists of two principal storeys. On the ground floor there is a small entrance hall, a big, richly decorated room at the north end of the house, two parlours facing west, and two family bedrooms at the south end. The upper floor has five bedrooms and the library, which fills the whole of the centre of the west front and looks towards the sea through its four round-headed windows. In Boswell's day there were also smaller attic apartments for the servants and for storing linen and lumber, while the basement contained the kitchen, laundry, dairy, brewhouse, and other utility rooms.

Even before he became laird on his father's death in 1782, Boswell delighted in entertaining his friends at Auchinleck, distinguished and not so distinguished. In September 1771 the guest of honour was General Pasquale de Paoli, the exiled leader of the Corsicans; legend has it that Lord Auchinleck contemptuously dismissed him as a 'land-louping scoundrel of a Corsican'. From 2 to 8 November 1773 Dr Johnson himself was the visitor, at the end of their tour to the Hebrides. At first it

Two of the pavilions at Auchinleck House

seemed as if the encounter between Boswell's biological and his spiritual father would pass without a hitch. On the first day Johnson revelled in the treasures of the library, with its fine collection of Greek and Roman classics. On the third and fourth days Boswell showed Johnson round the grounds. He was suitably impressed by the Old Castle and what he termed its 'sullen dignity', and by some 'venerable old trees, under which the shade of my ancestors walked'. On the fifth day, the explosion came. Lord Auchinleck was showing Johnson his collection of medals, among which was Cromwell's head. There followed an altercation about Charles I and Toryism. One story about the confrontation, perhaps apocryphal, derives from Sir Walter Scott. When Johnson asked what Cromwell had ever done for his country, Lord Auchinleck replied: 'God, Doctor! He gart kings ken that they had a *lith* in their neck' (he taught kings they had a *joint* in their necks). It is of a piece with another anecdote of Sir Walter's, Lord Auchinleck's jeering description of Johnson as 'a *dominie*, mon – an auld dominie; he keeped a schule, and cau'd it an acaademy'.

For the first few years after he succeeded as laird in 1782, Boswell spent a great deal of time at Auchinleck, and even after he took his family south in 1786 he spent four months there in 1788. At last he could truly be Baron Boswell, mingling with the tenantry, collecting their rents in person, sharing Presbyterian worship with them from the family pew despite his own Anglican persuasion, and patri-archally treating them to an annual dinner. It was at Auchinleck that Mrs Boswell died of consumption on 4 June 1789, apart from her husband, and where she was buried, as he movingly recounted in a letter to W. J. Temple:

> My two boys and I posted from London to Auchinleck night and day, in 64 hours [and] $\frac{1}{4}$. But alas! our haste was all in vain. The fatal stroke had taken place before we set out. It was very strange that we had no intelligence whatever upon the road, not even in our own parish, nor till my second daughter came running out from our house, and announced to us the dismal event in a burst of tears ... I could hardly bring myself to agree that the body should be removed, for it was still a consolation to me to go and kneel by it, and talk to my dear dear Peggie. She was much respected by all who knew her, so that her funeral was remarkably well-attended. There were nineteen carriages followed the hearse, and a large body of horsemen and the tenants of all my lands. It is not customary in Scotland for a husband to attend his wife's funeral. But I resolved, if I possibly could, to do her the last honours myself, and I *was* able to go through with it very decently. I privately read the funeral service over her coffin in the presence of my sons, and was relieved by that ceremony a good deal.

In 1794–5, shortly before his own death, he was at Auchinleck for over six months. After the hay-stacking in August 1794 he took the workers, men and women, 'up to the Hall, where they danced while Veronica [his daughter] played on the Harpsichord to them ... I with my own hand gave each of the rustick dancers a glass of Mountain Malaga'. During his last sojourn at Auchinleck there was much 'social glee', though Boswell as usual was often depressed and fretted for London. Some of the young women invited by his daughters stayed for a fortnight or even a month, and in mid-November officers of the Fourth Dragoons were invited to a fête at which twenty-two guests spent the night at Auchinleck and danced till four in the morning. The girls invited the officers and an equally large company to a similar party in December. Boswell was pleased that at his request the tenants had paid their rents ten days earlier than usual, so that he could pay off a bond – their last demonstration of what he liked to call 'feudal' loyalty, for by 19 January he was in London again, where he died on 19 May. His body was brought back to Auchinleck and interred in the family vault on 8 June 1795.

Auchinleck House remained the seat of the Boswells for most of the nineteenth century. In 1920 it was sold to Colonel John Douglas Boswell of Garallan, who was descended from the very branch of the family that Lord Auchinleck had insisted on excluding from the entail on the property. By 1986 the house was in an appalling condition, through no fault of the owners, and the then owner, James Boswell (the Colonel's grandson), agreed to sell it, together with thirty-five acres, to the Scottish Historic Buildings Trust. Since then their restorers have been at work. Dry rot has been eliminated; all the structural timber has been repaired or renewed; and further repairs are in hand. The Trust is currently seeking the 'right' purchaser for the house, either a private owner or an educational institution.

There is a small museum in what was once the parish church, which adjoins the family mausoleum. Among a few portraits of eighteenth- and nineteenth-century Boswells is a striking and rather Byronic bust of James's son, Sir Alexander Boswell, and a number of manuscripts, mostly by Sir Alexander, his widow, and a Dutch cousin of Boswell's, but there are only a few scraps in Boswell's own hand. The really interesting place to visit is Auchinleck House itself, which, quite apart from its historic connection with James Boswell, is important for its architecture alone. Its baroque-type wings and cupolas are unique in Scottish houses of this period and size, and it is the finest small Scottish country house of the villa type surviving from the eighteenth century.

THE BRONTËS

THE PARSONAGE, HAWORTH, W. YORKSHIRE

REBECCA FRASER

Charlotte Brontë, in a pretty country phrase, called her sister Emily 'a nursling of the moors'. It is a description that suggests something of that wild-bird quality common to all the Brontë children. A short-lived vulnerable species was created by the union of Maria Branwell and the Revd Patrick Brontë, incapable of surviving anywhere other than in the freedom of their Yorkshire wilderness. But there is also a magnificent, contemptuous strength to those tracts of bleak moorland which formed the Brontës' natural terrain. Such a backdrop bred a bone-deep indifference to the rest of the world and secured the family's extraordinary artistic autonomy. Despite the Brontës' nervous fragility, only uncompromising defiance would be displayed towards the massed ranks of the critical establishment when the vigorous realism of their novels was condemned.

Haworth Parsonage and its environs are unique because not only did they form the main scene (and in Emily's case practically the only one) of the lives of two of England's greatest novelists, but their isolation and wild ungovernable population gave a rare flavour to the Brontës' writing. After the din and hurrah that greeted *Wuthering Heights* and *Jane Eyre* had died down, eventually even the worldly and ambitious Charlotte was forced to acknowledge that there might be some good reason for the critics' outrage, that circumstances, at least, had made her family not quite as others. In her Preface to the posthumous edition of *Wuthering Heights* Charlotte would say that their surroundings were responsible for Emily's rugged originality, and a book that was 'moorish, and wild, and knotty as the root of heath'. As an ignorant, reclusive country girl, Emily had absorbed uncritically 'the rough strong utterance, the harshly manifested passions, the unbridled aversions, and headlong partialities of unlettered hinds and rugged moorland squires, who have grown up untaught and unchecked, except by mentors as harsh as themselves'. Just the same, for all Charlotte's own literary sophistication, there remained an inviolable core to her that was as raw and naïve and unyielding as her sister's, which her small experience of life outside Haworth would do little to change.

39

Although in 1820 the Brontë children could be considered as natives of the moors, they were actually the progeny of two Celtic intruders into the area. The Revd Patrick Brontë arrived at Haworth as part of the final thrust of the Evangelical movement to convert England back to godliness after the licence of the eighteenth century. For forty years he remained there, a widower, since his Cornish wife had died shortly after giving birth to her last child, Anne. The lack of a mother's softening, more sociable influence undoubtedly contributed to the Brontës' loneliness and eccentricity, and to their brilliance. During a particularly restrictive era for women, quite unusually all his children were able to roam as freely amongst the best creations of English literature as they did about the endless heath behind their house. Mr Brontë was a keenly intellectual man, the son of Northern Irish peasants, who had got himself entirely by his own efforts to Cambridge, and he fostered a spirit of real mental independence in his offspring. Under the influence of Byron, as well as other Romantics, an impatience with convention that was perhaps congenital would become Charlotte's own brand of Evangelism as she grew increasingly aware of the curbs imposed on female nineteenth-century life outside her hills.

Ever the analytical one, in early life Charlotte was not particularly enamoured of her home. As she would make clear in *Shirley*, the landscape near to Haworth is almost overwhelmingly industrial. Until you actually go to Haworth, though, and unless you have been paying very careful attention to Mrs Gaskell's *Life*, it comes as a great surprise just how much tall factory chimneys interrupt the wooded valley bottoms. Gulled by *Wuthering Heights*, our mental vision of the scenery is Emily's: it is that natural paradise of ousels and bilberry plants, of soft thaw winds and murmuring becks that Catherine Earnshaw preferred to Heaven. As Charlotte would point out, it is really only high up, deep amongst the ridges of the moors where Emily used to vanish to, with the footstool still in the Parsonage dining-room so that she could write *en plein air*, that the unromantic scenery does become grand, and 'Imagination can find rest for the sole of her foot'. According to Charlotte, if a visitor wanted beauty to inspire him, he must bring it inborn, for 'these moors are too stern to yield any product so delicate'. Without that, she said, 'the drear prospect of a Yorkshire moor will be found as barren of poetic as of agricultural interest'.

But of course the precocious Brontë children could bring the alchemy of their feverishly poetic sensibilities to the land. The dearth of entertainments and of other suitable young people forced the four at the parsonage back on to their inner resources; in no time at all their remarkable imaginations began to assume a power over them comparable to the genies of their adored *Arabian Nights*. The children's

The moors near Haworth

41

Haworth Parsonage, facing the church across the graveyard

tiny study over the hall became the harbour for great mental voyages to the imaginary countries of Glasstown and Gondal, which were traced on elaborate maps and whose ceaseless bloody chronicles became the focus of the Brontës' lives until long after adulthood. Still at the house is Goldsmith's *Grammar of General Geography*, whose ordinary Table of Contents is interspersed with the names in childish handwriting of the Brontës' own secret countries – like 'Gaaldine', which is 'a large island newly-discovered in the South Pacific'. The fantasy world took place in antique palaces of fabulous architecture inspired by Mr Brontë's reproductions of John Martin's paintings. But from Emily's laconic birthday diaries, inspired by Byron's method of describing events happening at the precise moment of writing, comes evidence of how easily it coexisted with the homely and everyday. While their maid Sally Moseley is 'washing in the back kitchin [*sic*]' the Gondals 'are discovering the interior of Gaaldine'. In amongst the potato peelings that Emily

The children's study

refers to were propped books of poetry. All the latest journals Mr Brontë could afford, like *Blackwood's*, were taken, detailing the goings-on in clubland and literary London, and of course at Westminster. For Mr Brontë was an immensely committed Tory, and he would read the debates out to his children. Aged thirteen, Charlotte passionately followed every nuance of the 1830 Catholic Emancipation Bill, which brought down the government of her hero, the Duke of Wellington. (His likeness is also to be found at the Parsonage, where it always hung in the dining-room.)

Blackwood's gave a certain rigour to Charlotte and Branwell's view of themselves as members of a literary brotherhood. It dictated the earliest versions of Brontë writing, with their miniature magazines, as well as firing the two elder children with ambitions to be figures in the great world, which through the magazines seemed so tantalizingly close. There would always be a side to Charlotte which revelled in what she called 'High Life', which was revealed so glitteringly in Byron's epics. The imaginary world she created with Branwell was always very aristocratic in tone. And that side to Charlotte would be uppermost in her for a very long time, until her experience of London as a celebrated author made her flee for the freedom of Haworth. (The copy of the portrait of Charlotte by George Richmond at the parsonage, commissioned by her publisher, is an indication of her celebrity by 1851.) Even when she was only fourteen, Charlotte poured scorn on the quality of life in one of Emily and Anne's castles, which is remarkably similar to Haworth and, to Charlotte, the humdrum life of home. The inhabitants don't crave a grand park, but enjoy running about the gooseberry and currant bushes – just like the ones outside the dining-room window – and eating a good Yorkshire dinner in good Yorkshire silence.

The extravagance of Charlotte and Branwell's youthful imaginations – the Byronic heroines clad in black satin they exulted about, the palaces they drew so frenziedly – were undoubtedly a means of escape from a childhood riven by loss. For within the space of four years their mother and two elder sisters, Maria and Elizabeth, aged ten and eleven, had died. Not only was there little emotional comfort from a father who confessed to finding it hard to deal with small children in the aftermath of his beloved wife's death, but the bleak, curtainless parsonage was just across the graveyard from the church where their mother and sisters were buried. The novelist Mrs Gaskell, Charlotte's champion and biographer, noted that when she met Charlotte twenty-four years after her sisters' death from tuberculosis, she still burnt with indignation when she mentioned their names. Her sisters' experience at the Clergy Daughters' School at Cowan Bridge, upon which the scenes at the terrible Lowood School in *Jane Eyre* were so closely modelled as to be almost indistinguishable, was perhaps printed all the more indelibly upon Charlotte's memory because they were buried so near. In her view, the authorities' sadistic neglect of their charges' all-too-mortal bodies, which was theoretically justified in terms of their immortal souls, was entirely to blame for the tragedy. And in this episode can be found the roots of *Jane Eyre*, with its theme of the hypocrisy of the clergy, which would bring the wrath of Victorian England down upon Charlotte Brontë's head.

Contemporaries in fact would be amazed when they found out that the infamous Bell brothers (the Brontë sisters' *noms de plume*) were really the ladylike daughters of a Yorkshire parson, and would always be absolutely astonished when they met Currer Bell, as Charlotte was known. Charlotte's modest dress and near-pathological shyness, which almost shouted her quiet life as a girls'-school teacher and governess, were the complete opposite of the bold, wicked woman it was considered must have written *Jane Eyre*. For the novel's passion and frankness both scandalized and delighted Victorian England; a bestseller, it became the sort of book that mothers would not allow their unmarried daughters to read, and Charlotte, like her idol, Byron, awoke to find herself famous.

The day dress on display with dim green and turquoise flowers is probably the one worn by Charlotte to a dinner given in her honour by Thackeray. It was a very awkward occasion, which disappointed all concerned. The sophisticated ladies who formed Thackeray's court were dismayed by Miss Brontë's lack of dress sense, and the gentlemen, who had been expecting something racier and more brilliant, a latter-day Madame de Staël, were bored by her shy small-talk and refusal to discuss her work. As for Charlotte herself, that incapacitating shyness was exacerbated by the knowledge that her work had made her notorious to the vulgar, which, alas, seemed to be the milieu that even her beloved Thackeray moved in.

Being scandalous was very far from Charlotte Brontë's original plan. Her aim was to reinvigorate the novel with her own brand of realism. That early obsession with Byron bred a hatred of cant that flourished under the peculiarly oppressive circumstances of Charlotte's life in her twenties; unsatisfactory spells as schoolteacher and governess chafed her proud spirit, as did the contrast between the conventions of polite society, where she was isolated as a near servant, and the convivial informality and intellectual freedom of Haworth. Her last experience of work in the outside world before she became a professional novelist, her two years learning French and training as a teacher in a girls' school in Brussels, only added fuel to the flames of her hatred for what she perceived as the falseness of contemporary manners, and contemporary feminine manners in particular.

For all Charlotte's impatience with Evangelical-led manners and mores, there was something in her attitudes akin to the Methodist preachers who had 'converted' her parents. The church of St Michael and All Angels, which stands so proximately to the parsonage, had been a byword for the fiercest kind of early Methodism in the middle of the eighteenth century under one of Wesley's most powerful lieutenants, the Revd William Grimshaw. He managed to convert most of the country round Haworth, and his harsh, branding religion appealed to a dour, naturally Non-conformist mountain folk, so that by the Brontës' time Haworth was still a centre of Methodist enthusiasm. Mr Brontë's sister-in-law was also a Methodist; Charlotte absorbed all that religious fervour, even if somewhat against her will, and transformed it into an abiding obsession with another kind of truth, the truth of the emotions. In the end she would be willing to endure the contemporary equivalent of an early Christian martyrdom for her beliefs. The Passions, as she called them with a capital P, were to her the most noble and beautiful part of man, and no novelist had done justice to them, particularly in their female personification. This abiding dedication to realism, if not naturalism, which she had felt since youth that fiction lacked, and her romantic impatience with convention, achieved in Charlotte's fierce, impulsive but ultimately unmovable character a missionary zeal as implacable as any Grimshaw's.

That temperamental lack of detachment meant that Charlotte Brontë's experience of London life could only be disappointing. Thackeray's satirical masterpiece, *Vanity Fair*, had come to her as a revelation, and was reassurance that at least one other kindred spirit existed in the world of letters. After the attacks on *Jane Eyre*, she clung to the idea that Thackeray was 'the High Priest of Truth', as she called him, and she venerated him humbly but ecstatically by the lonely dining-room fire. It was therefore a hideous shock to find that the hero she hailed as 'the regenerator of the warped system of things' loved the snobbish world he professed to see through. And Thackeray for his part found 'the little woman of genius', as he patronizingly called her, was too uncomfortable to have around. 'You see by Jane Eyre's letter don't you,' he wrote to an intimate, 'why we can't be very great friends? We had a correspondence – a little one; and met, very eagerly on her part. But there's a fire raging in that little woman, a rage scorching her heart which doesn't suit me. She has had a story and a great grief that has gone badly with her.'

But by the time that Thackeray knew Charlotte, which was after the publication of *Shirley*, there was not just *one* grief which had gone badly with her: her remaining siblings had all perished from tuberculosis in the space of nine months. Charlotte, at thirty-two the eldest, was left alone to keep house for her father, a duty that seemed to preclude any other destiny. Her reading by the fireside then assumed even more importance, the authors as much weight as they had in adolescence, now that those intimate, furious colloquies with Anne and Emily could never come again.

All those old rituals had gone – that strange march round the dining-room table inventing stories, arm in arm, the reading aloud of new chapters from their novels to while away the long northern nights, while Branwell raved next door. Charlotte poignantly confessed that she found it almost impossible to finish *Shirley* now that there were no familiar heads to raise from those small writing-desks on their laps to listen to the latest developments in the narrative, as they had with *Jane Eyre*.

Charlotte gives us a curious insight into the contrast between the characters of the enigmatic, almost brutal Emily and that of her sisters, who for all their affection could have no natural sympathy for the savagery of *Wuthering Heights*:

> If it was complained that the mere hearing of certain vivid and fearful scenes banished sleep by night and disturbed mental peace by day, Ellis Bell would wonder what was meant, and suspect the complainant of affectation.

If Charlotte's cultivated and naturally graceful muse took a more forceful form amidst her lonely mountains, Emily herself often seems more spirit than flesh. When we read her poetry, so often an image arises of her sitting expectantly at her window looking out over the moor. We seem to see her, as in Branwell's miraculous painting, where an invisible wind forever ruffles her hair, listening to the night sounds of that beloved universe. Then indeed, as the 'winds take a pensive tone, and stars a tender fire', did the visions begin that she had thrilled to ever since childhood. To her then 'the Invisible, the Unseen its truth reveals', and she would feel the godhead within her whose call became stronger and more alluring as tuberculosis ate her life away.

Unlike Charlotte and Anne, who both expressed disquiet at the hold the 'burning clime' of the dreamworld had over them, Emily had no wish to escape its toils. Though she reluctantly accompanied Charlotte to Brussels, that external experience which was so formative for her elder sister left no visible impress upon her imagination. Charlotte and Anne both made a bid for freedom. Little Anne resigned herself to governessing for five years in the vast manufacturers' halls springing up round Yorkshire as testament to their power and prosperity; they would provide the inspiration for *Agnes Grey* and *The Tenant of Wildfell Hall*. By going to Brussels Charlotte thought that she too had shaken off the compulsive 'infernal world' and also exchanged the society of her father's curates for a new world of light. But like all episodes in the Brontës' lives other than those set in Haworth, it was a mirage. It was as if some spell had been cast over the family, preventing anything of significance happening once the Brontës stepped outside the fairy boundaries of home, chaining them to Haworth forever.

The isolation of Charlotte's early life rendered her quite helpless to deal with the outside world. M. Heger, the progenitor of Mr Rochester and Mr Paul in *Villette*, to anyone other than Charlotte Brontë must have been a rather ordinary though dictatorial little Belgian. But that great blind force of Charlotte's imagination had for too long had its freedom, and would not be gainsaid. As she herself wrote, perhaps rather wearily:

> The writer who possesses the creative gift owns something of which he is not always master – something that at times strangely wills and works for itself ... to rules and principles it will perhaps for years lie in subjection; and then, haply without any

warning of revolt, there comes a time when it will no longer consent 'to harrow the vallies, or be bound with a band in the furrow' ... when refusing absolutely to make ropes out of sea-sand any longer, it sets to work on statue hewing, and you have a Pluto or a Jove, a Tisiphone or a Psyche, a Mermaid or a Madonna, as Fate or Inspiration direct.

Poor M. Heger was plucked up by the whirlwind, and life was never the same again.

For all her trembling sensibility, there was a ruthlessness in Charlotte which cut through the many ties restraining the professor from her embrace. When she couldn't have him in the flesh, her servant Imagination spirited him away from his schoolhouse in the rue Isabelle to become her plaything. When he would not respond to her letters in the way she wanted, and those mental conversations in French on which she existed in the grey winters of 1844 and 1845 had palled, why then he was put through his paces, with many changes of costume, in *Jane Eyre*, *Shirley* and *Villette*. And *Villette* reveals the depth of that obsession for her maître: Mme Heger is tormented in the character of Mlle Reuter, and Charlotte grants herself a kind of happy ending with M. Heger in the guise of Mr Paul.

With all that time hanging heavy on her hands, despite her habitual Sunday-school teaching and visiting the sick, it was impossible not to revisit the past. It had become increasingly obvious that there could be no future for her outside Haworth, and nothing there beyond an existence so uneventful that she several times compared it to being buried alive.

Amazingly, though, it was from Haworth that her husband was to appear. Unlike Mr Smith, her publisher, whose history may also be read in the pages of *Villette*, where he appears as Graham Bretton, and unlike M. Heger, Mr Nicholls, her father's curate, had been at Haworth long enough to fulfil the conditions that Fate demanded of all permanent features in Charlotte's life. And strangely, too – though he as a clergyman quite naturally had been the butt of Charlotte's pen in *Shirley* – the marriage proved remarkably felicitous, brief though it was. The ill health, both real and psychosomatic, which had dogged her since she was a young woman vanished. Living in the parsonage with a distinctly menacing father-in-law might not have been an obvious recipe for happiness, but it worked. The store-room behind the dining-room was transformed into a little den for the large and masculine Mr Nicholls, and hung very satisfactorily with a pretty green and white wallpaper and matching curtains. Its position was fortunately far enough away from where the blind white-haired parson sat amidst his pipe racks, facing over the churchyard, hearing the wind rush by from the east, its passage scarcely broken by the mountain ashes and hawthorns.

With marriage, some recognition of her position was accorded to Charlotte Brontë, she who had been described on her marriage licence as having no occupation. She and Mr Nicholls occupied her parents' matrimonial bed, and Mrs Nicholls at last assumed control of the parsonage purse, though it had long been filled mainly by her. So, before the end of her life, she did get a sort of measure of adult status, having had, at the age of thirty-eight, to ask her father's permission to marry.

It is perhaps incorrect to see Charlotte Brontë wholly as the spirited prisoner of female nineteenth-century life, trapped between the schoolroom and her father's will, but not entirely. She had written almost prophetically of her largely autobiographical heroine Lucy Snowe that the orb of her life was not to be so rounded, that for her 'the crescent-phase must suffice'. Charlotte's death when three months pregnant was a poignant physical fulfilment of that metaphor. All three Brontë sisters died before their time; it was almost as if the effort of giving birth to such extraordinary literary offspring had devastated those frail little bodies. They died at their artistic peak, still knowing very little of the world, unadulterated in the purity and intensity of their feelings. The parsonage reflects that purity, a lasting physical reminder of the isolation and poverty which produced a very idiosyncratic genius.

RUPERT BROOKE

THE OLD VICARAGE, GRANTCHESTER

MARY ARCHER

Grantchester, like most Cambridgeshire villages, is an ancient settlement, bearing traces of both Iron Age and Anglo-Saxon habitation. The Old Vicarage, the second of its four rectories or vicarages, was built shortly before 1685, in which year an ecclesiastical visitation referred to it as 'a good, new-built Vicaridge House'. It served as Grantchester's vicarage until about 1820 when, the incumbent being shared with Willingham, it was let to the Lilley family. In 1853 it was sold to Samuel Page Widnall, a local man who did much to shape the house and garden into their present form.

After Widnall's death in 1894, the Old Vicarage and the five other properties in his Grantchester estate passed first to his sister-in-law, Lally Smith, and on her death in 1908 to his niece, Emily Giles. Mrs Giles did not live in the house herself but installed as tenants Henry and Florence Neeve and their young son Cyril.

It was during the Neeves' time that Rupert Brooke entered the story. In 1906 he had come up from Rugby School to King's, his father's Cambridge college, to read Classics. Pursuit of political and poetical interests proved more absorbing, and Brooke took a Second in the Classical Tripos of 1909 instead of the First to which his mother, if not he himself, had aspired. His tutor advised him to change to English for further work aimed at a King's Fellowship, and to move away from the distractions of the city to work undisturbed on his chosen dissertation subject, the Elizabethan dramatist John Webster.

So Brooke came to live in Grantchester at the age of twenty-two. He first took lodgings at the Orchard, a house forming part of the original complex of farm buildings associated with the Old Vicarage. But in December 1910, complaining to his mother that 'horrible people' had appeared at the Orchard, he moved one door down to the Old Vicarage, renting from the Neeves two rooms on the ground floor and one on the first floor, plus full board, for thirty shillings a week.

Brooke formed a deeply romantic attachment to Grantchester – its woods, watermeadows and country ways – and above all to the house itself, of which he wrote to his cousin Erica Cotterill:

> This is a lonely, dank, ruined, overgrown, gloomy, lovely house: with a garden to match. It is all five hundred years old and fusty with the ghosts of generations of mouldering clergymen. It is a fit place to write my kind of poetry in.

Above all, there was the river. Reports of swimming recur in friends' accounts of visits to Grantchester. On one warm, moonlit night in 1911 during her stay at the Old Vicarage, Brooke took Virginia Stephen (later Woolf) upstream to Byron's Pool. 'Let's go swimming, quite naked,' he said, and they did. Virginia was disappointed that her London friends remained calm at news of the incident, although it may have contributed to the nickname of neo-Pagans which Bloomsbury conferred on Brooke and his Cambridge circle.

In the same summer, David Garnett trod the same path with Brooke. 'We went around midnight – for I had arrived rather late,' he wrote,

> to bathe in Byron's Pool. We walked out of the garden of the Old Vicarage into the lane full of thick white dust, which slipped under our weight as we walked noiselessly in our sand-shoes, and then through the dew-soaked grass of the meadow over the mill-wall leading to the pool, to bathe naked in the unseen water, smelling of wild peppermint and mud.

Brooke worked both on his Webster dissertation (which was to gain him the Fellowship at the second attempt) and on poems to be included in the first anthology of *Georgian Poetry*, among which 'The Old Vicarage, Grantchester' was to take pride of place. The poem itself was written, not in the gardens of the Old Vicarage, but in Berlin in May 1912, during his visit to Dudley Ward, a close undergraduate friend who was then an assistant editor of the *Economist* and shortly to be married to a German girl.

Brooke was out of sympathy with Germany and the Germans and homesick for England and the Old Vicarage. 'I've a fancy you may be, just now, in Grantchester,' he wrote to Katharine Cox. 'That river and the chestnuts – come back to me a lot.' At a table in the Café des Westens in Charlottenburg, he scribbled on four small sheets of paper the poem that has become 'The Old Vicarage, Grantchester', though that was not the immediate choice of title. First entitled simply 'Home', it became 'Fragments of a Poem to be Entitled "A Sentimental Exile"' and was published under that title in the June 1912 issue of the King's College undergraduate magazine, *Basileon*. It was at Edward Marsh's suggestion that the title was changed to 'The Old Vicarage, Grantchester'. Thus it appeared in the November 1912 issue of the *Poetry Review*, and thus it has remained.

The poem, romantic, satirical and whimsical though it is, is more factual than fanciful in its setting. Much of what Brooke recalls of the house and its surroundings

The Old Vicarage, Grantchester

The church clock

are here still. The chestnuts at the end of the garden by the Mill Stream still form a 'tunnel of green gloom' in summer, and poppies, pansies, lilac, carnations and pinks still adorn the springtime borders. But the May fields now 'all golden show' with rape, not buttercups, and the elm clumps sadly no longer stand. There were once great clumps of elm at the north end of the village, 'guardians of that holy land' of Grantchester, but they have all succumbed to elm-bark beetle.

53

Grantchester Mill burned down in 1928, and as for the mill at Trumpington, where

> Dan Chaucer hears his river still
> Chatter beneath a phantom mill,

that, as Brooke implies, had vanished long before his day.

The Old Vicarage has in a sense become a memorial to Brooke. When war broke out in 1914, he at first thought of becoming a war correspondent, but soon changed his mind and decided to join up. With Edward Marsh's help, he enlisted

The Granta near Byron's Pool

as a second lieutenant in the newly formed Royal Naval Division and briefly saw action at the fall of Antwerp. The story of his death in the Aegean in 1915 and subsequent beatification in the eyes of a nation mourning its youthful heroes is too well known to bear repetition here. But perhaps not so well known is the subsequent history of the Old Vicarage.

By the end of the war, Rupert's formidable mother had lost all three of her sons, and it was she who put into effect his wish, expressed in 1914, to buy the Old Vicarage. Dudley Ward and his German bride Anne-Marie came to live in it and Mrs Brooke bequeathed it to them on her death in 1931. The house was to stay in the Ward family until 1979, when I and my family acquired it. One does not need a lively belief in ghosts to sense the past generations, sacred and secular, that hover around the Old Vicarage.

EDWARD BULWER LYTTON

KNEBWORTH HOUSE, HERTFORDSHIRE

SIBYLLA JANE FLOWER

Edward Bulwer Lytton visited Knebworth for the first time in 1810, when he was seven. He and his widowed mother drove down from London shortly after she inherited the Knebworth estate from her father, Richard Warburton Lytton. The house, set on a hill and surrounded by parkland, was now partly occupied by tenants, but the furnished state-rooms had been unused for over forty years. To a child brought up in a terraced house in London as Bulwer Lytton had been, there was something curiously exciting about its spacious melancholy. Of his very early days he could remember little. His father, General William Earle Bulwer of Heydon Hall, Norfolk, had died in 1807, and the Heydon property was handed over to trustees by Bulwer Lytton's mother, who was anxious to turn her back on an unhappy phase of her life. The eldest son – Bulwer Lytton had two brothers – was sent away to school, and the second was brought up by his grandmother.

Nobody would have been more aware of the impracticality of Knebworth House as it stood than Mrs Bulwer Lytton, but a combination of pride in her Lytton ancestors and the enthusiasm of her youngest son encouraged her to embark on a radical programme of restoration. How radical this was can be deduced from old drawings. The Knebworth she inherited was a rambling quadrangular brick building, two storeys high, with a gatehouse in the courtyard. Most of this dated from the time of Sir Robert Lytton, a favourite subject of King Henry VII, who had purchased the reversion of the property in 1492. Mrs Bulwer Lytton decided to demolish three sides of the quadrangle, retaining the fourth which contained the Great Hall and an impressive withdrawing-room. This fourth wing, facing south, was transformed for Mrs Bulwer Lytton between 1814 and 1816 into a Regency country house by the architect John Biagio Rebecca. The old brickwork was covered with stucco, and battlements, turrets and an elaborate porch were added. After much deliberation, Mrs Bulwer Lytton selected Gothic tracery for the windows of the Great Hall.

Knebworth House from the north-east

Before and during the restoration of Knebworth House Mrs Bulwer Lytton lived in the manor house nearby. Bulwer Lytton was educated at a succession of small boarding establishments run by clergymen, refusing to attend a public school (one visit to Eton made up his mind on that point). In the school holidays he could immerse himself in the atmosphere of Knebworth and revel in its past. A copy of the latest Scott would be to hand, and at the age of ten or eleven he began to write poems and stories himself. In 1820, before he went up to Cambridge, his mother arranged for the publication of some of his verses. The slim volume entitled *Ismael, an Oriental Tale* has a precocious dedication to the 'British Public' and an address to Sir Walter Scott penned when Bulwer Lytton was thirteen. Scott professed to read this 'with great pleasure'. The book contains a tribute, written at fifteen, to Knebworth and to his mother's efforts to bring the house to life again. He addresses her in the following words: 'And mayst thou long live happy, to retrace/The faded honours of thy ancient race.' This wish was partially granted. Over a period of nearly thirty years, Mrs Bulwer Lytton recovered the prestige of the Lytton family in the county, and greatly enjoyed her role as chatelaine of

Knebworth. But from time to time her happiness was marred by the selfish actions of her favourite son.

At the time of his mother's death in 1843, Bulwer Lytton was at the height of his fame as a novelist. His political achievements, however, did not yet match his ambitions, despite the fact that he had successfully represented St Ives, Cornwall, in the House of Commons before the First Reform Bill of 1832, and the City of Lincoln from 1832 until his defeat in 1841. His radical sentiments, first articulated in the Union Society debates at Cambridge, found a counterpart in his early literary work in which the plight of the underdog and the criminal were favoured themes. In remarkable contrast was his social life, particularly after his marriage in 1827 to Rosina Wheeler, an emancipated Irish girl whom he had met through Lady Caroline Lamb. Bulwer Lytton's affectations, his rouged cheeks, his clothes, his parties and the interior decoration of his London houses were subjects of endless comment in fashionable society. His rash marriage alienated him from his mother, who reacted sternly by cutting off his allowance. To sustain his extravagant way of life he was forced to write for money. In this endeavour he was successful, but the toll was heavy. His health suffered; Rosina resented the long hours he spent at his desk, and his bouts of ill-temper terrified her. By the early 1830s their relationship had broken down, and when she discovered he had a mistress, she left him. Rosina's departure was followed by a reconciliation between mother and son.

Bulwer Lytton established his career as a novelist by the publication in 1828 of *Pelham, or Adventures of a Gentleman*. The book is a satire on the contemporary beau monde and the cult of the dandy. It was launched by an unprecedented advertising campaign, and readers had the fun of attempting to identify the individuals upon whom Bulwer Lytton had based his characters. This was the first and last time in his literary career that Bulwer Lytton was to draw so obviously from his own circle of friends. *Pelham* was followed by *Paul Clifford* (1830), *Eugene Aram* (1832), *The Last Days of Pompeii* (1834) and *Rienzi, or The Last of the Tribunes* (1835). The two historical novels set in Italy, one in Pompeii at the time of the city's destruction by volcanic lava in AD 79 and the other in fourteenth-century Rome, were the fruits of a visit to that country in 1833–4. They illustrate the great, almost obsessive, care Bulwer Lytton took to ensure that the facts in his narratives were accurate. Elements are often introduced that reflect his lifelong interest in the occult. In writing *Paul Clifford*, Bulwer-Lytton had a different purpose in mind. Paul Clifford is a highwayman, and the novel was planned as a vehicle with which to draw attention to the harsh penal laws of the time. In 1838 he received a baronetcy for services to literature in Queen Victoria's Coronation Honours List.

Bulwer Lytton was always a controversial figure among his contemporaries. In his early days as a novelist and journalist (for a time he edited the *New Monthly Magazine*), opponents such as W. M. Thackeray conducted a campaign of vilification against him in the press. But his books reached a wide and appreciative audience and were translated into all the major languages. He was delighted to hear that Goethe before his death planned to translate some of his work into German; Pushkin left unfinished a story entitled *The Russian Pelham* set in St Petersburg; and the young Wagner based the libretto of his opera *Rienzi* (first performed at Dresden in 1842) on Bulwer Lytton's text. The novels, too, remained popular, *Rienzi* selling the greatest number in Bulwer Lytton's lifetime. In 1853 George Routledge paid Bulwer Lytton £20,000 for the privilege of publishing a cheap edition of his works. 'My brother publishers think me mad,' he told Bulwer Lytton, but Routledge renewed the contract for a further five years after the initial ten-year period had elapsed.

The screen in the Great Hall

Bulwer Lytton's study, showing his portrait by E. M. Ward

Mrs Bulwer Lytton died in 1843. She had helped her son bring up his two children, Robert and Emily, and proved a wise counsellor and friend. A few months before her death, Bulwer Lytton published *The Last of the Barons* and announced that this would be his last work of fiction. His mother's long illness and her death affected him deeply, and he was bored with authorship. Furthermore, he had lost his seat at Lincoln and a quarrel with the Whig hierarchy made his chances of being selected for another constituency unlikely. Thus he turned to Knebworth, the catalyst of his youthful dreams. He had never criticized his mother for her restoration of the house, but there is no doubt that he regretted the manner in which its ancient character had been masked by a Regency veneer. He was stimulated to apply all the creative energy and careful research he would usually devote to a historical novel to Knebworth's resuscitation. Of his mother's alterations, he spared only her bedroom.

Within three months of Mrs Bulwer Lytton's death his plans for the house were under way. The architect was H. E. Kendall, Junior, and J. G. Crace was selected to decorate the interiors. As the theme of this decoration was the glorification of Mrs Bulwer Lytton's family, a genealogist was employed to trace the armorial bearings to which she was entitled. Meanwhile, antique shops were scoured for suitable furniture, arms and armour and paintings. Bulwer Lytton's considerable financial resources, almost entirely derived from his literary activities, were devoted to turning Knebworth into a frame, as it were, for his own portrait. Some of the results survive today, most notably in the State Drawing Room, a fine example of High Victorian Gothic, and his study, which remains much as he left it. There was an air of theatricality about his efforts which still lingers – and appropriately, because he was also a playwright. His best known play, *Money* (1840), a comedy written for the actor Macready, was successfully revived by the Royal Shakespeare Company in the early 1980s. A watercolour at Knebworth depicts Bulwer Lytton, exquisitely dressed, stepping into the Great Hall from between heavy velvet curtains as if to take his bow. When the house was finished he wrote an account of it for the benefit of visitors who had not known it in its earlier form. In this there was no need for him to be circumspect about the Great Hall, which is of late medieval origin and which retains to this day not only its panelling dating from the late seventeenth century but also its Jacobean screen; the architecture of the exterior he describes without qualification as 'the purest Tudor'. In fact, what he did was to retain the old plain brick structure and encase it in elaborate stucco decoration in the Tudor style. This stucco decoration – turrets, cupolas, gargoyles, armorial shields – has presented severe problems of maintenance, but much has been restored in the past fifteen years.

When Bulwer Lytton completed the initial work at Knebworth, and recovered from a serious breakdown in health, he resumed the flow of novels: *Harold, the Last of the Saxon Kings* appeared in 1848, two domestic novels, *The Caxtons: A Family Picture* (1849) and its sequel *My Novel* (1853), *A Strange Story* (1862), the pioneering work of science fiction, *The Coming Race* (1871), and *Kenelm Chillingly* (1873). In 1852 he returned to parliament as Tory MP for the County of Hertford, and in 1858–9 he served as Secretary of State for the Colonies.

His candidacy and election entailed much entertaining at Knebworth. In 1850 Charles Dickens was invited to bring his group of amateur actors for a series of performances of plays which took place on a portable stage in the Great Hall in front of an admiring audience of friends, local gentry and political allies. Wherever Bulwer Lytton was in later life – in the south of France, at Margate, or Brighton, or at his winter house overlooking Torbay – he was planning alterations at Knebworth, only a few of which were realized. Fortunately for his descendants, financial restraints restricted his most elaborate plans. 'A House is always eating a hole in one's pocket,' he once told his mother, but added, 'there never was a House that repaid what it costs half so well as dear old Knebworth.' Perhaps later in life he was happiest when he was away, sketching new ideas for additions and improvements, often on the backs of envelopes or in the margins of his manuscripts. His daughter died in 1848; his son's diplomatic career entailed long absences abroad, and a succession of mistresses from the demi-monde brought only inter-mittent domestic contentment. So he found Knebworth increasingly lonely and tended to leave after a visit of only a few days. A portrait of him at Knebworth by E. M. Ward painted in 1854 successfully conveys a mood of pensive sadness. In this he is shown seated at a table in his study, a book in one hand, a favourite Turkish pipe in the other, with a caged bird beside the open window. He died, as Baron Lytton, in 1873. His last wish, to be buried at Knebworth, was disregarded, and he rests in Westminster Abbey. Much of his work inside the house was effaced by his grandson, the 2nd Earl of Lytton, in partnership with Sir Edwin Lutyens (the grandson's brother-in-law). But Bulwer Lytton is once more the presiding genius, thanks to the efforts of a great-great-grandson, David (now Lord Cobbold), and his wife, Christine, who have lived in the house since the early 1970s and have embarked on a substantial programme of restoration. Knebworth itself and the literary, political and personal relics on display inside the house survive to recall a life of extraordinary stature.

JOHN BUNYAN

ELSTOW AND BEDFORD

JAMES RUNCIE

As I walked through the wilderness of this world, I lighted on a certain placewhere was a den, and I laid me down in that place to sleep, and as I slept I dreamed a dream ...

The opening sentence of *The Pilgrim's Progress* is rooted in the town of Bedford, where John Bunyan's statue, nine feet tall and green with age, stands at the top of the High Street in benign admonishment. Although there is no obvious focus of literary pilgrimage, it is here that the reader can start to uncover something of the heart of this fiercely Puritan man – converted brazier, 'immortal tinker', and passionately spiritual author – a man who recognized the need to find faith amidst the understandable rationality of doubt and despair; a man who was imprisoned for twelve years for his faith, and who knew that the principal purpose of his life was to come to an understanding of death.

Any Bunyan pilgrimage must begin with an act of the imagination. There is no equivalent of a Shakespearian theatre, Wordsworthian landscape or Haworth Parsonage to guide the visitor. Furthermore, Bunyan is a profoundly internal writer. His work is of the spirit, and the combined evidence of history, architecture and geography seems inadequate. Any investigation must of needs be a journey, an adventure of the imagination, a spiritual quest. There may be fixed points, signposts on the road to understanding, but there is much that remains mysterious and unfulfilled.

Yet there are clues. Bunyan's statue points the way to a journey through the town, and the visitor can make a modern Pilgrim's Progress, past the church in which he worshipped, through the museum which contains his work, over the bridge where Christian walked, and out to the village of Elstow, where he was born. We can embark on our own spiritual journey and begin, as Bunyan himself began, in the graceless reality of everyday existence. We can set out from the City of Destruction, pass through the Wicket Gate, ignore the advice of Mr Worldly

63

Wiseman and make our way through the Valley of the Shadow of Death towards the Celestial City.

> Who would true valour see,
>   Let him come hither;
> One here will constant be,
>   Come wind, come weather.
> There's no discouragement
> Shall make him once relent
> His first avow'd intent
>   To be a pilgrim.

Underneath Bunyan's statue are three plaques representing episodes in *The Pilgrim's Progress*: Christian with his burden of sin before the Wicket Gate; his wrestling with the demonic fiend Apollyon; and his meeting with three shining ones at the foot of the Cross. The Cross is Christian's still-point in a turning world, and it seems appropriate to begin this modern Progress in a church – not in a traditional, established, Church of England building, but in the Nonconformist Bunyan Meeting Free Church in Mill Street.

The Church of England, with its laws preventing preaching by unlicensed visionaries, was principally responsible for Bunyan's imprisonment. The charge against him was that he had 'devilishly and perniciously' abstained from attending official church services, that he could not fully understand the scriptures because he could not read Greek, and that he had preached to assemblies which were unlawful. To escape a long sentence, all he had to do was forswear his preaching. Yet this was something Bunyan found impossible, avowing to his judges, 'If I were out of prison today, I would preach the gospel again tomorrow, by the help of God.' Bunyan did not inherit his belief so much as possess the fierce and nonconformist convictions of the late convert; he felt that he had heard the Voice of God directly, and that he therefore owed his allegiance to a higher authority than that of Church or State. He did not follow the path of convention but that of righteousness, and sometimes these paths ran in different directions. Faith asks uncomfortable questions, and he did not shirk from the idea that the followers of God are often seen as 'a turbulent, seditious and factious people'.

The Bunyan Meeting was formed in 1650 by a group of twelve people who began to worship in a simple barn. Bunyan was its second pastor. The present church was built some time after his death, but its cool, classical interior has an appropriate simplicity; heavy bronze doors in imitation of Ghiberti's Baptistry doors in Florence and modern stained-glass windows both illustrate scenes from *The*

Houghton House, Bunyan's House Beautiful, Ampthill

Pilgrim's Progress; inscribed quotations from the work help to convey something of the sublime paradox at the heart of Bunyan's faith ('He hath given me rest by his sorrow and life by his death'). The original Communion table with a bread roll, a glass of water, the Bible and flowers forms a still life that might have come from a seventeenth-century Dutch painting. It is a restful, friendly, meditative place.

In the museum next door, an indenture of 1650 records the purchase of the garden and barn where the meetings began; there is the table on which Bunyan wrote while in prison; the anvil he carried while working as a tinker before he found his full faith and which some say was the physical burden referred to in *The Pilgrim's Progress*; the violin he made from tin; the flute he made from a chair leg; the door of the old gaol; the soup jug which his blind daughter, Mary, carried to him each evening; the chair which, as a minister, he used after his release; and the Church Book that records his death from a chill caught in London in 1688. It is

Exterior of the Moot Hall, Elstow

in this book, in a simple declarative sentence, that we can appreciate the affection with which he was regarded by the fellow members of his church:

> Wednesday, 4th September, was kept in prayre and humilyation for this Heavy Stroak upon us, the Death of deare Brother Bunyan.

In contrast to the church, the museum is located in a dark and sombre room, as if all time had stopped, but there is an equivalent simplicity about the arrangement of the objects, and a friendliness in the welcome that makes this seem the most appropriate place to begin any study of Bunyan. *The Pilgrim's Progress* is housed here in 167 languages, and there are copies of his other great works such as *Grace Abounding*, *The Holy War* and *The Life and Death of Mr Badman* for sale.

Seeing so many remnants of his prison life is a stark reminder that Bunyan spent a third of his adult life in gaol, and that his faith was hard fought. It makes Christian's statement to By-Ends all the more resonant, for, like Bunyan, he recognized the cost of faith:

> If you will go with us you must go against wind and tide, the which, I perceive, is against your opinion. You must also own religion in his rags, as well as in his silver slippers, and stained by him, too, when bound in irons, as well as when he walketh the streets with applause.

Bunyan knew what it was like to be bound in irons.

Leaving the church you pass the Swan Hotel, which housed the county assizes in the seventeenth century, where Bunyan's second wife Elizabeth pleaded for clemency during her husband's trial. You cross the bridge over the River Ouse, and mark the site of the Old Stone House, under the third pier east, which became the imagined 'den' where Bunyan dreamed his majestic dream. And you make your way to the House of the Interpreter, now the headquarters of the St John Ambulance in St John's Street. If you ring the bell, they will open up the room in which Christian and the Interpreter, alias Bunyan and John Gifford, his mentor, pastor and guide, discussed the essentials of the faith. ('Sir,' said Christian, 'I was told . . . that if I called here you would show me excellent things, such as would be a help to me on my journey.') The room is now an office, but the bare walls contain traces of fifteenth-century wall paintings, featuring the red and white roses of the Houses of Lancaster and York, and a series of single Prince of Wales plumes. The timber-framed partition walls support a roof of exposed beams with a strong central cross-beam – the sight of which, according to tradition, encouraged Bunyan in his meditation on the Crucifixion.

St John's Street leads straight to Elstow, Bunyan's birthplace, where the Moot Hall houses a Bunyan Room, early editions of his work and small domestic objects of the period. Originally built in the fifteenth century as a market house for the village fairs, the wattle-and-daub building was later used as a storehouse, a school

Interior of the Moot Hall

and a place of worship before it became a museum. Here it is possible to see something of the style of seventeenth-century everyday life – pewter chargers, trenchers and porringers are mixed with wooden dishes, platters and bowls on a long oak table. The period furniture, rather too lavish for a man of Bunyan's means, consists of oak chests, walnut presses and ash armchairs. It is a beautiful building, the leaded upper windows looking on to the green where Elstow Fair took place each year. It was here in 1645, during the Civil War, that the gathering of people of differing sympathies in close proximity led to considerable disturbance, and may well have provided the model for Bunyan's Vanity Fair, where

> there is at all times to be seen smugglings, cheats, games, plays, fools, apes, knaves, and rogues, and that of all sorts ... thefts, murders, adulteries, false swearers, and that of a blood red colour ...

Nearby stands the Abbey of St Helena and St Mary, where Bunyan was baptized on 30 November 1628, and where his mother, father and sister lie buried. The detached belfry is where Bunyan rang the bells for pleasure as a young man, a 'vain practice' he later abjured, fearing that God's anger at his sins would cause the bell to fall upon him.

The Abbey also contains the Wicket Gate through which Christian passed at the start of his spiritual journey, and even though it must be stressed that *The Pilgrim's Progress* is clearly a work of the imagination, existing outside any real geography, the neighbouring countryside contains frequent echoes of the book. Locals will have you believe that the dark and winding road through Millbrook Gorge was the model for the Valley of the Shadow of Death; fool's gold found at Pulloxhill may have made it the basis for his Hill of Lucre, and the town cross at Stevington is the location Bunyan had in mind when Christian lost his burden:

> He ran thus till he came at a place somewhat ascending; and upon that place stood a cross, and a little below, in the bottom, a sepulchre. So I saw in my dream that, just as Christian came up with the cross, his burden loosed from off his shoulders, and fell from off his back, and began to tumble; and so continued to do till it came to the mouth of the sepulchre, where it fell in, and I saw it no more.

The sepulchre, if we are to be literal about these things, is believed to be the Holy Well in the churchyard of St Mary's, Stevington, a spring whose waters never freeze or dry up.

In fact, the Bedfordshire countryside is alive with echoes of Bunyan. They are not laid out on a convenient Heritage Trail, but await discovery, and can all be found with a mixture of patience and imagination. All the visitor needs is a good map and a copy of the book. My own Progress ended at the Hill of Difficulty, underneath Houghton House some two miles from Ampthill.

As you walk up the hill, it is impossible not to think of Christian, 'where I perceived that he fell from running to going, and from going to clambering upon his hands and knees, because of the steepness of the place'. At the top stand the ruins of Houghton House, acknowledged to be the inspiration for Bunyan's House Beautiful. It was built in 1615 for Mary Countess of Pembroke, the sister of Philip Sidney, and records show that Bunyan himself visited the house to make and repair cooking utensils,

> and many of them meeting him at the threshold of the house said, 'Come in, thou blessed of the Lord; this house was built by the Lord of the Hill on purpose to entertain such pilgrims in.'

Standing on the top of the hill, looking at this ruined mansion, I remembered a *son et lumière* presentation of *The Pilgrim's Progress* I had once seen here, an amateur production that ended at nightfall with a magnificent firework display as Christian entered the Celestial City. Now it was late afternoon, and I could see the skyline of the City of Destruction, the smokestacks in the Slough of Despond, and the motorway that has flattened the land in the Valley of Humiliation. From the height of this Hill of Difficulty I looked out through the ruined windows of the House Beautiful and saw the sun breaking through a brooding, melancholic sky over the Chilterns, the Delectable Mountains of Bunyan's dream. I had come to the end of my journey. I picked up my copy of *The Pilgrim's Progress* and started to read:

> And behold, at a great distance he saw a most pleasant and mountainous country, beautified with woods, vineyards, fruit of all sorts, flowers also, with springs and fountains, very delectable to behold. Then he asked the name of the country; they said it was Immanuel's Land, and it is as common, said they, as this hill is to and for all pilgrims. And when thou comest there from thence thou mayest see to the gate of the Celestial City ...

I read on, turning the pages in the fading light, recognizing that even though this geographical 'progress' might have come to an end, my spiritual journey would last far longer, 'yea, even unto death'.

ROBERT BURNS

ALLOWAY, AYRSHIRE

DOUGLAS DUNN

Ireland, the 'Emerald Isle', has been verdantly named. England too, as a 'green and pleasant land', is identified with its fields and woods. Grassy epithets, however, were seldom among those that sped from the pre-industrial poetic pen when Scotland was evoked by its poets, and whose phrases have seeped into descriptive stock. These famous lines from Sir Walter Scott's *The Lay of the Last Minstrel* come close to matching their English and Irish equivalents:

> O Caledonia! stern and wild,
> Meet nurse for a poetic child!
> Land of brown heath and shaggy wood,
> Land of the mountain and the flood,
> Land of my sires! what mortal hand
> Can e'er untie the filial band
> That knits me to thy rugged strand!

Not much there suggests pleasant greenery. When Scott writes of 'shaggy wood', the colour that comes to mind is one of wrinkled, moss-colonized oak-bark. Leaves go unnoticed, or else the season is one of perpetual winter. It seems *peculiarly* brown, rugged and waterlogged.

Kyle, Robert Burns's native district of Ayrshire, which he turned into his Muse, Coila, has always impressed visitors as a green country. 'Brown heath' and local uplands can be found there, but its pasturage and good arable ground create a picture that is more fat, ample and prosperous. Of course, in Burns's time it was difficult terrain to farm. Drainage, machinery and agricultural skills have made life easier for those whose livelihoods depend on them. Green fields seen on a summer's day against a backdrop of a blue Firth of Clyde on that Ayrshire coast can become a memory not easily forgotten and confirmed on each return. John Keats, approaching Burns's birthplace from the south, was eager to the point of rhapsody for what he saw:

I had no Conception that the native place of Burns was so beautiful – the Idea I had was more desolate, his rigs of Barley seemed always to me but a few strips of Green on a cold hill – O prejudice! it was rich as Devon – I endeavour'd to drink in the Prospect, that I might spin it out to you as the silkworm makes silk from Mulbery leaves – I cannot recollect it – Besides all the Beauty, there were the Mountains of Arran Isle, black and huge over the Sea – We came down upon every thing suddenly – there were in our way, the 'bonny Doon', with the Brig that Tam O' Shanter cross'ed – Kirk Alloway, Burns's Cottage and then the Brigs of Ayr – First we stood upon the Bridge across the Doon; surrounded by every Phantasy of Green in tree, Meadow, and Hill, – the Stream of the Doon, as a Farmer told us, is covered with trees from head to foot – you know those beautiful heaths so fresh against the weather of a summers evening – there was one stretching along behind the trees.

Robert Burns was born on 25 January 1759 in that cottage in Alloway, two and a quarter miles south of Ayr, to which Keats was headed in mid-July 1818, his spirit ardent for the chance of communing with that of another poet whose work he held in passionate admiration. In Keats's day the cottage was a tavern, and so it remained until 1880. It is far from a disrespectful act to toast the memory of a poet like Burns, but if shrines of this sort are public places, it seems hurtful to permit them to be public houses. Small museums, though, devoted to a single personality, find it hard to avoid the atmosphere of a profane church. The modern Burns Cottage Museum is a serious place; but the nature of the house it preserves makes it a domestic memorial, as well as an archive of books, letters, documents and memorabilia.

However, the 'auld clay biggin' is tantalizingly poetic in itself. It is a metaphor. Those in the habit of associating one thing with another might find themselves unwilling to forget the significance of the material with which the house was built. With the exception of some stone lintels, masonry, braces and timbers, and the thatch with which it is roofed, it is made of clay, limed and harled. That is, it is constructed to a large extent of the substance with which Burns struggled for much of his relatively short life – clay, earth, dirt, ground. Because it was Burns who was born there, you could go a step further and connect earth and house with Ayrshire, language and song. Some of those who knew Burns were less keen on metaphors and stronger on pedantry. John Murdoch, who, as a teenaged dominie, was hired by Burns's father and four of his neighbours to tutor their children, referred to the cottage's clay structure as 'an argillaceous fabric'. Call it clay and the burden of toil that Burns was born to carry begins to become clearer.

The byre in Burns's cottage

The cottage at Alloway

William Burnes (to give the father the correct spelling of his name) was both architect and artisan of the house in which his son, the poet, was born. He came from Kincardineshire, and he was a gardener. Both he and his father before him had worked for the family of the Earls Marischal, whose greatest soldier was James, Field-Marshal Keith, who commanded armies in Russia and died in the service of Frederick the Great at the battle of Hochkirche in 1758. Burnes built the cottage in the summer and autumn of 1757 and married Agnes Broun (or Brown) on 15 December, in his thirty-sixth year. The seven and a half acres that he purchased leasehold in Alloway, by the River Doon – the name is Gaelic in origin, and means 'the steep river bank by the cairn' – were intended as a market garden, but the plan failed to come off. It was a time when, as Voltaire remarked, Europe looked to Scotland for philosophers and gardeners. In his *Autobiography*, Alexander Carlyle reported that 'It was at Bulstrode that we discovered the truth of what I had often heard, that most of the head-gardeners of English noblemen were Scotch.' Later on he noted that a Scotsman was head-gardener at Blenheim. When James Boswell put it to his Great Friend that 'England was obliged to us for gardeners', Dr Johnson brought forth his celebrated (or, if you like, notorious) reply:

> 'Why, Sir, that is because gardening is much more necessary amongst you than with us, which makes so many of your people learn it. It is *all* gardening with you. Things which grow wild here, must be cultivated with great care in Scotland. Pray now (throwing himself back in his chair, and laughing), are you ever able to bring the *sloe* to perfection?'

Despite his horticultural pedigree, Burns's father seems to have been less ambitious, or not so expert, as those of his countrymen who took their occupation to England and farther afield in search of advancement. Had he done so there might have been no 'auld clay biggin' in Alloway, no marriage to Agnes Broun, and no poet. Burnes was employed as chief gardener by Dr Fergusson, a local man who had made his fortune in a medical way in London and come back. There were as many Scottish medical practitioners in England as gardeners, 'bleeding their English neighbours', as Eric Linklater once remarked, 'more profitably than anyone since the Black Douglas'. Fergusson's estate at Doonholm offered parks and gardens, enough, at any rate, to suggest that William Burnes knew his trade.

Robert Burns was a winter-child. His nativity was well weathered, a coincidence that might help some Scots to their belief that it was the second most important nativity in the history of the world. Burns took the circumstances of his birth for all – perhaps a little more – than they were worth:

> Our monarch's hinmost year but ane
> Was five-and-twenty days begun,
> 'Twas then a blast o' Janwar Win'
> Blew hansel in on Robin

he wrote in the song known as 'There was a Lad'. In writing of how the January wind delivered its New Year offering, Burns allowed himself a degree of poetic, autobiographical licence. His brother Gilbert retold the event with more precision:

> When my father built his 'clay biggin', he put in two stone-jambs, as they are called, and a lintel, carrying up the chimney in his clay-gable. The consequence was, that as the gable subsided, the jambs, remaining firm, threw it off its centre; and, one very stormy morning, when my brother was nine or ten days old, a little before daylight, a part of the gable fell out, and the rest appeared so shattered, that my mother, with the young poet, had to be carried through the storm to a neighbour's house, where they remained a week, till their own dwelling was adjusted.

It was a fierce wind, and it could be, too, that William Burnes's handiwork left something to be desired. In two rooms, a 'but and ben', or kitchen and spence (parlour), it was a cut above the usual run of cottages in the neighbourhood.

Demonstrating a touch of the sentimentality with which accounts of Burns's story are often cloaked, James Barke in his novel *The Wind Shakes the Barley* (1946) has Burns's mother say to her husband-to-be:

> 'It's more nor I bargained on, William. It's a better house nor I was brocht up in at Kirkoswald. It's a palace of a place set by the cot-houses of the farms here ... And the ingle-neuk! That's a fireside ony woman in Ayrshire would be proud of. You've made a real snod job o' it, William.'

Snod, indeed – a big puff and the gable fell in. Burns was glad of an event that announced his arrival with more than his own howl. What poet wouldn't be? He was spared the necessity of imagining the auspicious visit of a wintry Muse. All he had to do was bring it forward by ten days.

Burns's birthplace, Burns himself, his life and poetry, tickle a racial nerve in many Scots, particularly those whose roots lie in the counties between the Clyde and the Solway. It is a difficult sensation to explain. Pride is part of it. When

Brig o' Doon, Alloway

allowed to run riot, it can take the unedifying form of local conceit and homespun swank. The late Christopher Murray Grieve ('Hugh MacDiarmid') girned and growled for over half a century at those Burnsians who elevated 'their' poet and condescended towards all others with a primitive, vainglorious candour that had the effect of distorting the Scottish notion of poetry with a belittling provincialism. Yet pride and the possessiveness that goes with it are understandable when you bear in mind that Burns speaks directly to those in a country who otherwise care little for poetry and literature, having sensed long ago that poetry and literature care little for them. When a Scot stands in the Alloway cottage among the memorabilia, at least a little of that angered or over-jaunty pride is likely to be felt. Humble scale and rustic particularity set up their own inevitable contrast between Burns's origins and the international spaciousness of his reputation – a posterity which, as it happens, has been peculiarly well tended in the United States, Germany and the Soviet Union as well as Scotland. Or, in the two-roomed cottage where Burns began, a visitor might have in mind images of the memorials that mark his end. A cenotaph can be seen nearby. Designed by Thomas Hamilton of Edinburgh and opened in 1823, it is unusually classical, in stark contrast to the figures in the same gardens of Tam o' Shanter, Souter Johnny and Nance Tannock in which James Thom, a self-taught local sculptor born in 1802, strove with glaring obviousness for vernacular, comic 'likenesses' and achieved them, although at the expense of exposing the essential differences between poetry and three-dimensional art. The Burns Monument at Kilmarnock is more baronial, as is the National Burns Memorial at Mauchline. Statues are far from being in short supply. For what subjective taste is worth, the one I prefer is in Burns Statue Square in Ayr, which dates from the early 1890s. Dumfries, where Burns died, offers a mausoleum in St Michael's churchyard in which there is a reworking in bas-relief of an original piece by Turnerelli (an Irish sculptor of Italian extraction) done by Hermon Crawthra and completed in 1936. It shows Burns at the plough before a vision of his Muse, Coila. 'The Poetic Genius of my country found me,' Burns wrote, 'as the prophetic bard Elijah did Elisha, at the plough; and threw her inspiring mantle over me.'

Should such an ostensibly fulsome statement be accepted literally? Could it be an enabling tactic, intended as both literal and ironic? That is, while open to be read as a Romantic or idealized truth, could it participate also in a self-aware, well-tutored and understandably self-defensive bluff? My opinion is that in the Preface to the Kilmarnock edition of *Poems, Chiefly in the Scottish Dialect* (1786), in some of his poems and letters, in the climate of his career, Burns's attitude to his poetry, what he says of it, can be stated something like this: 'I must demean myself to excuses, and apologies, because if I don't, society will not think of me as a poet at all, on the grounds of my origins – my own people, as well as the literati, and men

Mount Oliphant Farm

and women of importance; therefore, I appeal to inspiration beyond human knowledge, in which I believe, with all my heart, but I exaggerate the rusticity of the appeal, in order to make my poetry possible for you, but not for me.'

Thinking of Burns's poetry in his birthplace, or in the more substantial red sandstone, two-storey house in Dumfries where he died, is an exacting as well as an exhilarating exercise. There is a political and patriotic mood to these houses which is, or ought to be, part of the sensation felt by any Scot who visits them, or by anyone else who has read Burns's poetry and who knows something of his life. In the house in which he was born it flows from the poem 'The Cotter's Saturday Night', which Burns probably set there. Sir David Wilkie's painting of the same title catches the piety of the poem, but it could do nothing with Burns's championship of liberty or the Scottish grain in which he set it:

XIX

From scenes like these, old SCOTIA's grandeur springs,
    That makes her lov'd at home, rever'd abroad:
Princes and lords are but the breath of kings,
    'AN honest man's the noblest work of GOD:'
And *certes*, in fair Virtue's heavenly road,

78

The *Cottage* leaves the Palace far behind:
What is a lordling's pomp? a cumbrous load,
    Disguising oft the *wretch* of human kind,
Studied in arts of Hell, in wickedness refin'd!

XX

O Scotia! my dear, my native soil!
    For whom my warmest wish to heaven is sent!
Long may thy hardy sons of *rustic toil*,
    Be blest with health, and peace, and sweet content!
And O may Heaven their simple lives prevent
    From *Luxury's* contagion, weak and vile!
Then, howe'er *crowns* and *coronets* be rent,
    A *virtuous Populace* may rise the while,
And stand a wall of fire around their much-lov'd Isle.

XXI

O Thou! who pour'd the *patriotic tide*,
    That stream'd thro' great, unhappy Wallace' heart;
Who dar'd to, nobly, stem tyrannic pride,
    Or *nobly die*, the second glorious part:
(The Patriot's God, peculiarly thou art,
    His *friend, inspirer, guardian* and *reward!*)
O never, never, Scotia's realm desert,
    But still the *Patriot*, and the *Patriot-Bard*,
In bright succession raise, her *Ornament* and *Guard*!

'The Cotter's Saturday Night' is a flawed, passionately conventional poem in Spenserian stanzas; but its rapid transitions from rhetorical English to demotic Scots illustrate by themselves the contrast between the societies represented by them. It is as if Burns's instincts set Henry Hoare's Paradise or Pope's Grotto alongside 'The *lowly train* in life's sequester'd scene', as well as interpreted Gray's 'Elegy' for his local purposes. He would not have needed to look so far afield. As a pseudonymous correspondent pointed out when he wrote to the editor of the *Edinburgh Evening Courant* in November 1786, complaining about the apparent stinginess of patronage forthcoming in Burns's native shire, 'The county of Ayr is perhaps superior to any in Scotland in the number of its Peers, Nabobs, and wealthy Commoners.' He claimed, too, that 'This part of the kingdom has not produced many poets.' Perhaps both contemporary remarks should be kept in mind when visiting the house in which Burns was born, and the house in Dumfries in which he died. In the first house you might sense his unexpectedness as a poet, and, in the second, a measure of how his furtherance in the material conditions of life seems relatively unspectacular.

Life as an independent writer was never a possibility for Burns without the support of a generous patron, one who either agreed with the poet's political sentiments or was willing to ignore them, with the added eccentricity of being able to disregard the odium conveyed by rumours (many of them true) concerning Burns's erotic past – such a patron did not exist. It was through influence, however, that Burns obtained his post in the Excise in Dumfries in 1789 at a salary of £50 per annum. Schoolmasters in Scotland in the 1790s earned around £20 per annum. Clergymen did better, at £40 or less. By his death in 1796 Burns was earning £85. Excisemen were entitled to half the value of apprehended contraband and, as an additional inducement to official vigour, half the fines levied on smugglers. Even if 'Coin his pouches widna bide in', Burns earned enough for his needs, although at great cost to himself.

From 1788 to 1791 he leased the farm Ellisland on the banks of the Nith (where he wrote 'Tam o' Shanter'), a few miles north of Dumfries. He was reluctant to let go his inherited way of life as a farmer. Mount Oliphant (where the family moved from Alloway in 1766), Lochlie (1777–84) and Mossgiel (1784–8) in Ayrshire, and Ellisland in Dumfries offer an insight into the arduous physical work at which Burns spent the largest portion of his life. As agricultural landscapes, all four farms have changed; so, too, have their houses and outbuildings. Wandering round their fields, however, gives an impression, if not much more than that, of how it might have felt to 'drudge thro' dub an' mire/At pleugh or cart'. Expressions of fatigue and the effects of sore weather crop up frequently in Burns's poetry. 'Han'-darg', a day's manual work, was an experience with which he was more than familiar; he knew it intimately, from boyhood on. 'Forjesket sair, with weary legs,' he wrote of exhaustion, 'Rattlin the corn out-owre the rigs.' Significantly, that occurs in his second 'Epistle to John Lapraik', where Burns is concerned to defend his idea and practice of poetry. So does this statement from 'The Vision':

> The thresher's weary flingin-tree,
> The lee-lang day had tir'd me.

Burns was as self-aware a poet as he was a farmer. He knew more than enough about poetry and the precarious agriculture on which his family's livelihood depended – that is, he knew about life and the way the world turned – for him to make each activity articulate and defend the other. His birthplace, farms, and the house in which he died as an officer of the Excise encourage the overstatement of his humble origins and life of toil. It is necessary to emphasize them, just as any appreciation of Burns's life has to take into account his reputation as a carouser and womanizer, but not at the expense of his sagacity and intelligence, or the artistry and strategies of his verse.

80

Burns's poetry and song brought out the dignity of rustic labour and the decency of honest poverty. They entered the Scottish psyche with extraordinary thoroughness. The comfortably-off took to naming their houses after Burns's farms, especially Mossgiel. In all likelihood they approved of the virtuous family hearth, the Bible-reading, good-natured, hard-working ethos of the community that Burns represented and evoked. Yet Burns is the embodiment of transgressions of that same code through the covert, amorous merriment depicted by his songs and poems, or his plain-spoken, mischievous satire, his patriotism (although it is easy to tame it with distortions and caricatures) and his revolutionary sympathies.

Few poets' lives follow so closely an itinerary of tenancies and dwellings within such a socially and geographically confined range. It has invited pilgrimages ever since his death. William and Dorothy Wordsworth wrote of their feelings at Burns's grave in 1803 with a sorrow that suggests their understanding of Burns's destiny as one weighed down by misfortune. Keats struck a better note in the letter from which I have already quoted:

> One of the pleasantest means of annulling self is approaching such a shrine as the Cottage of Burns – we need not think of his misery – that is all gone – bad luck to it.

He, too, found it impossible to escape from the grievousness of Burns's career. After an encounter with 'a great Bore', a 'mahogany-faced old Jackass who knew Burns', and who called himself 'a curious old Bitch', Keats's hackles rose:

> O the flummery of a birth place! Cant! Cant! Cant! It is enough to give a spirit the guts-ache ... His misery is a dead weight upon the nimbleness of one's quill – I tried to forget it – to drink Toddy without any Care – to write a merry Sonnet – it wont do – he talked with Bitches – he drank with Blackguards, he was miserable – We can see horribly clear in the works of such a man his whole life, as if we were God's spies.

Opportunities for meeting curious old Bitches lessened in 1880 when the Alloway Burns Monument Trustees bought the cottage from the Ayr Corporation of Shoemakers for the sum of £4,000. Even by 1930, however, Burns's birthplace was insecure. In that year the Ayrshire Association of Federated Burns Clubs published a collection of letters and documents summing up their efforts to protect and preserve the cottage and its contents. One letter referred to threats of a few years before in the form of 'the undesirable attention which the Cottage and Museum are presently receiving from militant suffragettes and petty pilferers'. Suffragettes had tried to burn the place down. Relic-mongers had long since chipped away at the original stone marking the grave of Burns's father until next to nothing remained. Keats was right to be indignant at flummery and cant. Scottish literary opinion has echoed his responses, especially since 'Hugh MacDiarmid' questioned Burns's status – in my view, wrongly. Clearly, the house in which Burns was born (and others that still exist in which he lived and died) *ought* to be preserved. By 1991 the Birthplace Museum possessed the largest collection of Burns's letters, as well as other manuscripts and relics. It is a shrine for scholars as well as for everyone to whom Burns's poetry has spoken. As Emerson said of Burns's poems and songs, 'They are the property and the solace of mankind.'

LORD BYRON

NEWSTEAD ABBEY, LINBY, NOTTINGHAMSHIRE

PETER PORTER

In February 1823 Lord Byron was living in Genoa, in the Casa Saluzzo, the last of his Italian residences, and writing the last three Cantos of his unfinished parody epic *Don Juan*, 'Donny Johnny' as he called it in his marvellous letters home to friends in England, many of whom, including his publisher John Murray and the courtesan Harriet Wilson, disapproved of it. He had just entered his thirty-sixth and final year of life, and was the most famous poet in the world. Behind him he had a life of quite extraordinary activity and diversity – ahead lay his expedition to Greece to help the Greeks free themselves from rule by the Turks. The poet was about to become the man of action he had always wanted to be. But he was still occupied with his masterpiece, *Don Juan*. He had launched this long poem on the world five years previously, while living in Ravenna, recuperating from the excitements of Venice, and becoming embroiled in the Italian Nationalist movement known as the Carbonari. By 1823 Don Juan had experienced both first seduction and first love (in that order in Canto 1 and Cantos 2 to 4), followed by a set of farcical adventures in a Turkish harem, a Russian siege of a Turkish fortress (notable for Byron's realistic loathing of war) and the court of the Russian Empress Catherine. The poet, though not his hero, was tired and ready to die.

But before Missolonghi and the equally farcical events of the Greek war of liberation ('armies which won't march; fleets which sail away'), Byron had still to even scores with England, the land which had made him, fêted him and rejected him. England was now haunting his imagination. He was ready to tackle in verse the monstrous subject of English society, previously aired in his lively letters home from Italy, but ripe for the full force of his poetic satire. Byron was now writing poetry as sharp and entertaining as his prose had always been. Accordingly, from Canto 13 onwards, all Juan's adventures are in England. The high point of the English journey of the elegant Spaniard was to be none other than Byron's own country house, Newstead Abbey. First, there was an attempted robbery by footpads along Shooters Hill on the approach to London; then the encomium of the great

city itself, with its docks, grand dwellings and slums; two Cantos follow charting the London Season and the delights, hypocrisies and ebullient scenes of Europe's greatest capital, recalled with due savagery by a poet who had been the darling of this world until his summary expulsion from it.

At last Byron brought Juan down to an unnamed Norman abbey to join a house party of British worthies. The abbey is the seat of Sir Henry and Lady Amundeville, and Byron describes it with a relish testifying to detailed recall of reality rather than imaginative scene painting.

> An old, old monastery once, and now
> Still older mansion of a rich and rare
>   Mixed Gothic ...
>   ... It lies perhaps a little low,
> Because the monks preferred a hill behind
> To shelter their devotion from the wind.

> A glorious remnant of the Gothic pile
>   ... stood half apart
> In a grand arch, which once screened many an aisle.

> ... when
>   The Wind is winged from one point of heaven,
> There moans a strange unearthly sound ...
>   ... a dying accent, driven
> Through the huge arch, which soars and sinks again.
>   ... the distant echo ...
> ... harmonized by the old choral wall.

Sir Henry's country seat is Newstead Abbey, and from this point until the moment when Byron abandoned his poem, all the action takes place there. Cantos 15 and 16 amount to a guide to Newstead, so that almost two hundred years after they were written they conjure up the mansion in a form recognizable to the modern visitor.

Newstead Abbey, in Nottinghamshire, near Mansfield, had been the seat of the Byron family since 1540. Although Byron as a child had not expected to inherit it since he was not in direct line of descent, it had been the scene of many of the formative experiences of his youth and early manhood. Newstead was leased for periods during Byron's childhood and sold by him in 1817 (he was already living in Venice) to an Old Harrovian schoolmate, Wildman, for around £90,000, a colossal sum for the time. Much has been changed since Byron's time, but it is still a place of pilgrimage for visitors fascinated by the legend of England's most charismatic poet.

Byron's bedroom, Newstead Abbey

Following the house party from London to Newstead, we arrive at the abbey and its spacious grounds in the full splendour of an English autumn.

> The mellow Autumn came, and with it came
> The promised party, to enjoy its sweets.
> The corn is cut, the manor full of game;
> The pointer ranges, and the sportsman beats
> In russet jacket ...

The grounds of Newstead, with their lakes and formal gardens, were perfect for the entertainment of an early nineteenth-century house party.

> Before the mansion lay a lucid lake,
> Broad as transparent, deep, and freshly fed
> By a river ...
> ... The wild fowl nestled in the brake
> And sedges, brooding in their liquid bed ...

It was on this lake that Byron's eccentric grandfather, Admiral Sir John ('Mad Jack') Byron, had fought mock sea battles. Beside the house are the ruins of the Priory church; a venerable arch is all that remains of the body of the church, but the monument to Byron's Newfoundland dog, Boatswain, stands at a point he judged to have been the position of the high altar.

> Ye! who perchance behold this simple urn,
> Pass on – It honours none you wish to mourn:
> To mark a friend's remains these stones arise;
> I never knew but one, – and here he lies.

As well as these lines to Boatswain, Byron composed two poems about the abbey, 'An Elegy on Newstead Abbey' and 'Lines on Leaving Newstead Abbey'. But his true monument to the site will be found in *Don Juan*.

The main building was adapted from the priory living quarters and is catalogued thoroughly by Byron. Lording it over the grounds, this mansion is the very epitome of 'Gothick', that romantic ambience which sent such delicious shivers through literary persons at the end of the eighteenth century and the beginning of the nineteenth. From Horace Walpole's *The Castle of Otranto* via Beckford's *Vathek* to the parody Gothick of Thomas Love Peacock (*Nightmare Abbey*) and Jane Austen (*Northanger Abbey*), this revival of medieval spookiness captured the imagination of generations of readers. Byron, in Italy, piled on the colour to make Newstead worthy of its heritage.

> ... Now loud, now fainter,
> The gale sweeps through the fretwork, and oft sings
> The owl his anthem, where the silenced quire
> Lie with their hallelujahs quenched like fire.

Boatswain's monument, with the ruined west window of the Priory Church, Newstead

'Gothick' has the last word in the poem, as Juan, searching by night for the ghostly friar said to haunt the buildings, encounters an apparition in the darkness only to discover that his hand has come to rest on the bosom of the randy Duchess of Fitz-Fulke, disguised for an assignation. Byron wrote no more lines beyond this point, leaving his masterpiece poised in the air like Juan's hand, half-way between high romance and low comedy.

The statue of the Virgin remains in the west front of the church with the 'mighty window' and the Gothic fountain, though this is not now in the court but placed in the cloisters. Also in situ is the 'exquisite small chapel', though its present decorations are examples of Victorian medievalism. The styles of many centuries combine in Newstead to add the picturesque to the imposing:

Huge halls, long galleries, spacious chambers, joined
  By no quite lawful marriage of the arts
. . .
Yet left a grand impression on the mind,
  At least of those whose eyes are in their hearts.

Newstead is one of the most English of country houses, having been an Augustinian foundation before the dissolution of the monasteries, and thereafter the ideal embodiment of the way of life of the country gentry. Curiously, Byron did not live at Newstead very often or for very long. It's fair to say that today the atmosphere is not so much redolent of Byron himself as of the world he was born into, and of which he was so characteristic yet paradoxical a rebel. It is his museum and monument, though his spirit is that of a townee and a traveller: Newstead stands for the England which haunted him throughout his restless life.

When Juan alighted before the West Front, he would have gone straight into the Great Hall and the West Gallery by an exterior flight of steps which has now been removed. Today one can make one's passage instead through the crypt, with its memorials to the first Byrons, from nearby Colwick church, passing one side of the cloisters and getting a good view of the fountain in their midst. Circuiting the galleries, you encounter Byronic memorabilia of all sorts. It would not have been like this when the house guests used the rooms. Here were planned and arranged the diversions of ladies and gentlemen in the country.

The gentlemen got up betimes to shoot
  Or hunt; the young because they liked the sport,
. . .
The middle-aged, to make the day more short; . . .

The elderly walked through the library,
  And tumbled books or criticized the pictures,
Or sauntered through the gardens piteously
  And made upon the hothouse several strictures
Or rode a nag, which trotted not too high
  Or on the morning papers read their lectures, . . .

The ladies, some rouged, some a little pale,
  Met the morn as they might . . .
. . .
  Sung, or rehearsed the last dance from abroad;
Discussed the fashion which might next prevail
  And settled bonnets by the newest code
Or crammed twelve sheets into one little letter.

Byron's helmet

Passing into the South Gallery on the way to the Salon or Great Drawing Room, you get your first real reminder of Byron the great poet. Here are manuscripts of his poems from the earliest near-doggerel verses written in childhood, and at Harrow and Cambridge, and printed on a small press in nearby Newark, right up to the works of his maturity. His hand, in manuscripts, looks surprisingly modern, almost, one might say, Secondary Modern. He composed at enormous speed and wrote copiously. He certainly wasn't born writing poetry well. Not until the Italian years, when he produced *The Vision of Judgment*, *Beppo* and *Don Juan*, did he write poems the equal of the marvellous prose with which he had always filled his letters. But this was after the works which made him famous – *Childe Harold*, the heaven-storming dramas like *Sardanapalus*, *Cain* and *Manfred*, and the romantic narrative poems such as *The Bride of Abydos*, *The Giaour* and *The Corsair*. It was following the success of these long poems and *Childe Harold* that he lived as an adult at Newstead. They were the basis for his enormous subsequent European reputation, and an influence on generations of European writers – Pushkin, Lermontov, Stendhal, de Nerval among them. Here, at Newstead, we honour both the world-innovator and the English genius. The Romantic and the Apostle of Freedom attain a peculiar apotheosis in the helmet which Byron designed for himself to wear on the Greek battlefield. Faintly ridiculous, like a French fireman's helmet and yet clearly modelled on the neo-classical armour idealized by Revolutionary artists such as Jacques-Louis David, this helmet is a schizophrenic relic of the poet himself. His death did liberate Greece, since the fame of the event was instrumental in causing the English and French to move against the Turks at the Battle of Navarino. Byron was denied his chance to fall in battle and his helmet has come to rest instead in the museum of Newstead.

The North Gallery remembers the rakish young Byron – boxing gloves, foils, pistols and the brass collar worn by one of his many dogs, possibly Boatswain. Also one of his most unfortunate loves, Clair Clairmont, Mary Shelley's half-sister, and mother of his daughter Allegra, who was to die in childhood in the far distant convent of Bagnacavallo in Italy, is commemorated here, as is his first love of all, Mary Chaworth. First editions of his works are on display and a set of pistols, perhaps the ones he fired into a door at his house in Southwell when Mary rejected him. Such memorabilia as these are in fine oak bookcases in the Gothick style installed in this room by Wildman when he created his handsome library, recently restored. Here in 1850 Wildman is said to have introduced Byron's legitimate daughter Ada (then aged thirty-four) to the poetry of the father she had never known.

The Great Hall, with its minstrels' gallery, should be the heart of Byronic territory, but Byron lacked the necessary cash to restore it properly when he inherited Newstead. The whole abbey was in a pretty ruinous state, in fact, and was properly renovated only later by the Wildmans, who turned it into a model English country house of the grander sort. Byron was in possession for too short a time greatly to affect its appearance, though he knew it well enough and loved it sufficiently for the name Newstead to be indissolubly linked with his. It was in this Great Hall that he would sit at one end in solitary reflection and discharge his pistols at the facing door, though no longer for disappointed love. From the visitor's point of view, the Great Hall can act as a focus for thoughts on the glittering life Byron led as a fashionable young poet in London. And this is also the point of view of Juan in the poem, once he arrives at the abbey. Earlier in *Don Juan*, Byron had compared the exotic south, where he now lived in exile, with the moral north (essentially England).

> Happy the nations of the moral North!
>   Where all is virtue and the winter season
> Sends sin, without a rag on, shivering forth
>   ('Twas snow that brought St Antony to reason);
> Where juries cast up what a wife is worth,
>   By laying whate'er sum, in mulct, they please on
> The lover, who must pay a handsome price,
> Because it is a fashionable vice.

His own separation from his wife, Annabella Millbanke, rankles here, and now with Juan in England Byron is happy to catalogue the far from moral activities and inclinations of the English. Certainly, few poets of genius have been so firmly established in smart society as Byron was. He swam through London like a golden fish in a bowl, and the world of Juan's house party was the world of Byron's intrigues with Lady Caroline Lamb and Lady Oxford.

This was where the whole panoply of Lady Amundeville's guests, including Juan, would have met for meals. A fine parcel of Anglo-Saxon attitudes they make. They are essentially types, and at this distance there is little point trying to identify them from among Byron's acquaintance. But none would have been out of place in Newstead, and the scene is not hard to envisage today.

> The noble guests assembled at the Abbey
>   Consisted of – we give the sex the pas –
> The Duchess of Fitz-Fulke, the Countess Crabby;
>   The Ladies Scilly, Busey; Miss Eclat,
> Miss Bombazeen, Miss Mackstay, Miss O'Tabbey,
>   And Mrs Rabbi, the rich banker's squaw;
> Also the Honourable Mrs Sleep,
> Who looked a white lamb, yet was a black sheep . . .

> There was Dick Dubious, the metaphysician,
>   Who loved philosophy and a good dinner;
> Angle, the soi-disant mathematician;
>   Sir Henry Silvercup, the great race winner.
> There was the Reverend Rodomont Precisian,
>   Who did not hate so much the sin as sinner;
> And Lord Augustus Fitz-Plantagenet,
> Good at all things, but better at a bet.

Along the walls preside the ancestors of the Amundeville family – played up a little from what would have graced Newstead in Byron's time.

> Steel barons, molten the next generation
>   To silken rows of gay and gartered earls,
> Glanced from the walls in goodly preservation
>   And Lady Marys blooming into girls . . .

> Judges in very formidable ermine
>   . . .
> Bishops who had not left a single sermon;
>   Attorneys-General, awful to the sight . . .

> Generals, some all in armour, of the old
>   And iron time . . .
>   . . .
> Lordlings, with staves of white or keys of gold;
>   Nimrods, whose canvas scarce contained the steed.

Byron sums it up in one couplet:

> Society is now one polished horde
> Formed of two mighty tribes, the Bores and Bored.

Bored he may have been on occasion, but Byron was never out of society except when he retired from it deliberately as a selfconscious recluse. Even in his exile, Italian society sought him out. We should remember that he was a contemporary of Sheridan, had been briefly proprietor of Drury Lane Theatre, and, for all his dislike of Wordsworth, Southey, Coleridge and the Lake Poets, was the friend of Shelley and Peacock and could never fully make up his mind if he were an outcast of society or a worldly satirist with a host of literary friends.

Byron's dining-room, off the Great Hall, is where the poet wined and dined his own guests. Above this is his bedroom. Some of the furniture in both rooms was there in his time. Before the present rearrangement of the furnishings, his dining-room housed a section of a tree from the grounds in which the poet and his half-sister Augusta had their names cut into the bark. Augusta was probably the one true love of Byron's life, and the rumours which circulated of his near-incestuous (as well as adulterous) relations with her contributed to his refusal to return to England after 1816. Byron's bedroom is a chamber of singular charm, though less like a bower of Venus than a nature-lover's point of vantage. It looks out over the front lawn and the lake and in summer, with the birds singing and the sun streaming in, would have been an extraordinarily agreeable room.

Byron must be the first great literary man whose friends and acquaintances consciously collected anything connected with him *during* his lifetime. The great Byron exhibition at the Victoria & Albert Museum in 1974 (the 150th anniversary of his death in 1824, and celebrated much more comprehensively than the 200th anniversary of his birth in 1988, which perhaps reveals something of the English taste in anniversaries) demonstrated that he is one of the best-documented poets of all time. The V & A built replicas of the first-floor room he inhabited in the Palazzo Mocenigo in Venice along with his dogs, parrots and visiting mistresses, and from which he used to dive into the Grand Canal, and of the tent in which he died in Epirus (Missolonghi). Yet his personality remains something of a mystery. Not for him the one central devotion – whether Nature or Metaphysics, as with Wordsworth and Coleridge – nor, like them, one district or *genius loci* – the Lake District or the

Drawing of Byron, by Harlow, 1818

West Country. At home in Piccadilly and with the prizefighters he loved to watch, or at the theatre; in salons of great hostesses, or speaking in the Lords in support of the Luddites; roaming Turkey and the Eastern Mediterranean in search of exotic customs or drinking with British naval officers on duty; writing and womanizing voluminously in Italy; finally dying for the cause of freedom at the age of thirty-six; Byron is too chameleon-like to belong anywhere but on the page.

Nevertheless, Newstead Abbey is as good a place as any to seek his restless spirit. With its beautiful grounds, its combination of the practical and the romantic, its sheer talent for survival, it represents Byron well – for all the short span of his stay there. And, most of all, he made it the focus for the most sustained passages of good poetry he ever composed, the final cantos of *Don Juan*.

Newstead in its nineteenth-century heyday was more the work of the Wildmans than of Byron. But they remained conscious of its inheritance. Nowadays, as the major Byron museum in England, it has been recolonized by his remains and possibly by his ghost. The whole site, house and grounds, speaks of Byron. The place he romanticized but could not reside in has become his quintessence. In a youthful poem, his 'Elegy on Newstead Abbey', he hymned its charms in easy-going verse – lines as picturesque and unselfconscious as the subject.

> Newstead! what saddening change of scene is thine!
>   Thy yawning arch betokens slow decay;
> The last and youngest of a noble line
>   Now holds thy mouldering turrets in his sway.
>
> Deserted now, he scans thy grey worn towers;
>   Thy vaults, where dead of feudal ages sleep;
> Thy cloisters, pervious to the wintry showers;
>   These, these he views, and views them but to weep.

But this lachrymose versifying should not be allowed to be Byron's last word on Newstead or on England. It's better to recall the boundless energy of the Vanity Fair of English social life which Byron enjoyed as much as he enjoyed lashing it for folly and pretence. When Juan apostrophized the character of the English people, he, like his creator, was feeling as nostalgic as denunciatory:

> 'And here,' he cried, 'is Freedom's chosen station.
>   Here peals the people's voice, nor can entomb it
> Racks, prisons, inquisitions. Resurrection
> Awaits it, each new meeting or election.
>
> Here are chaste wives, pure lives. Here people pay
>   But what they please, and if that things be dear
> 'Tis only that they love to throw away
>   Their cash, to show how much they have a year.

Byron eventually had enough a year, after selling Newstead and receiving a legacy from Lady Noel, to equip an army to take an expedition to Greece. Some eight months after sailing from Italy he was dead. A magnificent and still unquenched legend had been born. His embalmed body was brought from Greece in a sarcophagus and was subsequently granted its own entombment near Newstead, in Hucknall church. At last, too, there is a tribute to him in Westminster Abbey. But this other abbey, Newstead, is an even better memorial to the poet, though his poems, especially *Don Juan*, are the best memorial of all.

THOMAS AND JANE CARLYLE

5 CHEYNE ROW, CHELSEA, LONDON SW3

ALETHEA HAYTER

On a cloudy day in June 1834 Thomas Carlyle, his wife, Jane Welsh, their maid-of-all-work, Bessy Barnet, and their canary, Chico, in his cage, drove across London in a hackney coach, piled with luggage, to take possession of their newly rented house, 5 (now 24) Cheyne Row, Chelsea. On the way Chico suddenly burst into song, which they saw as a good omen for their life in the new house. It was certainly an omen of stability: Cheyne Row was their home for the rest of their lives, thirty-two years for Mrs Carlyle, forty-seven for her husband.

For the previous six years they had been living at Craigenputtoch, a remote Dumfriesshire farm, but if Carlyle was to make a livelihood from his writing he now needed to be near London editors and publishers and libraries. The Carlyles had no regular income, but he had saved £200 made by translations and articles, and on that they intended to live for a year or so while his literary career was taking off. The rent of the Cheyne Row house (never raised throughout their long tenancy) was £38 a year; Bessy Barnet was paid £8 a year; their way of life was frugal, and Mrs Carlyle was an economical housekeeper, so their budget was not impossible.

The Cheyne Row house was built in 1708, one of a red-brick terrace of three storeys and basements, called after Lord Cheyne who owned the site. The street was at a right angle to the river, which in 1834 was unembanked and had a pebbly foreshore. From the back windows there was an eastward view over leafy open spaces and hay fields to the towers of Westminster Abbey. Central London could be easily reached by horse-omnibus or by boat from the old wooden Battersea Bridge, but Chelsea was still almost a village, once patrician, now unfashionable but picturesque.

Within a few days of their arrival in Cheyne Row, Mrs Carlyle's skilful management had got the house in order. Their possessions from Scotland – china packed in barrels, beds, fenders, a piano, carpets, chairs, saucepans, mattresses, hams, oatmeal, tobacco pipes – had been arranged in what seemed to the Carlyles a spacious measure of living-rooms and closets and kitchen quarters. Carlyle was

established in his library on the first floor, with his books around him, at his father-in-law's sturdy writing-desk, ready to start on his new book. His literary achievement so far consisted of studies and translations of German literature, hack-work for encyclopaedias, and the magazine publication of his *Sartor Resartus*. He had made some reputation and begun to influence some serious minds, but was known to the general public, if known at all, as a puzzling eccentric. He needed to show his power, and the book he now began, *The French Revolution*, was to do that, and to establish his fame.

Writing was rarely a pleasure to Carlyle. He felt he had a duty to say what needed saying, but he often felt like a galley slave scourged back to the task, and whenever he was working on a book he was preoccupied, restless, 'fidgeting and flurrying about all the while like a hen in the distraction of laying its first egg' in his wife's sardonic description. Sometimes he would be swept by a 'paroxysm of clairvoyance', what he called a 'sham-happy' excitement in which he could splash down, in broad masses of colour, his themes and narratives. But more often his whole morning's work – he tried to write two folio pages every morning – would be tossed on to the fire. When he did finish a section of his book to his satisfaction, he destroyed all the notes he had used, a practice which was to entail disaster in March 1835 when he gave his manuscript of the first part of *The French Revolution*, the only copy, to John Stuart Mill to read, and Mill's housemaid used it to light a fire. Carlyle had to start again from the beginning.

Mill was only one of the procession of distinguished literary figures who visited the Carlyles in the little ground-floor parlour and stayed for hours of scintillating talk. Leigh Hunt, Harriet Martineau, Monckton Milnes, Dickens, Browning, Thackeray, Tennyson, Forster, Ruskin, Mrs Gaskell, G. H. Lewes, Emerson – their visitors, who came again and again, are a roll-call of nineteenth-century literary eminence. Nor was it only writers who called; the actor Macready, the scientist T. H. Huxley, the composer Chopin, the dandy Count d'Orsay came; so did a group of foreign political exiles, Mazzini, Godefroi Cavaignac and others, to whom the Carlyles' hospitality was a godsend. Mrs Carlyle attracted unhappy men and women, even insane ones, by her power of eliciting confidences (which she did not always then respect). She had an inner circle of close allies – Erasmus Darwin (elder brother of Charles), Geraldine Jewsbury, the Sterling family, Mazzini, Countess Pepoli – whom she held enthralled by her wit, her anecdotes and a private coterie language of quotations and malapropisms. But she also had, as 'the Lion's wife', to cope with an increasing flood of unknown callers attracted by Carlyle's rising fame; it was her job to fend them off from Carlyle, to answer invitations and fan letters. It was

Carlyle's sound-proof room, Cheyne Row

5 Cheyne Row, Chelsea

not for lavish hospitality that the callers came; they were given tea, bread and butter, sweet biscuits. Sometimes the Carlyles would give dinners to two or three guests; only once did they give a soirée. But the feast for which their visitors came was their conversation. Emerson said that Carlyle's talk was one of the three things in Europe which impressed him most. It poured out in huge sustained harangues, thunderously excited, overbearing all interruptions, full of rich imagery and wildly original speculation, often ending in shouts of laughter at his own vehemence. Her talk, muted when he was performing but sparkling in diamond drops when she was in her own home among close friends, was sharper, less abstract, often more malicious than his. He paced about the parlour as he talked – a tall, lean, blue-eyed figure generally wearing a patterned dressing-gown. She, a small neat woman with a sallow, bony face, smooth black hair and huge dark eyes, sat in a chair by the fire. They are to be seen thus in Robert Tait's 1857 picture, 'A Chelsea Interior', which now hangs in the Cheyne Row parlour, and which shows the folding doors open into the dining-room and china-closet at the back of the house. These doors were generally left open, but in cold winters were pasted closed, as Mrs Carlyle suffered from the draughts produced by her husband's insistence on open windows, and was sometimes reduced to wearing a bonnet and fur pelisse even indoors. But the parlour, with its green curtains and wall-to-wall carpet (ingeniously eked out with strips of dyed blankets), its solid, highly polished furniture, its cream-painted waist-high wainscoting and flowered wallpaper above, was generally snug and welcoming.

The dining-room next door was also the home of Chico, whose cage was kept on a small table near the china-closet door. Chico was later provided with a consort, but as Carlyle grimly reported, he 'pecked his tattered and dispirited wife to death' and later died of ennui and old age – a somewhat sinister parallel. Carlyle also tolerantly accepted Mrs Carlyle's dog Nero, though neighbours' crowing cocks and barking dogs were anathema to him. Nero was a small, white Maltese part-mongrel, frisky but jealously devoted to Mrs Carlyle, on whose bed he slept and whom he followed everywhere, on a lead when they went out, for fear of dog-stealers, who nevertheless captured him twice. He disarmed Carlyle by dancing round him on hind legs, and Carlyle, though he addressed the dog as 'little villain', nevertheless took him on night walks and even bathed him, and when Nero was run over by a cart and had eventually to be put down, the whole household – Carlyle as well as his wife and the maid – were in tears. Nero was like a child to the childless Mrs Carlyle; she made up letters from him to Carlyle, told as many anecdotes about him as Mrs Browning did about her spaniel Flush, and declared when he died that nobody could have any idea what that inseparable companion had meant in her often lonely life.

At the oval table in this dining-room, the Carlyles in the early years at Cheyne Row ate their breakfast of tea or coffee, bread and butter, and eggs or ham, enlivened by Mrs Carlyle's 'tinkle of the finest mirth' about their everyday contretemps, as Carlyle remorsefully remembered forty years later. Here they dined on his preferred menu of beef or chicken broth, grilled mutton chops, old potatoes, steamed or boiled puddings, and supped on porridge, a simple diet but one which every successive cook had to be trained to get exactly right, or there would be loud complaints from Carlyle.

In the basement below the parlour and dining-room lay the servants' regions,

Thomas Carlyle, 1854   *Jane Carlyle, 1838*

the back kitchen with a shower-bath where Carlyle daily dowsed himself in cold water, and the front kitchen where cooking was done and the servant slept. In the thirty-two years of Mrs Carlyle's life in Cheyne Row, she had thirty-nine servants, one at a time till the last years. They were paid only from £8 to £16 a year, plus beer money, but this was normal for that time, and was nearly 10 per cent of Mrs Carlyle's whole allowance for running the house – food, heating, lighting, rent, rates, taxes – which was under £200 till late in her life. Mrs Carlyle was an exacting and sharp-tempered employer, fanatical about cleanliness and method, and her initial enthusiasm for new servants often rapidly changed to suspicions that they were hard, untruthful and idle, though in spite of this many of them felt an enthusiastic devotion to her. Carlyle demanded that his requirements should be exactly met, but otherwise he more or less ignored the servants.

However, the faults were not all on the employers' side: one servant was a dipsomaniac; one, a hysteric, threatened to have fits and stay in bed for a year; one secretly entertained men in the kitchen and actually gave birth to a child in the china-closet while the unsuspecting Carlyle was having tea in the next room. Mrs Carlyle was perhaps as much stimulated as exasperated by her problem servants; she and Carlyle invented nicknames for them – the Polar Bear, Sereetha

Carlyle in his garden, Cheyne Row

the Peesweep, Pessima, the Mooncalf. She made good stories out of their mala-propisms and treated them with a mixture of sharpness and affection, which probably suited both her and them better than aloof decorum on both sides.

Mrs Carlyle's meagre housekeeping allowance was nevertheless a reasonable share of the couple's very modest means, at least in the first years at Cheyne Row. In 1835 Carlyle had earned nothing at all from his writing for nearly two years.

101

In the late 1830s his earnings from giving lectures and from American sales of his books began to rise. In 1842 Mrs Carlyle inherited about £200 a year on her mother's death, but in 1848 Carlyle still estimated his fluctuating annual income from his books at an average of £150, though in some years it was as high as £800. It was not till the late 1850s that he could say he was 'rich enough for all practical purposes'.

Behind the basement lay a small garden with a grass plot, fruit trees and flower-beds, where Carlyle smoked his long clay pipes and sometimes weeded and mowed. But he had little time to spare for gardening; every day after breakfast he mounted the handsome spiral-balustered stairs to his library on the first floor, and with anguished wrestling set himself to practise the Gospel of Work which he preached. Nearly all his most potent and influential books were written in this room. When he finished *The French Revolution* in 1837, his next main project was his study of Cromwell, on which he battled morosely among dusty folios till 1845, but during that decade he was distracted by the preparation of four years of lecture courses, the last of them published in book form as *Heroes and Hero-Worship*, and by his anxieties about contemporary political and economic problems, which provoked him into writing *Chartism* and *Past and Present*. The working-class misery and food-riots which ushered in the Hungry Forties, the creeping evils of industrialization and squalor which he saw on his daily rides on his horses, Citoyenne and Fritz, all over ever-spreading London, filled him with prophetic dismay. He felt passionately that in a mechanistic and degraded age, dedicated to cant and *laissez-faire*, there was a crying need for reforms which would lead to an ordered society based not on democratic forms and universal suffrage, since men are not born equal in mental power, but on obedience to wise leaders and on dutiful acceptance of the Gospel of Work, the universal and divinely prescribed obligation to justify one's existence by labour. He deeply scanned the great moments and great men of history to diagnose the diseases and prescribe the panaceas of human society. He was truly concerned for the hardships of the poor, but his proposed remedies were para-doxically and eclectically his own.

His most powerful train of thought could always be jerked off the rails by any extraneous noise. Organ-grinders in the street, distant train-whistles, the neighbours' barking dogs, crowing cocks and screeching parrots drove him into a frenzy. Mrs Carlyle had to bribe and wheedle the neighbours into controlling their livestock's uproar, but the persistent piano-playing of the young ladies next door finally drove Carlyle into abandoning the library as a work-place; and alterations to the house, to give him the silence he needed, were set in hand, and lasted over ten years of disruptions and unsatisfying experiments. Partition walls were moved, new fireplaces installed, windows altered, panelling removed; a closet dressing-room was turned into a study, but Carlyle soon rejected that too. Carpenters, plasterers and paperhangers invaded the house for months together. Even when no structural alterations were going on, Mrs Carlyle's very high standards of cleanliness called for yearly 'earthquakes' of repainting and whitewashing. She herself was as dextrous as any workman: she could nail down carpets, paint cupboards, disinfect bug-ridden bed-curtains, make picture frames and chair-covers. During these earthquakes Carlyle generally absented himself on holidays with his family in Scotland, or on historical research expeditions for his books. Mrs Carlyle remained behind in the midst of household chaos.

This was not as unfair as it sounds; she preferred to have her husband out of the way and to be left to reign over exacting problems. She was not an exploited drudge, but an exceptionally efficient organizer who enjoyed being in charge of complicated operations and negotiations, and only wanted Carlyle to thank and praise her more often for her care of his comfort. She needed to be the centre of attention and admiration. Yet she often mocked the slavish devotion which she enjoyed from her men and women friends. One of these, Geraldine Jewsbury, who adored her with 'tigerish jealousy', nevertheless said after both Carlyles were dead, 'His was the soft heart, and hers the hard one.'

Ever since Carlyle's death in 1881, there have been rabid differences of opinion about the marriage. Froude, in his biography of Carlyle and his edition of Mrs Carlyle's letters, presented a picture of Carlyle as a gloomy, inconsiderate husband who treated his delicate wife as a useful housekeeper, while turning for intellectual companionship to Lady Harriet Baring. Carlyle's family, outraged by this travesty of their hero, published further editions of Mrs Carlyle's letters which presented her as a neurotic exaggerator and her husband as a paragon of devoted love. The truth probably lies somewhere between these two extremes. Carlyle was moody, irritable and unobservant of other people's feelings. Mrs Carlyle was jealous and sharp-tongued. They did undoubtedly have quarrels and misunderstandings which both these gifted writers described in far too memorable words. But Mrs Carlyle was proud of her husband's genius and protectively careful of his comforts, while Carlyle relied utterly on his wife and delighted in her wit. Probably both of them would have been bored by a more tranquil relationship. 'Woe to the house where there is no chiding,' Mrs Carlyle wrote in her commonplace book. Tennyson's comment that 'Mr and Mrs Carlyle on the whole enjoyed life together, else they would not have chaffed one another so heartily' probably comes nearest to the truth. The house in Cheyne Row often resounded to vociferous laughter as well as to complaints and laments. In one of her worst moments of mental and physical suffering, Mrs Carlyle wrote, 'Oh, my Dear, my Dear! shall I ever make fun for you again?'

Those worst moments were mostly passed in her bedroom on the first floor, behind the library. Here, in the red bed from her Scottish home in which she had been born, she spent long nights of sleepless misery. Insomnia was her worst complaint, but she also suffered from violent headaches, winter coughs and influenza which kept her indoors for months at a time, neuralgia in her arms and hands and – after a fall in the street in 1863 – intense nervous pain all over her body which made her afraid she was going mad. She frequently dosed herself with morphia, but still she could not sleep, and if she did briefly doze, she was likely to be woken by the thump of Carlyle's feet as he jumped out of his bed in the room over hers, furious at some neighbouring noise which had reactivated *his* insomnia – less bad than hers, for he was in the main a healthy, energetic man, though he considered himself a martyr to dyspepsia.

In 1854 a sound-proof room built on to the top of the house was at last achieved for Carlyle, and here he wrote his last great work, his life of Frederick the Great. It took him thirteen years. He loathed the tank-like room, lit only from above; he hated the grinding, uncongenial toil among mountainous heaps of books and maps and notes, which seemed irreducible to a finished whole. His satisfaction or dissatisfaction with what he had written was little affected by the international fame which he now enjoyed as the Sage of Chelsea, but his judgement had hardened and become more intolerant, and he was more contemptuous of anyone who did not share his opinions. The violence of his *Latterday Pamphlets* had alienated some of his admirers, but his influence was greater than ever. Fifty years after his death his ideas were condemned as fascist; today they are likely to be vilified as racist; but he had a dynamic power to make his readers re-examine their opinions and question their hypocrisies.

When *Frederick the Great* was finished in 1865, Carlyle abandoned the sound-proof attic, which became a maid's bedroom. His former library on the first floor was now the drawing-room, and there he and Mrs Carlyle, recovered from the miserable illness after her accident, were together for the brief Indian summer of their married life, eighteen months of renewed brightness. In 1866 Carlyle was in Edinburgh to give a triumphantly successful address on his inauguration as Lord Rector of the University. While he was in Scotland Mrs Carlyle, driving in Hyde Park, had a heart attack and died sitting in the corner of the carriage.

Carlyle, overcome with remorseful grief, could find consolation only in preparing her letters for publication and writing an atoning memoir. He was to live for another fifteen years, to be given the Prussian Order of Merit, to be offered and refuse a knighthood and a pension, to be devotedly cared for by his niece Mary Aitken who came to live with him – but to write nothing more of any substance. Early in 1881, when he was plainly dying – and public concern was so great that bulletins had to be pasted on the door of Cheyne Row – his bed was moved into the library, and there he lay with his wife's workbox and small treasures still on their table within reach of his hand; he would not allow them to be moved. He remembered how she had always praised and encouraged his work, and created the ambience in which he could write. His books seemed to him their only children, hers as well as his. Through his writings he scattered his seed to germinate in the works of Dickens, of Mrs Gaskell, of Ruskin; even those who, like John Stuart Mill, came to disagree strongly with him, felt his power. When he died, on 5 February 1881, George Eliot wrote: 'There is hardly a superior mind of this generation that has not been modified by Carlyle's writings.'

ECCLEFECHAN, DUMFRIES AND GALLOWAY; AND HADDINGTON, E. LOTHIAN

IAN CAMPBELL

Perhaps nothing more clearly illustrates the problems that lay behind the courtship of Thomas and Jane Welsh Carlyle than the houses in which they were born. Thomas arrived in Ecclefechan in 1795, and was already a schoolboy when Jane was born in Haddington in 1801. Thomas first saw Jane's birthplace in 1821 as a visitor. When Jane visited the Carlyles several years later as Thomas's prospective bride, they had long since moved away from the Arched House in Ecclefechan (which the family outgrew soon after Thomas's birth) to a succession of farms in the neighbourhood. Jane and her mother vacated the Haddington home of her birth at the time of her marriage in 1826, and it was sold.

Yet this is not the end of the connection of both houses with the eminent Victorians who were born in them. The Carlyle property remained in the family for many years (Thomas's father had been a builder, and the Arched House was partly his own work), and after the Sage's death in 1881 it came into public hands and was opened as a memorial. His statue sits at the top of the steep brae leading north from Ecclefechan, and it can just make out the widening of the main street where the Arched House still stands beside the running water of the burn which Carlyle remembered fondly in *Sartor Resartus*. The traffic and the electric trains rush by, out of sight but quite audible; Ecclefechan timelessly holds not only Carlyle's birthplace but his grave.

Haddington too is bypassed by both road and rail, and recently has regained much of its former distinction as an important Scottish market-town, the Lamp of

Jane Welsh Carlyle's birthplace, Haddington

Lothian Trust restoring Poldrate Mill and Haddington House, reroofing and bringing back into use the whole of St Mary's Kirk ('The Lamp of Lothian'), and most recently restoring and opening to the public the Jane Welsh Carlyle birthplace.

For Jane, there was a vanished childhood in Haddington which she revisited only once, in 1849, as a near-forgotten middle-aged tourist, reawakening her own painful memories of her father, who had died in her childhood, her strong-minded but impetuous mother, her sense of encirclement in Haddington and her recognition of its influence on her. By 1849 her mother was dead and buried in Crawford kirkyard, a place Jane could not face visiting: Haddington was as far as she could go, and her diary of that visit (in the form of a long letter to her husband in London) is the best thing she ever wrote – the best to survive, at any rate.

Her own ghost, she walked unrecognized up the main street from the inn and past her former home – the doctor's house at the top of the market street with its classical façade behind which she remembered vividly the private quarters, handsome rooms looking out on a secluded walled garden. Upstairs there was a formal drawing-room which impressed Thomas when he first saw it; downstairs a formal dining-room. Here Jane and her mother lived in genteel, modest style, ornaments and books aplenty, careful housekeeping taken for granted, visits taken and given, inexpensive entertainment every day. Jane's mother had style, and even her future son-in-law (with whom relations were rarely more relaxed than a grudging truce) admitted her way with furniture, entertainment and tasteful arrangements. Jane inherited these gifts, and used them to equal effect in Chelsea when she and

The view from the drawing-room

Thomas set up house in 1834 on his small income. Jane did not, so far as we know, go into her old home. She found her visit to Haddington distressing enough, and to see her childhood home might have broken her self-control completely.

Today Jane's Haddington house is open to the public on its top floor, where Thomas will first have walked into the drawing-room on a summer's evening in 1821, nervous among so many tables and ornaments, dazzled alike by the view of the setting sun over the garden, and his first meeting with young Jane Welsh who fascinated him from the outset, and remained his goal till their marriage in 1826. The house is beautifully restored, the entrance by way of a renovated conservatory and staircase, the noise of modern Haddington left behind when the visitor steps through the archway from the pavement.

Jane's perceptions of Thomas's house must have been very different. Though her letters are careful when they speak of his family, before and after marriage, she was never comfortable in his world of farm kitchens and working premises. Carlyle's was a large family with a working father – a builder, then a farmer. His mother was a working matriarch, her style the polar opposite of the elegant Mrs Welsh in Haddington. The kitchen was for living, eating and sleeping; there were not many spare rooms, though Jane would have had the best. This was the world of Mainhill and Scotsbrig, the farms to which Jane came first as Carlyle's fiancée, then as his wife.

The Arched House itself stands firmly in Ecclefechan, part of the town and its economy, a matched pair of houses connected by a central arch (hence the modern name) through which horses and carts could be driven for the builder's business which the Carlyle brothers conducted. The stream – stream and drain together, no doubt – which ran down the whole main street now runs down only the lower part past the Arched House, progress having roofed in the remainder to make a wider street. Trees, freshly planted saplings in early photographs of the house in the 1890s, are now gnarled veterans. The small outhouse at the back has been enlarged to give a home to the curator and his family. Yet to lift the latch and walk in through the front door is to step back in time, to a small kitchen with a window facing out on to the stream and the trees, a fireplace still hung with contemporary cooking utensils, cupboards, presses, an astonishing steep stair seemingly straight from Holland leading up to two bedrooms, a tiny one in the arch and a larger one where Thomas was born in 1795. There is still a bed, and a cradle which is the very one, we believe, that Thomas was rocked in.

Everywhere there are pictures, relics, hats hanging on pegs, a tobacco-cutter (Carlyle and his mother were both heavy pipe-smokers), a set of photographs of the house with Carlyle's own annotations, books, papers – the gathering-back of the traces of Carlyle's early life. The house is small and confining: one can see why the family moved (Carlyle was so young he could barely remember the move) to

The Arched House, Ecclefechan

a larger house up the hill, long since demolished. Like Chelsea, Carlyle's House in Ecclefechan has had the benefit of careful preparation in the 1890s for its role as a museum: the furniture and family belongings, long dispersed, were returned and restored. The National Trust for Scotland has filled the gaps with suitable matching items, and the Arched House (like Chelsea) is a time-capsule. No greater contrast could be imagined in styles.

In Haddington, Jane's own possessions are interspersed with carefully matched pieces, her own drawings and pictures among those of her friends, her own books among others'. In all the houses, the priceless collection of manuscript letters has been carefully catalogued and copied: over 10,500 surviving letters from the Carlyles have been found world-wide. They form the foundation of the great Duke–

The bedroom in the Arched House

Edinburgh edition of the *Carlyle Letters* (at the time of writing, they are almost half-way through the Carlyles' lives, with over twenty volumes still to go). It was the editors' fortune that the Carlyles moved rarely, and squirrelled away everything they received in the post: the archive of letters forms one of the greatest literary treasure-houses of the nineteenth century.

The Chelsea years cannot efface the importance of these first scenes, and Haddington and Ecclefechan provide a unique opportunity for the student of the Victorian age. For both Carlyles, the remainder of their lives was an onward movement, upward to city life, enlarged social experience, brilliant company and eventually to financial affluence. Even so, each remained fiercely loyal to early friends and family. Each acknowledged the debt they owed to their birthplace, even though they would visit it only rarely in middle and later life. It is right that their first homes should be open to the public, an explanation of the origins of the brilliant literary circle which came to animate 5 Cheyne Row in Chelsea.

WINSTON CHURCHILL

CHARTWELL, WESTERHAM, KENT

―――――――

JOHN GRIGG

Winston Churchill's acquisition of Chartwell Manor towards the end of 1922 coincided with one of the most important turning-points in his life. Nearing the age of fifty, and with a record of mingled success and failure that was already legendary, he had just fallen from power with the Lloyd George coalition and had then lost his seat at the ensuing general election. Out of office and out of parliament, he was also very conscious that the Liberal Party, to which he had defected from the Conservatives in 1904, was so weakened and divided that it was probably no longer capable of serving as a vehicle for his career. By the time he was established at Chartwell at the end of 1924, he was once again a Conservative (in fact, if not yet quite in name) and had returned to high office as Chancellor of the Exchequer in the second Baldwin government. Entering his new home he was, therefore, embarking on a new phase of his political career, a phase which was to lead to supreme power and eventual apotheosis.

His arrival at Chartwell also roughly coincided with his resumption of literary activity after a longish interval. What may be seen as his first period of authorship began with two books written while he was a young cavalry officer in India towards the end of Queen Victoria's reign (his only novel, *Savrola*, and his account of operations on the North-West Frontier, *The Malakand Field Force*), and culminated in the two-volume life of his father, *Lord Randolph Churchill*, which was published to general acclaim soon after he joined the Liberals and just after he was appointed to his first ministerial office, in the Campbell-Bannerman government formed at the end of 1905. There followed nearly ten years of power, including seven as a cabinet minister; a brief interlude out of office, part of it spent as a combatant on the Western front; and then five more years in high ministerial posts. Towards the end of this time he started to write his account of the First World War, on which he was engaged when he acquired Chartwell and whose last three volumes were composed there. *The World Crisis* marks the beginning of his second period of authorship, which ended with the publication of his *History of the English-Speaking*

111

Peoples between 1956 and 1958. (He died, aged ninety, in 1965.) This period of literary achievement was closely associated with Chartwell and, like his occupancy of the house, interrupted only by the Second World War.

Chartwell is an ugly house in a magnificent setting. When Churchill first saw it, the house was, if not uglier, certainly less distinguished, than after the drastic changes that he carried out in collaboration with the architect Philip Tilden. But it was for the view and the situation that he bought the place, and for those advantages above all that he continued to cherish it. To the east the land slopes down to a wide green valley, or combe, through which a stream flows from its origin in the Chart Well. There was already one lake in the valley, and Churchill's eye quickly grasped the possibilities for further use of the water, with another lake, a swimming-pool, and exotic fish and fowl. On the other side of the valley the rising ground was adorned, until the great gale of 1987, with a fine plantation of mature beech. To the south the landscape opens up in a marvellous panorama of the Weald of Kent.

So much for the bright side of Chartwell, on which Churchill never ceased to look. His wife, Clementine, was at first no less entranced by it, but before long became increasingly aware of the darker side, in both the literal and the metaphorical sense. The house is only eighty yards from the road, to the west of which the ground rises steeply, depriving the house of afternoon and evening light. The bank is covered with rhododendron, a shrub that Clementine particularly disliked, and along the top runs a public footpath overlooking the house. These flaws would have been enough to turn Clementine against the place, but in addition she was appalled by the likely cost of transforming and expanding the house, and fearful that it would always be a burden to run. Her apprehensions were justified. Nevertheless, Churchill went ahead and bought it without, in the end, even telling her that he was doing so, let alone obtaining her agreement. He hoped that she would later come round to it, but in fact she never did. Faced with a *fait accompli*, she did her utmost to make a success of Chartwell for his sake, and her contribution to it was indeed vital. But she suffered a lot in the process, and the strain was often apparent.

Churchill was, of course, a genius, and it is in the nature of genius to be self-centred. Exceptions to this rule are rare, and he was certainly not one of them. On the contrary, even among geniuses he was more egocentric than most. Clementine was a woman of intelligence and spirit, but where he was concerned she accepted the role of squaw. The idea that she influenced him profoundly, and that he was in the habit of deferring to her, is a myth. He loved her after his fashion, and wrote her flowery letters when they were apart, as they quite often

Churchill's desk with busts of Napoleon and Nelson

were. But their partnership endured because it was entirely unequal; because she subordinated everything, including herself and their children, to his interests. As their youngest child, Mary Soames, has written: 'Winston dominated her whole life, and once this priority had been established, her children, personal pleasures, friends and outside interests competed for what was left.'

The function of Chartwell was only incidentally that of a family home. As such it had obvious attractions for the young Churchills, ranging in age from thirteen (Randolph) to two (Mary) when they moved into the place. But above all Chartwell had to be, and was, a workshop with recreational amenities for its owner, only twenty miles or so from the heart of London. His political and literary work came first and occupied most of his time. Moreover, some of his recreations were alternative forms of labour: notably the painting to which he had taken as a pastime after the trauma of Gallipoli during the First World War, and the bricklaying of which conspicuous products at Chartwell were a cottage and a large garden wall. The choice of Tilden as the architect for refashioning the house owed much, no doubt, to the fact that he was currently designing a house for Lloyd George (at Churt in Surrey). Lloyd George had been a potent influence in Churchill's life since the early years of the century, when they were colleagues and radical partners in the pre-war Liberal governments. Tilden turned Chartwell from a dreary, grey, rectory-style building into a red-brick villa of more opulent and unusual, though scarcely more pleasing, aspect. There were, however, two major improvements. A wing was added on the eastern side to exploit not only the view but also the fall of the ground, which allowed the lowest level of the new structure to be below that of the front of the house. Here, on the bottom floor, the Churchills had their dining-room; the drawing-room was on the floor above, and Clementine's bedroom was on the top floor. After the Second World War the dining-room was converted into a cinema and a new dining-room created on the west side of the house. But when it seemed that Churchill and his friends might be observed, or even overheard, from the nearby public footpath, Clementine surrendered her bedroom for use as a dining-room, and moved to a ground-floor room at the front. Fortunately the National Trust has decided that the house should be laid out according to the original plan, and the public now sees the eastern wing essentially as it was in the 1930s, with its three main rooms commanding the splendid view over the garden, the combe and beyond.

The other big improvement was that the existing building was extended, and also modified, to uncover some features of an earlier structure which the Victorian owners had overlaid. In particular, in the room which was to be Churchill's study, a Victorian ceiling was removed to reveal handsome beams and rafters. Together with his small bedroom adjoining it (part of a Tilden extension to the main block), this study has rightly been described by Robin Fedden as 'the heart of Chartwell'.

Churchill's lectern desk (under picture)

In the study and bedroom he did most of his work, following the idiosyncratic routine to which those who served him had to adapt as best they might. His day started with a hearty English breakfast accompanied by the reading of sixteen newspapers. He then stayed in bed until lunch, dictating to a secretary, preparing articles or speeches, and working with one or more of his literary collaborators. After lunch he would potter around the garden with friends and relations, feeding his ducks and swans and golden orfe; or he would lay bricks; or he would do some painting in his garden studio. In the late afternoon he would undress and get back into bed for a siesta (a habit derived from his youthful adventure in Cuba covering the Spanish–American war), and he had the happy gift of being able to drop off at will. He would rise for more work and a bath before dinner, which he treated, like lunch, as a thoroughly convivial occasion, with invariable champagne and equally sparkling talk – much of it taking the form of monologues by him. At about midnight he would begin another long stint of work in his study, with a night-shift secretary to type (on a silent typewriter) or take dictation, and with a resident expert to help and advise on whatever book he might be writing. He could do with about four hours' sleep at night, though of course he also had the benefit of his earlier siesta.

Churchill's industry was no less prodigious as author than as politician. But were the results of comparable value? There have always been hostile views of his literary work, some critics dismissing his historical writing as hopelessly amateurish and prejudiced, others objecting to his style as overblown pastiche ('sham Augustan', in Evelyn Waugh's phrase). For the most part, however, competent judges have acknowledged that his qualities as an author were great, and that they included marvellous narrative power, command of dramatic effect, the capacity to give a lucid account of complex incidents and issues, epigrammatic wit and, not least, sheer vitality. He was a natural writer, with an intuitive response to the magic of language. As a small boy at Harrow he was in demand to write essays for older boys, and he took immense trouble in his early years to correct his grammar, widen his vocabulary and master the art of composition. He also made a close study of Bartlett's dictionary of *Familiar Quotations* which, as he put it, was 'a good thing for an uneducated man'. This was a useful, if superficial, substitute for the genuine literary culture that he never really bothered to acquire.

His passion was much more for writing than for reading. Few writers of his class can have been less well read. When he started writing, his ignorance of literature was almost total, and as time went on there continued to be enormous gaps that he either never filled or was amazingly slow to fill. His phenomenal memory enabled him to retain whatever he did read, but much that he read in his early years was second-rate. Apart from Gibbon and Macaulay, there were all too few major writers whose work deeply influenced him. He had a taste for epic poetry, often of a rather indifferent kind, which he could recite by the mile. Among poets of the highest rank, he certainly admired Pope and Byron and knew much of their work by heart; but Violet Bonham Carter found that when she mentioned Blake to him, in connection with poetry, he expressed surprise that the parliamentary admiral of that name had been a poet. As for Shakespeare, it seems that he lacked the sort of intimate rapport with our supreme writer that most English authors above the trashy level can normally be assumed to have.

116

Novels were almost a closed world to him until quite late on in his life. He had his first encounter with Jane Austen when he read *Pride and Prejudice* at the end of 1943 (recovering from pneumonia at Marrakesh), and his first encounters with Charlotte Brontë and Trollope in the 1950s. Dickens, whom many would regard as second only to Shakespeare among English writers, seems to have made no impact upon him at all.

Appropriately enough, his sole experiment in the novel genre was just about his only failure as an author. Nearly all his other books were successful with the public as well as with critics, and most were outstanding best-sellers, long before the Second World War transformed him into the literary equivalent of Picasso, whose slightest doodle could be turned to gold. During the interwar period, including the ten years when he was in the political wilderness and almost a pariah in the eyes of many of his compatriots, he was earning £20,000 a year from his books and journalism. This was a very large income indeed at the time (half a million a year by 1990 standards), but even so was not quite enough to sustain his recklessly extravagant way of life.

Chartwell itself made extremely heavy financial demands, as Clementine Churchill feared it would. The conversion alone cost far more than the original estimates, partly because the house was found to be riddled with dry rot. In the end the bill for making it as we see it today was about £18,000, on top of the £5,000 purchase price. By 1939 there was serious talk of selling the place. But during the Second World War he hardly went there at all, because he was advised that the lakes would make it an easy target for moonlight bombing; and after the war all financial problems disappeared. He had never been reluctant to accept favours from friends and strangers alike, and after 1945 he could live as spaciously as he liked almost entirely on the largesse of well-wishers. In particular, his position at Chartwell was secured when a group of friends, led by Lord Camrose, raised £50,000 to buy it from him for presentation to the National Trust, plus £35,000 to endow it, on the understanding that he would be allowed to stay there for the rest of his life, paying the Trust a rent of only £350 a year. In return he said that he and his wife would do their utmost 'to invest the house and gardens with every characteristic and trophy that [would] make it of interest in the future'.

His second, or Chartwell, period of authorship differs in one significant respect from the early period before he became a leading politician. As a young man he wrote his books in the strict sense, composing them in longhand. But when he returned to literary work after the First World War, he developed the habit of dictating the first draft of every book and then subjecting it to intense manuscript revision on a succession of proofs. He also became increasingly dependent upon the help of researchers, who provided him with facts and references, and whom he asked to advise him on points of interpretation without necessarily taking their

117

advice. The books remained unmistakably his, but all the same there was some loss of authenticity compared with the early period, varying in degree according to the extent of Churchill's direct acquaintance with the subject-matter. Thus, among his later works, the most authentic and, many would say, the best is *My Early Life* (1930), in the writing of which his need for assistance was minimal; the least authentic (and worst?) his *History of the English-Speaking Peoples*, of which a first draft was prepared before 1939 but which was then rewritten, with the help of many hands, after the war. When he is dealing with events in which he was a participant, he normally gives a special liveliness to the narrative, while also bringing to it the inside knowledge that often more than compensates for any scholarly weaknesses. But when he is dealing with periods remote from his own, and events in which he played no part, his work tends to be less compelling.

His *Marlborough*, published in four volumes between 1933 and 1938, is in a sense neither one thing nor the other, though nevertheless a powerful work. At the outset his knowledge of eighteenth-century Europe was superficial in the extreme. Yet he must have felt that telling the story of his illustrious ancestor was, by extension, a form of autobiography, and his own thoroughly Whiggish mentality in some measure helped him to understand the times as well as the character of his subject.

To my mind *The World Crisis*, for all its blemishes, is Churchill's best large-scale historical work, and certainly much superior to *The Second World War*, in which all the same faults are abundantly present, while some of the author's distinctive virtues are attenuated. When he came to compose the later work (mainly at Chartwell, though also in foreign villas put at his disposal by doting plutocrats), he was a quarter of a century older, but even busier, than when he wrote *World Crisis*. After 1945 he was Leader of the Opposition, eager to avenge his traumatic defeat at Labour's hands. He was also a cult figure throughout the world, and the West's self-appointed oracle. Inevitably he was more reliant than ever, in his literary work, upon researchers and assistants. Under pressure to produce the six volumes at top speed, he had too little time to ensure that every paragraph was vividly stamped with his own personality. No doubt the whole work was dictated by him, but much of the dictation must have consisted of too hasty paraphrasing of drafts prepared by aides. Moreover, the work displays even more shamelessly than *World Crisis* his bad habit of quoting his own letters and memoranda without giving any indication of how others replied to them.

Visiting Chartwell today, and standing in Churchill's study, we try to imagine him at work through so many long hours of day and night, producing his numerous books from *World Crisis* to *English-Speaking Peoples*. If he had done nothing else during the Chartwell years, this literary output would have been a formidable achievement for any man; but when we consider how much else he was doing at the same time we can only feel awe-struck. The room is full of inert reminders of his restless spirit:

the mahogany writing-table which belonged to his adored but unloving father; the portrait of that father writing with a quill pen; the Sargent drawing of Churchill's feckless mother, Jennie, and the bronze cast of one of her hands; the busts of Napoleon and Nelson; the painting of Blenheim Palace, where Churchill was born and within sight of which he is buried – these and many other authentic stage-properties are tellingly displayed. Most striking of all, perhaps, is the lectern-desk, successor to an earlier and simpler one that he designed himself in imitation of Disraeli's at Hughenden. On the sloping top he would spread his proofs and place books open at passages relating to a work in hand, while on the shelf below there were more books waiting to be used, with references flagged by his researchers.

Only the man himself is missing, and the vacuum is almost tangible. We begin to feel that all the energy that was once there will spring to life again at any moment. But the illusion passes, and we realize that what for a few decades was one of the most dynamic places on earth has reverted for ever to the placidity of an English country house which is now a perpetual shrine. The study is indeed the heart of Chartwell. But the heart is no longer beating.

WILLIAM COBBETT

FARNHAM, SURREY

MICHAEL FOOT

William Cobbett was one of the great self-taught masters of the English language. Emphasis on the self-tuition is necessary not only because of his own insistence but also because it confronts us at once with a proper challenge about the scale of his achievement. Whenever he stumbled on a new truth or an old one among the vast range of his interests – politics, economics, literature, beer-making, gardening, the education of children and the rest – he was gripped by a burning passion to tell everybody about it in words all would understand. He thought he could do this job better than anyone else, and he would turn his hand to it without delay. He was a kind of one-man Open University, always capable of adding a new item to the previous curriculum. So fresh and passionate was his ardour to teach that many of his books on non-political topics might have been expected to survive as satisfactory textbooks, and several of them do, but more and more, after his own original political conversion – a true Pauline or Bunyanite blinding revelation on the road to Damascus – his sense of political outrage came to dominate his mind, and he would take every available precaution to ensure that no method of expurgation would allow his victims to escape. But it is Cobbett the self-taught teacher who persistently returns to the centre of the stage.

He lived to the ripe age of seventy-three and until he reached his forties was literally still learning all the while the various conglomerations of political ideas which were to make him famous and unforgettable. He started his own weekly newspaper, his *Political Register*, in 1802, and kept it going by his own exertions until the day of his death in 1835. He was the son of a farmer and the grandson of a farm labourer, yet his boyhood vision was of a Merrie Eighteenth-Century England where his friends and fellow workers had at least enough to be able to eat, drink and make that Merrie claim something real. He served a short spell in the army and carried what he believed to be his High Tory principles across the Atlantic to young America. He would defend his King and Country wherever he went with all his might and indeed started to direct his budding literary talents to this end.

Lithograph of Cobbett belonging to Michael Foot

Over the years he would establish a reputation as pamphleteer, journalist, translator, author, publisher, bookseller, Member of Parliament. But he was also ploughboy, attorney's clerk, soldier, farmer, landowner, businessman, bankrupt, barrack-room lawyer, prisoner, fugitive, exile, traveller, gardener and arboriculturalist. Always the words and the action were mingled inextricably together.

Out of it all came a new way of conducting politics and a new way of writing English. Across the whole country, the arrival of the *Political Register* might be the most explosive event of the week, and his words could ferment like the beer he was happy to see enjoyed at these political festivals. Cobbett created 'a kind of fourth estate, in the politics of the country'. The phrase later became familiar, but the original application of it was William Hazlitt's measure of Cobbett's achievement. Let us glance first at the moment of conversion, the great crossroads in Cobbett's – and in England's – history.

The message was always more important than the medium. What would have become of Cobbett and his growing mastery of the language, if he had remained devoted to his Royalist High Tory standard, is impossible even to guess, but he would, supposedly, have taken his place among anti-Jacobin versifiers and polemicists of the Canning–Croker–Quarterly Reviewers school. It would have been a sad degradation, and it so nearly happened. He was often accused of being much too ready to rush headlong into a furious fight with friends and enemies alike. But what his critics failed to notice was how he would never close his eyes or his heart. He came to see what was truly happening in the England to which he had returned, in the Hampshire or Surrey villages which he knew so well. He saw what was happening to his own people; he drew the contrast with the memories of his own childhood – with considerable justice, as modern social historians have acknowledged. He described the event in a manner John Bunyan might have approved, although it was no mystical occurrence, but a great moment of political awakening:

> I myself, in the early part of my writing life was deceived . . .; but, when in [1804], I revisited the English labourer's dwelling, and that, too, after having so recently witnessed the happiness of labourers in America, when I saw that the clock was gone; that even the Sunday-coat was gone; when I saw those whom I had known the most neat, cheerful and happy beings on earth, and these my countrymen too, had become the most wretched and forlorn of human beings, I looked seriously and inquired patiently into the matter; and this inquiry into the causes of an effect which had so deep an impression on my mind, led to that series of exertions, which have *occupied my whole life, since that time,* to better the lot of the labourers.

Thenceforward, time and again – in the days of the Luddites in 1812, at the trial of Queen Caroline in 1820 and, most significantly, in the months of the 'Rural War', as Cobbett called it, which preceded the Reform Bill of 1832, Cobbett's furious powers of declamation swayed the opinion of his countrymen on the foremost issues of the age. Sometimes it was his political insight or foresight which gave him his following, and sometimes, as he himself would have been eager to testify, it was his unfailing zest as an educator of the working people whom he loved individually and whose cause he loved no less.

'When I am asked,' he said,

> what books a young man or a young woman ought to read, I *always* answer, 'Let him or her read *all that I have written.*' This does, it will be doubtless said, *smell of the shop*. No matter. It is what I have recommended; and experience has taught me that it is my duty to prove that recommendation.

Cobbett's birthplace, Farnham

He was often accused of an inordinate egotism and vanity, but these vices were usually mixed with a sly self-knowledge which mitigated the curse. With an equal lack of bashfulness he would recommend as the best of all guides to domestic happiness his *Advice to Young Men, And (Incidentally) to Young Women in the Middle and Higher Ranks of Life*, published in 1829 and destined to sell for the rest of the century and beyond – even though, according to his most recent biographers, his own much-vaunted domestic harmony was breaking up at just that moment. But he was no hypocrite; no one was ever fool enough to make that charge against William Cobbett. He would pour forth his opinions and judgements with unrelenting passion, even if they contradicted his own no less passionately held opinions of a few years or even months before.

One other volume with a beautiful long-winded title deserved and succeeded to rival his *Advice to Young Men*. It was called: *A Grammar of the English Language in a Series of Letters. Intended for the use of Schools and of Young Persons in General; but more especially*

Cobbett's tomb, St Andrew's parish churchyard

for the use of Soldiers, Sailors, Apprentices and Plough-boys. To which are added: Six Lessons, intended to prevent Statesmen from using false grammar, and from writing in an awkward manner.

The admonition was addressed not only to the politicians; he could be as easily provoked by the academic experts who should know better. 'My dear James,' he wrote to his son, the supposed recipient of the letters, 'let chambermaids and members of the House of Commons, and learned Doctors write thus [he cited a glaring misuse of common terms]; be you content with plain words which convey your meaning.' Then he cited some other solecisms, and continued: 'It is for monks,

124

for Fellows of English Colleges who live by the sweat of other people's brows, to spend their time in this manner, and to call the result of their studies learning.'

It is hard to know which to admire more: the courage of the defiance itself or the words in which he expressed his outrage at the use of such euphemisms as 'corporal infliction': '*Flog* is *flog* ... and it means to whip the naked back (and sometimes other parts) of a soldier with a thing called a cat; that is to say with nine strong whip cords, about a foot and a half long ...' Flogging in the British Army was not abolished then, but when the day of enlightenment came, Cobbett's choice of language had contributed to the victory.

The splendid insolence which incited Cobbett to attack Dr Johnson, the dictionary-maker, was part of a larger assault which changed the whole development of English literature; political literature at least, although no sharp distinction should be allowed. Three great prose-writers of the period found it essential for their political purposes to challenge the way in which the language itself was written. None of them at the time was accepted as a literary figure of any consequence; indeed, huge efforts were made to mock them off the stage altogether, to dismiss them as practitioners of a different trade. But all of them had the same urge, a common interest, to challenge the Johnsonian ascendancy and prove in practice that a much more flexible and potent means of political communication could be devised. William Hazlitt was the writer who did this demolition work most directly and who consciously forged the new weapon, but he had been preceded by two others of a slightly earlier generation: Thomas Paine and Cobbett himself.

Hazlitt wrote an essay in which he contrasted the virtues of Paine and Cobbett, and it is still in several respects the most observant criticism on the literary style of the two great radicals. He noted Paine's gift for the kind of memorable maxims which could start and finish arguments. He never underrated the power of Paine's writing and how it turned the scales at critical moments. All the more notable, therefore, is the even more glowing tribute which often in the same breath he would pay to the Cobbett who is remembered not for single phrases or passages easy to quote. Just after the phrase about the fourth estate, cited earlier, Hazlitt continues:

> He is not only unquestionably the most powerful writer of the present day, but one of the best writers in the language. He speaks and thinks plain, broad, downright English. He might be said to have the clearness of Swift, the naturalness of Defoe, and the picturesque, satirical description of Mandeville; if all such comparisons were not impertinent. A really great and original writer is like nobody but himself.

Cobbett was a true innovator, an original genius. He honoured the best traditions of his countrymen and was always eager to tell the story of how, as an eleven-year-old boy, he had bought for threepence, instead of his supper, a copy of Jonathan

Swift's *Tale of a Tub*, how he sat on a nearby Richmond haystack reading until it was dark and then fell asleep. He called that moment 'the birth of intellect'. Jonathan Swift and his three great pupils, Paine, Cobbett and Hazlitt, were determined to break down all the barriers which prevented the English (and Irish) people from talking to one another on all the subjects that mattered.

How that Farnham schoolboy learnt so early not to be intimidated by the boldest, plainest words and their true meaning is a moment of wonder in our literary and political history. Even before his political conversion, Cobbett had been learning a rudimentary love of truth from Swift. More and more, as the years passed, he learnt to appeal, like most great English Radicals, to history, to the Levellers, to Wat Tyler, to King Alfred; and to the endless tradition of English invective:

> 'Coarse!' the sons and daughters of Corruption will exclaim. 'Coarse!' will echo back the scoundrel *seat-sellers* ... 'Vary coarse, ma'awm!' will some grinning Scotch sycophant observe to some she-sinecurist or pensioner. 'Coarse as neck-beef' will growl out some Englishman, who has filled his bags by oppression of the poor ... Yes, it is *coarse* indeed, and coarse it ought to be in a case like this. Swift has told us not to chop *blocks* with *razors*. Any *edge* tool is too fine for work like this: a pick-axe, that perforates with one end and drags about with the other, is the tool for this sort of business.

Cobbett probably learnt more from Swift than from any other writer – even though Swift rarely preferred to use the pickaxe. They had many of the same hates, passions and primitive interests – for example, on food, and what people might do, and should do, if they saw their children starving.

> For my own part, I really am ashamed to ride a fat horse, to have a full belly, and to have a clean shirt upon my back, while I look at these wretched countrymen of mine; while I actually see them reeling with weakness; when I see their poor faces present me nothing but skin and bone, while they are toiling to get the wheat and the meat ready to be carried away and devoured by the tax-eaters.

As Hazlitt would insist, the writer of those sentences had a style of his own. However, let it also not be forgotten that the causes themselves – Cobbett's causes, as they should justly be called – and not merely the language in which they were expressed have their own grandeur. Time has not reduced them to the status of forgotten charades. Cobbett did not always range himself on the right or the most deserving side, even after his notorious conversion. The risk was always there that he might make terrible blunders or turn his uncontrollable wrath on his own followers or allies: 'If nobody else can argue with him,' as Hazlitt said, 'he is a very good match for himself.' But these cantankerous explosions, these descents into egotism, cannot be allowed to impair the recognition of his sustained intellectual achievement, which may be seen as a welding of three themes together. He saw what was happening in the England of his day: he understood the class war long before Karl Marx had ever written about it. And then he gradually devised a grand remedy, one which matched the scale of the disease – the reform of parliament. The Cobbett of the 1820s prepared the way for that victory more than any other single participant in the struggle. Then he placed the whole of his period in a new historical setting, one which first sanctioned and then gave a new impetus to the whole process.

No one of any sensibility can read his *Rural Rides* today without sharing the sense of shame which Cobbett expressed 'as an Englishman'. No single sentence or paragraph conveys his meaning; it is the rising, passionate, torrential description of what the oppression was truly like for the majority – and the rising fury that nothing was done, even after his exposures. So Cobbett both diagnosed the disease and expounded the remedy. He campaigned as others did for a reformed parliament: it was done with a scorn and an incisiveness which none could equal.

But there was something even more original than the power of Cobbett's invective directed to achieve immediate reforms. He wanted to overturn not merely the government of the upper classes but their imposition upon the English people of their history, their philosophy, their whole way of looking at society and at life. He wanted to show how all the supposedly decent institutions – the universities, the Church and the great aristocratic estates no less than the central government in London – had been twisted to serve their interest. 'Once convinced that this was the need of the time,' wrote the twentieth-century historian, J. L. Hammond, 'Cobbett threw himself into his task with great courage and with all the force of his versatile and exuberant mind.' It needed very real courage for a writer then to rewrite the history of the Protestant reformation. Not so long before, anti-papist mobs could be recruited by the government of the day to wreck the homes and activities of those who would dare plead for justice even for Roman Catholics. Cobbett was no Catholic, but he was quite ready to defy the suffocating orthodoxies of the Established English Church and the mobs they might seek to make do their dirty work. He saw what barbarities were perpetuated by the Protestant masters in Ireland (once he had backed or approved them himself) and he would sit quiet amid these infamies no longer. He would look back across the centuries and deduce a new moral. And, perhaps even braver and more remarkable, he would look back across his own revolutionary epoch and see a new vision.

He was a great agitator – that was the title G. K. Chesterton gave him: 'the noblest English example of the noble calling of the agitator'. But the combination of his new political vision and his capacity to express it in a new political language made him something larger still. I have had on my wall for years a contemporary lithograph portrait of a painting of 'Mr William Cobbett'. Every lineament of the self-confident, defiant style which Hazlitt discerned seems to be evident there. This was the face that was better known than that of any other Englishman of his time, except maybe those which figured in the Royalist parades. A little later, and for many years on end, Cobbett was caricatured more persistently and viciously than any other of the enemies of Church and State. But with his pen he established a closer association with the English people than anyone else. They would always remember what he wrote and what he stood for.

Today a visit to Farnham produces several reminders of William Cobbett. Although he would not recognize the centre with its modern shop-fronts and one-way street system, the many fine Georgian houses which remain in this once important corn-market town would have been familiar to him. He was born in 1763 in his father's pub, the Jolly Farmer Inn in Bridge Square, now renamed the William Cobbett, and is buried in the churchyard of the medieval parish church of St Andrew. Attractive, narrow lanes lined with original seventeenth- and eighteenth-century cottages lead to the church out of one of the town streets. A tablet with his portrait in relief on the inside south wall of the church tower commemorates him. As a boy, he worked for a time in the gardens of Farnham Castle, which is set on a rise to the north of the town, and was then owned by the bishops of Winchester.

Cobbett would have known Willmer House in West Street, which was built in 1718 and has a cut-brick façade among the best in the country. It is now a museum recording the history of the town, and has a room devoted to the memory of its most famous inhabitant, with displays of Cobbett's memorabilia – his chair, table, ink-well – and some of his manuscripts and letters. He returned to farm in the nearby village of Normandy for the last four years of his life.

Cobbett would never return to his native Farnham without renewing his faith. This was how he described it in 1818:

> I had to cross in my post-chaise the long and dreary heath of Bagshot. Then at the end of it to mount a hill called Hungry Hill; and from that hill I knew that I should look down into the beautiful and fertile vale of Farnham. My heart fluttered with impatience, mixed with a sort of fear, to see all the scenes of my childhood ... There is a hill, not far from the town, called *Crooksbury Hill*... It served as the superlative degree of height. *As high as Crooksbury Hill* meant with us the utmost degree of height. Therefore, the first object that my eyes sought was this hill. *I could not believe my eyes!* Literally speaking, I, for a moment, thought the famous hill removed, and a little heap put in its stead; for I had seen in New Brunswick a single rock, or hill of solid rock, ten times as big, and four or five times as high! The post-boy, going down-hill, and not a bad road, whisked me, in a few minutes, to the Bush Inn, from the garden of which I could see the prodigious *sand hill*, where I had begun my gardening works. What a nothing! But now came rushing into my mind all at once, my pretty little garden, my little blue smock-frock, my little nailed shoes, my pretty pigeons, that I

used to feed out of my hands, the last kind words and tears of my gentle-hearted and affectionate mother! I hastened back into the room. If I had looked a moment longer, I should have dropped. When I came to reflect, *what a change*! I looked down at my dress. What a change! What scenes I had gone through! How altered my state! I had dined the day before at the Secretary of State's in company with *Mr Pitt*, and had been waited on by men in gaudy liveries. I had had no one to assist me in the world. No teachers of any sort. Nobody to shelter me from the consequences of bad, and no one to counsel me to good behaviour. I felt proud. The distinctions of rank, birth, and wealth, all became nothing in my eyes; and from that moment (less than a month after my arrival in England), I resolved never to bend before them.

SAMUEL TAYLOR COLERIDGE

NETHER STOWEY, SOMERSET

ANTHONY QUINTON

If you drive west from Bridgwater in the direction of Watchet, Minehead and the north Somerset coast, the first place of any size that you come to – it is about eight miles along the road – is Nether Stowey. It is a little way off the main road to the left, a rather accidental-looking place, in a fairly flat region, but with rising ground behind it to the south, the northern edge of the Quantock Hills.

The main street of the village winds in an agreeably casual way beside the course of a small stream. Near the top end of the village is Coleridge's cottage, a building of no great intrinsic claim to attention, which one could easily miss if it were not for the National Trust notice that stands outside it. Although tidied up and in good repair, it is clearly much older than the new bungalows beyond it at the furthest extremity of the village. It must have been the last house to have been built in that direction when Coleridge came to live there in 1796. At that time he described it, cheerfully but no doubt accurately, as a hovel. But he grew to love it, being anyway not too fussy about his surroundings. At the time it was delightful to him as a refuge from all sorts of pressures: financial insecurity and the collapse of his sympathies for the ideals of the French Revolution in particular.

It is a simple two-up two-down affair, with four smallish windows looking out on to the street from a good deal of blank wall. There is a decent front door with an attractive little canopy over it. In Coleridge's time it was thatched, but is now covered with severe dark-red ridged tiles. It was none too well equipped in 1796. It had no oven, so Coleridge's wife, Sara, had to take things to be baked or roasted to the nearby baker's shop. Behind it there was – and to some extent still is – a patch of land on which Coleridge proposed to keep a pig and some ducks and to grow vegetables. There is reason to think that, like a great many of Coleridge's schemes, after an initial burst of enthusiasm this did not come to anything.

The place had been found for Coleridge by his friend Thomas Poole, who had not long before inherited his father's prosperous tanning business. Shortly before Coleridge moved in with Sara and their three-month-old child, Hartley, Poole was

Ash Farm, where Coleridge is thought to have written Kubla Khan

attacked by doubts as to whether it was not too primitive for the young family. Coleridge overrode these doubts with characteristically tumultuous enthusiasm. He was to remain there from December 1796 to September 1798. That is less than two out of the sixty-four years of his life, but they were by far his most productive as a poet. All his best-known poems – except, perhaps, for 'Dejection: an Ode' – were written then, in particular 'Kubla Khan' and 'The Rime of the Ancient Mariner'. In any reasonable selection from his complete poetic output the work of his twenty-one months at Nether Stowey is likely to take up half the space.

Thomas Poole had educated himself in defiance of his father's contempt for book-learning. He was an ardent and politically active Whig, of the democratic if not quite Jacobinical kind. His public spirit led him, in a way that is not all that usual among political extremists, to be a constant and substantial benefactor to his local community. His memorial stone is to be seen in Nether Stowey church.

Coleridge had first come to Nether Stowey in the late summer of 1796, soon after the collapse, with its tenth issue, of his periodical the *Watchman*. In the cold December of 1796, when he moved into the cottage, he was oppressed not only by that failure, but by intense eye-pain and facial swelling which drove him to opium for relief, with dire long-term consequences of addiction. He was suffering also from sympathetic distress on behalf of his friend Charles Lamb, whose sister, Mary, in a fit of madness, had recently murdered her mother.

Another unhappy person impinged more directly on Coleridge. Shortly before the move to Nether Stowey he had taken into his house in Bristol as a pupil a well-off young admirer called Charles Lloyd. Lloyd was, unfortunately, an epileptic, and a series of fits had made it necessary for him to go home to his father just before the Coleridge family's departure. In February 1797 he was back with the Coleridges, but he had more fits and had to go again in March. In a manner which was not uncommon among Coleridge's younger admirers, initial enthusiasm and devotion came to be replaced by disappointment and hostility. The first entrancing impact of Coleridge's personality did not endure. In Lloyd's case the most depressing result was a novel he published in the early part of 1798 called *Edmund Oliver*, which contained an unflattering and all too recognizable portrait of Coleridge.

Soon after Lloyd's departure an altogether more important and rewarding relationship developed, Coleridge's friendship with Wordsworth and his sister, Dorothy. They had first met in the autumn of 1795 around the time of his marriage to Sara Fricker and their honeymoon period at Clevedon on the Bristol Channel. In April 1797 Wordsworth called in on Coleridge in Nether Stowey while walking back from Bristol to Racedown in Dorset. In the same ardently pedestrian mode Coleridge returned the visit two months later. Racedown is some forty miles from Nether Stowey and Coleridge's walk there is evidence that he was just as strenuous a walker as Wordsworth, although less renowned as such. Indeed, he seems to have been a more adventurous and scrambling kind of walker than the more measured and deliberate Wordsworth.

Coleridge's first volume of poems had come out in April 1796 and went into a second edition, with poems by Charles Lamb and Charles Lloyd added to the text in the following year. A much more significant collaboration was soon to take place. The idea of Wordsworth and Coleridge combining the new kind of poems they were writing in a joint volume as a form of manifesto came to them in the course of one of their many walks in the Quantocks. The result, *Lyrical Ballads*, was published in September 1798, just as Coleridge was leaving Nether Stowey for good, at the outset of his trip to Germany. The famous introduction in which Wordsworth sets out their principles about poetic diction (that poetry should be written 'in the language generally used by men') and about the nature of poetry ('the spontaneous overflow of powerful feelings') was not added until the second

Coleridge's cottage, Nether Stowey

edition of 1800. But these ideas were illustrated by example in the poems themselves.

Coleridge's most important contribution was *The Rime of the Ancient Mariner*. For all its supernatural incidents and the atmosphere of magical glamour in which it is bathed, it is composed in ballad form, the simplest and most rustically unsophisticated of English poetic patterns, and its language is of the most straightforward character. Very few of the words in it are of more than two syllables: 'mariner', 'glittering', 'merrily', 'minstrelsy', 'tyrannous' and 'o'ertaking' are the only ones to be found in the first fifty lines. Some stanzas are as humble and rudimentary as *John Gilpin*:

> The ship was cheered, the harbour cleared,
>> Merrily did we drop
> Below the kirk, below the hill,
>> Below the lighthouse top.

The stanza that follows is composed almost entirely of monosyllables, like a song by Shakespeare:

> The Sun came up upon the left,
>> Out of the sea came he!
> And he shone bright, and on the right
>> Went down into the sea.

Wordsworth's finest contribution to the joint effort is surely 'Tintern Abbey'. More in conformity with his requirement of the language to be that generally used by men is 'The Idiot Boy'. The topic and its treatment gave great offence to many contemporary readers.

The relationship between Coleridge on the one hand and Wordsworth and his sister on the other was one of rapturous mutual enchantment. Coleridge was not in love with Dorothy (as he was to be later with Wordsworth's sister-in-law), but he admired the combination of intelligence and sensitivity which made her such a marvellous companion for her brother. By comparison, his own uninteresting, and understandably resentful, wife had little to offer but congested domesticity. The matrimonial breakdown to come is prefigured in the circumstances surrounding the writing of Coleridge's beautiful poem 'This Lime-Tree Bower My Prison'.

During the first summer at Nether Stowey Charles Lamb, with William and Dorothy Wordsworth, came on a visit. Sara spilt a pan of boiling milk over Coleridge's foot, so he was unable to go out walking with them. In the remarks with which he introduces the poem he says only, in the most gentlemanly fashion, that the author 'met with an accident, which disabled him from walking during the whole time of [his friends'] stay'.

> Well, they are gone, and here must I remain,
> This lime-tree bower my prison! I have lost
> Beauties and feelings, such as would have been
> Most sweet to my remembrance even when age
> Had dimm'd mine eyes to blindness! . . .

It is clear, I think, that he was distinctly annoyed and not merely regretful. That first line is unquestionably nettled.

Soon after this mishap the invaluable Thomas Poole had found a fine place nearby for the Wordsworths to rent. Alfoxden is a spacious country house (now some kind of hotel) only four or five miles on foot from Coleridge's much more modest establishment. The Wordsworths took it for a year at the amazingly low rent of £23, and for such walkers as they and Coleridge it was almost as if they were next door. For the rest of their time there they were constantly in and out of each other's houses.

What ensured that the Wordsworths' stay would not be longer was the communication to their landlord of suspicions about the political reliability, indeed of the patriotic loyalty, of their circle. Coleridge had arrived in Nether Stowey with the reputation of being a dangerous Jacobin radical. He had never really deserved it, for his concern for the oppressed was essentially humanitarian and only political in an accidental and transitory way. Poole was a radical as well, and he and Coleridge invited into their midst the radical agitator 'Citizen' John Thelwall, who had been remanded to the Tower of London for a spell in 1794 on a charge of high treason. When their walks, by night as well as by day, and their habit of sketching are taken into account, it is not surprising that Coleridge and the Wordsworths should have been suspected of some kind of complicity with the expected French invaders. An agent was set to spy on them. The incident is a parallel to that inspired by the presence of D. H. Lawrence and his unapologetically German wife in Cornwall in 1917.

The need of a regular income to support his literary career was always present to Coleridge's mind at this time. One possibility was to become a Unitarian minister, and now and again he went to preach in Taunton and Bristol. In January 1798 he was offered the post of minister at Shrewsbury and went there to deliver a specimen sermon. Among those in the congregation was the young William Hazlitt, who has left a brilliant account of this and later encounters with Coleridge in his essay 'On My First Acquaintance with Poets'. Just as Coleridge had agreed to accept, he received the strikingly generous offer of £150 a year for life from the Wedgwood family and quickly disentangled himself.

Hazlitt came to stay at Nether Stowey in the summer of 1798 for three weeks. Already Coleridge was planning a change of scenery. He and Wordsworth proposed to pay for a tour in Germany with the proceeds of *Lyrical Ballads*, which had been sent to their publisher, Cottle, in June. On 14 September he embarked in 'a spectacular greatcoat' (naturally with gigantic book-pockets) from Great Yarmouth on his first trip abroad. The Wordsworths were seasick, but Coleridge was not. By the time he got back from his German expedition, considerably extended from the three months originally intended to as long as ten, much had happened. Most important was his immersion in the literature and idealistic philosophy of Germany, which led to his translation of Schiller's *Wallenstein* and his continuing work to introduce German spirituality into the earthbound empiricist tradition of British thinking. His second child, Berkeley, who had been born four months before Coleridge's departure, died in February, but he did not hurry home. He was not to visit Nether Stowey again until around Christmas 1801, when he stayed for three weeks with Poole.

There are three main ways in which a poet can concern himself with nature. The first is by particular description, by the accurate recording of the detail of nature, of specific natural objects such as animals, birds, trees, flowers, rocks and streams. Secondly, there is the evocation of landscape, the recording of a general impression of the natural environment. Finally, there is the response to nature as a whole, an intimation of the place of man within it, an understanding of the moral or spiritual significance of nature, seen as something much more than a field for practical exploitation. Coleridge and Wordsworth were both poets of nature in the third sense, seeking to express in poetry a sense of man's connection to nature as the condition of his truest happiness and fulfilment. But they differed in the kind of description of nature from which they derived their general reflections about it. Coleridge, for all his reputation as an abstract metaphysician, is a master of particular description. Wordsworth, commonly thought of as the paradigm of a nature poet, is, by comparison, an impressionist.

These lines from 'This Lime-Tree Bower My Prison' are characteristic of Coleridge's exactness in the description of detail:

> Pale beneath the blaze
> Hung the transparent foliage; and I watch'd
> Some broad and sunny leaf, and lov'd to see
> The shadow of the leaf and stem above
> Dappling its sunshine! And that walnut-tree
> Was richly ting'd, and a deep radiance lay
> Full on the ancient ivy, which usurps
> Those fronting elms, and now, with blackest mass
> Makes their dark branches gleam a lighter hue
> Through the late twilight ...

That is the product of closely attentive observation. By comparison Wordsworth on the daffodils is vague and sketchy:

> When all at once I saw a crowd,
> A host, of golden daffodils;
> Beside the lake, beneath the trees,
> Fluttering and dancing in the breeze ...
> Ten thousand saw I at a glance,
> Tossing their heads in sprightly dance.

That is what happens if you wander lonely as a cloud and look at things only from a distance. Wordsworth's eye here is like Monet's; Coleridge's more like Dürer's.

Where Wordsworth appears to advantage is in his account of the leading features of a landscape. To take a homely example:

> The day is come when I again repose
> Here, under this dark sycamore, and view
> These plots of cottage-ground, these orchard-tufts,
> Which, at this season, with their unripe fruits,
> Are clad in one green hue, and lose themselves
> 'Mid groves and copses. Once again I see
> These hedge-rows, hardly hedge-rows, little lines
> Of sportive wood run wild: these pastoral farms,
> Green to the very door; and wreaths of smoke
> Sent up, in silence, from among the trees!

More glorious still is Wordsworth's handling of the grander scenery of the Lake District, as in the famous passage in Book I of *The Prelude* about taking a boat out on the lake at night:

> I dipped my oars into the silent lake,
> And, as I rose upon the stroke, my boat
> Went heaving through the water like a swan;
> When, from behind that craggy steep till then
> The horizon's bound, a huge peak, black and huge,
> As if with voluntary power instinct
> Upreared its head. I struck and struck again,
> And growing still in stature the grim shape
> Towered up between me and the stars, and still,
> For so it seemed, with purpose of its own
> And measured motion like a living thing,
> Strode after me . . .

A. N. Whitehead has suggested that Wordsworth's descriptive bias can be attributed to the typically unchanging character of his home region: mountains, waterfalls, hilly pastures, all varying little with the passage of the seasons. Coleridge's West Country is altogether more mutable.

Coleridge did not become a nature poet – or, one might add, a natural poet – in one bound. His first writings are for the most part rhetorical, verbose and conventional. Only two years before his most creative period he wrote a widely noticed group of sonnets 'on eminent characters' of which this passage of fustian is representative:

> Stanhope! I hail, with ardent Hymn, thy name!
>   Thou shalt be bless'd and lov'd, when in the dust
> Thy corse shall moulder – Patriot pure and just!
>   And o'er thy tomb the grateful hand of FAME . . .

137

But in the same year the first clear signs of a new, more natural poetic manner, freed from Zephyrs and Muses and capitalized abstractions like Pity and Solitude and Mirth, were shown by his 'To a Young Ass':

> Poor little Foal of an oppresséd race!
> I love the languid patience of thy face:
> And oft with gentle hand I give thee bread,
> And clap thy ragged coat, and pat thy head.

His descriptive exactness appears in some lines about the ass's tied-up mother:

> Or is thy sad heart thrill'd with filial pain
> To see thy wretched mother's shorten'd chain?
> And truly, very piteous is her lot –
> Chain'd to a log within a narrow spot,
> Where the close-eaten grass is scarcely seen,
> While sweet around her waves the tempting green!

By the time he came to Stowey he had essentially liberated himself from the kind of decayed Augustan formalism which he had at first supposed to be the proper vehicle for poetry. But, being a nature poet of the minutely descriptive type, rather than a poet of landscape like Wordsworth, his work of the Nether Stowey period does not contain all that much in the way of direct evocation of the surrounding scenery. But there are suggestive passages.

In 'This Lime-Tree Bower My Prison' he thinks of his friends 'on springy heath, along the hill-top edge' and of their getting a view of

> The many-steepled tract magnificent
> Of hilly fields and meadows, and the sea,
> With some fair bark, perhaps, whose sails light up
> The slip of smooth clear blue betwixt two Isles
> Of purple shadow!

No doubt he is imagining them looking towards Watchet, which is presumably the port of the Ancient Mariner's departure.

'Christabel' is full of standard Gothic romance material: a castle at night with owls, a thick forest, a moat, a massive gate, a toothless mastiff. All that has nothing whatever to do with the Quantocks and Nether Stowey. But in 'Kubla Khan', for all its exotic theme and furnishings, there are touches of Somerset. The 'deep romantic chasm' might well have been inspired by a stream hurling itself into the Bristol Channel between narrow banks and down a steep cliff somewhere between Porlock and Lynton. It was in that region that the poem was written. Coleridge, feeling ill in the course of making his long way home from Lynton on foot in October 1797, put up at a lonely farm near Culbone, probably Ash Farm, half-

Overlooking Porlock Bay, above Culbone Combe

way between Lynton and Porlock. In Culbone Combe the neighbourhood is equipped with an appropriate romantic chasm. The 'person from Porlock' on whose interruption Coleridge blames the poem's incomplete state would have had to come a distance of only about five miles, if, indeed, there was such a person.

The cottage at Nether Stowey is alluded to in one of the first poems to be written there: the dedicatory lines to his eldest brother, George, that were sent to him with some poems.

> Or when, as now, on some delicious eve,
> We in our sweet sequester'd orchard-plot
> Sit on the tree crook'd earthward; whose old boughs,
> That hang above us in an arborous roof,
> Stirr'd by the faint gale of departing May,
> Send their loose blossoms slanting o'er our heads!

In 'Frost at Midnight' the opening movement describes the poet sitting at night by his son's cradle in the cottage 'with all the numberless goings-on of life inaudible as dreams'. He thinks back to his childhood in rural Ottery St Mary, his exile at school in London, and promises his son a country upbringing: 'all seasons shall be sweet to thee'. In 'France: an Ode', written in February 1798, there are obvious references to the Somerset coast:

> On that sea-cliff's verge,
> Whose pines, scarce travell'd by the breeze above
> Had made one murmur with the distant surge!

That poem registers his deliverance from the French Revolution and its way of realizing the ideal of human freedom. Like those English Stalinists who swallowed the Russian invasion of Hungary in 1956 but could not tolerate the invasion of Czechoslovakia in 1968, Coleridge, who had managed to digest the Terror without any sign of distress, boggled at the invasion of Switzerland.

Possibly the best evocation of the scenery of the Quantocks in Coleridge's work is contained in the opening passage of his 'Fears in Solitude', written in April 1798, and even more in its closing lines in which Stowey is mentioned by name.

> And now beloved Stowéy! I behold
> Thy church-tower, and, methinks, the four huge elms
> Clustering, which mark the mansion of my friend;
> And close behind them, hidden from my view,
> Is my own lowly cottage, where my babe
> And my babe's mother dwell in peace!

The presence of the natural surroundings in which all Coleridge's great, and much of his good, poetry was written is not a dominant feature of the work he produced during his short stay there. But there is enough evidence of the effect of the place upon him to invest it with an attraction over and above that exercised by its visible beauties.

WILLIAM COWPER

ORCHARD SIDE, OLNEY, BUCKINGHAMSHIRE

ELIZABETH MAVOR

'On Monday last,' wrote William Cowper to his aunt, 'we went to see our Friend Newton at Olney and to take a view of the Place where we trust the Lord has fix'd the Bounds of our Habitation.'

It was August 1767, Cowper was thirty-six, an unsuccessful barrister and not fully recovered from an appalling plunge into insanity three years before. Then, riven by the terrifying revelation that he was eternally damned, he had tried repeatedly to kill himself; had been taken by his despairing brother to Dr Cotton's Collegium Insanorum at St Albans where, so he tells us, locked up and bound, he endured a mental agony of eighteen months before he at last began to recover.

The recovery had been due to the skill of Dr Cotton, to Cowper's reading of the poems of George Herbert, but mainly to his conversion to Evangelicalism, which Dr Cotton himself professed.

A period of convalescence had followed in timorous retirement at lodgings in Huntingdon, where he proved totally unable to look after himself. Happily all this changed when at church one morning he made the acquaintance of William Unwin, son of the Revd Morley Unwin. Companionable cups of tea were drunk, an affinity of religious belief established, and Cowper introduced to Mary Unwin, the young man's mother. 'Suddenly I think, I cannot say how, suddenly it occurred to me that I might possibly find a place in Mr Unwin's family as a boarder.'

This duly came to pass, and for almost two years Cowper enjoyed an increasing confidence and contentment until the cosy Evangelical domestic idyll of which he had become a part was rudely broken by Mr Unwin being killed in a riding accident.

Where should they go? For by now Cowper had formed a close and dependent tie with Mary Unwin, and both longed to settle in a 'faithful' neighbourhood (Huntingdon being deficient in this respect), where their modest private incomes would suffice.

Orchard Side, Olney

It was now that Thomas Newton entered their lives. One-time shipmaster, deserter from a press-gang and a slaver, he was a passionate convert to the Evangelical faith, had become a clergyman and was currently making the small Buckinghamshire market town of Olney into a centre of the Evangelical world. The parties took to one another immediately. Within a week this dynamo of a man had written offering Cowper and Mary Unwin the possibility of renting one of three houses in Olney.

By September 1767 Cowper, Mrs Unwin and Mrs Unwin's daughter (the last an unwilling chaperone to her mother) had taken up temporary accommodation in the town. By mid-February the following year they had moved into Orchard Side.

On first seeing the gaunt red-brick house, Cowper was put in mind of a prison. Built sixty years earlier, it was adjacent to Silver End, the worst and most insalubrious part of the town. Its windows faced north, its garden was restricted. Cowper would complain how 'the fishy smelling fumes of the marsh miasma' ineluctably seeped up from the River Ouse in winter, and how the paths round Olney were so deep in mud that he and Mary were imprisoned in their tiny parlour from September to March. Events in the little town, moreover, were 'as scarce as Cucumbers at

Christmas'. Yet over the next twenty years Orchard Side would be the setting for his becoming a poet, for his universal success, for the dearest friendship of his life; and when he left it for somewhere grander and with south-facing windows, his eyes, in spite of himself, would mist with tears.

For the time being, however, Olney had at least two great advantages. Its dreamy river landscape, its willows, its soft blue hills, reminded him of the country round his father's rectory at Berkhamsted in Hertfordshire; and Orchard Side, with all its drawbacks, was not far from the church, and couldn't have been closer to his friend Newton. Cowper had only to open the gate at the end of his garden, cross a small orchard and there was the handsome, newly built vicarage with Thomas Newton in it.

At Newton's electric instigation there now began for Cowper a rigorous programme designed both to combat Cowper's blue devils and further the Lord's work in Olney. 'For nearly twelve years we were seldom separated for seven hours at a time,' Newton later recollected of their daily preaching, praying and teaching. Perhaps more tellingly, Cowper wrote to his aunt just before Christmas 1767 of verses

> composed Yesterday Morning before Daybreak, but fell asleep at the End of the two
> first lines, when I awaked again the third and fourth were whisper'd to my Heart in
> a way which I have often experienced.

It was the beautiful hymn 'Oh! for a closer walk with God', and it became one of the collection of *Olney Hymns* that he and Newton were currently writing together.

Otherwise Cowper attended church with Mary, and wrote, when time allowed, letters of a heavily religious cast. So those early Olney days passed, and he seemed better. But in August 1769 he wrote significantly to a friend, that 'the Vacancy I left at St Alban's [the Asylum] is filled by a near Relation', for although he seemed cured, the awareness that his malady might recur was ever present. Variously thought to have originated in early childhood with the sad loss of his mother, or perhaps caused by the knowledge of a private physical abnormality which has never been specified, but which led to unmerciful bullying at his first school, it now seems more likely to have been inherited. Certainly, lesser symptoms of depressive illness appear to have been exhibited by his brother John, who, by the time Cowper had been not quite three years at Olney, had become mortally ill.

John's deathbed, attended by a spectacular conversion to Evangelicalism, chiefly brought about by his brother's agonized prayers that he should see the light, certainly went far to unhinge Cowper. His state of mind was further exacerbated by a domestic crisis. Miss Unwin, Mary's daughter, was about to marry. Her absence from Orchard Side necessitated, for propriety's sake, so Cowper thought, that he should marry her mother, and he and Mary Unwin became engaged.

His anguished knowledge that he had a physical abnormality may have played its part, as must a nightmare in which he heard the frightful words 'Actum est de te periisti' (It is over with thee, thou has perished). At all events, by the beginning of 1773 the engagement was broken off, and for the third time poor Cowper went mad. Orchard Side was abandoned, and they went to live in the vicarage with Newton. For a long time there are no letters. Silence falls.

They went back home on 23 May the following year. Cowper returned to normal life slowly, very slowly, and when seen again is feeding his eight pairs of pigeons in the little garden at the back of the house or attending to his cucumbers and melons in his greenhouse. Now he has three tame hares, Puss, Tiny and Bess, who are allowed out into the parlour each evening to play, emerging through the specially designed pop-hole, which can still be seen in the Orchard Side hall.

'The necessity of Amusement,' he writes to a correspondent, 'makes me sometimes write verses – it made me a Carpenter, a Bird Cage maker, a Gardener, and has lately taught me to draw ...' He and Mary rarely see company, preferring 'Quiet walks under the same hedges' to nearby Weston Underwood, where the kind Throckmortons who live there have given him the key to the Wilderness in which he loves to wander. But he has no illusions about his state of mind, telling Mrs Newton:

> If I were in a Condition to leave Olney too [the Newtons had by now just left] I certainly would not stay in it ... I lived in it once, but now I am buried in it, and have no Business with the World on the Outside of my Sepulchre; my Appearance would startle them, and theirs would be shocking to me.

All he can do is face 'the usual routine of circumstances that meet us daily'.

Of these he writes in letters that are no longer ecstatically religious, but pleasantly humorous evocations of their quiet life; how poor Puss has for a time escaped into the town; how he and Mary have converted the little greenhouse into a summer parlour where they spend their time listening to the wind in the trees and the singing of the birds in preference to the incessant barking of dogs and crying of children at Silver End.

Meanwhile the *Olney Hymns* have been published; and, encouraged by Mary, he is writing secular poetry:

> I have no more Right to the Name of Poet than a Maker of Mousetraps has to that of an Engineer, but my little Exploits in this way have at times amused me so much that I have often wish'd myself a good one.

By May 1781, with 'Table Talk', 'The Progress of Error', 'Truth' and 'Charity' having excitingly gone to press and been appreciatively received, an unusual sense of well-being sweeps over him, and in his gaiety he begins writing rhyming letters to his friends. It must have been in similar mood that he looked out of the Orchard

Side parlour window one July morning and saw two ladies emerging from Mr Palmer's, the draper, opposite. One he recognized, but the other was so instantly and compellingly interesting to him that he asked Mary Unwin to find out who she was and to invite the two ladies for tea. They accepted, and Lady Austen bounded into Cowper's life.

Sprightly, charming, inventive, more than a little brushed by the fashionable cult of Sensibility, she effected a revolution in their humdrum Olney lives. Before they knew it, they were returning the visit, planning an excursion with Lady Austen to Weston.

> Lady Austen's lacquey and a lad that waits on me in the garden, drove a wheel-barrow full of eatables and drinkables to the scene of our fête champêtre. A board laid over the top of the barrow served us for a table, our dining-room was a root house lined with moss and Ivy. At Six o'clock the Servants who had dined under a great Elm upon the ground at a little distance boiled the kettle, and the said wheel-barrow served us again for a tea-table. We then took a walk from thence to the wilderness about half a mile off, and were home again soon after eight, having spent the day together from noon 'till Evening, without one cross occurrence, or the least weariness of each other.

By August Lady Austen, now head over heels in love with the idea of Retirement, was contemplating moving to Olney to be with her new friends. As Cowper explained in a letter to Newton, she intended repairing and beautifying the other half of Orchard Side, 'at present occupied by Dick Coleman, his wife, child and a thousand rats . . .' In the event she wisely took a lease of the vicarage instead, and for the next eighteen months the friends filed back and forth through the intervening door at the end of Cowper's garden, to dine alternately at the vicarage and Orchard Side, from then onwards enjoying each other's company until bedtime.

For the time being the ever-present Lady Austen proved a blessing. She played the harpsichord charmingly, commissioning the entranced Cowper to set her music to words, though as the year turned down into autumn, Cowper began showing unmistakable signs of oncoming depression, and one October afternoon nothing could rouse him from total despair. Lady Austen now became a saviour and set herself to banish his depression by recounting a childhood story of the absurd adventures of a London linen-draper who attempts to celebrate his wedding anniversary in a manner something above his true station in life. To begin with nothing happened, but, as Lady Austen gallantly persevered, Cowper's stony face softened, then he smiled, began to laugh. That night he went to bed, and, still laughing, so he tells us, began the ballad of 'John Gilpin'. It went to London, was printed in broadsheet, became an enormous success. John Gilpin had saved Cowper's reason.

145

The following October (now to be always an anxious time) the three friends were sitting cosily round the parlour fire one evening when Lady Austen suggested her friend should now try a work in blank verse. If she would provide the subject, he promised, he would write the poem.

'Oh! you can never be in want of a subject – you can write upon any: Write,' she impetuously cried, 'upon this Sofa!' (still to be seen in the parlour at Orchard Side).

The project grew with writing, split into six books, among them 'The Sofa', 'The Time Piece' and 'The Garden'. He called the whole *The Task,* and in it celebrated all the quiet Olney days of the last fifteen years. So that to read this quaint yet charming work is not only to be allowed into the private thoughts of this most gentle of men – a man for our own times, hating slavery, detesting cruelty to animals, averse to sending small children away from home to school – but to take a magic step into an aquatint of past Olney and its landscape and into the very domestic life of Orchard Side.

There was his beloved greenhouse:

> The seed, selected wisely, plump and smooth,
> And glossy, he commits to pots of size
> Diminutive, well-fill'd with well-prepared
> And fruitful soil, that has been treasured long.

There was that delicious moment in the parlour on a winter afternoon:

> Now stir the fire, and close the shutters fast,
> Let fall the curtains, wheel the sofa round,
> And, while the bubbling and loud hissing urn
> Throws up a steamy column, and the cups,
> That cheer but not inebriate, wait on each,
> So let us welcome peaceful evening in.

And their tranquil walks to Weston:

> Here Ouse, slow winding through a level plain
> Of spacious meads, with cattle sprinkled o'er,
> Conducts the eye along his sinuous course
> Delighted. There, fast rooted in their bank,
> And never overlook'd, our favourite elms . . .

It is not great poetry, but it is pleasantly evocative of moment and place, and, what was then novel, made poetry from quiet domestic pleasures and simple lives – even poor lives.

Indeed, like his contemporary George Crabbe at Aldeburgh, Cowper saw the poor of Olney with true and unsentimental eyes. He had peered in at the cottage

*The parlour at Olney with the sofa in the foreground and
a portrait of Cowper by George Romney*

doors of the Olney lacemakers noting the frugal half-eaten brown loaf on the shelf, the pathetic implication of the poor little fire of brushwood, which for a moment blazed up so cheerfully, only to die down. His poetry could paint this for his readers, and the same tender sympathy enabled him to evoke for them a more true peasant than the cardboard figures of the old Sensibility. For he could see, while the woodman's dog joyously snatched at the snow and plunged about in it with his snout, how his poor master relished

> ... the fragrant charge of a short tube
> That fumes beneath his nose.

The writing of *The Task* took Cowper so completely out of himself that when an unforeseen crisis arose in his relationship with Lady Austen, it affected him rather less than it might have done. Little is known of this drama, only that by the spring of 1784 Mary Unwin had made it plain that Cowper must choose between her and Lady Austen.

Cowper had probably been unwise; he had written to Lady Austen:

> ... when a poet takes the pen,
> Far more alive than other men,
> He feels a gentle tingling come
> Down to his finger and his thumb,
> Derived from nature's noblest part,
> The centre of a glowing heart ...

She no doubt had suffered misapprehensions. Sometime in the early summer of 1784 Cowper braced himself to write an explanatory letter. The letter is lost, though in later years Lady Austen confessed it was a good letter. But its effect was immediate. Lady Austen left Olney and Cowper for ever.

The Task was completed that October. The following July it was published. It made Cowper instantly famous. He informed a correspondent:

> I write in a nook, that I call my *Boudoir*. It is a summer-house not much bigger than a sedan chair, the door of which opens into the garden, that is now crowded with pinks, roses and honeysuckles, and the window into my neighbour's orchard. It formerly served an apothecary, now dead, as a smoking-room; and under my feet is a trap-door, which once covered a hole in the ground, where he kept his bottles ...

Cowper's summer-house is there still, and although the view from his window is now obstructed by a fence, it is possible to raise a floorboard where, perhaps, the apothecary's trap-door once was. Was it here that he wrote those later poems which have delighted generations, the affectionate poems about his dogs and cats, his hares and the pet birds of his friends and, perhaps because one would like to think it, his fine requiem for the felled Olney poplars?

> The poplars are fell'd, farewell to the shade,
> And the whispering sound of the cool colonnade ...

For Cowper is nothing if not a 'green' poet.

Lady Austen may have gone, but he was already making new friends, with the young Throckmortons who had succeeded to Weston Park – pretty Mrs Throckmorton particularly. Equally pleasing when he came down to breakfast one morning was to find on the table a letter from his cousin Lady Hesketh. They had not met for years, she had recently read *The Task*, had loved it and now wanted to get into touch with him again.

The following June her coach drove into Olney to a peal of happy bells. She refused to stay at Orchard Side, however, lest she be a charge on her cousin's slender purse; instead, as poor Lady Austen before her, she rented the vicarage. Now, as once with Lady Austen, there was again established that happy routine of dining together every day and spending the remaining time *à trois* till bedtime.

Lady Hesketh, kind, warm-hearted, with a brilliant complexion, delighted Cowper. Being cousins, there was happily no likelihood of embarrassing romantic tangles, and, unlike Lady Austen, Lady Hesketh did not interfere with his morning work. Sharing a youthful past, there was much to discuss and laugh about, and she was, moreover, generous, and Cowper was soon writing a poem which testified to her kindness.

> This cap that so stately appears,
> With ribbon-bound tassel on high,
> Which seems by the crest that it rears
> Ambitious of brushing the sky;
> This cap to my cousin I owe:
> She gave it, and gave me beside,

The summer-house in the Wilderness at Weston Underwood, and Cowper's summer-house at Olney

149

> Wreathed into an elegant bow,
> The ribbon with which it is tied.

The poem also tells us that she gave him a 'wheel-footed' studying-chair, carpets, a dressing-table mirror to shave in, bookshelves, stoves, curtains, not to mention a pretty horn snuffbox with pictures of Tiny, Puss and Bess. Indeed she appears to have completely refurnished Orchard Side.

They were not to remain in their old home much longer, however. Not long before, the young Throckmortons had tried to persuade Cowper and Mary to rent a pleasant house called The Lodge, which had fallen vacant at Weston. When she heard, Lady Hesketh enthusiastically promoted the idea, promising to help with the rent, and by the time she quitted Olney that November they had fixed to go.

After so long at Orchard Side Cowper found the move had 'a terrible effect in deranging the intellects' and couldn't write for a time. But it wasn't long before he was informing Lady Hesketh that

> when poets tell of cottages, hermitages and such like things, they mean a house with six sashes in front, two comfortable parlours, a smart stair-case, and three bed chambers, of convenient dimensions; in short, exactly such a house as this.

One would have liked the drama of poor Cowper's life to have ended here, content at Weston, among the scenes he loved. What actually followed is another story, and a sad one.

In Olney he has never been forgotten. When he and Mary Unwin left Orchard Side, it was for a time occupied by a Mr Haddon, who much treasured a looking-glass Cowper left behind, and who no doubt collected, and lovingly preserved, as did those who came after him, every tiny memento of the poet. Some are to be seen at Orchard Side today, eccentrically touching: a pinch of horsehair from the poet's wig; a square from a fruit net woven by him; a neat ball of Mary's worsted wound by him; saffron feathers from the poor goldfinch who, in his poem, was found starved to death.

Olney itself remains much as Cowper knew it. Across the square from Orchard Side is the Bull, where the postboy with 'spatter'd boots' dropped the eagerly awaited mailbag; further down on the same side is the house where Cowper's friend, Mr Wilson the barber, lived; opposite Orchard Side is Mr Palmer's, the draper, where Cowper saw Lady Austen that July afternoon. Weston village is even less changed, save that the Wilderness has curiously become a flamingo park – something that possibly would have intrigued Cowper.

In 1900 its then owner gave Orchard Side to the town of Olney as a Cowper museum. It has remained so ever since, supervised by a succession of devoted caretakers, and surely, in all England, there is no more evocative, no more poignant memorial to a man of letters.

CHARLES DARWIN

DOWN HOUSE, DOWNE, KENT

MICHAEL NEVE

Down House stands about a third of a mile to the south of the small Kentish village of Downe, a village which until the early nineteenth century was spelt without an 'e'. The addition of an 'e', for administrative reasons, has led to endless confusion for visitors to the home of England's most famous naturalist. When Darwin moved into Down House in 1842, he was looking for a place to live that embodied country quiet and a peaceable idea of England. 'Down' is a word that carries those echoes, and he insisted on retaining it. Darwin was not a man of Kent, having been born in Shrewsbury in February 1809, but by the time he came to live in Downe, many of the formative events of his life were over, and he wanted to study in peace while not being entirely removed from the metropolitan world that he both needed and mistrusted. Sixteen miles from St Paul's, Downe was perfectly situated, near and yet far. Down House, an ugly flat-fronted property (*circa* 1778) whose previous incumbent had been the Revd James Drummond, had been a parsonage. Inside this ex-parsonage, insulated from ordinary life, Charles Darwin set out to produce an entirely Godless account of the origin of species and of man's animal ancestry.

In 1836 Darwin returned from his famous voyage on board HMS *Beagle*. In December 1831, at the age of twenty-two, he had set off on this journey in a speculative and open-minded way, without any real idea of how to make a career or where the adventures that he might have would lead. He travelled as a self-financing, upper-class gentleman, able to pursue his own interests and to dine with the young and difficult captain of the vessel, Robert FitzRoy. All through the journey, as the superb edition of his *Correspondence* now shows us, he kept in touch with England, with family and friends. Letters from home brought news, above all of contemporaries getting married and quite often settling down to the country life. Meanwhile he was suffering from isolation, sexual deprivation and anxiety, while at the same time becoming absorbed in natural history and especially in geology. Personal loneliness was the driving force for the research which resulted in his

eventual fame. Darwin saw spectacular feats of nature on the other side of the world, and he also made considerable natural history collections in the course of his travels. On his return to England he was ready to be received into the network of gentleman scientists who had encouraged him to undertake the *Beagle* voyage, many of them members of the Anglican church, or Unitarians, like the geologist Charles Lyell. From October 1836, Darwin socialized with this community, partly in what he called 'dirty, odious London', with his mind mostly on other things.

First, he had to marry. It is worth recalling that Darwin never had to take a job in the course of his adult life, coming as he did from a background of wealth and leisure. In early 1838 his father was supporting him to the considerable tune of £400 per annum, while Darwin pondered his future and his prospects of marriage. He had to make a respectable choice, but also to decide whether he might make a reputation out of writing natural history. And here lay a great and troubling problem.

We now know that from early 1837 Darwin had become committed to a series of doctrines about nature that were scientifically disreputable and subversive of the standard political and social beliefs of virtually all his social circle. He was slowly establishing, in private, a belief in scientific materialism. This belief, and the argument ('one long argument' as he put it later) upon which it rested, would become his life's work. Yet it had to be kept from sight. Until the time was ripe, and that might even mean until after his death, Darwin's evolutionary theory and its implications must remain his private, internal world. But he could not possibly carry on alone after the emotional and sexual deprivations he had experienced on the *Beagle*, and by November 1838 he was engaged to his first cousin Emma Wedgwood, of Maer, Staffordshire. Emma was to be the intimate of a man who was constructing a view of the world that implied the destruction of some of her dearest beliefs. And she knew it.

Married in January 1839, Charles and Emma began to look for places to live, firstly in Upper Gower Street in London, and then elsewhere, out of the metropolis, out of the world of controversy. Emma and her husband needed to raise their children in peace somewhere where seclusion did not mean exile.

They needed this, not least, because the time of Darwin's marriage was also the time when the full extent of his mysterious 'illness' became apparent. For reasons that are still not understood, and which will probably never be settled, Darwin spent his entire adult life in various states of physical discomfort, nausea, and dyspeptic malaise. He never left England again; some of the longest journeys he made thereafter were to Malvern, for the spa waters and hydrotherapy. Darwin, the naturalist who removed God from the order of nature, was permanently

The Sandwalk

*Down House from the garden, with the worm-stone used
by Darwin in one of his experiments*

unwell, and Emma, his wife and nurse, both gave birth to ten children and
mothered her husband in his valetudinarian atheism. It was in Down House that
all these contradictions were acted out; it was an epitome of the home of the
'parson/naturalist' and, at the same time, the address to which Marx and Engels
allegedly sent a volume of *Das Kapital* in the hope that Darwin would accept a
dedication (which he did not).

154

Having reached Downe village, the visitor would do well to visit the parish church of St Mary the Virgin (next to the bus stop) before proceeding to the house itself. It contains the graves of Emma Darwin, of her daughter Emma (buried October 1842) and of Emma's sister Sarah, among others. The contradictions that Down House embodies in itself (the retirement home of a revolutionary thinker) are also brought out by the Darwin family's interest in and indeed often support for the activities of the parish church, although these varied with the conduct of the incumbent of the curacy. Part of the peaceful idyll that sustained Darwin was that England continued to be the world of Gilbert White's Selborne, and the church in Downe still carried that significance, even in the climate of the *Origin of Species*. The Darwins were respectable: after the abolition of slavery, which he hated with all his heart, Darwin never questioned the order of society, whatever the radical conclusions that might be drawn from his theory of evolution. He might be ill, closeted in his study, or worried about the way his theory was being received. He was also a county magistrate, a treasurer of the parish Sunday school, the founder

Bust of Darwin by Charles Hartwell

155

Darwin's study

of a Friendly Club. He was devoted to his wife, his children, and to his terrier dog, Polly. Few English villages, churches or houses tell a more intriguing story: of materialist, scientific work nestling inside an old Anglican settlement; of a lifetime's labour that led to worldwide fame authored by a man so anxious to avoid the world that he had a special mirror made, so that he could see back down the road from the entrance of his house and avoid visitors who happened to call and were not welcome. This mirror can still be seen in his study today. He wrote in 1844, one of the years when he thought he was going to die, 'I am almost convinced (quite contrary to the opinion I started with) that species are not (it is like confessing a murder) immutable.' This was the plot that Darwin hatched in his study in Down House.

For Darwin and his family, the house came to represent the world of family harmony and happiness. Whatever the concealed difficulties – with his sons' education, or the insanity of one of the governesses, Miss Pugh, in 1856, or the death of his beloved daughter Annie in 1851 – it was the home of children's laughter, the evocative smell of tennis rackets and croquet sticks, and the place of refuge. As Sir Hedley Atkins showed in his definitive *Down: the Home of the Darwins* (1974), the daily routines of the house followed those which Darwin established for himself and rigidly observed. He did no more than two concentrated hours' work in a day, although he spent at least that long dealing with correspondence. In the hours before lunch, and especially between 10.50 am and 1.00 pm he retired to his study, and at noon walked the Sandwalk (which visitors can still do). It is fair to say that the two bouts of labour would have involved intense acts of concentration, the one to do with setting down thoughts and queries, the other with very detailed observations of tiny events in the garden or in the wood at the end of the Sandwalk. There can be little doubt that some of the lazier parts of the day – smoking cigarettes, listening to Emma reading a novel or playing the piano, chats with his children – would have been times to reflect on the concentrated thinking of the period before lunch. This went on every day for nearly forty years.

The heart of Darwin's theory of evolution is that nature represents a world of permanent struggle – of selection – but that the rate at which this proceeds is often very slow; it is therefore a process observable only by the patient and diligent. A visit to Down House (which is partly a museum, administered by the Royal College of Surgeons) allows a glimpse into this world of nature and this world of routine. The study, the drawing-room, the dining-room (now called 'the Beagle room') all speak of domestic order, bourgeois comfort, and a life built around the work of the father. It is a very Victorian story, reflecting the monied status of the family and some crucial aspects of Victorian life: reading aloud; the frequent death of children; the long, Tennysonian afternoons; the problem of servants. Darwinism was built on the accumulation of masses of small observations – the speed at which climbing plants circle a line – and the peace of Down House reflects this slow, careful experimentation. It would be quite wrong to suggest that no visitors came to the house. There were many, famous and not so famous, scientists and other admirers. But this is above all a family house built around the need to protect the admired father.

As Emma Darwin sheltered her husband, so Down House sheltered them. It protected the family from the struggle of life which Darwin saw at work in all of nature, an incessant combat that selected the fit and eliminated the unfit. But while the house was a haven of peace, the author of the theory of natural selection often found himself unspeakably exhausted, sick and worn out. He needed a parish community and a provincial life to have the strength to put together the most influential account of man's place in nature since the scientific revolution of the sixteenth and seventeenth centuries. Darwin was meticulous (not least about money, where he was the quintessential balancer of books) and his house allowed him to write up the work that saw nature as savage, competitive and yet full of terrible splendours and wonders. The visitor to Down House comes away with a powerful sense that the house was where Darwin and his family survived the implications of his own theory.

At Down House Darwin completed his task and died. He is buried in Westminster Abbey, the secular hero of a still formally Christian culture. Although he would of course deny ever having a spirit, one small detail may contradict him. His beloved dog Polly could not survive the death of her master. Within days of his own death, her remains were buried under the 'Kentish Beauty' apple tree in the garden, and who is to say that some part of him is not there with her?

CHARLES DICKENS

DICKENS HOUSE
48 DOUGHTY STREET, LONDON WC1
BIRTHPLACE MUSEUM, PORTSMOUTH, HAMPSHIRE

CLAIRE TOMALIN

For anyone with a wisp of imagination, the spirit of Charles Dickens, bright-eyed and very fast on his feet, may still be encountered walking at night, or dusk, or early morning, anywhere along the river from the Docklands to Greenwich to Richmond, or up the Hampstead Road through Mornington Crescent and Camden Town; through the mazes of Seven Dials, Covent Garden and the Inns of Court; or hurrying westwards from Shepherd's Bush, or south into the Borough, and rambling further afield into Hatcham and Peckham. Dickens, like Shakespeare, is simply too large to be contained or defined in any one house or collection of objects, although the best museum by far – the Dickens House Museum – is, very properly, in the heart of London.

London is Dickens's city above all others, so much so that foreigners are still sometimes surprised not to find it just as he described it, shrouded in fog, with booming river traffic and ancient inns, and child crossing-sweepers to remove the nuisance of horse droppings from the feet of ladies in long skirts. In fact we are reverting in the 1990s to Dickensian London in certain respects, our streets again full of the mad and destitute, our schools almost as poor as the ragged schools of the nineteenth century, and filth and squalor to rival the dirt of his day. But if the whole of London remains some sort of memorial to Dickens and his characters, the most appropriate single memorial might be sited in a railway junction or on a platform at Charing Cross or Waterloo; for he was the most restless of authors, always on the move between his various homes and semi-homes or perching places, between what he called his 'gypsey camp' over the office and opposite the Lyceum in Wellington Street, and the succession of seaside holiday houses in which he installed his large family; ready to cross and recross the Channel as the whim took him, eager to speed from city to city all over the British isles to give readings to his adoring public; even prepared to tour the United States, once in the 1840s

The drawing-room at 48 Doughty Street

when travel conditions were far from easy and again twenty-five years later when his own health should have deterred him.

Energy is the key to his character – the energy of a boy who knew himself to be exceptionally endowed, and knew also that he could depend on no one but himself to come into his birthright – and he was no more capable of slowing his pace than a racing car with a jammed accelerator. He speeded on until the engine exploded, and even as he dropped to the floor, felled by a brain haemorrhage at the early age of fifty-eight, he was muttering about travelling to London.

Dickens was born at 387 Mile End Terrace, Portsea – part of Portsmouth – on 7 February 1812, in a small red-brick Georgian terrace house with three floors and a basement, and a little patch of garden front and back. He was the second child and first son of a naval pay clerk and his lively wife, Elizabeth, who is said to have spent the night before the birth out dancing. Within months they were obliged to move; John Dickens was in financial difficulties – they were to be the main feature of his life – and the family had to make do in a more modest house in Hawke Street (this was bombed to bits in 1941). Soon they left Portsmouth altogether.

Dickens had so little recollection or feeling for the place that, on visiting it during a reading tour in 1866, he was unable to locate his own birthplace. Portsmouth figures in his work only once, as the city to which Nicholas Nickleby walks from London with the vague idea of finding shipboard work, but instead joins the acting troupe of Vincent Crummles. He finds cheap lodgings for himself and Smike on the Common Hard, and visits the actress Miss Snevellicci at her lodgings above a tailor's shop, with the scent of ironing rising up the stairs and her stockings drying on the fender. The Crummleses are endowed with a more picturesque landlord, Mr Bulph, a pilot, who keeps the little finger of a drowned man on his parlour mantel-shelf 'with other maritime and natural curiosities', a mast topped by a weather-vane in his back garden, and has a 'boat-green' door and windows. You can sense Dickens's imagination exciting itself over Bulph, but he fails to reappear, and soon Nicholas and Smike are on their way back to London, this time in a coach.

So much for Portsmouth: but it was his birthplace, and in 1903 – thirty-three years after his death – the mayor and council of Portsmouth decided to acquire the little house in Mile End Terrace and make it into the Dickens Birthplace Museum. It was duly opened the following summer, and has remained open to the public ever since, surviving the bombing which flattened most of the surrounding area during the Second World War.

It now stands in a small oasis consisting of the few remaining contemporary houses, with neat front gardens, railings and lavender plots, a late Victorian chapel and a pub, the Oliver Twist, but surrounded – almost engulfed – by high post-war housing estates. The shape of the old streets has been lost, and the address changed to 393 Old Commercial Road. The Dickens Fellowship has done its best by planting a row of trees to shield the view somewhat; the house is as shipshape and spick and span as Dickens would have wished but, inevitably, there is a slightly melancholy feeling of contrivance about the arrangements.

Inside the museum, the rooms are furnished with antiques, mostly from the period of Dickens's birth, though perhaps rather finer than the family would have possessed. There is a handsome four-poster in the front bedroom to which his mother returned after her dance, and in which he first saw the light. In the back room stands the most affecting object in the house, a *chaise-longue* covered in green velvet, on to which he was lifted fifty-eight years later, and on which he lay dying, throughout a short summer night and a long summer day, in the dining-room of his house at Gad's Hill in Kent. No one felt able to move him from it on to a bed; and on this surprisingly slight piece of furniture he died in the evening of 9 June 1870. The sofa was given to the museum by his devoted sister-in-law, Georgina Hogarth, in 1909.

There are a few mementoes in a glass case – a pen stand, a piece of his hair, a letter in his hand – and on the walls some prints of the best-known characters from his books; also a copy of the portrait painted by his friend Maclise, showing the young, handsome Dickens, clean-shaven and with long curly hair. In the basement you can buy pencils, paperbacks, postcards, posters and beer mats with Dickensian motifs.

Those interested enough may, after visiting the museum, like to make their way the mile or so to the Highland Road cemetery in Southsea, where, by a coincidence that no writer of fiction would allow, lie buried four women with whom Dickens was closely associated. One is Maria Winter, *née* Beadnell, whom he loved to distraction in the years before his marriage, the original of both Dora Spenlow and Flora Finching; she died in 1886. The others are the three Ternan sisters, Fanny, Maria and Ellen, in whom he became intensely interested in 1857. Their crumbling gravestones bear their married names, respectively Trollope, Taylor and Wharton Robinson; the youngest of the sisters, and the last survivor, died in 1914. During the last twelve years of his life Dickens not only did all he could to help them in their stage careers, he also published many of Fanny's novels in *All the Year Round*; he had particular admiration for Maria's powers as an actress and mimic, and with Nelly he maintained a private and passionate relationship until his death. When she joined her sisters in Southsea in old age, the past was strictly unmentionable, and she is thought never to have visited the museum.

The Dickens family moved to London when Charles was four, to Chatham when he was five, and back to London when he was ten, in 1822. Chatham and the adjoining city of Rochester, with its castle and cathedral and ancient houses, marked his imagination first, and then London, and particularly Camden Town, then a modest suburban development, with the Bedford estates and Regent's Park to the south, and the main road running north through market gardens and hayfields to Kentish Town, Hampstead and Highgate. From Camden Town it is not a long walk into Bloomsbury, and not much further to the Strand, the theatres and law courts, the river and the City. The story of his boyhood is probably the best-known thing about him: how his father's debts caused him to be put into the Marshalsea prison in the Borough – the prison has gone, but the site is still marked, just off Borough High Street in Southwark, where the old prison wall now forms the limit of a public garden – and how Charles, barely twelve, was sent to work sticking labels on bottles in a wretched black-leading warehouse beside the Thames, separated from his family and hardly able to get through the week on his own earnings; and worse, as he never forgot to the end of his days, how his mother saw no great need to rescue him from this degradation even after his father left the Marshalsea.

Fortunately, he was sent back to school for a few years, at the Wellington House Academy near Mornington Crescent; there is a cab drivers' snack bar on the site today. At fifteen he began to work in a lawyer's office; he was a slight but handsome boy, always smartly turned out, something of a dandy, with a taste for bright

Gad's Hill, near Rochester, which Dickens bought in 1857

colours, a fine head of curling hair and large, short-sighted but highly observant eyes. He was quick, clever and high-spirited, and his fellow-clerks soon found that he knew not only the position of every shop in the West End, but the whole of London 'from Bow to Brentford'. Like his mother, he was a brilliant mimic; he had serious hopes of becoming an actor, and almost every night he took himself to the pit of one or another of the London theatres, rowdy, boisterous places in which the evening's entertainment might start before seven and continue into the small hours. He also set up amateur productions of his own, with the help of his musical sister, Fanny, and their friends. Dickens was a superb organizer, and could sing and dance, paint scenery and drill his fellow players as enthusiastically as he acted.

When he was twenty he applied for an audition at Covent Garden, and prepared in front of a mirror, teaching himself to imitate the famous 'polymonologues' given by the foremost comedian of the age, Charles Mathews, who would impersonate a whole series of characters, sometimes playing all the parts in a farce. These virtuoso performances were exactly to Dickens's taste, and he made himself both word- and song-perfect. When the day came for him to be vetted by John Kemble and the manager, Dickens had a cold in the head and lost his voice, and the audition had to be postponed, as it turned out, indefinitely; but his passion for the theatre is obvious in his writing from the start. The funny voices of the characters in *The Pickwick Papers*, which seized the imagination of the nation at once, are instantly established and, although pushed to the very limits of absurdity, never fail to strike true. It took genius, and the confidence of genius, to carry off these impersonations – for such, in a sense, they were – and the genius was supported by the technical lessons he had learnt in the theatre. All his greatest characters present themselves through their speech patterns: Jingle, Pecksniff, Quilp, Mrs Gamp, Skimpole, Squeers, Micawber, Pip. When he fails with a character, the failure is associated with a failure to give him – or more often her – a credible speech pattern.

When Dickens started on *Pickwick*, he was a shorthand reporter working for newspapers, with experience in the law courts and the House of Commons; he had a score or so of magazine articles and theatre reviews to his credit and was hoping to establish himself as a playwright. Indeed he wrote two farces and a libretto for an operetta, with some success; but the overwhelming triumph of *Pickwick* steered him decisively into novel writing. Ironically, like most of his subsequent stories, it was immediately adapted for the stage by other hands and played in theatres all over the country, ensuring that even the illiterate became familiar with his characters.

The first number of *Pickwick* coincided almost exactly with his marriage to Catherine Hogarth, daughter of a Scottish music critic, in the spring of 1836; and before the last number had appeared, Dickens was the father of a son. He had also moved his family into 48 Doughty Street, in Bloomsbury. Together with the adjoining No. 49, this is now the Dickens House Museum, where all Dickens lovers and scholars sooner or later find themselves. It holds a marvellous collection of books, pictures, papers and Dickensiana, as well as a small shop in which new and second-hand books can be bought alongside the souvenirs and postcards. Among its most interesting exhibits are Dickens's own reading copies, with stage directions to himself, and the velvet-covered desk, designed by himself, with which he travelled. The museum has a reading-room, facilities for students and researchers, and an excellent curator and staff ready to answer questions and give assistance.

Dickens leased the house in Doughty Street – then a private road, closed at each end by a gate with a livery-attired porter in attendance – from April 1837 until December 1839, during which he wrote the last of *The Pickwick Papers*, most of *Oliver Twist* and the whole of *Nicholas Nickleby* (dedicated to his much-loved friend, the actor Macready), as well as the anonymously published *Sketches of Young Gentlemen*; he also edited and rewrote the *Memoirs* of Grimaldi, the famous clown of his boyhood, and turned out a farce for Macready, *The Lamplighter*. The only failure was the last, which was never performed; but as the product of a period of just over two and a half years, this output approaches the phenomenal. Catherine was kept busy too, for there were constant dinner parties, and two more children were born to her in Doughty Street: Mary (known as Mamie) in March 1838, and Katey in October 1839; there was a miscarriage in between.

There is an account by Dickens's publisher Bentley of a dinner at Doughty Street just after the family moved in, which gives a vivid impression of their way of life:

> Dinner in Doughty Str. I the only stranger. Mr Dickens sen, Mr Hogarth, Miss Dickens, the Misses Hogarth. It was a right merry entertainment; Dickens was in force, and on joining the ladies in drawing-room, Dickens sang two or three songs, one the patter song, 'The Dog's Meat Man', & gave several successful imitations of the most distinguished actors of the day. Towards midnight, it was Saturday, I rose to leave, but D. stopped [me] & pressed me to take another glass of Brandy & water. This I wd. gladly have avoided, but he begged Miss Hogarth to give it me. At the hand of the fair Hebe I did not decline it.

As Lionel Trilling put it, 'the mere record of his conviviality is exhausting'; but these gaieties were brought to an abrupt end for a while when, very shortly after the dinner with Bentley, Catherine's younger sister Mary was taken ill after a family visit to the St James's Theatre and died the next day of heart failure. She had lived almost constantly with Catherine and Dickens since their marriage; she was only seventeen years old, and his grief was violent. 'Thank God she died in my arms, and the very last words she whispered were of me,' he wrote to a medical student friend, adding, 'I solemnly believe that so perfect a creature never breathed.' He immediately made plans to be buried in her grave, and for years he dreamed of her. The innocent, delicate girls such as Rose Maylie and Little Nell in his novels are assumed to be modelled on her; altogether she became, by dying, the focus of an intensity of feeling that failed to attach itself to his wife.

After this tragedy Doughty Street was not likely to become a favourite abode. And there were other reasons for turning against it, notably the drains, which gave constant trouble; 'a serious annoyance', wrote Dickens, complaining that innumerable visits from plumbers did nothing to cure the smell. Still, his working and convivial life re-established itself. He and Catherine went briefly to a cottage in rural Hampstead (now known as Wyldes, a pretty timber-hung house at North End, opposite Golders Hill Park) and then his diary records a resumption of his habit of long walks, steady pressure to keep up with the instalments of his current book, and enough other business to keep three men occupied. In the autumn of 1838 he made a trip to Wales; in the spring of 1839 he travelled to Exeter to rent and fit up a cottage for his parents, whom he decided to banish to Devon

Dickens lined the door of his study at Gad's Hill with the spines of imaginary books. Other titles include: History of a Short Chancery Suit in Twelve Volumes, Growler's Gruffiology *and* Life and Letters of the Learned Pig

166

Broadstairs with Fort House in the Distance

in an attempt to limit their demands on his income. On his return he took a cottage at Petersham for the summer, and in September installed his wife, children and servants in a 'dear little house' in Broadstairs, from which he travelled busily to and fro to London by steam boat, often bringing friends with him to stay.

Broadstairs became a favourite summer resort for more than a decade, although it was replaced by Boulogne in 1852. Several of its houses claim Dickensian associations, and one in which he took summer lodgings in 1850 and again in 1851 can be visited. Dickens always knew it as Fort House, but it has rather confusingly been renamed Bleak House, in reference to the novel, although the house in the novel is of course set somewhere quite different (in Hertfordshire), and bears no relation to the Broadstairs house. Fort House was in fact where he wrote a good deal of *David Copperfield* and planned some of *Bleak House*. He described it as 'a good bold house on the top of a cliff, with the sea Winds blowing through it, and the gulls occasionally falling down the chimneys by mistake'. It has been altered and very much enlarged since Dickens stayed there, and is privately owned; but several of the rooms used by him, most notably his 'airy nest' of a study, are open to the public, and contain some memorabilia, including playbills and pictures, a Russian postage stamp commemorating Dickens in 1962, a printer's proof with his corrections, cheques signed by him, etc. Some of the exhibits have a touch of Flaubert's parrot to them: there is a bed he is thought to have slept in at the Bull Hotel, Rochester, and one of the several chairs that match the chair in the famous Luke Fildes painting, 'The Empty Chair', showing Dickens's study at Gad's Hill just after his death, though no one knows which is the original (perhaps Dickens used more than one chair?). But the Broadstairs view, air and atmosphere are indisputably genuine, and they inspired one of his most charming pieces of occasional journalism, 'Our Watering Place', in 1851.

Broadstairs is the place where he described himself as 'a kind of salmon-coloured porpoise' emerging from a bathing machine to enjoy the sea water; and where, in 1840, he spent a memorable evening recounted many years later by one of the participants, a Miss Eleanor Picken, then about nineteen:

The next night we were all assembled on the little pier or jetty which ran out into the sea, with an upright spar fixed at the extreme end. At the beginning was a railed-off space with seats, which he called the family pew. Mr Dickens was in high spirits, and enjoyed the darkness of the evening, because he escaped the curious eyes of the Broadstairs population. We had a quadrille all to ourselves, the music being Frederick Dickens's whistling, and Mr Dickens's accompaniment on his pocket-comb ... Dickens seemed suddenly to be possessed with the demon of mischief; he threw his arm around me and ran me down the inclined plane to the end of the jetty till we reached the tall post. He put his other arm round this, and exclaimed in theatrical tones that he intended to hold me there till 'the sad sea waves' should submerge us.

'Think of the sensation we shall create! Think of the road to celebrity which you are about to tread! No, not exactly to *tread*, but to flounder into!'

Here I implored him to let me go, and struggled hard to release myself.

'Let your mind dwell on the column in *The Times* wherein will be vividly described the pathetic fate of the lovely E[mma] P[icken], drowned by Dickens in a fit of dementia! Don't struggle, poor little bird; you are powerless in the claws of such a kite as this child!'

By this time the gleam of light had faded out, and the water close to us looked uncomfortably black. The tide was coming up rapidly and surged over my feet. I gave a loud shriek and tried to bring him back to common sense by reminding him that 'My dress, my best dress, my *only* silk dress, would be ruined.' Even this climax

*Dickens's writing chalet, originally at Gad's Hill but now in the grounds
of the museum in Rochester*

did not soften him; he still went on with his serio-comic nonsense, shaking with laughter all the time, and panting with his struggles to hold me.

'Mrs Dickens!' a frantic shriek this time, for now the waves rushed up to my knees; 'help me! make Mr Dickens let me go – the waves are up to my knees!'

'Charles!' cried Mrs Dickens, echoing my wild scream, 'how can you be so silly? You will both be carried off by the tide' (tragically, but immediately sinking from pathos to bathos) 'and you'll spoil the poor girl's silk dress!'

'Dress!' cried Dickens, with withering scorn. 'Talk not to me of *dress*! When the pall of night is enshrouding us in Cimmerian darkness, when we already stand on the brink of the great mystery, shall our thoughts be of fleshly vanities? Am I not immolating a brand-new pair of patent leathers still unpaid for? Perish such low-born thoughts! In this hour of abandonment to the voice of destiny shall we be held back by the puerilities of silken raiment? Shall leather or prunella (whatever that may be) stop the bolt of Fate?' with a sudden parenthetical sinking from bombast to familiar accents, and back again.

At this point I succeeded in wrestling myself free, and scampered to my friends, almost crying with vexation, my *only* silk dress clinging clammily round me, and streaming with salt water . . .

Few descriptions of Dickens catch so well his high spirits, his physical delight in play-acting (and in young women), and the way he could slip from boisterous fun into something almost demonic – from Nickleby to Quilp – in a moment, becoming unable or unwilling to control his fantasy.

Although Dickens visited Broadstairs very little after 1852, he was there in August 1859 for a week at the Albion Hotel, in order to be near his friend Wilkie Collins, who was spending the summer with his mistress, Caroline Graves, in Church Cottage, on the Ramsgate Road. It was a troubled time for Dickens; he had separated from his wife, put his children in the care of his sister-in-law Georgina, and was obsessively in love with Nelly Ternan; and it was just at this time that she gave up her career as an actress and disappeared from public view.

The break in Dickens's family life coincided with a change of direction in his working habits. The majestic sequence of great novels of social criticism – *Dombey and Son*, *Bleak House*, *Hard Times*, *Little Dorrit* – came to an end. He began to give public readings, which brought him a far bigger income than his writing had done, and which allowed him full scope for his love of performance and the theatre. Of his late novels, *Great Expectations* is without a doubt the greatest, and for many the best of all his books. It was written in 1860 and 1861, when he had many griefs, including his mother's senility, his daughter Katey's marriage, which he believed to be loveless on her side and entered into to get away from an unhappy home; and, not least, his own guilt feelings about what he was doing to Nelly Ternan, who was almost exactly the same age as Katey.

An essay of this kind cannot begin to encompass the breadth of Dickens's life, work, travels and experience. It can at best point in one or two directions. The places associated with his name are evocative and worth visiting, but the best way of getting close to Dickens is to read his words – the novels, the collected journalism and the letters. Among the thousands of books devoted to him, two stand out: the ongoing Pilgrim Edition of *The Letters of Charles Dickens*, published by the Oxford University Press, which has reached the year 1852 and Volume VI at the time of writing; and Philip Collins's superb two-volume *Dickens: Interviews and Recollections* (Macmillan, 1981), both of which I have made use of here.

Dickens was buried in Westminster Abbey. He hated pomp, and had hoped to be laid in a Kentish graveyard, at Rochester, near Gad's Hill, but he was not allowed his own choice. As so often happens to great men and women, his public not only loved him, it wanted to fix its own preferred image on to him. But the real Dickens lives, and laughs, and endures, in his own words.

BENJAMIN DISRAELI

HUGHENDEN MANOR, HIGH WYCOMBE, BUCKINGHAMSHIRE

VERNON BOGDANOR

The historian A. J. P. Taylor once began a lecture on Disraeli by reciting the well-known story of the man who, visiting a zoo, saw a giraffe and exclaimed, 'There is no such animal.' Over a hundred years after his death, that still seems the only response to the remarkable life of Benjamin Disraeli, Earl of Beaconsfield (1804–81). There is no stranger political career in the annals of British history.

Disraeli was, from 1849 until his death in 1881, leader of the Conservative Party, the party, as it then was, of country gentlemen whose central principle was to preserve the influence of the landed interest in politics. His political colleagues were mainly great landowners, and he himself spent much of his life amidst a society of aristocrats. Yet Disraeli himself was very far from being a country gentleman. Indeed, he had no connection with the land at all. Born in 1804, the son of a moderately well-to-do Jewish man of letters, Isaac D'Israeli, he was baptized in 1817. He was the only Victorian prime minister, except for the Duke of Wellington, not to attend university, leaving school in 1819 or 1820, after which he was articled for a short time to a firm of solicitors. His real vocation, however, or so he thought, was for literature, and during his twenties and thirties he wrote a number of rather flippant society novels, 'silver-fork' novels as they are generally known.

Disraeli's background, then, was very different from that of the grave statesmen who ruled in Victorian England; but, far from trying to minimize his disadvantages, Disraeli seemed, in his early years, to be doing everything possible to increase the number of obstacles which stood in his way, perhaps for the sheer pleasure of showing that he could overcome them. His numerous relationships with women, and especially with married women, scandalized respectable society; he came to be involved in a speculative deal which collapsed almost as dramatically as the South Sea Bubble; and he spent nearly all of his early years, indeed much of his life, in debt.

In 1837, after four defeats, Disraeli finally managed to get himself returned to the Commons as a Conservative. His maiden speech was a disaster and was howled

Hughenden Manor

down. He was not taken seriously by the leaders of his party, and was not even considered for office when the Conservatives won power in 1841. As a frustrated back-bencher, Disraeli became the leader of a small group of youthful and aristocratic Tories known as Young England, which attacked Sir Robert Peel, the prime minister, for deserting Tory principles and allowing the party to degenerate into a clique of concessionaries and place-seekers.

In the 1840s Disraeli published a political trilogy, intended to be the manifesto of this rather curious coterie – *Coningsby, or The New Generation* (1844), which he called 'the secret history of my feelings', *Sybil, or The Two Nations* (1845), and *Tancred, or The New Crusade* (1847). The first two of these, at least, can still be read with pleasure today.

In these novels Disraeli argued against Utilitarianism and against the rationalistic approach to politics, which he saw as characteristic of the Peelite attitude: only through the imagination, he declared, could politics be truly understood. The heroes of his middle-period novels are young men in search of an ideal through which they might organize their lives. This ideal could be found only by truly absorbing the lessons of the past; a political creed could be sound only if it was based upon 'the use of ancient forms and the restoration of the past'. 'That's the true spring of wisdom,' Coningsby is told; 'meditate over the past.'

Disraeli's political message was intended to be constructive, and he argued for a Conservatism based on social reform. He sought to achieve 'One Nation' in place of the two which then existed, the two being, of course, the rich and the poor. This should be done by renewing the feudal principle of social responsibility, a principle which could transform relationships between employer and employed so that they could be joined by something other than a mere cash nexus. Yet Disraeli's message is anything but clear, and it is embedded in long passages of cloudy theorizing and religious speculation.

In 1845 Disraeli's political fortunes underwent a startling transformation. Peel, after much reflection, decided to repeal the Corn Laws, the laws which imposed duties on corn. The trends of the times were in the direction of Free Trade, and at first it seemed that Peel, supported by all the great names in his party as well as by the opposition, would triumph once more. Yet the Corn Laws, and the hegemony of the landed classes which they symbolized, were of crucial importance to Tory back-benchers. Disraeli saw his chance; and, in a series of slashing House of Commons speeches, speeches probably unequalled in parliamentary annals, he utterly destroyed Peel's credibility. The Corn Laws were repealed, with the aid of the opposition, but Peel was hounded from office and his supporters – who included almost all the men of talent in the party – followed him out of the Conservative Party. The landed interest desperately needed someone who could look after their needs, and who could be relied upon not to betray their cause. That person could

174

only be Disraeli, and he became, in effect, the party leader in 1849. 'I think,' said the exiled French statesman Guizot, 'your being the leader of the Tory Party is the greatest triumph that Liberalism has ever achieved.' And indeed, this strange, exotic, raffish figure would never have been accepted by the gentlemen of England had they not been in a desperate condition, bereft of leadership, smarting from the wounds of betrayal, and determined to fight back hard.

But if Disraeli was to be the leader of the party of the landed gentry, and to be of real use to them, he had to have a country residence. As he wrote to his wife on 18 October 1848: '... it would be no object to them and no pleasure to me, unless I played the high game in public life; and ... I could not do that without being on a rock'. The 'rock', however, was to be paid for, not by Disraeli himself, who was hopelessly in debt, but by the leader of the Protectionist Tories in parliament, Lord George Bentinck, who, with his two brothers, put up £25,000. A further £10,000 was found from Isaac D'Israeli's estate. So it was that in 1848, after protracted negotiations, Disraeli was able to purchase Hughenden Manor.

Hughenden Manor lies about a mile north of High Wycombe, on the road to Missenden. Although at that time a house of no particular size or architectural significance, it had a history which must have appealed to Disraeli. It had formed part of the possessions of Edith, the queen of Edward the Confessor, but after the Norman Conquest it had been granted by William the Conqueror to Odo, Bishop of Bayeux, and it appeared in the Domesday Book.

In the thirteenth century, Richard de Montfort, youngest son of Simon de Montfort, leader of the baronial revolt against Henry III, settled in the parish though not in the manor itself. There remains in the nearby church a de Montfort chapel with family monuments. In the eighteenth century the manor had passed to the fourth Earl of Chesterfield, author of the famous *Letters*.

That the manor was situated in what Disraeli called his 'beloved and beechy Bucks' was highly agreeable to him. He had stood three times, unsuccessfully, for the Commons as candidate for Wycombe, but in 1847 he had become MP for Buckinghamshire, the constituency for which he sat until in 1876 he was created Earl of Beaconsfield and became a member of the House of Lords. There was also a family connection. For Disraeli's father, Isaac, had retired to Bradenham in 1828, a couple of miles away in the direction of West Wycombe, and lived the life of a country gentleman there until his death. Chapter XI of Disraeli's final novel, *Endymion*, published in 1880, begins with a charming and nostalgic description of 'Hurstley', which is in fact Bradenham, his father's home.

Hughenden Manor, if truth be told, was not then, nor is it now, a house of much grandeur or architectural beauty. When Disraeli purchased it, the manor was an oblong eighteenth-century house of three storeys, built of brick but whitewashed. It can be seen as it was then in three pen drawings made by

175

R. Green in 1840, and in three sepia drawings by John Norris, both in the Berlin Congress Room at Hughenden, and also in a water-colour of the house painted in 1852 by Lord Henry Lennox, MP, to be found on the left of the fireplace in the Disraeli Room.

In 1862 the house was ruthlessly 'done up' at Mrs Disraeli's suggestion by E. B. Lamb, the Gothic architect, who had previously built the Obelisk, a monument to Disraeli's father, to be found one mile to the west of the manor. Mrs Disraeli also created the garden, with its statues and vases, at the south front of the house. Lamb's reconstruction gave the manor the appearance it has today, although the west wing, now used as regional offices of the National Trust, was added after Disraeli's death by his nephew, Coningsby Disraeli, early in the twentieth century. Lamb embellished the manor with red brickwork, constructing a new parapet with pinnacles and redesigning the windows to make them appear Jacobean. To modern taste, Lamb's reconstruction has little to commend it. In Pevsner's words, 'Lamb's details are excruciating, everything sharp, angular, aggressive ... the window-heads indescribable.'

The interior of the manor today is not very different from what it was when Disraeli lived there, except that the library, to the left of the entrance hall – which retains its late eighteenth-century fireplace and the plaster ceiling installed by Disraeli – was used as a drawing-room, while the drawing-room was used as a library. The entrance hall and staircase, where Disraeli, in his last years, hung portraits of his friends and political associates, calling it his 'gallery of friendship', and Disraeli's study on the first floor, which he called 'my workshop', remain as they were in his time.

A short distance from the manor, near the Aylesbury Lodge, lies the church of St Michael and All Saints, occupying the site of a twelfth-century church and almost completely rebuilt in 1875 by Sir Arthur Blomfield, the Victorian architect. Disraeli, together with other members of his family and his great friend Mrs Brydges Willyams, lies buried at the east end of the North Chapel. Inside the church, above the seat in the chancel which Disraeli used to occupy, can be found the monument erected in his memory by Queen Victoria, the only memorial ever erected to a subject by a reigning sovereign. The inscription on the monument reads: 'To the dear and honoured memory of Benjamin, Earl of Beaconsfield, this memorial is placed by his grateful Sovereign and Friend, Victoria R.I. "Kings love him that speaketh right." Proverbs XVI, 13. February 27, 1882.' Disraeli's Garter banner lies nearby.

Whatever the deficiencies of the manor from the point of view of architectural taste, Disraeli loved it. He found in Hughenden the haven which he needed from the hurly-burly of political life. Of a nervous disposition, and subject to frequent debilitating illnesses – bronchitis, asthma and gout – he found solace amongst his

Disraeli, by Millais, 1881

books and his trees. In the nineteenth century it was very rare for there to be an autumn session of parliament, and so every year when he was not in government, Disraeli would repair to Hughenden. When the Conservatives were in office, his stay at Hughenden would be curtailed, and he would find himself compelled to return to London for cabinet meetings in late October. But, even when he became prime minister, first in 1868 and then from 1874 to 1880, he spent as much time as he could in the house which he persisted in calling 'the prettiest place in the county'.

In a letter to Lady Bradford, dated 29 August 1878, Disraeli described how as prime minister he spent his day at Hughenden:

You asked me where I generally lived. In my workshop in the morning and always in the library in the evening. Books are my companions even if you don't open them ... I am called every day at seven o'clock when my bag and general letters arrive. I get through all these and find myself in my cabinet by nine o'clock and work very well till the second post comes in at noon which always disturbs me, for it brings the newspapers which are fortunately dull enough but which must be looked at. I make my chief meal at two, and an hour afterwards get out when it is not a thunderstorm ...

Disraeli completed three books at Hughenden. The first, *Lord George Bentinck: A Political Biography*, published in 1851, was a life of his friend, the leader of the Protectionist revolt against Peel. This biography is his only mature work of non-fiction, and it was to be nearly two decades before Disraeli published anything else. In 1870 he wrote *Lothair*, the first novel ever to have been published by a former prime minister, and described by his biographer, Robert Blake, as 'perhaps the best of all Disraeli's novels'. And ten years later *Endymion* appeared. At the time of his death in 1881, Disraeli was working on yet another novel, which would probably have been named after its main protagonist, Falconet. The character of Falconet was based upon none other than Disraeli's hated rival, W. E. Gladstone, leader of the Liberal Party, who had recently defeated the Conservatives in the general election of 1880. Only nine chapters of this book were completed, together with a fragment of the tenth; they can be found in Disraeli's official biography by G. E. Buckle.

'My books,' Disraeli told Lady Bradford, 'are the history of my life; I don't mean a vulgar photograph of incidents, but the psychological development of my character. Self-inspiration may be egotistical, but it is generally true.' Disraeli's later novels are those of a mature Conservative. The experience of power had altered him. He had become respectable at last, and Hughenden had given him a new-found security. It is for this reason that *Lothair* and *Endymion* are more detached than their predecessors. The early novels, from *Vivian Grey* (1826–7) to *Venetia* (1837), were frivolous *jeux d'esprits*, immature reflections of an overwhelming ambition. The trilogy of *Coningsby, Sybil* and *Tancred* had been a political statement, informed with an ideological intensity rare in the English novel. *Lothair* and *Endymion* are also political statements, but their message is subtler and more mellow; they have less of the manifesto about them and more of the satire.

But these two later novels also make explicit Disraeli's conception of the connection between political authority and the ownership of land. In an early work, *Vindication of the English Constitution*, Disraeli had argued that the great statesmen of English history had

looked upon the nation as a family, and upon the country as a landed inheritance. Generation after generation were to succeed to it, with all its convenient buildings and all its choice cultivation, its parks and gardens, as well as its fields and meads, its libraries and its collections of art, all its wealth, but all its encumbrances.

For Disraeli, property, like the monarchy and like the Church, was an institution which, by helping to maintain an ordered society, helped also to preserve liberty. For only a nation with a strong and independent landed class would have the self-confidence needed to operate free institutions. Thus the whole purpose of Disraeli's political life was to strengthen the landed interest, something he believed essential if a sense of responsibility was to be instilled into the depositories of political power.

Much of the action in *Lothair* and *Endymion* takes place in great houses, representative symbols of that ordered society which Disraeli devoted his political life to preserve. Disraeli's descriptions of the great houses in these novels are lavish and fulsome, but they fulfil their purpose of drawing attention to the particular model of government which he favoured. For these great houses reflect a social order, hierarchical but open to talent, an order based on tradition and yet, for Disraeli, the surest guarantee of liberty that had ever been found.

Disraeli did not succeed in his political aims. Admittedly, the Conservative Party became, after his death, the dominant party in the state; and admittedly, its political success owed much to the doctrines which Disraeli adumbrated, so much so, indeed, that he may be regarded as the founding father of the modern Conservative Party. But, nevertheless, the fundamental cause for which Disraeli stood, the cause of the landed interest, was doomed. The agricultural depression which occurred during the 1870s, even while Disraeli was prime minister, and the development of new and radical doctrines requiring high progressive taxation and death duties, rendered the dominant position of land in British politics quite untenable.

In Act 1 of *The Importance of Being Earnest* (1895) Lady Bracknell asks Jack Worthing:

> 'What is your income?'
> 'Between seven and eight thousand a year.'
> 'In land, or in investments?'
> 'In investments, chiefly.'
> 'That is satisfactory. What between the duties expected of one during one's lifetime, and the duties exacted from one after one's death, land has ceased to be either a profit or a pleasure. It gives one position, and prevents one from keeping it up. That's all that can be said about land.'

Only thirty years after Disraeli's death, in 1911, the Conservative Party elected a Glasgow ironmaster, Andrew Bonar Law, as its leader; and since then it has been dominated more often by its industrial or commercial wing than by the landed interest. Disraeli would hardly have recognized the Conservative Party of today, with its emphasis on competition, on the role of the market, and on economic modernization, as the political force which he had nurtured in the nineteenth century.

Where does Disraeli's place in English literature lie? He was uninterested in the traditional furniture of the English novel. His concern with the development of character was perfunctory and his plots are melodramatic and preposterous. Yet he had a profound insight into political ideas, and succeeded in grafting on to the framework of the 'silver-fork' novel a political content. This makes him *sui generis* amongst novelists writing in the English language.

Disraeli's last novels, *Lothair* and *Endymion*, which were written at Hughenden, provide the best picture that we have of the Indian summer of the Victorian aristocracy before the agricultural depression was to destroy the supremacy of the land in English life and render unattainable Disraeli's conception of British society. But they offer more than this, for they provide a clearly thought-out and consistent philosophy of Conservatism. Disraeli, in fact, represents a genuine and vital link in the history of English Conservative thought – a link between Burke and Coleridge, in the eighteenth and early nineteenth centuries, and T. S. Eliot in the twentieth.

Disraeli's view of life was deeply influenced by Burke, as well as by Carlyle. Like them he sees human existence as impalpable, as something not to be grasped in any set of abstract formulae or rules of living. 'Utilitarians in politics,' Disraeli had written in his early *Mutilated Diary*, 'are like Unitarians in religion. Both omit imagination in their systems and Imagination governs mankind.' And in *Lothair* Disraeli tells us that the philosophers 'accounted for everything, except the only point on which man requires revelation'. It is this insistence that life is not to be understood in terms of dogmatic philosophy that gives Disraeli's novels their characteristic exuberance and optimism.

And yet, at the end of his life, what did Disraeli really believe? After destroying Peel, he had spent almost all of the next twenty-eight years in opposition, powerless to influence events. He did not become prime minister until 1868, by which time he was already sixty-three. The 1868 government in any case had no majority in the House of Commons, and lasted only nine months. The only majority government which Disraeli led did not reach office until 1874, by which time he was sixty-nine and a lonely widower, and it lasted until 1880. A year later, he was dead.

Power, Disraeli told Lady Bradford, had come to him too late. 'Everything,' he told her on Christmas Day 1878, 'comes too late. It is something if it comes. However, I won't complain of life. I have had a good innings and cannot at all agree with the great King that all is Vanity.' But was there nothing above power and worldly ambition? In the last few months of his life, a young secretary came into the library and found Disraeli, seemingly asleep in front of the fire, murmuring 'dreams – dreams'. Reality, agreeable though it had become, was always a very poor substitute.

GEORGE ELIOT

NUNEATON

A. L. BARKER

Mary Ann Evans was born in 1819. 'George Eliot' entered the world in 1857, when she wrote to her publisher:

> I shall be resolute in preserving my incognito, having observed that a *nom de plume* secures all the advantages without the disagreeables of reputation. Perhaps, therefore, it will be well to give you my prospective name, as a tub to throw to the whale in case of curious inquiries ...
>
> Yours very truly,
George Eliot

She had put the pseudonym together from the Christian name of the man who was to inspire her finest work – George Lewes – and the not uncommon 'Eliot' which, as she said, was 'good, mouth-filling and easily pronounced'. It is also rather elegant and evokes a man of substance and the world. Its main purpose was to get her books judged on their merits, not dismissed as the work of a mere female.

She has been called a woman of contradictions, divided and divisive. There are personality splits in any creative writer who lives in visionary worlds yet never loses touch with the real one. Marian Evans's life (she abridged her baptismal names) was complicated early on by her rigorous religious concepts. They caused rifts with her family and friends. 'I cling strongly to kith and kin, even though they reject *me*,' she wrote in one of her letters. When she became a free-thinker and an independent woman, the change was no more acceptable to her family, nor to society. And there was her liaison with Lewes, who was still legally married to another woman.

It was Lewes who brought George Eliot into being. He saw the promise in the body of work – essays, reviews, translations, poems – which she had done as Marian Evans, and encouraged her to try writing fiction. He said:

> It may be a failure – it may be that you are unable to write fiction ... or it may be just good enough to warrant your trying again ... You have wit, description and

philosophy – those go a good way towards the production of a novel. It is worth while for you to try the experiment.

He was loving and caring. He gave her the emotional support she needed as a woman, and the confidence she lacked as an artist. A portrait of her dated 1860 shows a heavy-featured, sad-eyed face with deeply cleft chin and something both vulnerable and disdainful about the lips. George Lewes was described by contemporaries as an ugly little man, vivacious, volatile and an excellent mimic with a flow of 'well-informed and perceptive conversation'. He was socially acceptable, whereas their unorthodox 'marriage' meant that she was not. Polite society considered that she had grievously sinned against the current code of social morality. But a deeper, corrosive trouble was that she was flaunting conventions which she herself respected and would wish to live by. This and the snubs of people she admired in literary as well as general circles caused her great unhappiness. At the same time it might be claimed that such an inner conflict kept her supremely aware as a writer of fiction. She did not aspire to be a clever novelist creating a world better than the one she lived in, and turning a cold indifferent eye on breathing men and women. For her, sympathy was not enough; there had to be empathy too.

Marian Evans and George Lewes lived together for twenty-four years, and within two years of the start of their union she had begun her first published story, 'The Sad Fortunes of the Rev. Amos Barton'. This, with 'Mr Gilfil's Love Story', based on her childhood memories, and 'Janet's Repentance', was published in *Blackwood's Magazine* in 1857, and eventually the three came out in book form as *Scenes of Clerical Life*.

George Eliot sustained Marian Evans, but how did she sustain *him*? The account of the tea-party at the beginning of 'Amos Barton' leaves me in two minds: it is written with male gusto and feminine finesse, and in the same pages is a gentlemanly reference to 'late dinners with enigmatic side-dishes and poisonous port'. Yet poor Milly Barton's make-do-and-mending is detailed with the authority of a needlewoman and the raciness of a mere male.

George Eliot, male or female, unmarried, childless, knew and loved the ways of children. There's a moment when little Tommy Bond's top is just beginning to 'sleep' and the Revd Gilfil has to be stopped, irreverently and peremptorily, from treading on it, and vignettes of two tiny girls, one posturing in her new frock put on to honour a visit from the vicar, the other steeped in naughtiness and greedy for cherries, indulged by her doting mother, the redoubtable Mrs Poyser in *Adam Bede*. And surely Eppie, the 'tramp's child' who comes to bless Silas Marner, could not be more vividly and naturally portrayed if she had been George Eliot's own and observed from babyhood. And besides tender evocations of motherhood, there

The medieval painted figures in the choir stalls at Astley church

is such familiarity with the details of ladies' dress, their bonnets, hair-dos, cannon-curls and ringlets, all declaring George Eliot to be female. Yet it is a manly appetite which looks forward to dinner at Milby Vicarage where there will be no risk of guests required 'to be brilliant on ill-flavoured gravies and the cheapest Marsala'. There's an ambivalence which must have engaged readers at the time. Eventually, some ridiculous pretenders to the name and fame of George Eliot began to appear and she was obliged to come into the open and state her rightful claim to the pseudonym.

Mary Ann Evans had the countrywoman's love of the land. Wherever she went in her travels, she was mindful of the soil and the weather which governed the harvests. She herself preferred the meadows and farms of her native Warwickshire above romantic views of mountains and sea. To her awareness of people's looks, good and bad, was added her awareness of the ambience, good and bad, of places.

The present-day traveller, battered by airports and motorways and stupefied by ribbon development, will find refreshment in George Eliot country – as she pictures it. There the hedgerows grow tall, a riot of pink and white may-blossom, dog-roses, buttercups, honeysuckle, wild parsley and hemlock, foxgloves and ox-eye daisies. Her fields are bright with corn and scarlet poppies, or lie in shining furrows newly turned by horse and plough; the working streams run clear between banks of water-mint and cress, driving the mill-wheels to grind the corn; old orchards are tall with grass. The mild cows wait for milking-time at the field gate, and the sight of speckled hens industriously scratching for grain in the farmyard does 'more for a sick heart than a grove of nightingales'. On the other hand, the voice of the wood-pigeon 'saying do-do-do all day and never setting about any work itself' vexes the farmer who has been hard at it since daybreak. But she has also seen the blight of industrial areas, black with coal-dust, dingy with smoke, and the northern counties, 'hungry country', where the sky hangs dark over the hills. And she has felt a malign influence in dense woods, something old and oppressive. Arthur Donnithorne found his 'evil genius' among the trees.

George Eliot's country people speak their sense and nonsense in a vernacular that is fresh and vigorous. Mrs Poyser's, in *Adam Bede*, is a special joy. There is wit and wisdom and rough poetry in her speech. When she ridicules people's follies and frailties, she spares no one, not the clumsy dairymaid nor the saintly Dinah who preaches on the village green. Even the gentry cannot check her flow, for once she is over her preliminary awe of captain or squire, she breezes along with the fullest confidence. Queen Victoria herself esteemed Mrs Poyser and fancied she could see something of the 'dear Highlanders' in her.

George Eliot also reverenced things past. Maggie Tulliver, in *The Mill on the Floss*, cannot face the prospect of beginning a new life; she would feel like a lonely wanderer cut off from her past. And her father couldn't bear to think of living on

Arbury Hall

any other spot than his old home, where he had grown up to the sound of every gate and door and knew the shape of every roof and weather-stain. Throughout *The Mill* there is this sense of the influence of the past on the present and the future.

In Chapter One of 'Amos Barton', writing of the so-called improvements to Shepperton church, she laments the loss of that 'dear old brown crumbling picturesque inefficiency'. She has tenderness for old abuses, and sighs for the 'departed shadows of vulgar errors'. How would she describe the living errors which have been made in her countryside, the vulgarities she could not have dreamed of?

Nuneaton was described in a magazine of 1885 as being surrounded by fields, lopped elms and sprawling villages of weavers' shops – so many of these that it was thought they might engulf the town. The market-place then was 'sleepy', orchards intruded into the heart of the town and almost every street ended in vistas of green fields. A 'general tone of slowness pervaded the whole place ...' This is how it must have been when she renamed it Milby for the setting of her first published book, *Scenes of Clerical Life*.

Today it would be hard to find a livelier place. Commerce, industry, super- and hyper-stores have arrived; brick and glass fantasies replace the weavers' shops and the vistas of green fields. There are still fields, but you have to go farther to see them. The 'general tone' is far from slow; it is regulated by the pace of the traffic flow sweeping on to Rugby, Birmingham and the north.

If Nuneaton was rather late in acknowledging its links with arguably the greatest woman novelist of her time and ours, the omission has been rectified to a large extent. Most of the credit for that must go to the George Eliot Fellowship, founded in 1930 to honour her and promote interest in her life and work. It is organized now by a dedicated husband-and-wife team supported by tireless members and patrons. They hold regular meetings and programmes of readings, an annual memorial lecture and a luncheon to mark her birthday in November. Four newsletters are published each year, and a magazine. The fellowship campaigned to raise money for the statue in Newdigate Square. John Letts, a Warwickshire sculptor, was commissioned to do the statue, and it could not have been better done. He has shown her seated, a book laid down at her right hand, face averted from Debenham's, Fads and the Britannia Building Society. Her eyes are lowered but intent, as if she has just come across something arresting in her reading. She wears one of her own dresses which can be seen in the George Eliot collection of memorabilia in the local museum. Her major works are listed on the plinth, and there is a very brief but serviceable biography in the stone for those who choose to have only a nodding acquaintance.

George Eliot, her face averted from Debenham's, by John Letts

In Bridge Street, leading off the Market Place, there was a hostelry in George Eliot's day which went by the good old country name of the Bull Inn. It has been identified as the inspiration for the Red Lion in 'Janet's Repentance', third of the stories in *Scenes of Clerical Life*. From the upper windows Lawyer Dempster incited the mob against the Revd Edgar Tryan and his supporters. Today, a portrait of the novelist appears as the inn-sign of the George Eliot hotel. The building itself is bright with shiny white and butterscotch paint, and in the summer pink geraniums cascade from the sills. There is a George Eliot Suite and a Mill Restaurant, all cheerful and welcoming to the tourist, though Mary Ann Evans probably never set foot inside.

St Nicolas parish church, Nuneaton, has a rather troubled exterior of dark Warwickshire stone. But inside, it is all light and air, serene white arches, a timbered ceiling in a beautiful geometric design, and superb vaulting like the ribs of a Viking ship. When the wind is in a certain direction, a sonorous roar fills the nave with the sound of the sea. In the porch a white and gold panel confirms that this is the Milby church referred to in *Scenes of Clerical Life*. The memorial tomb of Sir Marmaduke Constable, who received Nuneaton priory and its lands from Henry VIII, is wonderfully carved in alabaster. George Eliot would, I feel, have been agreeably surprised to hear, as I did, a woman curate in full canonicals preaching from the pulpit at the family service.

Arbury Farm, as it was then called, is within the grounds of Arbury Hall in the parish of Chilvers Coton, Nuneaton. Mary Ann Evans was born in the room over the bow window. The outside appearance of the house has scarcely changed since then, though it is now called South Farm. This was the home of Robert Evans, Mary Ann's father. He was the farmer, surveyor and land agent for the Astley and Arbury estates. Much of his character as a conscientious, valued and successful manager is recognizable in the fictional Adam Bede, and in Caleb Garth in *Middlemarch*.

Mary Ann was christened in the parish church of Chilvers Coton, which she realized as Shepperton church in *Scenes of Clerical Life*. The character of Amos Barton, curate of Shepperton, is believed to have been founded on the life and hard times of the Revd John Gwyther, curate of Chilvers Coton, who lived in the vicarage but received an inadequate salary from the absentee vicar.

Mary Ann went regularly to Sunday services at the church with her family, and years later recalled some of its 'dear old quaintnesses', such as the Benefactors' Boards which commemorated sundry charities to the poor of the district. These can still be seen in the porch and inside the church. Her parents and her brother Isaac are buried in the churchyard. The stone tomb of Mrs Gwyther, wife of the curate and reckoned to be the model for the lovely but luckless Milly Barton, can just be discerned in the depths of an ancient yew tree. The George Eliot Fellowship has placed a tablet in the north wall, commemorating the novelist's association with the church. It was unveiled in 1972 to coincide with the centenary of the publication of her greatest novel, *Middlemarch*.

Griff House, which stands a mile south of Chilvers Coton, was her home from the age of four months until she was twenty-one years old. In *The Mill on the Floss* she evokes it for the childhood of Maggie and Tom Tulliver, drawn from the early days of her brother Isaac and herself. Griff has been enlarged and today is a comfortable Beefeater Steakhouse and residential hotel. A photograph of George Eliot presides from over the fireplace in the extension building, and one of the dining-areas has been given a literary atmosphere, cosily furnished with shelves of assorted books. The old stone-flagged floor, polished by countless feet, was in the entrance-hall in her day, and is quite undisturbed. So is the ancient yew in the garden. The Griff House pond, assumed to be the Round Pool in *The Mill*, has been landscaped. But Robert Evans's small study, where he sat to do his paperwork, is still identifiable in the old part of the house, and the dining- and drawing-rooms can be traced. Some readers have supposed that the Hall Farm garden in *Adam Bede* was based on the big fruit-and-vegetable garden which used to be attached to Griff, and that the garden walk to the summer-house was resited at Lowick Manor in *Middlemarch*.

Arbury Hall is surely one of the most beautiful houses in this country. A Gothicized mansion with an exterior of sombre stone, it stands at the end of a mile-long drive among lawns, woods and meadows, overlooking a waterfall and lakes. The town and all its bustle stop at the round towers of the main gateway. Beyond is serene country.

The fabulous fan-vaulting of the ceilings and walls, wedding-cake white and delicate as lace, has to be seen to be believed. George Eliot saw, and remembered ever after. She had often visited the Hall as a child with her father. In 'Mr Gilfil's Love Story' she envisages Arbury as Cheverel Manor and describes the architecture of the interior and its treasury of paintings, ceramics and furniture. The library, which she probably remembered best, having been given the use of its books, is not open to visitors. (Part of the extensive stable-block was designed by Sir Christopher Wren for a fee of two silver candlesticks with a value of about £11.)

In Astley village, which is just outside the Arbury estate, is the 'wonderful little church' which George Eliot described as Knebley church in 'Mr Gilfil's Love Story'. Recreating it in memory, she recalled twelve apostles 'painted in fresco on the walls'. (There are in fact nine apostles and nine prophets, but otherwise her memory, and her imagination, served her well.) She remembered the coats of arms in clusters on the roof, and the 'marble warriors and their wives without noses' by the west doorway. Her parents were married here, and there remains an affectionate tribute on one of the Newdigate family memorials to Robert Evans's first wife, Harriet Poynton, who died while still a comparatively young woman. She was 'for many years the faithful friend and servant of the family of Arbury'.

Nantglyn, the school in Coventry which George Eliot attended until she became a teenager, used to be the last house in town. Beyond it lay open country. The city has now swallowed the fields and woods, and the house itself, 29 Warwick Row, is portioned out between an Indian restaurant and an estate agent's. Only a plaque on the wall identifies it as a place she knew so well.

Bird Grove, another house she came to know intimately, was at Foleshill, just outside Coventry, where she was housekeeper for her father after he retired. The house still stands in what is now called George Eliot Road. In her day it consisted of two semi-detached dwellings. One of these has gone; the other has lost much of its Victorian charm – such features as the pleasing Ionic columns inset at the corners of the walls, and the elegant roof-balustrades. The remaining area of garden is minimal. Happily, the magnificent church of the Holy Trinity in Coventry, where Robert Evans was sidesman and his daughter attended with him for many years, has altered scarcely at all. There, too, she is remembered by a plaque in the nave. The richly historic Great Hall of St Mary's Guildhall in Coventry is thought to have been the setting of Hetty Sorrel's trial for murder in *Adam Bede*. 'A mirror of local history', the Hall was the meeting-place of the powerful Merchants' Guilds in the fourteenth century. George Eliot identifies it by her description of the great tapestry, the suits of armour and the Minstrels' Gallery.

In Nuneaton public library (situated in Church Street, featured as Orchard Street in 'Janet's Repentance') the George Eliot collection contains unique first and Fine Art editions of her major works, many of them lavishly illustrated and bound, and some original letters and manuscripts, locked away behind glass. But there are also shelves of interesting editions of all her novels, as well as criticism, biographies, essays by and about her, translations, novels about her, a Who's Who in George Eliot, critiques of Victorian literature in general, and so on. These you are at liberty to take down and leaf through.

Nuneaton Museum and Art Gallery, set in the beautiful Riversley Park, has a completely new display, a room-setting depicting a specific time in George Eliot's life. The period chosen was perhaps her happiest and most successful, while she was writing *Middlemarch* and living with George Henry Lewes in London. The drawing-room is furnished with authentic copies of the original wallpaper, fabrics and furniture of their home in Regent's Park. The panelling and fireplace have been recreated from drawings in the archives of the Victoria & Albert Museum. Other irreplaceable items on display are her piano and the only existing dress she is known to have worn, displayed on a character figure. Her writing cabinet, desk and armchair are there, together with small personal items such as her gloves, shoes and books. Robert Evans's glasses and two of his diaries, 1832 and 1833, containing his day-to-day accounts, events in the area and details of their family and social life, are also included in the collection. From these she drew much of the background material for *Mill on the Floss*, *Adam Bede* and *Middlemarch*.

The George Eliot Memorial Garden was established by the fellowship in 1952 in conjunction with Nuneaton borough council, and is the setting for a granite memorial to the novelist. It is in Vicarage Street, part of the garden of Lawyer Dempster's house in 'Janet's Repentance', a pleasant retreat lovingly maintained in honour of a woman who, a critic once said, had been 'disturbed enough by life to come near to greatness'. Her finest work surpasses greatness: it has that quality of heart and mind which makes it supreme.

ELIZABETH GASKELL

KNUTSFORD, CHESHIRE

JENNY UGLOW

Elizabeth Gaskell was thirty-eight when she was thrust into public attention – and fierce controversy – in 1848 on the publication of her first novel, *Mary Barton*, a drama of love and murder, and class antagonism in Manchester. More uproar followed when she made the young mother of an illegitimate child the heroine of *Ruth*, in 1852, and, to a lesser extent, when she returned to the struggle of masters and men in *North and South*, published in 1854. Her later novels, *Sylvia's Lovers* and the marvellous *Wives and Daughters* (left unfinished at her death in 1865), caused less of a storm. In addition she wrote many short stories, spinning tales of ghosts and mysteries and strong, solitary heroines. All her writing was packed into a busy life as the wife of a Unitarian minister in Manchester, where she also brought up four daughters and was active in innumerable social causes.

Her fiction, varied in subject and style, resists simple classifications. Marked by deep convictions, firm faith and a passionate concern for the disadvantaged, it can be tragic or comic, realistic or fantastic, but it always reveals an eye for the telling detail, an ear for the curious tone of voice and turn of phrase. A reader can trace many literary influences – from the Bible and fairy-tales to the novels of Scott, the poems of Wordsworth and Crabbe, the polemics of Carlyle – but can also feel her pleasure in pure listening and talking. Wherever Elizabeth was – in Wales, the Lake District, the slums of Lancashire, the salons of Paris – she collected anecdotes, local histories, personal memories, customs, folk-tales. Perhaps none of her work shows this more than *Cranford*, which appeared as a series of episodes in Dickens's *Household Words* from 1851 to 1853, and which depicts the lives of a group of women in a small country town. Cranford, of course, was Knutsford, in Cheshire, where she herself grew up.

The house that Elizabeth Gaskell lived in as a girl is not open to the public – but this hardly matters, for the whole of Knutsford was her childhood home, 'my dear adoptive native town'. She was actually born in London, in Lindsey Row, Chelsea (now 93 Cheyne Walk), where her father, who was Keeper of the Records

Heathwaite, Knutsford, where Elizabeth Gaskell grew up

at the Treasury, had settled after an erratic life as a Unitarian minister, farmer and writer. Her mother never fully recovered from Elizabeth's birth (it was her eighth pregnancy in twelve years and only one other child, John, had survived). Her widowed sister Hannah Lumb came down from Cheshire to care for her, but she died on 29 October 1811, when Elizabeth was thirteen months old. Hannah's invalid daughter, Mary Anne, immediately thought of the baby and wrote pleadingly to her mother: 'Poor little Elizabeth. What will become of her? She has been the constant subject of my thoughts ever since – and it is about her I have taken up my pen, to write to you. Do you think she could come to us?'

That was how Elizabeth came to Knutsford, which she recreated nearly forty years later in *Cranford* as a town 'in possession of the Amazons' where 'all the holders of houses, above a certain rent, are women'. Aunt Lumb's house, The

The church of St John the Baptist, where Elizabeth Gaskell was married in 1744

Heath, stood slightly apart from the town in Northwich Road (now renamed Heathwaite, and Gaskell Avenue). After Mary Anne died a year later, another aunt, Abigail Holland, joined the all-female household, although she may have lived in nearby Heath House – once the home of the famous 'Highwayman Higgins', hanged at Carmarthen in 1767, whose adventures Mrs Gaskell used for 'The Squire's Story'. Both houses looked across an unfenced road to the broad triangular heath stretching away into the country. Knutsford races were held on this heath from the seventeenth century until 1873, and here too the local people kept their cows, horses and flocks of geese. The ladies of Cranford, however genteel, were

194

'quite sufficient for ... rushing out at the geese that occasionally venture into the gardens if the gates are left open'.

Heathwaite is a Queen Anne house of red brick with fine oak-panelled rooms. It has a square of garden in front and, as in Mrs Gaskell's day, the drawing-room windows at the back look out over lawns surrounded by flower-beds and shaded by a huge cedar, with vegetables and fruit trees beyond, although the poultry and the paddock with two cows and a pony have gone. The story 'My French Master' gives a glimpse of her life here, taking lessons in an arbour in the garden from M. Rogier (a refugee from the French Revolution and a great local character, like the fictional French master). Life with Aunt Lumb – 'my more than mother', as Elizabeth called her – was far from lonely as it drew her into her mother's large extended family, the Hollands, who belonged to the old Dissenting community established in Lancashire and Cheshire since the seventeenth century. Elizabeth's grandfather Samuel Holland farmed at Sandlebridge, five miles from Knutsford in the lanes off the Macclesfield road, on land which had been in the family since 1718. The farm was over 300 acres and Samuel combined his work as land-agent and farmer with that of a lay-preacher, as Farmer Holman does in Mrs Gaskell's *Cousin Phillis*.

The smithy and mill, though converted, still stand in their hidden valley by the brook, but the old three-storeyed house, with its oak beams and flagged passages, was demolished in the 1960s. It was as familiar to Elizabeth as her own home, and she and her cousins often slept in the huge bedrooms with room for three or four beds in each. She loved its neat parlours, its vast loft, its casement windows and walls, 'over-run with roses, honey-suckle and vines', and was proud of its history, telling the novelist Geraldine Jewsbury in 1849 how, as a child, she heard the story of young Robert Clive (who had Holland relatives) jumping across the gap between the great stone balls on the entrance gate. 'Of course this made him into a hero before I knew there was such a place as India.'

Sandlebridge became a prototype of Wordsworthian harmony. In 1836, four years after she married and moved to Manchester, she stayed there with her baby, Marianne, who was at 'the very tip-top of bliss' because of its 'chickens and little chickens, pigs & cows & calves & horses & *baby horses* & fish in the pond & ducks in the lane & the mill & the Smithy & sheep & baby sheep & flowers'. Elizabeth, meanwhile, was working privately, scribbling notes on Coleridge and Wordsworth (*'fit place for the latter!'*), sitting in a corner of a shady field, 'crunching up my paper, & scuttering my pencil away, when anyone comes near'.

Although set in this rich countryside, Knutsford itself was far from sleepy. It was an important centre and an assize town. When Elizabeth was eight, the imposing classical Sessions House was completed, and later a gaol was built for seven hundred prisoners. (Her cousin's husband, Edward Deane, was doctor to the gaol.) The town's prosperous past shows in its two main streets, Princess Street and King

Street (known as Top Street and Bottom Street), with their Georgian houses of mellow Cheshire brick. They run parallel along the side of a gentle hill sloping down to a marshy valley called The Moor, where Tatton Mere peters out in tall reed-beds, and are linked by cobbled alleys, whose names conjure up history – Red Cow Yard, Slater's Yard, Silkmill Street. Apart from some obtrusive modern shop-fronts and signs, the heart of the town is almost unchanged from Mrs Gaskell's Duncombe in 'Mr Harrison's Confessions', where, 'here and there a bow window, every now and then a gable, cutting up against the sky – occasionally a projecting upper storey – throws good effect of light and shadow along the street'. But the 'pink blotting-paper' tinged whitewash has disappeared and so have most of the limes and chestnuts which sheltered the townsfolk from summer showers.

The Hollands were among Knutsford's leading citizens. Elizabeth's uncle, Peter Holland, was the town doctor, and his two daughters by his first marriage, Mary and Lucy, had some of the characteristics (combined with memories of older aunts) which Mrs Gaskell gives to Cranford's Deborah and Matty Jenkyns. Cranford women were known not only for chasing geese but 'for kindness (somewhat dictatorial) to the poor': Peter Holland's first wife founded a Female Benefit Society in 1806 (like the Benefit Society for the Poor which Deborah Jenkyns and her mother start) and both Mary and Lucy ran their own infant schools. Dr Holland lived with his large family and his apprentices in Church House, which overlooked the churchyard, so people joked that the 'the good Doctor never loses sight of his patients'. Church House still stands (though it is now called Hollingford House, in memory of Dr Gibson in *Wives and Daughters*), but its fine garden has long since vanished, and the house is hemmed in by new buildings beside a busy main road. It was in the solid, dignified church next door, St John the Baptist, built in 1744, that Elizabeth married William Gaskell on 30 August 1832, since dissenters were not allowed to be married in their own chapels until 1844. Her uncle gave her away, the wedding breakfast was held at Church House and Knutsford paid tribute with its old custom of 'sanding'; the ground outside almost every house was strewn with red sand, sprinkled with white in patterns of flowers and verses, a tradition unique to the town and continued on special occasions today.

Since the Hollands were Unitarians, the centre of their religious life was not this church, however, but Brook Street Chapel, beyond the lower end of King Street. One of three dissenting chapels built in the area after the Act of Toleration of 1689, Brook Street is moving in its simplicity, resembling a long brick cottage, with outside steps at each end where, perhaps, look-outs stood to watch for trouble in early days. Mrs Gaskell described it vividly as Mr Benson's chapel in *Ruth*, sheltering in a 'hidden' part of town, its lattice windows covered with ivy, 'full of nesting birds', creating a green gloom inside. Here she worshipped and taught in Sunday school, and here she was buried, among her forebears, in November 1865.

Brook Street is on the opposite edge of Knutsford from Heathwaite, and a circling walk back through the town is crowded with places associated with Mrs Gaskell. Just round the corner from the chapel was Brook House, where Lady Jane Stanley lived, a figure still remembered in the town (in her will she left money to the town to pave a footpath but insisted it should be only a single flag wide, to prevent young couples linking their arms in an unseemly fashion). The sedan chair she used, like Mrs Jamieson in *Cranford*, still turns out for May Day processions. You walk back from Brook Street (alias 'Darkness Lane') into King Street under the bridge built for the railway, which reached Knutsford in 1862, three years before Elizabeth's death. Opposite the seventeenth-century houses at the bottom of King Street is a large white house, No. 15, where Captain Hill lived, a Waterloo veteran, adjutant of the Cheshire Yeomanry and the model for *Cranford*'s Captain Brown. Further up is the astounding Gaskell memorial, built in 1907 by the eccentric Ruskin-inspired glove merchant Richard Harding Watt, who embellished Knutsford with Italianate buildings quite in line with *Cranford*'s sense of the bizarre, though not with its sense of discretion. (Watt's buildings include a row of houses on Legh Road which Pevsner calls the 'maddest sequence of villas in England' and a laundry in Drury Lane modelled on a Damascus mosque whose green-tiled tower used to proclaim, 'Let thy garments be always white'.)

In the middle of King Street is the Royal George Inn, where the London and Birmingham coaches, called the 'Bang-up' and the 'Express', like those which Roger Hamley and Cynthia Gibson take in *Wives and Daughters*, rolled up the cobbles under the high archway. At the back of the hotel, a real surprise, is a set of small eighteenth-century Assembly Rooms. Their moulded ceilings and Adam fireplaces are still visible, although their elegance has suffered from their conversion into a bar – the bar itself taking up most of the space in the room. The Assembly Rooms were built by joint subscription of all the county families, as explained in 'A Dark Night's Work', and the gentry held card parties and winter dances here, like the Charity Ball in *Wives and Daughters* (except the takings did not go to charity, but to fund the summer races). When Elizabeth was small they were less exclusive and were used by M. Rogier for his dancing classes. Their early glory had faded, as it has in Cranford when the town gathers to see Signor Brunoni, the travelling magician:

> The salmon coloured paint had faded into a drab; great pieces of plaster had chipped off the white wreaths and festoons on its walls; but still a mouldy odour of aristocracy lingered about the place, and a dusty recollection of the days that were gone made Miss Matty and Mrs Forrester bridle up as they entered, and walk mincingly up the room, as if there were a number of genteel observers, instead of two little boys, with a stick of toffy between them, with which to beguile the time.

Near the Royal George (at 84–86 King Street) stood Jacksons, the general store, which appears disguised in both *Cranford* and *Wives and Daughters* as 'Johnsons', where Miss Matty discovers she has been ruined by a bank failure. (Knutsford Library and Barclay's Bank have 839 'cheques' of the failed bank.) And so it goes on: at the top of King Street is Marble Arch, the former site of the Angel Inn where Lord Maulever stayed while visiting Captain Brown; at the very end, before a footpath winds under the trees towards Tatton Park, the Towers of *Wives and Daughters*, is the Old Vicarage, fictional home of Peter, the Cranford vicar's son, who ran away to sea but miraculously returned after many years (unlike Elizabeth's own sailor brother John, who vanished without trace on a voyage to India in 1829). At 22 Princess Street is a house commonly called 'Miss Matty's Tea Shop', which actually belonged up to the mid-1830s to a Miss Harker (Cranford's Betty Barker) whose cow really did fall into a lime-pit on the heath and was given a grey flannel waistcoat.

The web of connections spread outwards, to Sandlebridge and to the two large estates each side of the town, Tatton Park and Tabley. Tabley was the home of the Leicester-Warren family from 1272 until 1976, when the last of the line died. Tabley Hall, a strong, elegant mansion built by Carr of York in 1760, with a vast portico supported by four columns of Runcorn sandstone each cut in a single piece, gazes across the meadows to a lake twice painted by Turner. Part of the house, including the picture gallery, is now open to the public, as is the beautiful panelled chapel nearby. Built in 1675 for the original Tabley Old Hall, which stood on an island in Tabley Mere, this chapel was carefully moved to its present site when subsidence made it unsafe in 1927. Elizabeth knew the Old Hall well. It had been partly rebuilt in the seventeenth century but had kept its old medieval hall, over forty feet long, with a gallery on three sides, a fine timbered roof and walls hung with weapons and armour. As a girl she and her friends spent summer days in the park and drifted on the lake in old boats 'which would only float', to be summoned by the chapel bell when the picnic was spread. At Christmas there were carols and dancing in the hall. Memories of Tabley appear in a letter of 1838 to her friend Mary Howitt, and in 'Mr Harrison's Confessions', where a party from Duncombe travel to the hall by cart, down a sandy lane between high hedges and overarching elms:

> There was a moat and a lake, with a boat; and there was a gallery in the hall, from which music sounded delightfully. The family to which the place belonged were abroad, and lived in a newer and grander mansion, when they were at home.

Now the ruins of Tabley Old Hall are screened by a tangle of trees, rising amid the water-lilies of the broad, ancient moat. But in a room attached to the chapel

Brook Street Chapel, where Elizabeth Gaskell worshipped and is buried

stands a strange, powerfully carved Elizabethan fireplace, rescued from the hall, which gives a haunting idea of its vanished grandeur.

Tatton Park, which now belongs to the National Trust, is larger and more imposing than Tabley, built on a rise overlooking a thousand acres of gardens, parkland and lakes. There is an Old Hall here too, restored to illustrate medieval life, but the 'new' house was designed by Samuel and Lewis Wyatt and completed in 1813. With its lavish furnishings and paintings by Van Dyck and Canaletto, this was the model for the Towers in *Wives and Daughters*. The park was landscaped by Repton in 1791 and the velvet lawns, hot-houses and spreading cedars are still much the same as those that so impress Molly Gibson when she goes to Lady Cumnor's garden party. The Egerton family lived at Tatton until 1958, and the Egertons of Elizabeth's childhood had much in common with her Cumnors. A recent Gaskell Society newsletter points out that Wilbraham Egerton, MP from 1812 to 1832, was followed into parliament by his son, as Lord Cumnor was, and, like Lord Cumnor, was well known for pottering about his farm (to the great irritation of his steward) and for carrying pockets full of halfpennies for the school-children. Lady Egerton, like her fictional counterpart, had no qualms about interfering in the lives of the town and founded a school at the park gates, known locally as Lady Mary's School and supported by the Egerton women for nearly a hundred years. The aristocracy of Knutsford, as well as its shopkeepers and single women, thus found their way into fiction.

After her marriage Elizabeth Gaskell moved to Manchester, where William was minister at Cross Street Chapel. Manchester was the setting for several stories as well as for *Mary Barton* and *North and South*. The city captured her imagination. But the rural myth, the sense of a vanishing way of life and a lost innocence linger behind all her writing, even her powerful novels of industrial strife. She returned constantly to Knutsford, especially in the early years of her marriage. Aunt Lumb died in 1838, and Aunt Abigail ten years later, her death finally closing the doors on Elizabeth's childhood home and, perhaps, releasing a flood of memories, for the following year she sent an article called 'The Last Generation in England' to *Sartain's Magazine*. In this she gives as 'fact' some of the stories to be found in *Cranford*, which appeared two years later. *Cranford* always remained her own favourite among her books, and in the last year of her life she told Ruskin: 'Whenever I am ailing or ill, I take "Cranford" and – I was going to say, *enjoy* it! (but that would not be pretty!) – laugh over it again!'

THOMAS HARDY

HIGHER BOCKHAMPTON; AND MAX GATE, DORCHESTER

RONALD BLYTHE

The Higher Bockhampton cottage and the Dorchester villa stand some three miles and eighty-five years apart, although with Thomas Hardy there was never any kind of separation. Both emotionally and imaginatively, his two homes remained interconnected. Between them there had been a number of other addresses in which poems and stories had been written, but all of these were in effect ante-rooms to Bockhampton and Max Gate. His great-grandfather had built the cottage in 1800 on ginger sand and the author and the third Thomas had built Max Gate in the cemetery of Durnonovaria (the Roman Dorchester). Hardy's, as the cottage was known before Hardy was born in 1840, is the Georgian version of the type of cottage in which the countrymen of Dorset had lived for centuries, a snug shelter of cob and boughs. To one side stretched the plantation which supplied its open hearth with limitless fuel; to the rear stretched the powerful heathland he was to call 'haggard' Egdon. Woods and wastes, the Frome valley pastures and stony cornfields provided the ecology and the mystery for both houses. Late in life Hardy continued to walk or bicycle between them, for his mother, Jemima, lived until 1904. She was his original muse: the seeds of much of his finest work, *Tess*, *The Dynasts* and many of the poems, had been sown by her. Hardy called himself a Victorian, but through Jemima, who died aged ninety, he reached back in his conversations with her to Napoleon and to the horrors of the Georgian countryside, to the implacable nature of the English class system and to the huge old melodrama of human existence as villagers had always witnessed or endured it.

Hardy's fate, like that of so many great writers, was to be caught between two cultures: that into which he had been born and that into which he was led by his genius. Bockhampton and all that it represented was what made him a novelist and poet. But when, eventually, he set up house for himself on the outskirts of the county town, Hardy's went with him. Max Gate has drawn some of the strongest responses ever to a writer's house. Maybe Hardy, when he designed it and got his brother Henry to build it, sharp Broadmayne brick and slate throughout, thought

that its sheer conventionality would deflect the remorseless interest in his background which, almost from the start, had become such a worry to him. Or maybe, and this is something which none of his biographers appears to have considered, his wife, Emma, determined what their first real home should be like. In the ten years since their marriage in 1874 her little architect had become a famous novelist who could afford to give her a respectable house with maids and a gardener, something in the line of the new parsonage houses which the Church of England was building everywhere. If Max Gate suggests anything, it is a nineteenth-century rectory, and this would have delighted Emma. But in whatever way this unforgettable and hauntingly strange yet ordinary house came into being, there is no doubt at all about the kind of life which Thomas and Emma lived in it. Literature apart, it was one of severe bourgeois order and respectability. The determination on both their parts was to live, not as artists – and Emma was in her own muddled and sometimes impressive way unorthodox and free-spirited, as well as the 'onlie begetter' of one of the most profound sequences of love-poetry in the language – but as gentry. Max Gate thus confronts everyone who enters it with its never-to-be-solved puzzle. Why such a façade when everything he wrote allowed such open access to the very source of his being, socially and imaginatively? He and Emma were forty-five when they moved into it, there to lead an existence which, for all that has been written about it, remains a mostly untold tale. Hardy often allows vivid glimpses of the hidden life behind what he would have called 'the front elevation' of a house. In his courtship novel *A Pair of Blue Eyes* we have a writer calling out, '"Come in!" from distant penetralia.' He and Emma were famously welcoming to their visitors, maintaining the façade of their marriage in the approved Victorian manner. Max Gate retains its formality and its welcome. It is not only the succession of studies used by Hardy which are so overwhelmingly inviting, but every stick and stone. It is a 'calling' house whose unusual voice can be heard above the traffic now rushing past it. Set back among what remain of the thousands of trees which Hardy planted round it, it is as instantly recognizable to the literary traveller as is the Taj Mahal to the tourist, and its physical reality as surprising.

Thomas Hardy was born in the cottage that his great-grandfather had built at Higher Bockhampton, a hamlet which was part of the parish of Stinsford. His father was a self-employed mason and his mother, Jemima Hand, was a servant girl whose family had suffered crushing poverty. Her mother was a well-read woman who had come down in the world by falling in love with and marrying a servant. Jemima Hand was four months pregnant when Thomas Hardy II married her on 22 December 1839. Their son was born in the middle bedroom of the cottage on 2 June 1840 after a desperate labour, and then cast into a basket as dead. A few

Thomas Hardy's cottage at Higher Bockhampton

203

minutes later the midwife rescued the boy and exclaimed, 'Stop a minute: he's alive, sure enough!' From then on Hardy's young parents, his handsome father, his pragmatic mother, appeared to have had an understanding of the special nature of this child, filling his early years with the richest kind of rural culture and, before long, daring to offend the lady of the manor by seeing that he received an education which would take him out of village toil and into one of the professions. Hardy remained never anything less than embarrassed by the informality of this education, but it did for him what 'Christminster' could never have done, kept him at the heart of all rural experience whilst giving him a unique language and philosophy in which to describe it. Taught music by his father, story-telling by his mother, poetic form by the Anglican liturgy, the true depths of local speech by William Barnes, architecture by both provincial and London standards, and classical drama by a young friend whose own life was as tragic as anything to be found in Sophocles, Hardy's culture could not have been more perfect for his purpose. Added to which was his minute interest in everything which had happened to him personally, so that the reader enters both the cottage and the villa, as well as Hardy's private life, painfully and brilliantly well-briefed. He is the supreme poet of regret, of what was and what might have been.

The Hardys were 'liviers' or life-holders of a property, rural craftsmen and businessmen whose position had a certain independence from both the local farmers and the gentry. Most of their relatives, however, were less free and worked as labourers and domestic servants. As was common with sprawling Victorian families, Hardy maintained strong links with just a few of those close to him and ignored the rest. Chief among the former were his mother, his sister Mary and his cousin Tryphena. Beautiful Tryphena, later a headmistress, was his first great love. Quiet Mary, also a teacher, occupied a role in his development, it has been suggested, similar to that of Dorothy Wordsworth in the art of her brother William.

Although his family modestly extended the Bockhampton cottage, Hardy's imagination expanded it in various ways, first to accommodate scenes from *Under the Greenwood Tree*, in which it is Tranter Dewy's house, and, towards the end of his life, to accommodate a part-factual, part-dream notion he was anxious to purvey of his ancestry. But now and again the architect speaks, as when Hardy describes the actual making of such a building. He was supporting an appeal by the Royal Society of Arts to correctly understand and preserve England's ancient cottages which at that moment, the 1920s, were being torn down in their thousands as unhygienic and being replaced by brick and slate.

By merest chance I was able, when a child, to see the building of what was probably the last of these old-fashioned cottages of 'mudwall' and thatch. What was called mudwall was really a composition of chalk, clay and straw – essentially, unbaked brick. This was mixed up into a sort of dough pudding, close to where the cottage was to be built. The mixing was performed by treading and shovelling – women sometimes being called in to tread – and the straw was added to bind the mass together, a process that had doubtless gone on since the days of Israel in Egypt and earlier.

It was then thrown up by pitchforks on to the wall, where it was trodden down, to a thickness of about two feet till a 'rise' of about three feet had been reached all round the building. This was left to settle for a day or two, and then another rise was effected, till the whole height of the wall-plate was reached, and then that of the gables, unless the cottage was hipped, or had a 'pinion' end, as it was called. When the wall had dried a little the outer face was cut down to a fairly flat surface with a spade, and the wall then plastered outside and in. The thatch projected sufficiently to prevent much rain running down the outer plaster [rain pouring from roofs was a desolating sight to Hardy], and even where it did run down the plaster was so hard as to be unaffected, more lime being used nowadays. The house I speak of is, I believe, still standing, unless replaced by colder brick-and-slate . . . I have never heard of any damp coming through these mudwalls . . . Yet as everybody, at any rate every builder, knows, even when brick walls are built hollow, it is difficult to keep damp out entirely in exposed situations.

Landowners who have built some of these latter express their wonder that the villagers prefer their dingy old hovels (as they are regarded) with rooms only six feet high, and small dormer windows with little lead squares, to the new residences with nine-feet rooms and wide windows with large panes. The explanation is the simple one that in the stroke of country winds a high room is not required for fresh air, sufficient ventilation entering through the door and window, and that the draught through the hollow brick wall makes the new cottages cold in winter.

I would therefore urge owners to let as many as are left of their old cottages remain where they are, and to repair them instead of replacing them with bricks, since, apart from their warmth and dryness, they have almost always great beauty and charm.

As with virtually everything Hardy wrote, there is no private detachment from this public advice. He had passed from mudwall and thatch to bricks and slate, and had felt the chill. He had loved Bockhampton, but what he felt for Max Gate could not be put so simply. In the defensive autobiography which he wrote in the third person under his second wife's name, he says that the old homestead is only a fragment of what it was, although the reverse is true. The cottage he knew was nearly twice the size of that built by his great-grandfather. Moreover, the original cob had been bolstered with brick and cement. Up until 1857 there were in effect a pair of cottages, one of which was the home of his widowed grandmother. When she died that year, it is probable that these two little houses were turned into one. Forty years later it was altered once more, and the lean-to was given cavity walls! Country people will always do the domestic best for themselves as their families swell and as what they believe to be improved building materials arrive in the district. Young Hardy ruined St Juliot's church with his 'restoration'; and many a devoted cottage-dweller in the 1990s is ruining some old home with his DIY improvements. Each man kills the thing he loves.

The teenage Hardy celebrated the unity of his birthplace with his first poem, 'Domicilium'. In it the cottage itself barely exists, only its setting. His real home is landscape, not a roof.

> In days bygone –
> Long gone – my father's mother, who is now
> Blest with the blest, would take me out to walk.
> At such a time I once inquired of her
> How looked the spot when first she settled here.
> The answer I remember. 'Fifty years
> Have passed since then, my child, and change has marked
> The face of all things. Yonder garden-plots
> And orchards were uncultivated slopes
> O'ergrown with bramble bushes, furze and thorn:
> That road a narrow path shut in by ferns,
> Which, almost trees, obscured the passer-by.
>
> 'Our house stood quite alone, and those tall firs .
> And beeches were not planted. Snakes and efts
> Swarmed in the summer days, and nightly bats
> Would fly about our bedrooms. Heathcroppers
> Lived on the hills, and were our only friends;
> So wild it was when first we settled here.'

The poem is full of undercurrents. It would be in his maternal grandmother's bedroom, now connected with his paternal great-grandfather's cottage, that Hardy would write *Under the Greenwood Tree* and *Far from the Madding Crowd*, and from which, in 1870, he would set out for 'Lyonnesse' and all its consequences. And those 'ferns, which, almost trees, obscured the passer-by' point to *The Return of the Native* and to Hardy's recognition that people living in certain ecological circumstances are in a trap. And it was also in this small room under the eaves which he shared with his brother Henry that he would define his literary territory and write the name Wessex for the first time. In his eighties he wrote a vivid description of his home hamlet, showing the changes during his lifetime, and including the come-down from cob to brick.

The domiciles were quaint, brass-knockered, and green-shuttered then, some with green garden-doors and white balls on the posts, and mainly occupied by life-holders of substantial footing like the Hardys themselves. In the years of his infancy, or shortly

206

preceding it, the personages tenanting these few houses included two retired military officers, one old navy lieutenant, a small farmer and tranter [carrier], a relieving officer and registrar, and an old militiaman, whose wife was the monthly nurse [and to whom English literature owes an incalculable debt for noticing that the stillborn Thomas was in fact faintly breathing]. These being mostly elderly people, the place was at one time nicknamed 'Veterans' Valley'. It was also dubbed 'Cherry Alley', the lane or street leading through it being planted with an avenue of cherry-trees. The life-holds fell into hand, and the quaint residences with their trees, clipped hedges, orchards, white gatepost-balls, the naval officer's masts and weather-cocks, have now perished every-one, and have been replaced by labourers' brick cottages and other new farm-buildings.

Hardy had an eye for the conditioning of people by what he termed 'meditative solitude', something a poet or a religious would pursue as a necessity, but which was part of the lives of the villagers of his day without their knowing it. The cottage at Bockhampton was filled with it, even when it was full of Hardys. Those seven little rooms with their chestnut floorboards and bumpy whitewashed ceilings, ancient adze-marked doors from another house, fragile stairs and solid flags, exuded it. It was in the porch that his mother had discovered him sleeping with a snake on his chest. Inside, the watching boy would wait for the westering sun to fire the Venetian-red wall of the staircase and then sing Watts's 'And now another day is done'. The Max Gate study would be given this rich colour, which was both vital and elegiac. Both houses were where the living doubled up with the dead.

> Here is the ancient floor
> Footworn and hollowed and thin,
> Here was the former door
> Where the dead feet walked in.

On his forty-fourth birthday – the year before he moved into Max Gate – he had walked from the cottage to what would be the setting of *The Woodlanders*, his own favourite among the novels, and into what as children he and Henry had called 'the birds' bedroom', and written:

Alone in the plantation, at 9 o'clock. A weird hour: strange faces and figures formed by dying lights. Holm leaves shine like human eyes, and the sky glimpses between the trunks are like white phantoms and cloven tongues. It is so silent and still that a footstep on the dead leaves could be heard a quarter of a mile off.

Soon it would be:

> The change to a high new house,
> He, she, all of them – aye,
> Clocks and carpets and chairs
> On the lawn all day ...

Hardy had published nine novels by the time he moved to Max Gate and the tenth, *The Mayor of Casterbridge*, was completed just a few weeks before the wagons carried his furniture up the newly made drive. An earthwork called Conquer Barrow had been flattened to make this drive, during which operation a row of skeletons had been decapitated. Two of them lay clasped together like lovers. They were Romano-British but he placed them in pre-history.

> So long, beyond chronology,
>   Lovers in death as 'twere,
> So long in placid dignity
>   Have you lain here!

Years later, taking a spade from the shed to bury one of his beloved cats – they sometimes came to grief on the nearby railway line – he wondered if some passer-by might think he was doing a bit of archaeology. Instead, was he not laying to rest 'a little white furred thing' whose existence had meant more to him than the whole of the Roman empire? Interring among the legions' dust Comfy, Snowdove, Tippety, Marky and all the others when their time came spoke to him, as every other thing did, of human vanity.

When Hardy and Emma came to Max Gate, they had been married for eleven years and had lived in a succession of rented houses, both in London and in the country. Max Gate set the seal on Hardy's becoming a popular novelist with an assured income. His stories were serialized in the best magazines and he was being accepted as a distinguished figure in the literary world. Also, that interest of his readership in his background as well as his books, and which caused him so much anxiety, was running high. Max Gate stood at the very centre of what he was and what he knew. An early visitor found it stark and reported, 'The place is as lonely as it is elevated.' At first Hardy himself seemed to shrink from what he had created on an acre and a half of Duchy of Cornwall wasteland just outside Dorchester, and complained:

> The house is bleak and cold
> Built so new for me!

Its name derived from Mack's toll-gate, which had stood on this spot. One of Hardy's first tasks was to create a windbreak to protect his property from the coastal gales roaring across Egdon. He built a garden wall and planted a forest of Austrian pines, between two and three thousand in all. Their function would be not only to protect him from the weather, but to hide him away from ever more inquisitive eyes. Also they could be a birds' bedroom for Emma, a great bird-watcher. Soon after moving in, he began work on *The Woodlanders*, which acted as a bridge between his seedling pines and the soaring plantation at Bockhampton, crowded with 'figures formed by dying lights'. Hardy uses trees as a haven against the 'he'th', as the

208

Max Gate, Dorchester, c.1900 showing Emma, her nephew
and Hardy with his bicycle

Dorset people called their pitiless moor, although his pine shelter round Max Gate was to prove excessive:

> I set every tree in my June time,
> And now they obscure the sky.

The house remains tree-ringed, but not to the melancholic extent it was when all the pines closed in on it, and the Hardy-reader's first sight of it is among the great associative experiences.

The regular emergence of bones and stones from the garden gave Hardy a time pattern which helped to console him for the loss of the Christian calendar, which for him became that latest of things. One of his immediate intentions was to fix a sundial on the Max Gate turret which read 'Quid de Nocte?' ('What of the night?'), a question from Isaïah – but it was never achieved until his second wife, Florence, saw to it after his death. It hangs there still, telling good time. What he called 'the Druid Stone' was dug out of the garden while he was finishing *Tess*. It took seven men with crowbars to heave it out of the earth and erect it opposite to what was

Thomas Hardy

to be his last study. It had lain for thousands of years among burnt bones and ashes, and now it faced the sun. 'I want to see the deeper reality underlying the scenic, the expression of what are sometimes called abstract imaginings.' Extensions to the house over the years allowed Hardy to write facing new directions and Emma to find privacy from the sight and sound of his fame. Their final work-rooms, his above the kitchen and hers in the roof, are intensely affecting. She, writing the memoir which would after the long, faltering marriage hurry him back to their courtship and a flood of poems, had even managed to cut herself off from the domestic noises of Max Gate. He, on the other hand, wrote *The Dynasts* and most of his best poetry to the muted accompaniment of the maids' chatter and

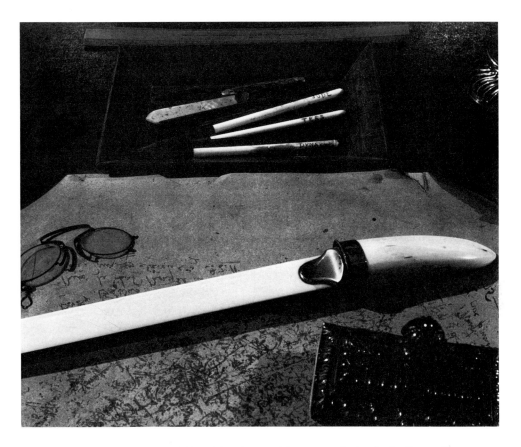

Hardy's study was removed from Max Gate and is now on display in the Dorset County Museum, Dorchester. His pens still lie on his desk

games of ring-board from below. In this room Hardy found his ultimate greatness. The gardener would glimpse the old man from the corner of his eye, wearing a shawl and staring at the Druid Stone and then towards Rainbarrow.

Emma died in her attic boudoir. Her last act – astounding to him – was to break his heart. Florence introduced a bathroom and her own kind of light. But Max Gate now reflects that of the two tough personalities who created it in their middle age. By keeping it in normal homely use, it says more about the lives of Hardy, Emma and Florence, and more about Tess and those other immortals, than ever it could had there been an attempt at keeping everything as it was and roped off. Max Gate had its drawbacks, but it does seem that during Hardy's lifetime it was the done thing to mock it. After a chilly start he and Emma grew to love it. Neither knew much about comfort but they knew everything about symbols, about spirits and about the way in which what lay outside looked in at the window. Max Gate pays homage to the magic of the imagination, and also to the ennui of married life.

> Within the common lamp-lit room,
> Prison my eyes and thought;
> Let dingy details crudely loom,
> Mechanic speech be wrought.

It has often been said that Hardy's famous sense of irony and of the macabre would have been exercised had he known that his heart and the rest of him would lie some 135 miles apart. To have known that his red study would be cut out of his house and made what he would have called 'a show' in Dorchester Museum might equally have amused and shocked him. But there it is, his study in a glass case for us to gaze into, rather as into an icon, our eyes boring through the smooth surface of his handsome desk to the wonders he created on it. His pens, each marked 'Tess', 'Casterbridge', etc. and put away, lie in their tray. His fiddles and academic robes are respectfully arranged. The calendar is stopped at 1928. The museum itself, like a tiny Liverpool Street station, all fretted cast-iron and galleries, which holds this heart of Max Gate was built by Crickmay, Hardy's old employer. Nearby on a shelf lie fibulae and shards which Hardy preserved from the mounds of soil which his brother's workmen dug out to lay Max Gate's foundations. That he should be laying his own stratum to the remorseless yet beautiful pressed-down stratifications called history thrilled him. At first he and Emma had watched gloomily as the Roman bones were tossed to the surface. What an omen. In the spring of 1884 the cleared plot became a sheet of primroses and then of 'graegles' – wild hyacinths – and they were cheered.

Holding these two houses in trust, the cottage and the villa, and each of them so much more than this, could have presented untold difficulties had it not been realized that Hardy's 'own people', as it were, should be left to care for them. Bockhampton is a lesson in the understanding of the fragile elements which make up a sturdy Dorset homestead. Max Gate continues its original role of prim bourgeois residence, and wholly fails to conceal the fact that it is still one of the world's most potent literary shrines. Writers' houses sometimes have little to do with the books written in them, but these buildings were in Hardy's blood and so in his work. His sister Kate bought Max Gate for £2,250 when Florence died in 1937 and left it to 'the Nation' in 1940. It was just a century after Thomas's birth. She also endowed a scholarship of £3,000 so that a Dorchester grammar school boy could go to Oxford. In his eighties Hardy was still being driven over to Bockhampton, once to look at 'fencing, trees, etc. with a view to tidying and secluding the Hardy house'.

HENRY JAMES

LAMB HOUSE, RYE, E. SUSSEX

ALAN JUDD

Henry James was fifty-five when he moved into Lamb House, Rye, in 1898. He had never owned a house and had never before settled with any idea of permanence. Now he confessed to a 'long-unassuaged desire for a calm retreat' and described his find as

> the very calmest and yet cheerfullest that I could have dreamed in the little old cobble-stoned, grass-grown, red-roofed town, on the summit of its mildly pyramidal hill and close to its noble old church – the chimes of which will sound sweet in my goodly old red-walled garden.

He often remarked on the 'essential amiability' of Lamb House and to A. C. Benson, a future occupant, he wrote that

> the merit of it is such that I may, when pressed by the pinch of need, retire to it with a certain shrunken decency and wither away ... It is really good enough to be a kind of little, becoming, high-door'd, brass-knockered façade to one's life.

As often with James's remarks about himself, this is both misleading and revealing. It is misleading because he did anything but retire and wither and never intended that he should. When he took possession he had great work still to come: his three late major novels, *The Wings of the Dove*, *The Ambassadors* and *The Golden Bowl*, were composed there, as were some lesser works, the prefaces to his collected edition and numerous stories and articles. Nor was there any social withering. Always a keen visitor, he now became a man much visited and within months was writing to H. G. Wells of how 'my little house has been stuffed with people' who had 'strikingly numerous wants ... The bump of luggage has been frequent on my stair ... I should have sought a drearier refuge.' His literary guests alone included Wells himself, Edmund Gosse, Edith Wharton, Rudyard Kipling, the Benson brothers, George Gissing, Ford Madox Ford, Stephen Crane, Joseph Conrad, Max Beerbohm, Violet Hunt, Hugh Walpole, Rupert Brooke, Logan Pearsall Smith and Hilaire Belloc.

Lamb House, on the corner of West Street, Rye

The revealing part of James's description is the 'little, becoming, high-door'd, brass-knockered façade to one's life'. It was that and more. The phrase is accurate in the sense that the house is not large for a Georgian building; it is a four-square, three-storeyed, red-brick structure at the corner of a narrow cobbled street. It has a fine, light, panelled interior and an imposing, elaborately bolted front door. The rooms are not large, but their perspectives and proportions make this seem not to matter, while the hall is spacious and welcoming and the staircase broad. It is like one of the larger town-houses scaled down and is both homely and, as James said, 'becoming'.

His description was not, however, confined to the physical but had a pointedly social reference. As a frequent and sought-after guest, he had arrived at a time of life when it was appropriate to offer hospitality as well as to receive it. He wanted to be established and his choice had good claim to be the first house of Rye, at that time a 'little hilltop community, bound together very like a modest, obscure and impecunious, but virtuous and amiable family'. 'Society' in Rye then comprised about a score of households, plus shopkeepers and tradesmen. As well as being able to entertain friends from the wider literary and social worlds, the acquisition of Lamb House meant that James became a local figure, owner of a family pew in Rye church, supporter of the golf and cricket clubs (he was offered and refused the vice-presidency of the latter; his interest in both had more to do with tea and talk in the pavilion than with trying to knock balls into 'some beflagged jampots') and discreet participant in local gossip. 'I think a position in society is a legitimate object of ambition,' he had once observed; with 'becoming, high door'd, brass-knockered' Lamb House he had acquired an important accessory.

'Façade' is an apt choice of word not only in the sense of front or appearance. It had for James a deeper purpose in that it provided a shield for his essential privacy, a degree of social and domestic stability and a structure of life within which he could work. By thus publicly establishing himself as a benign local bachelor with independent means and good connections, a sociable but private man, he was able to remain of the world without being too much with it.

His use of the word 'little' is also revealing. He often applied it to Lamb House, and even when ill and near the end of his life wrote that he still cherished 'the blessed, the invaluable, little old refuge-quality of dear L. H.'. When revisiting America, he said that he would give 'the whole bristling State of Connecticut' for 'the old battered purple wall' of 'poor dear little Lamb House garden'. What 'little' suggests, however, is not only the affection he felt for his home but also what his close friend Edith Wharton identified as 'the pride that apes humility', which in him 'concerned itself (oddly enough) with material things'. He lived, she said, 'in terror of being thought rich, worldly or luxurious, and was forever contrasting his visitors' supposed opulence and self-indulgence with his own hermit-like asceticism …'

215

His protestations do indeed frequently sound like the sort of oriental courtesy in which self-deprecation, even abasement, is part of the ritual of politeness. It may also have been an extension of his extreme desire not to impose upon others. Whatever its origins, though, there is little doubt that he often felt himself to be poorer than he ever was, and may have half believed some of his own humble posturings.

There is no doubt at all, though, of his feeling for Lamb House. Edith Wharton touchingly describes how 'he who thought himself so detached from material things tasted the simple joys of proprietorship when, with a deprecating air, he showed his fine Georgian panelling and his ancient brick walls to admiring visitors'. It was more than a home, more than a way of life; it was of a piece with the culmination of his artistic achievement. It was there that he finally and most fully achieved himself, a work of art, perhaps, the equal of any he produced.

The house dates from about 1723, when it was built by James Lamb, a collector of customs who was to be thirteen times mayor of Rye. He founded a local dynasty which virtually monopolized Rye's public affairs for over a century (two of his descendants achieved the mayoral office twenty times each) and future occupants of Lamb House continued the tradition until well into the twentieth century (E. F. Benson, the novelist, was mayor from 1934 to 1937). The house incorporated the kitchen and cellars of an earlier building and the acre of garden was at one time brewery, stables and 'deese', a structure in which herrings were dried. Fishing was for many years the only industry in Rye and is still a considerable one. James Lamb also built what came to be known as the Garden Room, an attractive, bow-windowed addition a few yards from the house, overlooking the street. Henry James did much of his work there.

The house came to him by a blend of chance, coincidence and longing. During the summer of 1896 he rented a property outside Rye, explored the area by bicycle, liked it and liked the town. In particular, he liked Lamb House and its Garden Room, having already admired a water-colour of the latter in the London home of his architect friend Edward Warren. He determined to remain in the area and took a short lease on the Old Vicarage, adjacent to Rye church. He found he worked well in Rye, but the lease could not be extended beyond October 1896 and there seemed no question of Lamb House becoming available.

In September the following year he was staying on the Suffolk coast and was joined by Warren for a day's cycling. James enthused about Rye and Lamb House. He had already told his brother that he was 'tired of oscillating between bad lodgings and expensive hotels' and that he sought to 'put my hand on some lowly refuge of my own for which, from year to year, I thirst'. Rye was the perfect semi-rural retreat and it had the essential prerequisite for anyone as metropolitan as James: a good rail link to London (the journey time was about two hours, roughly

Bust of Henry James, by Derwent Wood, 1913

the same as now). When he returned from Suffolk to his London lodgings he found a letter from the Rye ironmonger – 'to whom I had whispered my hopeless passion' – informing him of the death of the owner of Lamb House and 'the preference (literal) of his son for Klondike'. (It was the time of the gold rush.) James secured first refusal and hurried down with Warren to survey the property. Warren pronounced it basically sound and James signed the twenty-one-year lease, which was well within his means but which nevertheless seemed to him an enormous step.

He was delighted. The obliging Warren oversaw the alterations, principally a matter of panelling, fire-surrounds and plumbing, and installed french doors opening from two ground-floor rooms to the garden, as well as a built-in bookcase. James attended to the furnishings: 'I am developing ... the most avid and gluttonous eye and the most infernal watching patience in respect of lurking "occasions" in not too-

217

delusive Chippendale and Sheraton . . .' He subsequently described his possessions as 'a handful of feeble relics'. There was also the question of some five thousand books to be removed from London.

He described himself as 'densely ignorant' of gardening and charmed a lady in neighbouring Winchelsea into advising and supervising George Gammon, the gardener he had inherited (and who was still working when E. F. Benson occupied the house in the 1930s). James never became an authority on gardens but he took a keen interest, and in the first novel he wrote at Lamb House, *The Awkward Age*, described both house and garden. Two years later, on the death of the unlucky Klondike adventurer, he bought the freehold. But before that he had nearly lost everything when a fire broke out:

The morning-room, looking into the hall, at Lamb House

218

I sat up late writing letters – in the Green Room – most unusually late by the blessing of providence, and towards 1.30 in the small hours of the morning, after an odour that had long puzzled me, found smoke coming up through the boards of the floor …

The beams beneath the fireplace had caught light. The fire brigade was prompt and effective and Warren was engaged to carry out substantial rebuilding of chimneys and fireplaces.

The Green Room, where Henry was working, is on the first floor at the rear of the house. It is still a sitting-room and study, though not open to the public. He composed in it during the winter months, and at other times used it mainly for reading and letter-writing. It adjoins a bedroom that became known as the King's Room after George I stayed for four nights in 1726, having been shipwrecked on nearby Camber Sands. During the first night Mrs Lamb gave birth to a son and James Lamb, ever mindful of family advantage, persuaded the king to be god-father.

The royal connection was renewed thirty years later when the king's grandson, the Duke of Cumberland, also stayed a night. Lamb lived to be host again on this occasion, despite an attempt on his life some years earlier. This occurred one wet night when, feeling unwell, he decided not to attend a dinner with one of his sons and asked his brother-in-law to go in his stead, lending him his cloak. Returning, drunkenly, through the churchyard some hours later, the unfortunate brother-in-law was attacked and stabbed by a local butcher called Breads, who had lain in wait and mistaken him for Lamb. (Breads had conceived a hatred of Lamb ever since being fined for giving short measure and had earlier gone about the town shouting, 'Butchers should kill Lambs.') Fatally wounded but without knowing it, the victim reached his house nearby and died sitting before his own fire, probably asleep and probably from loss of blood. Meanwhile, a few yards away in Lamb House, Lamb dreamt three times that his dead wife appeared to him and urged him to get up and go to her brother. When he eventually did so, accompanied by a servant, they found the apparently slumbrous body still in the fireside chair, a pool of blood beneath it.

Nearly two centuries later E. F. Benson, who had an interest in psychic phenomena, held a seance in the Garden Room during which the medium pointed to a chair, not knowing it was believed to be the one in which the victim had died, and described a man in a cloak. On another occasion Benson saw a ghost in the garden, witnessed also by the vicar, but James seems not to have seen any such visitations. He may, however, have had this aspect of Lamb House's history in mind when writing 'The Third Person', a story about two ageing spinster cousins living in a town called Marr, which is clearly Rye.

James worked hard most days. He had begun dictating his novels before moving to Rye but once there continued the method in earnest. He dictated to a typist, straight on to a machine, and had a series of amanuenses, chief amongst whom were a taciturn Scottish man called Macalpine, an obliging Miss Weld and the devoted and more literary Miss Bosanquet. He worked them hard. In three and a half years Miss Weld took down four novels, a biography and many articles and stories. Of the novels, James reckoned that *The Wings of the Dove* came easiest, with 194 days of dictation, while he worked on *The Golden Bowl* every morning for thirteen months. As already noted, summer sessions tended to be in the Garden Room, winter in the Green Room. He would pace up and down as he worked, smoking during the pauses; his amanuenses were permitted to smoke, knit, crochet or read. His long sentences and the click of the typewriter were familiar sounds in the quiet cobbled streets (then also grass-grown) around Lamb House.

Miss Weld, whose daughter still lives in Rye, said, 'He dictated beautifully. He had a melodious voice ... Typewriting for him was exactly like accompanying a singer on the piano.' His sentences 'seemed to spread out across the page like a beautiful architecture of this medieval town ...' Sometimes in the afternoons they would walk or cycle together and in the evenings he would make notes for the next day's work. Behind that 'brass-knockered façade' was a drive and a concentration of purpose that few of his neighbours guessed at.

Partly because he dictated, his later prose-style is more involved and diffuse than his earlier. His brother William, the psychologist, pointed out the disadvantages in an unanswered, and perhaps unanswerable, letter:

You know how opposed your whole 'third manner' of execution is to the literary ideals which animate my crude and Orson-like breast, mine being to say a thing in one sentence as straight and explicit as it can be made, and then to drop it forever; yours being to avoid naming it straight, but by dint of breathing and sighing all round and round it, to arouse in the reader who may have had a similar perception already (Heaven help him if he hasn't!) the illusion of a solid object, made (like the 'ghost' at the Polytechnic) wholly out of impalpable materials, air, and the prismatic inferences of light, ingeniously focussed by mirrors upon empty space. But you do it, that's the queerness! ...

But it's the rummest method for one to employ systematically as you do nowadays; and you employ it at your peril. In this crowded and hurried reading age, pages that require such close attention remain unread and neglected. You can't skip a word if you are to get the effect, and 19 out of 20 worthy readers grow intolerant. The method seems perverse: 'Say it *out*, for God's sake,' they cry, 'and have done with it.' And so I say now, give us *one* thing in your older directer manner, just to show that in spite of your paradoxical success in this unheard-of method, you *can* still write according to accepted canons. Give us that interlude; and then continue like the 'curiosity of literature' which you have become.

220

James acknowledged it to Theodora Bosanquet, who fled from typing the lengthy index to the Report of the Royal Commission on Coast Erosion to join him in 1907. In her brief memoir, *Henry James at Work*, she described how his sentences became increasingly like free, involved, unanswered talk. Also,

> His own speech, assisted by the practice of dictating, had by that time become so inveterately characteristic that his questions to a railway clerk about a ticket or to a fishmonger about a lobster might easily be recognized as coined in the same mint as his address to the Academic Committee of the Royal Society of Literature ...

He, on the other hand, believed that what he called his 'Remingtonese' gave more in freedom and expressiveness than it cost in concision. Indeed, he disliked composing to the music of any other make: 'During the fortnight when the Remington was out of order he dictated to an Oliver typewriter with evident discomfort, and he found it impossibly disconcerting to speak to something which made no responsive sound at all.'

Ford Madox Ford, his sometime Winchelsea neighbour, described dictation in progress. Not all of Ford's anecdotes are reliable, but the impressions he gives usually are:

> ... he could never let his phrases alone ... How often when waiting for him to go for a walk haven't I heard him say whilst dictating the finish of a phrase: 'No, No, Miss Dash ... – that is not clear ... Insert before "we all are" ... Let me see ... Yes, insert "not so much locally, though to be sure we're here; but temperamentally, in a manner of speaking".' So that the phrase, blinding clear to him by this time, when completed would run: 'So that here, not so much locally, though to be sure we're here, but at least temperamentally in a manner of speaking, we all are.'

There was also a domestic routine. He was looked after by a staff of four, all of whom lived on the top floor, plus the gardener, who lived out. When James arrived he was accompanied by the Smiths, a couple of drunkards who had been with him for twelve years and whom he put up with for another four before the 'domestic cyclone ... a whirlwind of but 48 hours' duration' compelled him to pay them off; their incapacity had become too public and too inconvenient. They were replaced by a cook-housekeeper called Mrs Paddington, whom he reckoned 'a pearl of price', and Burgess Noakes, a diminutive houseboy who became his faithful valet and was with him to the end (and also became bantamweight boxing champion of Sussex).

He seems to have been a good and generous employer, inspiring loyalty but perhaps too easily taken advantage of. One of Mrs Paddington's many virtues was that she saw to it that this happened no longer. There were, however, limits to his tolerance, one of which was his housemaid's dress. Catching sight of her in the street one day while dictating in the Garden Room, he interrupted himself to fulminate against the 'incongruous, incoherent shoddiness' of the lower class of Englishwoman, contrasting her with her French counterpart. It was one of his pet grievances.

He was quite frequently absent-minded, especially, it seems, during his constitutionals around the town (for which hat and stick were carefully chosen according to whom he intended to visit). His cook told the badly dressed housemaid how she had approached him in the High Street one day, 'but she could tell as she went towards him that he hadn't the faintest idea who she was, and that he was obviously racking his brain to place her; and that only after she had spoken to him did recognition appear'. There were other occasions when apparent strangers would arrive for lunch and he would move from cheerful incomprehension, through consternation to horror as he recalled having met and invited them some weeks before.

His favourite food was fish, particularly sole, and when there were no guests he would often walk about the house eating (he believed thorough chewing to be the answer to many ills). Although he had long since lost his American accent, he still wore an American civil war belt and cuff-links designed as miniature cannon. He drank sparingly. He was fond of dogs, generally small breeds such as dachshunds, and buried four in a corner of the garden. He was less fond of cats and once described how 'under the extreme provocation of its obscene caterwauling' he had killed one on the lawn: 'The act was followed by nausea and collapse.'

In appearance he was portly and imposing, though not tall. He had a domed brow, sensitive lips and piercing grey eyes. He could be cruel – 'He was too intent on his own particular aims to be lavishly sentimental over surrounding humanity,' observed Ford – but also perceptively and ingeniously kind. He was a good host, considerate and correct, and as a companion he was engaging and entertaining, if sometimes exasperating. Edith Wharton recalled his verbose and bewildering attempts to render navigational assistance to her chauffeur; also the games he made of local Kent and Sussex place-names, telling stories about such imaginary families as the Dymmes of Dymchurch, one of whom married a Sparkle and was the mother of little Scintilla Dymme-Sparkle.

His last years were spoiled by ill-health and he spent more time in London. He grew lonelier and the winters in Rye seemed more of a trial, though on his death-bed, in 1916, he apparently imagined he was back in Lamb House and spoke of his pleasure at being there.

After his death the house passed to his nephew, Henry James, Jnr, who let it. The lease came eventually to E. F. and A. C. Benson, and both brothers did much of their later work there. It was whilst in Lamb House that E. F. Benson conceived and wrote the 'Miss Mapp' and the 'Lucia' novels. A few months after he died, the

Garden Room received a direct hit from a German bomb, destroying it utterly and with it Henry's pictures and over two hundred of his books, many of them presentation copies. The house itself was damaged badly enough to be uninhabitable until after the war. When Henry James, Jnr, died in 1948, his widow generously presented it to the National Trust. The contents, including most of James's furniture and books, were unfortunately sold at public auction.

Now fully restored by the National Trust, Lamb House and its garden are open two afternoons a week in the summer. Three of the ground-floor rooms are on view, along with the hall and staircase. There is a certain amount of James memorabilia, and the garden is as peaceful and pleasant as he described it.

The house has retained its 'essential amiability' and its 'refuge' quality. The cobbled street is still quiet, if no longer grass-grown, the view of the church is the same, the great brass knocker still functions as a latch (a device that always pleased James) and the high red-brick façade still calms, concentrates, protects and stimulates.

SAMUEL JOHNSON

BIRTHPLACE MUSEUM, LICHFIELD, STAFFORDSHIRE
17 GOUGH SQUARE, LONDON EC4

────────

JOHN WAIN

Samuel Johnson, during the seventy-five years of his life, occupied a fair number of houses. But the two he lived in the longest, and where the most crucial things happened to him, are both still standing, both carefully maintained, and both open to the public. They are the birthplace in Breadmarket Street, Lichfield, and the London house in Gough Square, off Fleet Street, where he compiled the dictionary that established his fame.

There is a certain similarity between the two houses – large, solid buildings dating from the early eighteenth century; commodious because they had to serve as places of work as well as of residence; dignified, ample and well proportioned. Visiting them, however, offers contrasting experiences. The London house is the richer in what it contains – pictures, furniture, objects. The Lichfield house, while putting on a brave show, inevitably lags behind in these matters. Once outside the four walls, however – before entering and after leaving – the advantage is all the other way. Modern Fleet Street contains nothing to remind you of Johnson. Its all-pervading ugliness and noise can only get in the way when one tries to think oneself back into his world. In Lichfield, not only the house but the entire neighbourhood is calm, spacious and rich in history.

Both houses belong to the years of effort and struggle, before Johnson's life emerged into comparative ease. The moment of transformation came suddenly, with the award of his pension in July 1762. It came (almost) out of the blue, with no anxious period of waiting, and it changed everything. Before it, Johnson's life was one of relentless work, meeting deadline after deadline, never earning enough to put by any savings, always with the pavement waiting for him if he fell behind through illness or weakness of any kind. After it, he became understandably reluctant to put pen to paper, preferring to share his wisdom and learning with other people in hours of relaxed and infinitely memorable talk.

Lichfield Cathedral seen across Minster Pool

Less than a year after the award of his pension, Johnson met James Boswell, whose temperament and gifts made him entirely suited to the mission of attaching himself to some major figure and conveying in words the flavour of his mind and personality to a wider circle of people – a circle that went on widening, indeed, until it gathered in virtually the entire civilized world. But even Boswell can only give us half the picture. He never knew Johnson during the years of trial, only in the years of acclaim. And both the houses we can visit today belong to that first period. Boswell never visited him in either.

Johnson left Lichfield for London in 1737, at the age of twenty-eight, to try his luck as an author. They were lean years in that profession. If a writer wanted to eat every day he had to write every day, and get someone to buy what he wrote. No wonder that Johnson did not see Lichfield again for a quarter of a century. The cost of travel, plus the time away from his desk, were doubtless enough, taken together, to keep him in London. There are, however, other, more shadowy, considerations that would have to be faced if we were concerned here with Johnson's psychology rather than his dwellings. His poverty was worst in the early days; after about ten years it had probably eased enough to make it possible for him, if he had really tried, to get down to Lichfield for a day or two. In 1754 he spent some weeks in Oxford, doing research for the dictionary; from there to Lichfield, by the route he would have taken, is seventy-eight miles, an unhurried journey of a couple of summer days. But by that time it was so many years since he had visited his widowed mother that he had probably built up a huge backlog of guilt about her and needed to hypnotize himself into the belief that it simply wouldn't have been possible. She died in 1759; later that same year he spent at least seven weeks in Oxford, again without going on to Lichfield; finally, in the early weeks of 1761, the long-deferred homecoming took place.

For whatever reasons, then, Johnson did not visit Lichfield for nearly twenty-five years, and if the obstacles that kept him away were partly psychological in nature, they were effective obstacles nevertheless. For all that time, the three graceful spires of the cathedral, the quiet streets still laid out in their medieval pattern, the wide pools, Stowe and Minster, calmly reflecting the changing Midland sky, and the green meadows surrounding the town, saw nothing of him; nor did the bookshop where he had grown up, nor the church where his parents and his only brother were buried, nor the handsome house in the cathedral close, the Bishop's Palace no less, where he had enjoyed evenings of good talk and mind-stretching disputation with his friend of an older generation, Gilbert Walmsley, whose encouragement he remembered all his life. That he thought of these things during the long years of drudgery is certain, and equally certain that he thought of them with affection and sometimes with longing. There is a touching little piece of evidence for this in the great dictionary itself. One day, slogging away as usual in his study at Gough

226

Bust of Dr Johnson, by Joseph Nollekens, 1777

Square, he arrived at the word 'lich' (nowadays more usually spelt 'lych', and in any case only found in compounds such as 'lychgate'). Having correctly given its derivation from Anglo-Saxon, Johnson defines it as 'A dead carcase; whence *lichwake*, the time or act of watching by the dead; *lichgate*, the gate through which the dead are carried to the grave'. That, one would have thought, would do as a definition; the word is now perfectly clear, and illustrated twice over: it must have been a sudden tug of local patriotism that made Johnson add, '*Lichfield*, the field of the dead, a city in Staffordshire, so named for martyred Christians'. And then, doubtless with the ink still wet on the pen in his hand, he went on to add, impulsively, three more words, '*Salve magna parens*', hail, great parent.

Johnson in his maturity was one of the most celebrated men in England; respected by the populace in general (to whom he was 'Dictionary Johnson'), by the scholars at the universities, by the lawyers at the Inns of Court, by members of the aristocracy in so far as they were literate enough, and by King George III, who allowed him to read in the library at St James's Palace and gave instructions that he was always to be told when Dr Johnson was there so that he might go and have a few words with him. Johnson was in fact philosopher and sage to the nation. But his social background – his original background, in the early Lichfield days – was interestingly mixed. His father came from the working class, the son of a farm labourer. His mother was from a family, the Fords, who owned land in the county and had connections with the Midland gentry and even the minor aristocracy. (When Johnson had his famous clash with the Earl of Chesterfield, neither man realized that the other was his distant relative.) His social position was, in a sense, ambiguous, misty. But it is hardly a conventional case of poor-boy-makes-good.

Clearly, Michael Johnson, at the outset of his trading career, did not intend to be a poor man. He expected to do well. He knew he was able and energetic, he had solid achievements behind him which had already brought him from the world of field labour to the world of bookselling – he was a competent Latin scholar, for

The bookshop in Johnson's birthplace

228

instance – and he was not afraid of spending money on a good address and a good stock. In 1706 he had purchased the entire library of the Earl of Derby, an ambitious venture for a man with his business still to establish. In fact what happened thereafter was the old story. Michael Johnson had expanded too fast, borrowed too much money, and never quite got on top of things. As his son put it in a private memorandum of his early life, written in middle age (*Annals*, probably early 1770s), 'My father, having in the early part of his life contracted debts, never had trade sufficient to enable him to pay them, and maintain his family; he got something, but not enough.' He tried everything; he rode hundreds of miles round the county obtaining orders from the local gentry and clergy; he ran market stalls in two local towns; he had a factory outside the town, on the fringe of Stowe Pool, where he manufactured parchment and vellum; his shop on the ground floor of the house stocked stationery, ribbons, paints and patent medicines as well as books. It was all not quite enough. The business slid steadily downhill, until in 1731 we read that the Conduit Lands Trust, a charitable fund which still exists in Lichfield, granted Michael £10 as 'a decayed tradesman'. He had once been one of the administrators of this Trust, and indeed he continued to be active in municipal affairs, and to have the respect of his fellow townsmen, all through his long decline. He died before the end of the same year in which he received the £10. Perhaps having to accept charity from his neighbours was the final blow to an exhausted spirit.

All this, however, was far in the future, and unguessable, in the year when Michael proudly built the fine house and made room in it for the stock of the bookshop and for his wife and servants; the following year, for a son, and three years later another son, Nathaniel. In those early days there was still bustle, and stir, and optimism. In the year of Sam's birth, Michael was elected sheriff, a position of honour in the town, and he celebrated by entertaining lavishly. In his early formative years, Samuel would have no sense of coming from an under-privileged household. Michael, a tradesman of obscure origins, could give his family no aristocratic aura of romantic snobbery. But the family were decent, respectable, solid people rooted among neighbours who were the same. Johnson's background, in fine, is very much the same as Shakespeare's.

And now, after that long but necessary preamble, we are ready for the house. Until 1909 it was a private house; it was then bought by the City of Lichfield, who opened it as a museum. Under the able and knowledgeable guidance of its curator, Dr Graham Nicholls, the house has been refurbished in recent years. The bookshop on the ground floor has been handed over to independent management ('franchised' is, I believe, the expression) so that one can combine a visit to the house with a browse through an ample stock of second-hand volumes, never a bad thing.

Other features of the new styling will strike different people differently, depending on how far they go along with the late twentieth-century fashion for explicit visual and aural presentation. The basement kitchen, for instance. Johnson in middle life recalled that his childish reading of the ghost scenes in *Hamlet* made him so nervous that he suddenly ran up the stairs to the street door 'that he might have people about him'. From this we deduce that he was reading the play in the daytime, since an eerie empty street, in darkness, would have made his imaginative dread all the worse. It is a touching detail, and easily enough imaginable; all the more easily when one is in the house and sees the cavernous kitchen, the short flight of stairs, the street door opening on the market-place. But go into the kitchen nowadays and you find a mock-up of an eighteenth-century kitchen (fair enough), with stage lighting to give the glow of firelight (fairish enough), a clutter of dirty plates on the table (why? They had domestic servants), a waxwork figure of a child in a nightgown sitting reading by the fire (oh, no!) and a tape-recorder grinding out some actor's reading (presumably) of the ghost's speech beginning 'I am thy father's spirit'. One doesn't wish to be hypercritical, and it may be that the school parties like it; but people capable of using their own imagination, of whom there are still some left in the world, will find that wonderful faculty no use to them here, disabled by all the paraphernalia.

Going up the stairs, we find another mock-up, showing Michael Johnson's work-room or office; innocuous, this one, and, given Dr Nicholls's careful scholarship, doubtless situated exactly where Michael had it. Anyone interested in grasping the range of Johnson's experience should pause to recall, while in this room, that after Michael's death there was a period of some three years in which the business was run by the widow and the two sons, Samuel and Nathaniel. During these years, however reluctantly, Sam Johnson must have learnt more or less everything about how to run a small business. Perhaps it was at this time that he acquired the slightly disillusioned view of commerce that led him to remark, many years later, to Hester Thrale, 'Trade could not be managed by those who manage it, if it were difficult.' The business did not prosper, but at least it never went under; Sarah Johnson continued to run it till the end of her life, and after that it was carried on by Lucy Porter, Johnson's step-daughter.

Nathaniel, sadly, disappears from the story. Perhaps the shop did not yield enough profit to support a young man as well as two unambitious women. He drifted away, tried to establish himself in various trades, vaguely contemplated emigrating to America, and died at twenty-four. He is the forgotten man of Johnson studies.

The remaining rooms are all frankly exhibition spaces, with show-cases and framed prints. In one there is a thirteen-minute video, 'In His Native Place', informatively written and engagingly spoken by Dr Nicholls.

Speaking as one who has been familiar with the house since childhood (and my first visits there must have been half a century ago), what most delighted me about the new styling of the place was the fact that the two rooms on the topmost floor, which hitherto had never been open to the public, are now accessible. (Doubtless they had previously been used as store-rooms or something of the sort.) Now, going up to the top floor, one is greeted by a magnificent roof-top view of Lichfield. They are poky little rooms – servants' bedrooms, for a certainty, into which Sam and Nat would go only by rare invitation or, with the mischievousness of children, on explorations into forbidden territory while the occupants were elsewhere. But from one of them, the one facing north-west, there is a striking view of the cathedral, which fairly bursts on the sight as one enters, stately, venerable, and breathtakingly close at hand. To sit in that room and look across at the cathedral on a calm summer evening must be as conducive to deep thoughts on spiritual matters as a gentle walk around the close itself. No wonder that this house saw the growing-up of a passionate defender of the Church of England, staunchly orthodox, suspicious of Methodists and other innovators in religion.

Johnson in boyhood was not an example of religious devotion. He found his bad eyesight a handicap in moving about the church, and when his parents sent him to the service on Sunday mornings he would go and walk in the fields instead, allowing it to be supposed when he got home that he had attended worship. This backsliding continued until in later boyhood he became virtually a sceptic – as he put it later, 'a sort of lax talker against religion' – until, while still in his teens, he was converted by reading William Law's *Serious Call to a Devout and Holy Life*, a book that has made many converts beside Johnson. But all the time the great cathedral was doing its work. Whatever may have happened to the top layer of Johnson's mind, his sensibility and his emotions were profoundly influenced by that solemn brooding structure, its main outlines established in the fourteenth century though its foundation was in the eighth, lifting its three spires to that heaven to whose authority it bore witness – and visible from a window in his own dwelling.

One doesn't, of course, want to make the naïve suggestion that Johnson's mature political and social opinions can be deduced from the fact that as a child he could see Lichfield Cathedral from an upper window at home – just like that. But it seems fair to give this consideration its weight among the others. Johnson admitted to Boswell that he would 'stand before a battery of cannon to restore Convocation to its full powers'. (Convocation, the governing body of the Church of England, had been shorn of some of its authority because the Hanoverian regime distrusted what were taken to be its Jacobite elements. That is a simplification, but not a very gross one.) On another occasion, speaking of a strange character named George Psalmanazar, who among his other exploits had perpetrated a series of monstrous and entirely successful hoaxes, Johnson remarked that in the days when he knew Psalmanazar his wild antics were long outlived and he had become a thoughtful and pious, almost saintly, character. He never, Johnson affirmed, interrupted when Psalmanazar was speaking: 'I would as soon have thought of interrupting a bishop.' Interrupting a bishop was the example that came most readily to his tongue to describe an unpardonable lapse from correct behaviour. We may surely conclude that not only the cathedral, but the cathedral clergy, and indeed the whole Church, gained in respectful and reverent submission from the pattern laid down early in Johnson's mind. Throughout his life, anyone who spoke disrespectfully of the Church of England was certain of a rebuff. Once, in the Hebrides, he and Boswell met a Presbyterian minister whose low opinion of the Anglican Church came out in scoffing remarks about 'fat bishops and drowsy deans'. 'Sir,' said Johnson, 'you know no more of our Church than a Hottentot.' The predictable response was part of a total position on Johnson's part. By sneering at the Church dignitaries, the rustic minister was lining himself up with the Roundhead soldiers who had smashed the images from the cathedral walls.

The English Puritan movement of the seventeenth century was not only anti-ecclesiastical but revolutionary in general. Johnson was too pragmatic to accept the notion of revolution, with its tendency to empty out the baby with the bath-water. Hence his disapproval of Cromwell, and incidentally also of Milton, whose work is the supreme literary expression of the Puritan ideal. (On reading Johnson's *Life of Milton*, the poet Cowper exclaimed in a rage, 'I could thrash his old jacket till his pension jingled in his pocket!') Here again we may see the marks of childhood impressions. The Civil War of the 1640s raged with particular fury in the Midlands. Lichfield was the only cathedral damaged in that war, and the damage was terrible. It was left completely ruined. Built on a lump of rock and surrounded by water, it was a natural point for fortification, and it was taken and retaken three times, each time with colossal damage. During their spells of occupation of the building, the Puritan soldiers, in accordance with their belief that such things were idolatrous, disfigured and smashed as many of the statues and images as were within their reach.

Those ravages, and the destruction of houses and walls, were of course made good in the sixty years between the Civil War and the birth of Sam Johnson. But there were many visible remains, and many tales handed down from grandparents. Lichfield was not alone in this. In Victorian Oxford, for instance, Civil War earthworks were still plainly evident in the area that is now North Oxford and Summertown. T. S. Eliot remarked in 1947, speaking of the English Civil War, that he doubted whether it had ended. Certainly when Sam Johnson was growing up in Lichfield it had not ended. Many people felt that the Hanoverian settlement was the product of an exhausted lull rather than a decisive victory. If they were Jacobites, they openly wished to see the Stuarts back on the English throne. Johnson, who valued political stability too much to be a Jacobite and encourage actual

17 Gough Square, London EC4

insurrection, was nevertheless far from being unsympathetic to their feelings. He
described the Master of his Oxford college, Dr Panting, as 'a fine Jacobite fellow'.
Sooner a Jacobite than a latter-day Cromwellite!

Turning now to 17 Gough Square; it is reached by a narrow footway leading

233

The attic in Gough Square, where the dictionary was compiled

off Fleet Street, on the left as you go towards St Paul's. Sir John Hawkins, an acquaintance and early biographer, said that Johnson tended to find his habitations in 'the courts and alleys about Fleet Street', and it is true that this area still has a maze of narrow streets and walkways that open out into small squares or afford glimpses into 'courts'. But it is only the grouping of the buildings, not their nature, that retains any traditional flavour. The handbill put out by the trustees of Johnson's house calls this area 'a legacy of old London worthy of exploration'. I am afraid this handbill will have to be redesigned and that sentence taken out. The unrelieved hideousness of the buildings that have been shoved up in every available space in the 1970s and 1980s has made nonsense of any talk of legacies and explorations. Johnson's fame has protected No. 17 from the developers, and this is his last and best gift to the city he lived in. One fine building is better than none.

Once inside, everything is a delight, starting with the heavy but beautiful, because plain and well-made, chain that secures the door itself – made, we learn, by women iron-workers in Cradeley Heath. Cradeley Heath is a town in south Staffordshire, in that belt of the county associated during Johnson's later life and throughout the next century with the iron-working trades. There is food for meditation in this chain, for these must have been skilful workers. What would Johnson have said if he had seen women forging white-hot iron? Would he have said, as he once sportively said about the sight of a woman preaching, that the interest lay not in whether it was well done, but in the novelty of its being done at all? Or would he have said, in one of his bursts of local patriotism, that the women of Staffordshire work better, even at a man's trade, than the men of any other county?

The house has two rooms on each landing, and we mount by a handsome staircase, still in its original condition. Each room has its portraits of people important in Johnson's life – Boswell, Mrs Thrale, Reynolds, Goldsmith, all the way down to fringe characters like his Italian friend Giuseppe Baretti – and its display cases.

Johnson enjoyed the long friendship of Sir Joshua Reynolds, who painted numerous portraits of him, copies of many of which are to be seen here. Reynolds was often unfortunate in his choice of technical ways and means, in particular the mixing of materials with different rates of drying and the choice of non-durable pigments (cf. P. and L. Murray, *The Penguin Dictionary of Art and Artists*, 1968: 'The faces of his sitters are often deathly pale because the carmine has faded out completely'). The evocative portrait of Anna Williams in one of the upper rooms, not by Sir Joshua but by his sister Frances, sadly exemplifies this; Miss Williams was doubtless pale, but not as pale as that.

After three floors and six rooms, one arrives at the top floor and beholds with reverence (if one has any inkling of the stupendous nature of that achievement) the attic, running the width of the house and with plenty of light from ample windows, where the eight years' labour was performed that made him 'Dictionary Johnson' and steadied the English language for a hundred years, settling definitions and usages at a time when English was just becoming a world-wide language, and therefore benefiting not only the inhabitants of these islands but millions of people in places Johnson would never see or hear about. Here, at stand-up desks (for the place was 'fitted up like a counting-house'), his six assistants, five Scotsmen and one Englishman (but not, one gathers, all at the same time, some coming and some going during the long march of the enterprise), toiled at transcribing, cutting and pasting, copying out the words Johnson had underlined and the definitions he had arrived at, preparing the vast work to go to the printer sheet by sheet.

The labour, which no one nowadays would dream of undertaking single-handed, was long and the burden heavy. Our own common sense would tell us that; we also have the testimony of Johnson's noble Preface. Most of this is concerned with the ordinary business of prefaces, to introduce the book to the public who will be using it, to explain its scope and its principles; but Johnson does not shrink from mentioning the human price that has had to be paid. He had slogged on through a dark valley of fatigue, ill-health, disappointment and bereavement. Assistance that he might reasonably have looked for had not been forthcoming; the immensely wealthy Earl of Chesterfield, who allowed it to be understood that he would act as patron of the work (i.e., help Johnson out with hard cash), in the end did nothing of the sort. In the sixth year of his labour his wife died; his friend Gilbert Walmsley, back home in Lichfield, had died the year before. He must have realized, sadly, that if his work should be crowned with success, the original circle who had given him support and love would not be there to share in it and to see their judgement vindicated. When he thought of this, he felt surly, defiant. He knew he had done his best; let the world take it as they would; since their praise would come too late now, he cared nothing for their dispraise. Some passages in the Preface read like the throwing down of a gauntlet.

> In this work, when it is found that much is omitted, let it not be forgotten that much likewise is performed; and though no book was ever spared out of tenderness to the authour, and the world is little solicitous to know whence proceeded the faults of that which it condemns; yet it may gratify curiosity to inform it, that the *English Dictionary* was written with little assistance of the learned, and without any patronage of the great; not in the soft obscurities of retirement, or under the shelter of academick bowers, but amidst inconvenience and distraction, in sickness and in sorrow.

In the same spirit he wrote to Lord Chesterfield, who once the work was complete was eager to jump on the bandwagon of its fame, that he had done without His Lordship then and could do without him now.

> The notice which you have been pleased to take of my labours, had it been early, had been kind; but it has been delayed till I am indifferent and cannot enjoy it, till I am solitary and cannot impart it, till I am known and do not want it ... Having carried on my work thus far with so little obligation to any favourer of learning, I should not be disappointed though I should conclude it, if less be possible, with less.

At last, after slightly more than ten years in this house, Johnson, in the spring of 1759, decided to move on. (The place was, of course, rented, not owned, as

Michael Johnson owned the birthplace. Samuel Johnson never did own a house.) 17 Gough Square had served its purpose. As well as the dictionary, it had seen the composition of his bi-weekly series of essays, *The Rambler*, austere and deliberate lay sermons on ethical questions and the conduct of life, which sold slowly in periodical form but, when collected into volumes, sold and sold for a hundred years and remain a memorable contribution to the literature of wisdom. In this big, bare house (for whatever it is like now, it was very bare in his time), he mourned the death of his 'Tetty'; he gave a permanent home to her friend Anna Williams, the cultivated and intelligent but sharp-tongued Welsh lady reduced to blindness by an unsuccessful operation for a cataract; he took into his service the Jamaican lad Frank Barber, who served him (desultorily, it has to be said) for the rest of his life and finally became the chief beneficiary of his will; wrote his immortal letter to Lord Chesterfield; embarked on his monumental edition of Shakespeare. Anyone who has seen these two houses, here and at Lichfield, and perhaps called in at Pembroke College, Oxford, on the way from one to the other, has seen the physical setting of the pre-Boswell Johnson, the Johnson we cannot see in the beautifully managed and brilliantly lit theatre of Boswell's *Life*, but must try to imagine for ourselves.

JAMES JOYCE

JAMES JOYCE TOWER, SANDYCOVE, DUBLIN

―――――

ANTHONY CRONIN

The facts of Joyce's stay in the tower now so firmly associated with his name are rather surprising; and they remind us, among other things, that he was a writer of imaginative fictions, not a historian or autobiographer. They also tell us something about the sort of fictions he was interested in creating.

To begin with, he was not there on what is now called Bloomsday, 16 June 1904. True, 16 June 1904 was a memorable day in the life of James Joyce, but he did not wake up in the tower at Sandycove, nor hear Oliver St John Gogarty chanting 'Introibo ad altare Dei' to the sunlit waters of Dublin Bay on that date.

On most mornings in June he woke up in the large room he had rented on the first or upper floor of 60 Shelbourne Road, a very typical Dublin lower-middle-class house in a terrace of identical houses in Ballsbridge. It was owned by a family called McKernan, who had advertised for a lodger and had got the greatest writer of the twentieth century. For a few weeks after moving in the individual in question taught in a private school which was conducted in Dalkey by a Mr Francis Irwin, who was to become Mr Deasy in *Ulysses*, but he had hopes of earning his living as a professional singer, so he had hired a piano. However, to avoid tipping the delivery men he absented himself from the house on the morning it was to arrive; and his little stratagem misfired, for the men, finding no one in to receive it, took the piano away with them again.

Prior to renting the room in Shelbourne Road he had been living – staying is perhaps a better word – in the house his father occupied at 7 St Peter's Terrace (now 5 St Peter's Road), Phibsborough, described by Stanislaus as 'the house of the bare table'. This is a familiar type of red-brick, Dublin north-side house, with a little garden in front and a bow window on the ground floor. From the outside such houses seem the acme of respectability, but inside in 1904 the reality was otherwise.

The Martello tower, Sandycove, Dublin

239

It was the fifteenth house John Joyce had occupied since his marriage twenty-four years before. Social mobility, like much else that we think peculiar to our time, is not a new phenomenon; and it was the fourteenth house in which his son had been able to observe him with that mixture of amused fascination, objective scorn and filial love which was eventually to result in the portrait of Simon Dedalus in his work.

John Joyce's long-suffering wife had died the year before and this had accelerated his grandiloquent progress along the downward path. Most of the furniture had been sold or pawned and part of the stair banisters had been burned for firewood. When he was drunk (which according to his second son, Stanislaus, was on 3.97 days of every week) he terrorized his six daughters if not his three sons. When he was sober and penniless his irate presence spread gloom at the kitchen table. And of course they all, including James, were still suffering from the shock of May Joyce's death.

Nevertheless, throughout these months James was working. The later poems in *Chamber Music* belong, for what they are worth, to 1904; he had begun an extended narrative essay called 'A Portrait of the Artist' which, after intermediate transmogrification into *Stephen Hero*, would eventually become *A Portrait of the Artist as a Young Man*. And, in response to AE's (George Russell's) urgings he would write three of the stories of *Dubliners* ('The Sisters', 'Eveline' and 'After the Race') before the year was out. In all the abodes he fetched up in, this necessarily hole and corner activity must be assumed to have continued.

There is, however, an extraordinary contrast between the poems he was still writing and the prose he would have written before the year's end. 1904 was an important year for James Joyce in several respects, but not least because in that year he began to find his true subject matter. Up to this point he had been writing only the sort of poetry which George Moore, when he was shown it in the National Library by AE, had rightly dismissed as being derived from Arthur Symons.

Joyce did not believe that poetry could encompass ordinary living. On one side was 'life' in all its sordidness, the life of St Peter's Terrace, the life he was leading himself; and on the other was 'beauty', something to which poetry might attain. According to Stanislaus the poems he had been writing up to this time were 'evidence of the struggle to keep the spirit within him alive in the midst of the all pervading squalor and disintegration' which he saw everywhere in Dublin; they were an 'attempt to seize the elusive eucharistic moments in life and express them in songs for his own relief and comfort'. The result is apparent in *Chamber Music*: a vague, cloudy poetry, burdened with an inchoate romantic yearning. He told Padraic Colum around this time that poetry was 'a simple liberation of rhythm'; the liberation unfortunately had to be attained at the expense of almost everything else: circumstantial detail, exactness of imagery, even syntax, even meaning.

The *Dubliners* stories are a different matter. Here for the first time is the life that was all around him and that he really knew, the life of hopeless people trapped in hopeless circumstances, with, as in the case of the young man in 'After the Race', its brief gleams of an escape which nobody had the strength or determination to effect.

Because he believed that the life of the soul was separate from all this he was still writing poems like 'From dewy dreams my soul arise ...', apparently composed in Shelbourne Terrace that summer. In time he would realize that it was a mistake to think that there were two kinds of experience: 'squalor and insincerity' on the one hand, 'beauty' on the other; and the wonderful intertwined epic of his life and work was an acknowledgement of this mistake. There was not a separable beauty. There was not an escape from the everyday life one had to live into some sort of

7 St Peter's Terrace (now 5 St Peter's Road), where Joyce lived with his father for part of 1904

ideal life where the soul would triumph over circumstance. There was not something outside the ordinary conditions of living for which it was in any way admirable or poetic to yearn. As Stephen Hero would say: to believe so is 'the starkest of pessimisms'.

There was only life. Interwoven with life there was courage, humour, compassion, tenacity, will, even love and honour. Indivisible from the rest of life were visions and wonders enough, but they were surrounded and coloured, if never finally discredited, by the 'squalor and insincerity' which he would not only explore but which would prove to have, like Rembrandt's flayed ox, its own sort of beauty.

To embody all this he needed an inclusive art. So he took to prose; and after 1904 there would be only brief returns to poetry. A poet is tempted to say that he fell back on prose, but this would not be true either. For the great thing about Joyce is that if he did not know or did not care whether the 'squalor and insincerity' could be expressed in poetry, he certainly believed and was amply to prove that all of life, including its poetry, could be put into prose.

But this was in the future. In the meantime, as well as working, he spent a lot of time in the pubs and a lot of ingenuity cadging money from various sources, including people he despised. He stayed in bed till four o'clock in the afternoon. He staggered off to Dublin's notorious brothel quarter with his boon companions when he or they could afford it. According to Stanislaus's sharp-eyed account of things he was drunk almost as often as his father was in St Peter's Terrace; and in March he had occasion to ask Oliver St John Gogarty's advice about finding a doctor for a venereal complaint.

The break came when John Joyce sold the piano on which James and his mother had so often played. In retrospect the wonder is that the instrument had lasted so long, but in any case James walked out and took the room in Shelbourne Road. This was not entirely a sentimental gesture, nor was the attempt to install a piano in his new lodgings a piece of wilful extravagance. He really did have ambitions to be a professional singer and he borrowed some money from his acquaintances to pay for lessons from Benedetto Palmieri, reputed to be the best teacher in Dublin. He got occasional concert engagements and in May he competed in a Feis Ceoil, a competition in which the great John McCormack won the first prize. It is virtually certain that Joyce himself would have won it except that after singing his two set pieces, Sullivan's 'The Prodigal Son' and an Irish air arranged by Moffat, he refused to sing the required third piece at sight and walked off the platform. Years later his sister Eileen was to explain to the present writer the difference between his voice and McCormack's. 'John McCormack,' she said, 'had a wonderful voice, but Jim's voice would break your heart.'

He told his friends that singing at sight was unworthy of an artist, but the truth is that he had never learned to read music for the voice and so could not attempt the piece. If he had, he would undoubtedly have found backers to pay for his training, as they paid for McCormack's. If the career which would then have opened out before him had been anything like that of his great rival, it is difficult to see how he could have combined it with the sort of dedication he gave to the art of words. 1904 was certainly a year of decision in more than one respect.

But the most important event of his non-literary life was still before him. Since his schooldays he had been a little in love – perhaps more than a little – with Mary Sheehy, the prettiest of the four daughters of David Sheehy, a Member of Parliament who welcomed supposedly suitable young men to his Georgian house in Belvedere Place on the second Sunday of each month. The formalities of the time, added to the middle-class status of the beloved and the temperament of the poet, ensured that this love was unexpressed except in very vague, fugitive poems which Mary probably never saw and which of course did not name their object. To declare anything for such a girl would have been half-way to entering into a contract of marriage. So, though Mary may have wondered sometimes, she probably never knew. And of course in any discussion of Joyce's dichotomies, let alone those of the human heart generally, one must remember that at the same time as he was writing such lyrics as the one beginning

> Go seek her out all courteously
>   And say I come,
> Wind of spices whose song is ever
>   Epithalamium.
> O, hurry over the dark lands
>   And run upon the sea
> For seas and lands shall not divide us
>   My love and me . . .

the youthful poet was a regular visitor to the stews of Tyrone Street.

However, on 10 June 1904 Mary Sheehy vanished from Joyce's literary consciousness for the time being – though she would recapture some of the lost ground in the closing pages of *A Portrait* – for on that date, as he was walking along Nassau Street, he met another young woman. Her name was Nora Barnacle. She was a working girl, a maid in the adjacent humble establishment known as Finn's Hotel, and she had come to Dublin from Galway, the daughter of a drunken baker who had separated from her mother. As Mary Sheehy would never have, Nora proved amenable to being accosted in the street by a young man wearing a yachting cap and tennis shoes. He was twenty-two. She was nineteen.

There is of course a touch of Tony Lumpkin about Joyce's behaviour here, for the hero of Goldsmith's comedy is also more at ease with women of inferior social station. Anyway, he did well enough in that first conversation for Nora to make an assignation with him. They were to meet in front of Sir William Wilde's house at the corner of Merrion Square four days later. It was visible from where they stood, so it would have been easy for this brash young man to point authoritatively to it; but in the event she did not turn up.

On the 15th he wrote to her asking with some humility for a new appointment and on 16 June, afterwards a sacred date for James Joyce, they met. The mechanics of how she transmitted her reply are obscure, but the fact that she was able to do so and that they did meet raises a difficulty. His note is sent from 60 Shelbourne Road; but it would appear that on the very day he wrote it Joyce, who was very much in arrears with his rent, decided that he could no longer face his landlord and left, spending the evening of the 15th and subsequent days at the house of a theosophistic poet called James H. Cousins, whose musical wife had offered him the use of her piano. The Cousins lived at 35 Strand Road. Ellmann described this as a tiny house and said it was in Ballsbridge; but neither of these statements is true. Like most of the houses in Strand Road, 35 is quite substantial and Strand Road is in Sandymount.

The progress of Joyce's courtship of Nora has been chronicled several times, though Ellmann's account is incomplete in some important respects. Nora's biographer, Brenda Maddox, thinks she may have been involved in 'a mild form of soliciting' when she met his glance in Nassau Street, adding rather unkindly that 'if Nora was intending to exchange sexual favours for money, she had the wrong man'. Joyce was 'a genius of a scrounge'; and: 'It was more likely that he took money from her.' What this leaves out of account is that Nora had come to Dublin from the less commercial Galway, where a form of the *paseo* was a recognized way for young people to get acquainted. When she met him she was certainly lonely and glad to be accosted. On that first evening's rendezvous they walked to Ringsend, where, probably by the bank of the Dodder, she granted him the same sexual favour that Molly was to grant to both Lieutenant Mulvey and Leopold Bloom, suddenly slipping her hand inside his trousers to do so, while, as he was to put it in his famous 1909 letter, 'all the time bending over me and gazing at me out of your quiet saintlike eyes'. It was the first important sexual contact he had had with any woman not a whore, and in *Ulysses* it was commemorated twice. Bloom remembers Molly on Howth Head: 'Cool soft with ointments her hand touched me, caressed: her eyes upon me did not turn away.' Molly remembers the first time, with Lieutenant Mulvey in Gibraltar: '... O yes I pulled him off into my handkerchief pretending not to be excited ...' This double commemoration is important. As Joyce thought the matter over he unworthily concluded that if Nora had been so free with him in Dublin, she must have been just as free with some chap over in Galway. The saving grace, as often, is in art and in the irony with which he puts his typically male reaction into his book.

244

James Joyce, 1904

Unfortunately for romantics, in the immediate aftermath of 16 June his way of life did not change. On the 20th of the month he was so drunk at a gathering of the National Literary Society, a body which Yeats had founded and an important nub of literary Dublin, that the ladies had to step over him in a corridor as they left. The following night he accosted another young lady in Stephen's Green and was beaten up by her escort. Although abandoned by his friend Vincent Cosgrave, subsequently the model for Lynch in *A Portrait*, he was cleaned up and taken home by a man called Alfred Hunter, reputed in Dublin to be Jewish. This act of non-Christian charity was to be given its due importance in *Ulysses* also.

Home was still the Cousins's vegetarian household in Sandymount, but within a few days he was back in 60 Shelbourne Road, having been poisoned, he said, by 'a typhoid turnip'; and presumably now able to discharge the arrears of rent.

It was from here that his notes to Nora during the succeeding weeks were addressed. Her impulsive generosity of the first night was not repeated and he finds it necessary to reassure her about her boldness while urging her to be bolder still, rashly gives her his views on the Catholic Church and even more recklessly regales her with an account of his sexual life before their meeting. He will not use the word love – though she soon does – and being, as we know, a master of literary resource, he does well enough without it, quoting verses by Yeats and Henry VIII, both, as Stan Gebler Davies says, 'gentlemen who had trouble with women'.

Meanwhile they were walking out together as a couple on a more or less regular basis. The news of this soon spread through his acquaintance in Dublin and most people disapproved, including the redoubtable Cosgrave, who managed to disapprove while making a pass at Nora himself, thus providing Joyce with one of the betrayals he found so necessary, and earning for himself the privilege of doubling with Judas in *Ulysses*. 'He was Irish, that is to say, he was false to me' was a proposition enunciated to Nora in late August with reference to another of his former intimates.

By now the rent for the room in Shelbourne Road was sadly in arrears once more; and the McKernans, who were locking up the house and going on holiday, perhaps intimated that enough was enough. Joyce stayed two more nights with the Cousins; went to his Aunt Josephine's for a night or two; stayed with a medical student he knew for one night at least; and finally wound up – at last, the reader may say – in the Martello tower at Sandycove.

It is difficult to know how much introduction Oliver St John Gogarty, the lessee of the tower, needs nowadays for any audience. The once famous wit and the once gleefully recounted pranks have, like most wit and pranks, paled with the years. The eloquent lyric poems are rarely anthologized, the salacious limericks attributed to others. The involvement in the Civil War on the side of the Free State needs a lot of explaining to people who are vague about what the Irish Free State was.

But as Ulick O'Connor makes clear in his biography, Oliver Gogarty was once a famous man, much more famous, in Ireland anyway, and to some extent even beyond, than James Joyce. Mr O'Connor has also spotted the 'joyous dactyls': Oliver Gogarty – Malachi Mulligan chime in together very neatly. And Joyce has had the enormous good sense to make Buck Mulligan a joyous character; he counterpoints the brooding Stephen in exactly the same way that Blazes Boylan counterpoints Leopold Bloom: accenting his isolation, making a mockery of his difficulties, representing a worldly glitter and a sexual flamboyance which neither Bloom nor Stephen possesses:

246

Wit. You would give your five wits for youth's proud livery he pranks in. Lineaments of gratified desire.

Stephen may be, after Bloom, the most important male person in the book; but the spectacular lift-off achieved on the very first page is entirely due to Mulligan. Nevertheless, to the bus loads of tourists who debouch there it is now 'Joyce's tower'. Many may have only a hazy idea of who James Joyce was. Fewer still have heard of Gogarty.

So one of the most surprising facts about the matter is that Joyce was in residence for only six days, arriving probably about 9 September and departing, it would seem, on the 15th. Gogarty had leased the tower from the Lords Commissioners of the Admiralty in August. It was always intended that Joyce should stay there, 'to finish his novel', for they were after all close friends and literary comrades in arms, allied in their scorn of 'the rabblement', a familiar sight as they walked Dublin's streets together, often arm in arm. One of the reasons why the virtually homeless Joyce did not turn up earlier in Sandycove may have been Nora, whose advent had led to a cooling off with all his friends. There had certainly been a cooling off with Gogarty, perhaps about mid-August when the tower became available, which would account both for a reluctance to move in and a half-heartedness about his tenancy when he did.

Of course the shortness of his stay makes the appropriation of the tower a superbly daring act, but it is important to realize that it has little personal symbolic significance. It was Gogarty, not Joyce, who called the tower *omphalos*, the centre of the world. Yeats's tower in Galway, from which a cross-gartered arrogant soldiery had asserted the right of the strong man to rule by violence, had suited his somewhat dubious symbolic needs superbly. Joyce had no such feelings about this relic of the Napoleonic wars. But he gets great mileage out of it all the same, reminding us of Empire, both Roman and British, and of the subservient position of the Irish (including Stephen, curiously representative of that people in spite of his scorn for them), while its position by the sea brings Homer's *Odyssey* into the book as if on the very tide.

Another daring act of course was to leave out all description of the tower and its purposes in the world. Any other novelist would (like the writer of this essay) feel some necessity to inform the reader that Martello towers were built to repel an expected invasion by the French in the early nineteenth century; to describe their squat ugly shape and their interior arrangement of one large circular room over a cellar; to position the thing at Sandycove overlooking Dublin's superb bay. Not so Joyce. He knew that commentary (including such pieces as this) would do all that for him.

And finally, on the subject of arrogance, there is the disdainful rejection of drama.

The facts of Joyce's departure after such a short stay were much more interesting in the ordinary sense in which we use that word than those recounted in his novel. Gogarty had another guest besides Joyce, one Samuel Chenevix-Trench, an Oxford acquaintance so in love with all things Irish, including the Irish Literary Revival, that he signed his writings Diarmuid Trench and spoke Irish to all and sundry. Trench had a revolver and on the night of 14 September he used it.

Waking from a nightmare to imagine a black panther about to spring on him, he discharged several shots which ricocheted around the fireplace a few inches from where Joyce was sleeping. Still raving about panthers, he was about to shoot again when Gogarty seized the gun and fired at the pans which hung above Joyce's head, bringing them down on the bed with a clatter. Joyce got up in terror, dressed, departed and walked all night through the deserted streets, interpreting the gun play both as an affront and as a dismissal from the tower.

To any other novelist this would be riches, at least in retrospect, and the temptation might be to embellish it: indeed Joyce was fond of telling this real life story and probably did improve it as time passed. In his fiction, however, he reduces Stephen's departure from the tower to the trivial business about the key and the obscure episode at Westland Row station. As a novelist, he was against drama, confrontation, violence and even – or so he thought, at least – the extraordinary.

One thing we may be glad of, though. He was no great man for formal description, still less of nature; and beauty, whether natural or moral, had to be accompanied and coloured by other perceptions. So of course the sea has to be 'snot-green' and 'scrotum-tightening'. Nevertheless he does permit himself the beauty of the Latin liturgy; Mulligan blessing gravely 'the tower, the surrounding land and the awaking mountains'; the woodshadows from the fire floating seaward through the morning peace; and, further out, the mirror of the water whitening, 'spurned by lightshod hurrying feet'.

He never went back to the tower so far as anybody knows. For his remaining month or so in Ireland he alternated between St Peter's Terrace and his Aunt Josephine's house in Fairview, finally departing, with Nora, on 8 October. His final hurried notes are to ask for a loan of ten shillings from one person and a toothbrush, a nail brush and a pair of black boots from another. They bear no address.

JOHN KEATS

WENTWORTH PLACE, HAMPSTEAD, LONDON NW3

MARGARET DRABBLE

The house which we now know as Keats's house was built as a joint enterprise in the winter of 1815–16 by two one-time school-friends, Charles Wentworth Dilke (1789–1864) and Charles Armitage Brown (1786–1842), both of whom were to play an influential part in the poet's brief life. They were cultivated 'men of letters' and Hampstead suited their tastes. In those days it was still a village, renowned for the mineral waters that gave Well Walk its name, and famous for its fresh air, fine prospects and pleasant walks. This was the romantic age, and nature was in fashion; the district was much sought after by writers and artists. It was also a popular retreat for summer visitors from the city, and Brown was from time to time to supplement his small private income by letting his half of the house.

Dilke and Brown at the time of this shared venture were both easy-going young men in their thirties, fond of company, and the very design of the home they called Wentworth Place suggests a happy and informal intimacy. It was designed to look like one dwelling, but was in fact divided into two, in an early and elegant version of the semi-detached so popular in later periods. Dilke, as a family man, had the front door, and bachelor Brown had a door at the side, but the garden was to be shared. It was and is a welcoming house, with a smiling aspect, and although it has undergone several alterations and improvements it remains very much the house that Keats knew. It has been in public ownership since 1921, and currently is open (free) to the public. I can see some of the public sitting in its garden as I write, for my study overlooks it.

Time has spared the house, and it has not dealt too harshly with the neighbourhood either. There is no longer a pond at the bottom of Pond Street, South End Green is only faintly green, and cows no longer graze beyond the garden fence, but Keats Grove itself remains an interesting little street, full of character and characters. It now has houses of all periods (including some post-modernist surprises), but it retains a pleasing idiosyncrasy and a lingering rural charm. Cars and lorries engage in complicated confrontations and jostle for parking spaces in

Bust of John Keats, by Anne Whitney

its narrow thoroughfare, and roadworks seem endlessly self-perpetuating. But the pedestrian can still with a little care wander idly and gaze at cottage gardens and well-trained shrubs and Ancient Lights and Victorian stained-glass windows. There is more here than pious association with the name of John Keats: poets, musicians, painters, philosophers, radicals, Bohemians and eccentrics still find a refuge here. And I myself, walking home at one in the morning, have heard the nightingale.

Keats knew and wrote about Hampstead before he came to live here. He enjoyed an escape from his damp, corpse-smelling medical student's lodgings in Southwark and Cheapside, and looked forward to the luxury of a day's walking on the Heath, with a prospect of Kenwood. His early poem 'I stood tip-toe upon a little hill' was suggested, according to his friend the poet and editor Leigh Hunt, 'by a delightful summer-day, as [he] stood beside the gate that leads from the Battery at Hampstead Heath into a field of Caen Wood' (*Lord Byron and Some of His Contemporaries*, 1828). It paints a rapturous pastoral portrait of bluebells, dandelions, hawthorn glades, goldfinches, laburnum, brooks, primroses and 'sweet peas, on tip-toe for a flight; With wings of gentle flush o'er delicate white' – all of which may still be encountered, though not perhaps in such poetic profusion.

In 1816 he visited Leigh Hunt's white-painted cottage in the Vale of Health on the Heath, and was delighted by the disorderly creative muddle of books, flowers, music and sculpture. Hunt introduced him to the painter Benjamin Haydon, who was staying in Hampstead for a fortnight for health reasons, and Haydon in turn introduced him to other like-minded spirits. His circle of friends grew, and his connections with Hampstead became stronger. His poems of this period capture the happiness of youthful affection and good society, and Keats would often find himself 'catching the note of Philomel' as he made the long walk home to the city after convivial evenings 'brim full of friendliness'.

But the walk was long, even though it was enlivened by stars and nightingales, and in the spring of 1817 Keats abandoned South London and his medical career and opted for poetry and Hampstead. He was newly of age, and free from the legal and financial control of his not wholly sympathetic guardian and trustee, Richard Abbey. He was now a published poet, with a real possibility of fulfilling his poetic ambitions. His first volume appeared on 3 March, and in the same month he and his two brothers, George and Tom, took lodgings at 1 Well Walk with the postman Bentley's family. It has been suggested that the move was connected with the growing ill-health of Tom, or possibly with that of Keats himself, who was already unusually susceptible to cold and damp: and it also represented escape from the lowering neighbourhood of Abbey. Keats was to tell Brown that 'in no period of my life have I acted with any self-will, but in throwing up the apothecary profession', and on the day of his removal his hospital appointment at Guy's came to an unmarked end.

All three brothers were soon welcome guests of Charles Dilke and his charming, hospitable wife, Maria, calling at Wentworth Place 'three times a week, often three times a day', according to Dilke. Maria became a sister to them, and although Dilke was six years older than Keats and more philosophical and opinionated (Keats called him a 'Godwin perfectibility man'), the relationship was close and informal. Letters (mostly to brother George, who emigrated to America in June 1818) tell of walks and wanderings, of claret feasts and dinners and gifts of game and hops to the tunes of the pianoforte, of jokes and horseplay and above all of conversation – 'I have been over to Dilke's this evening – there with Brown we have been talking of different and indifferent matters – of Euclid, of Metaphisics, of the Bible, of Shakespeare, of the Horrid System and consequences of the fagging

The back of Keats's house, Hampstead

at great Schools ...' (letter to Mr and Mrs George Keats, October 1818). Keats had clearly found a home from home.

Dilke was a civil servant in the Navy Pay Office, a radical and an antiquarian who also reviewed for the serious periodicals of the day; Brown had been rescued from a chequered business career (in bristles) by a legacy which enabled him to invest in Wentworth Place and his infectious passion for the theatre. (In 1814 he had a musical play performed at Drury Lane, and Keats and he were to collaborate on the verse drama *Otho the Great*.) Brown too became intimate with the poet, and

252

*Brown's sitting-room, where Keats was nursed during his illness
in February and March 1820*

they set off together in the summer of 1818 for an exhilarating but exhausting tour of the Lakes and Scotland.

While they were away, Brown let his home to a widowed Mrs Brawne and her three children. She was in her thirties, living in a small but comfortable way on money from the 'West Indian connections' of her brother John, who had died in 1816. The Brawnes must have liked Hampstead, for on Brown's return they took lodgings only a few minutes' walk away, at Elm Cottage on the corner of Rosslyn Hill and Downshire Hill.

Young Tom Keats had been seriously ill in his brother's absence, and John, arriving home from Scotland in high spirits, 'brown and shabby' from his adventures, called first at Wentworth Place, where Maria Dilke took on the task of breaking the bad news. Keats returned at once to Well Walk, and spent much of the next few months by Tom's bedside, in ominous ill-health himself and plagued by an unpleasant personal attack in *Blackwood's* magazine. As his biographer Robert Gittings noted, 'The strain of these weeks with every detail of death seen at close quarters was to dominate the rest of his own life and thought.'

Tom died on 1 December, some two weeks after his nineteenth birthday. Brown, immediately, and with a characteristic mixture of generosity, sensitivity and self-interest, suggested that John should leave the melancholy associations of Well Walk and join him as paying guest in Wentworth Place. Keats gratefully agreed, and his little library of some one hundred and fifty books was carried down the hill by his ex-landlord Bentley in a clothes-basket. And thus, by mid-December, the scene was set for the next two years of extraordinary intensity and creativity.

These were years of death, poetry and love, of a life's work passionately cramped into a tiny space. As Tom lay dying, Keats had first met the eighteen-year-old Fanny Brawne, and had found her 'beautiful and elegant, graceful, silly, fashionable and strange'. This oddly mixed response was soon transformed into ardent admiration. In the spring of 1819 the Brawnes moved back into Wentworth Place as Dilke, an anxious father, took himself off to live in Westminster for the sake of the education of his nine-year-old son, Charley. So there, now, was Fanny, inescapably, in the shared garden, through the party wall, under the same roof, eternally present and eternally vanishing, in an agony of tantalizing domestic proximity.

Keats fell deeply in love with her. Their relationship, by hindsight doomed, has a kind of tragic lightness to it, a playful brittle terror. On the surface, life was crowded with parties, dinners, dances, flirtations, birthday celebrations, kisses, tokens and promises: a happy courtship in a happy house. An unofficial engagement became, by the end of the year 1819, official. The world was all before them, although some of their friends frowned on the match and muttered about lack of prospects on both sides.

But the prospects were worse than anyone feared, and the poetry itself foretold a different ending to the story. 'La Belle Dame sans Merci' had Keats in thrall, and in February 1820 he suffered his first haemorrhage in the cold sheets of his cold bed in the back bedroom at Wentworth Place. Brown was with him, and records the terrible moment of recognition:

> 'Bring me the candle, Brown; and let me see this blood.' After regarding it steadfastly, he looked up in my face, with a calmness of countenance that I can never forget, and said – 'I know the colour of that blood; it is arterial blood ... that drop of blood is my death warrant; – I must die.'

And Keats, the ex-medical student, was correct in his unsparing self-diagnosis.

Little time was left, and much was still to be gleaned. Some of the greatest work had already been written, here, at this house, in this garden – most notably, perhaps, the 'Ode to the Nightingale', composed the previous summer, as Brown records, under the plum tree in the first happy weeks near Fanny. But now the hours pressed, and Keats could not tell whether Fanny's presence gave him more pain or comfort, more anguish or more inspiration. His movements express his misery and uncertainty; he kept helplessly leaving, then finding himself helplessly drawn back to her presence.

Brown, who had at first nursed him with devotion, vanished to Scotland for the summer, and Keats took refuge with Leigh Hunt in nearby Kentish Town. He knew he was dying and could prolong his life a little only by leaving all he loved and wintering in Italy; in these last bitter months he turned against Dilke, Brown and the carefree days of the past and was seen one day by a stranger 'sitting and sobbing' on a bench at the end of Well Walk, gazing towards the Heath. On 12 August 1820 he wrote to Fanny:

> I shall never be able any more to endure the society of any of those who used to meet at Elm Cottage and Wentworth Place. The last two years taste like brass upon my Palate. If I can not live with you I will live alone.

That same day he appeared, feverish, on the doorstep of Wentworth Place and was taken in by Mrs Brawne. There he spent his last days in Hampstead, nursed by Fanny, until his final departure for Rome with his friend Joseph Severn, who had stepped in as companion to fill Brown's place. Fanny records, on Wednesday 13 September, in pencil, in a copy of *The Literary Copy Book* which he had given her, 'Mr Keats left Hampstead.' He departed, with keepsakes, forever. He and Severn set sail on 18 September and Keats died on 23 February in Rome. A few days before his death, Severn, foreseeing the appalling and rapidly approaching end, wrote to Mrs Brawne, saying that they should never have left Hampstead.

The conscious torment of Keats's last days makes almost unbearable reading, and there are times when I look over my garden wall and feel that the very stones and trees must be impregnated with unresolved suffering. One night as I stood on my lawn, reflecting on my father's view (inaccurate, as I later discovered) that my garden must occupy space once belonging to Wentworth Place itself, I suddenly found myself repeating lines from Keats that I did not know I knew by heart: words which some have thought to be his last lines of verse.

> This living hand, now warm and capable
> Of earnest grasping, would, if it were cold,
> And in the icy silence of the tomb,
> So haunt thy days and chill thy dreaming nights
> That thou wouldst wish thine own heart dry of blood
> So in my veins red life might stream again,
> And thou be conscience-calm'd – see here it is –
> I hold it towards you.

And yet, despite the sadness of a life cut short and the bitterness of un-consummated love, Keats House remains in most of its moods a happy house. It is a pleasure to visit, with its well-proportioned rooms, its pretty, well-polished period furniture, its authentic manuscripts and its inauthentic conservatory. There are touching relics – a sampler and a fichu made by Fanny Brawne, her gold bracelet, and a gold brooch commissioned by Severn in the form of a Greek lyre with the strings made of Keats's hair 'intended as a present to Fanny Brawne, but never given to her' – an aptly poignant comment on their unfulfilled relationship. But there is also the lingering memory of parties and laughter, of Maria Dilke and Fanny singing to the pianoforte. These characters were not cut out for tragedy.

This is not a tragic neighbourhood – no dark windswept moors, no gloomy romantic caverns here. Keats's critics have accused him and his poetry of a schoolboy greedy eagerness, of a Cockney craving for ostentatious lushness: Carlyle called him 'a miserable creature, hungering after sweets which he can't get', and it was Yeats who famously remarked that he was like a boy with his face pressed against a sweet-shop window. It is true that the verse is full – occasionally cloyingly full – of dainties and creams and sweets and junkets and spices and fruits and 'luxuries bright, milky, soft and rosy'. So, too, still is Hampstead. It is not an austere district, despite its reputation for intellect. It is a place of good food and cheer, of cake shops and conversation, of gardens vulgarly crammed with suburban flowering cherries and laburnum and sweet pea. In healthy, happy Hampstead, literary figures well into their eighties and nineties throw garden parties amidst the blooming roses. And here, perhaps, is the real poignancy – that a poet who enjoyed the good things of life with such unashamed rapture should have been torn away from them so soon.

RUDYARD KIPLING

BATEMAN'S, BURWASH, E. SUSSEX

PHILIP MASON

'At very first sight, we said: "That's her! The Only She!"' That is how Kipling and his wife first reacted to Bateman's. 'We entered and found her Spirit ... to be good. We went through every room and found no shadow of ancient regrets, stifled miseries nor any menace.' They had to wait nearly two years before they could buy the house and soon afterwards, in 1902, Kipling wrote to C. E. Norton, a close friend in Massachusetts:

> Behold us now lawful owners of a grey stone lichened house – A.D. 1634 over the door – beamed, panelled, with old oak staircase, and all untouched and unfaked ... a good and peaceable place, standing in terraced lawns nigh to a walled garden of old red brick, and two fat-headed oast-houses with red brick stomachs, and an aged silver-grey dovecot on top.

In the same letter he says that while house-hunting:

> We discovered England, which we had never done before ... England is a wonderful land. It is the most marvellous of all foreign countries that I have ever been in. It is made up of trees and green fields and mud and the gentry and at last I'm one of the gentry ...

These are significant words, which need to be considered against the background of the unsettled gypsyish life Kipling had led until then. He was born in Bombay on 30 December 1865. His parents had been married on 18 March of that year, and since their ship sailed unexpectedly a day early, had left for India straight from the church, without even going to their own wedding reception. This suggests that Rudyard was probably begotten at sea. As a child, he lived, as the children of the British in India usually did, very much in the company of servants, talking the kitchen-Hindustani that was the lingua franca of Northern India. He remembers being told: 'Talk English when you go into the drawing-room to see Papa and Mamma.' Earlier than was usual, when he was only six and his sister only three,

Bateman's

they suffered the fate of most such children and in 1871 were left behind in England with strangers. At that time it was thought best that the children should not be warned of what was to happen. Kipling spent six years without seeing his parents at what he later referred to as the 'House of Desolation' and there is a story, 'Baa Baa Black Sheep', which is undoubtedly based on this experience. It is a very poignant and moving account of a little boy's misery. Of course it is fiction and opinions differ as to how far it can be taken as describing actual events, but for my part I have no doubt that it describes what Kipling later thought he had *felt*. Emotionally, the story, published when he was twenty-five, tallies with the account he gives forty years later in *Something of Myself*. He felt deserted; he was bereft of love; he believed that he was actively disliked by the woman to whose care he had been entrusted as substitute for a mother.

From 1878 to 1882, Kipling was at the United Services College at Westward Ho! in Devon, a public school founded by army officers in order to get their sons into Sandhurst without the heavy expense of a London crammer. Here again, there are different views about how far Kipling himself is to be believed in what he wrote later, but again I believe that emotionally *Stalky & Co.* is good evidence, not necessarily of what happened, but of what it felt like to be there. It was much better than the 'House of Desolation'; the headmaster was a civilized man and a friend of Poynter and Burne-Jones, two painters of the Pre-Raphaelite school who had married two of Mrs Kipling's sisters. But the United Services College existed to get boys into the armed forces and cannot have been altogether different from other public schools of the period. Games were important, and Kipling was so extremely short-sighted that he was excused all games. He was the only boy in the

A corner of Kipling's study

school to wear spectacles and was known as Gig-lamps or Gigger. Nor did he shine at Latin or maths, the two most important school subjects. He was never in the sixth form or a prefect. He says he was bullied at first, but portrays himself in his later years as a tolerated eccentric, a kind of amiable butt, accepted, even liked, but clearly on the margin or outer fringe of school life. It is important for an understanding of the writer to notice that he admired the aims of the school, that he admired the headmaster, but was very critical of some of his subordinates, including the housemasters. But I feel sure that at school he was odd man out – and he knew it.

He was odd man out again when he went back to India. He was still only seventeen, a reporter on the *Civil and Military Gazette* at Lahore. His father, though personally liked, was merely the curator of a museum, low-paid and on the fringe of the official hierarchy. Kipling was part of a society that was almost entirely official and in which seniority was of the first importance. But he meant to be known as a writer and to be known he had to shout. Shouting was not done – not by anyone, least of all by a very young man, younger than the youngest subaltern. So he was considered brash and conceited. Once again, he admired the aims of the institution of which he was part – British rule in India – though often he was highly critical of the men who made it work, as he had been of the assistant masters at school. But he had to be careful; he must not offend his readers nor the proprietors of his newspaper. If you read with care some of his very early stories – 'The House of Suddhoo' or 'Beyond the Pale', for example – you will see that he is deeply interested in the people of India and their ways but very anxious to convince his readers that he hasn't gone native altogether. 'Seven Years Hard' was how he described his time in India. He worked hard, he was often ill, he lived in other people's houses; he had no home and spent his time inquisitively poking his nose into other people's business, like the mongoose Rikki-Tikki-Tavi of his later story.

He came to England in 1889, living by himself in lodgings near the Strand; at twenty-five, he began to be famous. He became engaged and broke it off; he pursued another girl, who would not have him; he married Carrie Balestier. All that is another story and has little to do with Bateman's except that it suggests he was looking for permanence.

With his bride he started on a trip round the world, but when he was in Japan his bank broke and most of his savings vanished. The Kiplings made for Carrie's home at Brattleboro in Vermont, USA. Here they stayed six years and seem sometimes to have meant to settle but again he was odd man out. He had odd English ways such as dressing for dinner and not mixing with his neighbours; above all, he thought he had a right to privacy. Reporters came and pestered him when he wanted to work. Carrie could not get on with her brother, one of those genial rascals liked by everyone except their bank manager. Rudyard made an indiscreet remark that reached his ears. There was an angry scene and on Carrie's advice Rudyard took his brother-in-law to court for assault and threat to murder. It was a bad mistake; everyone laughed at him. The man who admired courage and action had been scared! The Press seized on it; there were caricatures and lampoons. The Press did not like Kipling because he had wanted privacy – and because he criticized America. The Kiplings fled; they left the United States bruised and hurt and only once returned. On that disastrous visit, Kipling himself almost died of pneumonia and his adored daughter Josephine did die, aged six – a loss from which he never recovered.

That is the background to his settling at Bateman's. He wanted very much to find a permanent home, to put down roots, to 'belong' somewhere. But he was a far more complex character than is often supposed and was full of unresolved contradictions. He knew – as the letter I have quoted shows – that he did not 'belong' in Sussex, even in England. England was a foreign country. His mother was a Macdonald – mixed Scottish, Irish and Welsh; his father was Yorkshire. He himself was by upbringing of that class the British Empire developed in Victorian times, men and women who served in the army or in an administrative service, who spent long spells abroad and whose English roots often withered. But even to that class he did not belong by temperament because he was above all a writer.

But he *wanted* to settle when he found Bateman's, just as he had wanted to marry. Did that affect his judgement when he and Carrie were bowled over by the house? It is indeed a house of singular external beauty, from whatever angle it is seen. The sharp pitch of the roof, the angles of gables and main ridge, the tall stack of chimneys, are deeply satisfying. It is all of a piece. As his own thumbnail sketch suggests, the oast-houses and their weathered brick add a touch of domestic warmth. Inside, the house is undoubtedly dark for modern taste and the heavy old oak of furniture and panelling make it darker. But the furnishings are altogether in keeping with the date over the door and with the Kiplings' desire that it should be 'untouched and unfaked'. The National Trust aims at keeping the interior today as nearly as possible as it was when Kipling lived there and – if it is now inevitably more of a museum – on the whole they succeed. Above all, the Kiplings liked it as it was. They found it 'peaceable', and they were very sensitive to atmosphere in a house. He once wrote that a man may be able to lie successfully but a house never.

It has been claimed that the house described in the story called 'They' is Bateman's. This needs qualification. In 'They', the narrator of the story – in this case rather more to be identified with Kipling himself than is usual – finds a house as beautiful as a dream 'on the other side of the county' and there meets the spirit of his dead daughter, a child of six. But it would be wrong for him to go again to

Bateman's, in the Burwash valley, with Pook's Hill to the right

that house; he must go back to the real world. The house is indeed very like Bateman's – but it is not quite the same. In every respect the description is a shade exaggerated, a little more than lifesize, heightened as poetry is from prose. It is a mysterious story – I think a parable of his own resolution to look forward.

On two collections of stories, *Puck of Pook's Hill* and *Rewards and Fairies*, there can be no doubt about the direct influence of Bateman's and its surroundings. Dan and Una are not unlike Kipling's own surviving children, John and Elsie; they live in a house like Bateman's, with a mill and a stream like the Dudwell, a governess and a daily routine like theirs. The surrounding countryside is hardly disguised. Ostensibly meant for children, these stories are 'worked at different levels', as Kipling said himself, so that though children would enjoy them, grown-ups too would come back to them at all ages. The children meet Puck of *A Midsummer Night's Dream* and he introduces them to a variety of people, whom most of us would think long dead – a Norman knight, Queen Elizabeth, a Roman centurion. They learn something of the continuity of English history, but there is much more than that. The centurion defends Hadrian's Wall in loyalty to an emperor he knows to be dead, the Queen sends young men to almost certain death with her kiss on their lips; their reasons are by no means simple. Why do they behave as they do? In all these stories, the characters believe in personal honour; they believe that man is responsible for his acts; they display courage or loyalty or cheerfulness in danger and privation. They are compelled to act by the nature of their being.

One reason why the Puck stories have been so widely loved and admired is that while the children have to go home at bedtime and Dan may be kept in over his lessons, while the familiar routine of a comfortable upper-middle-class household goes on – in the story itself, so long as it lasts, there is a note of conspiracy, a conspiracy from which grown-ups and settled ways and 'folk in housen' (it is Puck's own term) are shut out. In this conspiracy, Kipling himself shared. The feeling is strong in 'Cold Iron', the first story in *Rewards and Fairies*. The People of the Hills – whom most of us call fairies – try to bring up a mortal boy 'on the far side of Cold Iron', which stands for custom and settled ways and all that lies between the People of the Hills and 'folk in housen'. Once he touches Cold Iron, the Boy will lose his magic and his youth; the spell will be broken. Of course he is bound sooner or later to meet Cold Iron – and he meets it in the worst possible form. He picks up an old slave-ring – and snaps it home on his neck and has to go back to 'folk in housen' – just as Kipling had done when he bought Bateman's and when he married, just as everyone does when youth ends. But we snap on the ring ourselves; we have to. What else can we do? Those words are the recurring theme of *Rewards and Fairies*. This is a very important story for understanding Kipling.

Kipling lived at Bateman's from 1902 till his death in 1936. It was the base from which he explored Sussex – and sang its praises with something of the zeal of a convert. But he was still odd man out, never quite part of Sussex – neither one of the landed gentry nor one of the villagers. There is a story, 'An Habitation Enforced', published in 1909, which underlines the point. An American couple, almost by chance, stumble on an empty house with which they 'fall in love'. It is of great beauty but not at all like Bateman's, a Georgian house, light, airy and graceful. They buy the house and the estate that goes with it, and the house and the countryside and English ways begin to assimilate them. But in *their* case, there is a difference, because the American wife discovers that she is a descendant of the people who had lived there and owned the farms of the estate; and gentry, farmers and cottagers all take the two strangers to their hearts. But that never happened to the Kiplings.

He listened though. He had listened all his life. There are two stories told in Sussex speech which I would put among the dozen best that Kipling wrote. These are 'Friendly Brook' and 'The Wish House'. A friend of mine, who was brought up in West Sussex and lived there all his life, told me that the language of these stories was recognizably East Sussex not West, and most impressive. Kipling had learnt it by listening as he went round the farms on the small estate he built up round Bateman's.

These two stories with a Sussex background are only a small part of his output during the years at Bateman's. It is uneven but includes his finest work. Here it was that he endured the burden of the war with the Kaiser's Germany which he had dreaded and predicted, and it was worse than he had believed it would be. Here too he bore the death of his only son – missing in France, destroyed by a shell – and here he faced the growing onset of gastric pain, an ulcer undiagnosed until too late. In the late stories, his most frequent themes are suffering and healing and what he calls breaking-strain, the point at which suffering becomes too great and the normal controls of the human spirit give way. He was deeply concerned about what was then called 'shell-shock', when the personality disintegrates 'Because they laid on My Mother's Son/More than a man could bear.' Increasingly, he expresses the redemptive power of suffering and particularly of suffering willingly borne for someone else. 'It do count, don't it, de pain?' says Grace Ashcroft in 'The Wish House', of the cancerous pain that is killing her and which she had accepted on behalf of the lover who had deserted her. These late stories – 'The Gardener', 'A Madonna of the Trenches', 'Fairy-Kist', 'The Church That Was at Antioch' – reveal a man of deep compassion very different from the vulgar little figure with a flag and a tin trumpet shown in Max Beerbohm's well-known cartoon. But that was the figure he sometimes showed the public.

These late stories, apart from 'Friendly Brook' and 'The Wish House', say nothing directly about Bateman's. But Bateman's gave him the first-floor study, the lightest room in the house, where he could sit at his desk undisturbed, dreaming and brooding on his writing, now and again getting up from the chair to lie on the day-bed and get the full rhythm of a sentence exactly right. I do not believe that Carrie ever quite understood much of what he was brooding and hatching but she guarded like a dragon his privacy in those sacred hours he spent in the study. He believed that for his best work he was 'only a telephone line'; what he wrote was dictated to him by what he called his 'Daemon'. The Daemon was not always present in the same degree, but never more so than in the *Jungle Books*, *Kim* and the Puck stories, the most widely loved of all he wrote. In none of these is the reader conscious of that posturing that is sometimes distasteful. Of all that has been written about him, the most discerning remarks were made by André Maurois, who said that the true secret of his 'hold on men's hearts' was his 'natural and permanent contact' with the 'oldest and deepest layers of human consciousness'. I question the word 'permanent'; I think his contact was intermittent. But it *was* with the oldest and deepest layers that he had contact when the Daemon was there; he had a sense of the collective unconscious, an understanding of the tribe, of vengeance and honour, of such concepts as sacrifice and the Law, and the sacredness of rocks and snakes. Mowgli had to be bought into the wolf-pack by the death of a bull. As a child I puzzled over the reason for this but I saw its necessity. It was a sacrifice, a redemption, sealed by blood. 'By the Bull that bought me!' Mowgli would swear for the rest of his life.

The study at Bateman's gave Kipling the chance to plunge into these ancestral and magical depths and dredge up some of what he found. But when he came out of the study he was back among 'folk in housen' and he put on the shiny outward surface that reflected and even intensified the opinions of the outside world – just as long ago he had put on that outer carapace when he had taken his meals in the Lahore Club and striven to convince his readers that he hadn't gone native. His study at Bateman's was a hermitage into which he could retire and hear strange music. But when he stepped outside the study, the house, though he loved it and it gave him the background he had always wanted, stood for the slave-ring he had snapped home on his neck as the sign of his servitude to Cold Iron and 'folk in housen' and to things as they are.

D. H. LAWRENCE

EASTWOOD, NOTTINGHAMSHIRE

RICHARD HOGGART

The township of Eastwood and its surroundings incorporate to a remarkable degree some major elements in English social and cultural life. They can still remind the visitor of the old rural England of farm and forest (Robin Hood operated nearby); they recall a people and a landscape greatly damaged by a thoughtless and often grasping capitalism (from the mid nineteenth century coal-mining on a large, industrialized scale got under way in those parts). Their working-people were squalidly housed in what came to be known – and such housing was put up in many parts of the country as the Industrial Revolution reached its height – as 'the barracks of industry'. The men were overworked and ill-paid by the big landowners who owned also the mining rights under their land and exploited their labourers as a matter of course. Their fine mansions were often in sight of the miners' huddled dwellings, but far enough away to have their own, enclosed large gardens.

Above all, Eastwood in D. H. Lawrence's day exemplified the resilient culture of the working-class people themselves, a culture which held a complex balance between the men and the women but in which, on the whole, the women were usually the stronger. They embodied a determination to survive respectably, and in that effort the twin principles were self-help and neighbourliness. They held fast to church or, more likely, chapel. Most of them would not allow themselves to be brutalized by living conditions hardly better and in some ways worse than those their forebears had known as pre-industrial workers – above ground – on that same land.

In this place in 1885, and into a miner's family, D. H. (David Herbert – but known to Eastwood as Bert) Lawrence was born. Frail, sickly but, with his mother unshakeably behind him, hugely determined to make his own kind of life in his own kind of way; so he wrote ceaselessly, to become one of the greatest writers in English of the twentieth century. An old miner said to me in 1990, as one offering remarkable and hardly-known information to a visitor strange to such things:

'Lawrence lived by 'is pen, you know. That tek's some doing for a miner's son.'
Yes, indeed.

Eastwood sits on a hilly spine of land nine miles north-west of the large industrial
city of Nottingham. The main street runs roughly along the spine, and its north-
west-facing slope looks over the last half-mile of the county of Nottinghamshire to
Derbyshire, the demarcation marked by a small and sluggish river, the Erewash.
To a visitor it seems a mongrel of a river but, like most mongrels, it is loved by
those who know it well, as Lawrence did. It figures in his writing as powerfully as
do the larger rivers of Europe in some continental novels. Even today the view
from the top of the town, over the fields, hills and woods of what Lawrence called
'the country of my heart', is little changed from his time. But there is one major
change; even where their buildings have not been knocked down, and many have,
the mines are silent, worked-out, dead.

Eastwood's population has grown to 12,000 from the 3,000 of Lawrence's day.
Yet again it is remarkable how little the general appearance of the town has
changed. There are, of course, the new chain-store shops – outfitters for women
and men, chemists, video and electrical shops, fast-food outlets (but still the old,
characteristic fish-and-chip shops); and there are new housing areas on the fringes.
But Lawrence would have recognized the heart of the town at once; its odd
geographical position has kept much of the centre largely as it was a hundred years
ago. True, there is a White Peacock café, named after Lawrence's first novel, a
small factory called the Lawrence something or other, and a few similar fribbles.
But the main frame of the town is instantly recognizable and its main Lawrence
landmarks easily traceable. Most striking of all: the four houses in which the
Lawrence family lived are all still there and can all be seen in a circular walk of
less than a mile. Two of them can be visited, and luckily they are the two most
interesting of the four.

Any visit to the town should now start at the modern public library, set just back
from the main street. The old library was a good repository of Lawrence material
but the new one has a special Lawrence room which contains, among much else,
the Hopkin collection. William Hopkin was a prominent local socialist and writer
who befriended the adolescent Lawrence, remained a friend for life and was sent
copies of most of the books as they appeared. There is much else in the library,
notably a clear and helpful fifteen-minute audio-visual slide-show introducing us to
Lawrence's Eastwood. That makes much the best start.

From the library it is only two or three hundred yards up the same side of the
street to Lawrence's birthplace, 8a Victoria Street. It is a typical street of miners'
houses, each opening directly on to the pavement and looking across at its
neighbours opposite. 8a is slightly different in that its front window is larger than
usual, an oblong. An English visitor from a similar background knows at once that

8a Victoria Street, Eastwood, Lawrence's birthplace

8a was once a shop, of the sort which appeared at intervals in working-class terraces. Mrs Lawrence made use of the facility by selling linens and baby clothes from a display in that window.

The front door opens directly into the living-room and that in turn to the kitchen. They and the bedrooms are furnished as nearly as possible in the style of the Lawrences' time there (they left in 1887, when Lawrence was two years old). There are two identified pieces of furniture from the Lawrence home itself, a chiffonier and one of those single-legged bedside tables which can be adjusted up and down and across, so that the table's surface can be placed over the bed. Both pieces, slightly genteel for a miner's home, poignantly remind us that Mrs Lawrence was from a 'better-class' family than her husband; she had been a schoolteacher. Presumably most of the Lawrence furniture passed, when the family home was broken up, to the children or other relatives, or was sold for a few shillings.

The local district council has been at pains to recreate the house as it very likely

The living-room, looking through to the kitchen, at Victoria Street

looked at that time, and successfully sought authentic pieces; it is a sympathetic recreation. The council was shrewd, too, in recruiting a core of well-informed and helpful local ladies to act as a team of curators.

8a Victoria Street is not the poorest kind of miner's dwelling (nor are the other three Lawrence houses). It is, in comparison with a typically basic miner's home, quite substantial, the living-room a good size with a warm and solid feeling, the bedrooms not cramped either; and a large attic runs across the whole floor area. The 'main' or front bedroom, its big iron bedstead and simple bedspread, are deeply evocative. You may easily imagine the knocking on the party wall to tell the neighbour that labour has started and the local midwife had best make haste. David Herbert came into the world here as the fourth child and third son. Mrs Lawrence was to have her fifth and last child, a second daughter, in their next home.

269

Through the main bedroom, in a room which did not form part of the Lawrences' home, is a collection of very good photographs and another short audio-visual show, this one focusing particularly on Lawrence's works and the inspiration the area gave him.

Just below the house, dropping down the hillside, were in Lawrence's day rectangles of mean miners' dwellings known as the Squares. Lawrence hated them and with good reason. They were what the colliery owners, secure in their comely mansions, had thrown up to corral their workers. Compare the beauty of the hill towns of Italy, Lawrence cried, in a passage which is often regarded as excessively romantic. But he had a point. Grouped housing, even for people who cannot pay much in rent, does not have to be as basic, as ugly, as uniform, as defiant of the surrounding natural features, as this. This was housing by people whose only God was Mammon, who regarded their workers as little more than beasts of burden, and whose interest in grace and beauty stopped just within their own park gates. Areas such as the Squares, squalidly planned, squalidly thrown up, encouraged squalid living.

It is no wonder – but not a sufficient excuse, especially to women such as Mrs Lawrence – that many miners spent too much of their spare time and their wages, after a long hot day down the pit, in the male camaraderie of the public houses; such as the one Lawrence called the Moon and Stars in his first major novel, *Sons and Lovers*. It still stands, in a back street only a couple of hundred yards from the public library, its real name the Three Tuns. It has a Lawrence room now, and a few other bits of self-conscious catchpenny nonsense. But the atmosphere, at least from the outside, survives, and easily evokes the shade of Lawrence's father, stumbling out and heading for home and a tongue-lashing.

Of the Squares, one row of houses has been retained though now pedestrianized and artificially cobbled, so that it is a feat of the imagination to recreate the noise and the clinkered dirt of the streets as they were. You have walked 150 yards down from 8a and, as you turn right along the gentrified street, are heading directly for the second home of Lawrence's childhood, in a group of houses called the Breach. The family lived there from 1887 to 1892, from the second to the seventh year of his life. In *Sons and Lovers* the Breach is called the Bottoms and the Lawrences' time there memorably described – the house itself and the melodramatic life they lived within it – in the first half of that novel. The Bottoms is a more accurate name than the Breach for the group, since the houses sit almost at the bottom of the ridge on which the town stands. A field away is the Erewash and Derbyshire.

These houses were, again, larger than the general run of miners' dwellings, and in size a step up from 8a Victoria Street; 'substantial', Lawrence said. Much of the group still stands, though now surrounded by more modern houses. Lawrence could look from the back bedroom over the fields to Derbyshire, or from the front at the slope up to the town, then parcelled into allotments the miners tended. The allotments have given way to semi-detached houses and a school, and the road has become, entirely unsurprisingly and unimaginatively, Garden Road. At least it hasn't been called Lawrence Road; but the house has been renamed Sons and Lovers Cottage and its upper part is let to holidaymakers, most of whom want to explore the surrounding countryside and have not heard of Lawrence.

Mrs Lawrence was pleased that hers was an end-house and so only half-attached to the rest of the terrace, even though it cost sixpence a week more (two and a half new pence), since it gave her slightly more privacy and a bit of side garden, and was not entirely overlooked. But she came to dislike the house intensely since it shared with the block opposite a dirty and noisome alleyway (still traceable). Her gentility made her constantly strive to pull her family and especially her children out of the drab, often brutal and totally unperspectived life of the miners.

It is worth walking to the bottom of the narrow little garden to a little brick shed which recalls the harrowing scene in *Sons and Lovers* when Morel (based on Lawrence's father), drunk and violent, locks his wife out of the house and she wraps round her an old rug from the coal-house at the bottom of the garden until she can get into the house again.

The ground floor of the house is open to the public by appointment. Arrangements change from time to time, so it is best to check first with the library. Here, too, is a recreation of a miner's home of the 1880s and 90s: the 'best front room', only open on special days – say, for weddings, funerals or Christmas. Most of the time it would have looked, as it does today, chill and formal, frowned over by an upright piano out of proportion with the size of the room itself. But that recalls Lawrence's haunting poem 'Piano':

> Softly, in the dusk, a woman is singing to me;
> Taking me back down the vista of years . . .

The back kitchen, where the family would live almost all the time, has a black-leaded range, a centre table and a few simple chairs. It is best to enter by the back door, as the family would, coming from the pit or from school, through the tiny scullery with its simple utensils for the washing of clothes, to the heart of the house. The front door would have been opened only for posh visitors and, again, weddings and funerals. A coffin would be taken in that way and placed on trestles in the front room until it left again by the front door for the cemetery; as it is in the most poignant of all scenes in *Sons and Lovers*, after the death of the central character's (Paul's) older brother William.

These two, 8a Victoria Street and the house in the Breach, are the two places to see before all others. But two remaining Lawrence homes, both within a quarter of a mile, add to the atmosphere. You climb three hundred yards up the hill

271

The kitchen range at the Breach house

towards the town and find Walker Street. Here the Lawrences lived, whether in No. 8 or No. 12 is not sure, until 1902. Mrs Lawrence's slow but steady climb to gentility is exemplified in the bay-window, a very important signifier to those who know the codes in such things. Being high, these houses have a splendid view over that country of Lawrence's heart, and indeed inspired the phrase. This is not the claustrophobic setting for family fights like those of the Breach. As you look over the road at the sweep of countryside you remember more the settings of Lawrence's first novel, *The White Peacock*, as well as passages in many another novel, short story and essay.

The Walker Street house has no plaque and visitors are not received. The fourth of the houses has at least a plaque. It is even further up the hill, just behind the town centre, and has no view, being in a street whose houses face each other at right angles to the panorama: 97 Lynn Croft Road. But it was, in the finely-graded terms of such communities, yet another step up, and even Lawrence was proud of its style and standing. He was still young enough for such pride, being only sixteen when they moved in. It was here that the family lived until 1910, the year of Mrs Lawrence's death. This house, we may say, marked the end of Lawrence's early life, just as Paul after his mother's death moves out and away, and *Sons and Lovers* ends.

We are now back near the Three Tuns and the library. There are still other buildings which Lawrence knew, all of them identified in booklets available at the library; but the above is the crucial Lawrence town-walk. Meanwhile the modern town, largely unaware of Lawrence and his achievements, or aware only that he wrote a 'dirty book' called *Lady Chatterley's Lover*, or simply wondering what all the fuss is about, goes on with its perennial business as, in a phrase from Lawrence about the banal inevitability of most of our emotional life, 'it has to do'.

Yet a visit to Eastwood which did no more than tour the town would be too truncated. If at all possible, the visitor should make two short trips by car or bus out of town, one to the north-west, the other to the south-east.

The north-west trip takes you on the Mansfield Road, past the home of the Walkers who, with the Barbers, owned the local mines (it now houses National Coal Board offices), past the mine offices where young Paul Morel queued miserably for his father's wages, up the hill towards Underwood, down a lane off which a private gate leads to the ruins of Haggs Farm (the Willey Farm of *Sons and Lovers*, where Lawrence formed his relationship with Jessie Chambers, on whom the character of Miriam is based). A quarter of a mile on, you can leave the car on the verge and walk in woods Lawrence knew well. Then you head for Moorgreen Reservoir, the setting for the water party chapter (14) in *Women in Love*. On a slope nearby is Lamb Close, still the home of the Barbers and not open to the public. But it can be glimpsed through the trees and figures as 'Shortlands' in *Women in Love* and elsewhere. This trip will take no more than an hour unless you join the walkers and their dogs who wander in the area every day of the week. It will, like the second tour, greatly enhance the sense of Lawrence's countryside, of what it gave his imagination, and of how his imagination transmuted it.

The second, south-easterly, trip goes above all to Cossall; still a virtually untouched village with comely houses grouped around an old church. Though nearer Nottingham than Eastwood, and within sight of the motorway between London and the North, it sits quietly there as it has done for centuries. The cottage to the left of the church, double-fronted and well-proportioned, was the home of the Burrows family to whose daughter, Louie, Lawrence was for a short time engaged. More important for the reader as reader, the cottage was the home of Will and Anna Brangwen in *The Rainbow*.

D. H. Lawrence, 1908

If there is still time, one may go a few miles further east, cross the motorway and come to the hamlet of Strelley, which also is untouched and looks much as it must have looked when Lawrence knew it and had the Brangwens see it from across their fields. This second trip, too, will take about an hour, halts excepted.

So what does all this wandering add up to in terms of our understanding of Lawrence's work? Can such a visit actually do anything to increase our appreciation of those works? Or is it a harmless form of biographical gawping, intrinsically no different from ignorant shufflings through country houses about whose history and the lives of its inhabitants we learn only a little and that on the surface? Wouldn't it be all too easy to gain the false impression that we have learned much about Lawrence's work, rather than a little about the early life of the man himself? Not surprisingly, to such questions some scholars give entirely negative answers. Read the books, they say, do not seek such adventitious aids.

It is true that there is no substitute for trying to grapple in all their complexity with the works themselves, and in that effort there are no real short cuts. Yet though the family backgrounds of some authors may be entirely irrelevant to an enhanced understanding of their works, with Lawrence the case is somewhat different. To see Eastwood and the mining countryside is to understand a little better, visually and imaginatively, the culture from which Lawrence came and its contribution to his work – in all that culture's crudenesses and complexities, its weaknesses and its strengths, its brutalities and its pieties. Our eyes do not see into the meanings of those lives as penetratingly as Lawrence's did – that is part of the case for the novels, for all good novels.

It follows, very importantly, that a visit can bring home to us with renewed force the way in which a great writer can take material which looks to an outside and unendowed eye simply poor and deprived and can see in it, and recreate by his imagination, the power and passion, the splendours and miseries, of those lives. And can do so in such a way that we cannot any longer, if we have been so tempted, write off such lives as of little interest. So one may from such a visit learn more about the working of the creative imagination and have a chastened sense of one's own comparative impercipience; both great gains.

Similarly, to see the countryside Lawrence loved so much and to recall his recreation of it makes us realize how relatively blind most of us are, and what an exceptional ability Lawrence had to respond to landscape. The eyes and ears and touch and smell which he learned to exercise in that pleasant but undramatic home landscape were later to blossom in Australia, Sicily, New Mexico, Sardinia. More dramatic landscapes, all those; but hence a visit to Eastwood reminds us also that, properly seen, inwardly seen, no landscape is in itself uninteresting, dull.

Lawrence was a great evoker of landscapes, a fine essayist and critic, a considerable poet and short-story writer and a superb novelist. His greatest single achievement was in the exploration of complex human relationships, especially those between men and women, in love or in hate. It would be hard to name another English novelist who has so penetrated the constant ebb and flow of such relationships. To appreciate this, one must read above all *Women in Love*. But his work is in the end all of a piece. The second half of *Sons and Lovers*, with its explorations of Paul's relationships with Miriam, with Clara and with his mother, grows inextricably from the first part and is also inextricably part of that astonishing process which led to the even more complex relationships of the later novels.

To stand in the Breach house does not in itself help us see further into Lawrence's achievement in that respect. But if we come to know the novels and to know, partly as a result of a visit, something of the crowded and unprivileged life of such homes, then we realize even more sharply than before that, though passions of the most complex kind can be played out anywhere, only a genius – of whatever parts of a society he writes – can transmute those events, those styles of life, into universality.

T. E. LAWRENCE

CLOUDS HILL, WAREHAM, DORSET

MALCOLM BROWN

The year 1923 began badly for T. E. Lawrence. In January his first attempt to slip out of the skin of 'Colonel Lawrence of Arabia' failed when he was ejected from the Royal Air Force, in which he had served since the previous August as John Hume Ross. The press furore caused by the revelation that the famous war-hero was lurking in the ranks as an ordinary aircraftman was too much for his service superiors. He immediately embarked on a second, more successful, disappearance, emerging in March at the Army Tank Training Camp at Bovington, Dorset, as Private Thomas Edward Shaw – the alias he was to retain until his death twelve years later.

He hated the Army from the outset, however, and his mood soon deteriorated to one of near despair. His enthusiasm for the RAF, which he saw as having an exciting future, had sustained him during his months as an aircraftman, and he had found his comrades decent and congenial – 'the cleanest little mob of fellows' he called them in a letter to his Oxford friend Lionel Curtis, in spite of their being 'foul-mouthed'. His new barrack-mates were also foul-mouthed, but in a crucially different manner. 'Behind their mouths,' he complained, 'is a pervading animality of spirit, whose unmixed bestiality frightens me and hurts me.' He would later find good friends among these men, but to begin with he saw them as a crowd of uncongenial drop-outs and failures and, if for his own different reasons, himself as no better than they. Adding to his distress was the knowledge that if he wished he could leave the Army at any moment. 'It's terrible to hold myself voluntarily here,' he wrote to Lionel Curtis in the letter referred to above, written from 'Tanktown' on 14 May, 'and yet I want to stay here till it no longer hurts me: till the burnt child no longer feels the fire.' In the same letter he stated: 'Sometimes I wonder how far mad I am, and if a mad-house would not be my next (and merciful) stage.'

Fortunately, his next stage was not to be a mad-house, but the half-derelict one

Clouds Hill

which he was shortly to discover near Tanktown at Clouds Hill (strictly the name applies not to the building but to the geographical area). It stood on a piece of land recently leased to an Army sergeant, Arthur Knowles. The story told in the Knowles family is that one day in the second half of 1923 Lawrence with some other soldiers came walking up to Clouds Hill and found the sergeant at work on the building's roof. Knowles was in process of constructing his own bungalow on the other side of the road, but was fulfilling a legal obligation to put the old house to rights at the same time. Lawrence saw its potential at once, opened negotiations and soon agreed terms. By November that year he was writing to an RAF friend: 'I'm not wholly resourceless in Bovington: found a ruined cottage near camp and took it for 2/6 a week. Have roofed it and am flooring it. At present one chair and a table there ... Scruffy place. About a dozen good books already.'

At first he had no plans to live in it – as a private soldier he had to sleep in Camp – but he could go up there in the evenings and it would be ideal for the literary activities for which it was becoming increasingly important to find time. That summer he had struggled through the translation of a French novel for the London publisher Jonathan Cape. Beyond that, however, lay the challenging task, which became a firm project at this period, of producing a private, subscribers' edition of his war-book *Seven Pillars of Wisdom* to the highest possible standards of printing and design; he would need somewhere to work on revising the text. He had, however, found much more than convenient office-space. Ascetic as he was, he saw that Clouds Hill offered the prospect of solitariness and ease. 'I covet the idea,' he wrote to a wartime colleague, 'of being sometimes by myself near a fire.' It had one other key attraction, defined in a letter to Mrs George Bernard Shaw dated March 1924: it allowed him the opportunity 'to hide a quiet while in a cloud-defended cottage'.

The visitor to Clouds Hill today can appreciate at once why Lawrence found it a marvellous place to hide in. The cottage stands in its own secluded dell, an arena of grass and gravel dominated by high hedgerows, bushes and trees. The range of growth is remarkable. There is gorse in abundance, broom, laurel, bush heather, honeysuckle; daffodils, primroses and periwinkles in season; and, like Assyrians poised over the fold, ranks of rhododendrons. Among and beyond these loom tall oaks, half a dozen elegant silver birch, plus fir trees of numerous varieties which heap to a remarkable height eastwards to the summit of the hill. In spring and summer the rhododendrons, as they always did, take total, arrogant control. In June 1924 Lawrence, initially suspicious of their aggressive presence, yielded to them. He wrote to Mrs Shaw: 'The cottage is nearly closed in with mountains of rhododendron bloom, of the screaming blue-pink which I used to dislike: now they are my plants I love them.'

278

By contrast the house itself is distinctly ordinary; a place that would catch no one's interest if it had not had a notable occupant. 'As ugly as my sins,' Lawrence once described it, in affectionate disparagement, 'bleak, angular, small, unstable: very like its owner.' Today, with its gleaming white walls and its flutter of dormer windows, it is not quite the plain labourer's dwelling which it originally was, but it still appears slightly out of place in all that luxuriance. In fairy-tale terms, it's a woodcutter's cottage in a rich man's garden. It almost seems to touch its forelock at its own good fortune.

There was much for Lawrence to hide from here. He was thirty-five when he became the tenant of Clouds Hill and already had lived several strenuous careers. Illegitimate, he was the son of an Anglo-Irish landlord who had decamped with his children's governess and founded a new family, eventually settling in respectable middle-class north Oxford. The name 'Lawrence' was an invention – the father's real name was Chapman – which helps to explain why the beleaguered war-hero would feel no compunction in changing it. The second of five brothers, he had received a sound education in Oxford at the City High School and at Jesus College, where he got an outstanding First in History. The scholar had then mutated to an archaeologist, spending several years in the Middle East at a major dig sponsored by the British Museum. Next and crucially, he had been a successful if off-beat soldier, who, in the parlance of the times, had had a 'good war' – in fact an astonishing one, in that after two years in military intelligence in Cairo he had been seconded to help the Arab Revolt against Turkey, becoming the principal liaison officer between the leading Arab field-commander, Prince Feisal, and the C-in-C of British forces in Egypt and Palestine, General Sir Edmund Allenby. During this time he had ridden on raids, blown up trains and generally lived the stuff of which legends – and, ultimately, movies – would be made. He had carried his identification with the Arab cause forward to the Peace Conference in Paris, once more in the capacity of right-hand man to Feisal. Later in 1921 he had again been active in Middle Eastern diplomacy, this time as adviser to the then Colonial Secretary, Winston Churchill.

Meanwhile he had also become an international celebrity, thanks to a brilliant American publicist, Lowell Thomas, who had met him during the war and who from mid-1919 onwards presented an illustrated travelogue about the Middle Eastern campaigns which played to packed houses first in New York, then in London and subsequently around the world. Thomas swiftly turned Lawrence, not without the latter's initial cooperation, into a quasi-film-star. In modern terms, Lawrence became tabloid fodder – though when he saw what he had connived at, he realized with dismay that he had helped to release a genie that he would never be able to control.

279

T. E. Lawrence on his motor-cycle at Clouds Hill, 1935

From his childhood onwards, however, he had lived another life as well – that of a would-be writer. It was the persona he cared for most of all. His supreme ambition was to produce a classic, memorable work. The books he particularly admired were monumental ones: Nietzsche's *Zarathustra*, Melville's *Moby Dick*, Dostoevsky's *The Brothers Karamazov*. 'Titanic' books, he called them. His hope from his youth up, confessed to the novelist and critic Edward Garnett in a letter of August 1922, was to make 'an English fourth'. (A second list, in a letter to E. M. Forster in September 1924, admitted *War and Peace, Don Quixote*, Whitman's *Leaves of Grass* and the great work of Rabelais to his canon.)

In a curious way the possibility of realizing this ambition had virtually fallen into his lap. The war not only made a guerrilla genius out of him but also offered him an amazing literary opportunity. Quite early in the Arab campaign he had become aware that he had a subject evolving daily around him about which a 'titanic' book might be made. In effect, he was a significant participant in a non-fiction story which promised the qualities of the fiction he most revered.

This, in essence, is why *Seven Pillars of Wisdom* became what it is, and why it bears its grand, if obscure, name. He had conceived the title before the war for a book about seven oriental cities which he had started and subsequently destroyed. He had coined the phrase from the Old Testament – Proverbs 9:1: 'Wisdom hath builded her house, she hath hewn out her seven pillars.' He had carried the title over to the new work, he once told a friend, 'out of sentiment', but he also saw it as providing an appropriate metaphor for what he had attempted, and partly achieved, in his wartime activities in Arabia. If he had been content with a lesser work with a lesser title, say, *Memoirs of a Middle Eastern Intelligence Officer*, or *By Camel and Rolls-Royce Tender to Damascus*, he would have been lucky to sell 2,000 copies and the book would now be found only in the British Library, the Imperial War Museum or in the lists of specialist military booksellers. *Seven Pillars of Wisdom* isn't just an account of one man's war. It is an attempt to turn experience into literature. And in that it has been one of the century's steadiest best-sellers, who is to say that he did not achieve his aim – to some extent at least?

The keynote statement in this context is in the book itself:

> I had had one craving all my life – for the power of self-expression in some imaginative form – but had been too diffuse ever to acquire a technique. At last accident, with perverted humour, in casting me as a man of action had given me place in the Arab Revolt, a theme ready and epic to a direct eye and hand, thus offering me an outlet in literature, the technique-less art.

Now it must be said at once that if ever a writer laboured to find a technique it was Lawrence. He approached *Seven Pillars* as if it were a sculpture or a painting – a Sistine Chapel almost. He agonized over his text, constantly rewriting. The result (here I declare my personal view) is a quasi-Wagnerian work; often superb, but sometimes hard pounding, with its definite *longueurs* and its areas of verbal clutter. Yet it's a book that one might well take to a desert island along with the Bible and Shakespeare. Despite its weaknesses it has passages that stay in the mind like fine music: read his description of Wadi Rumm in Chapter LXII, or its stunning opening chapters – including the moving Introductory Chapter which Bernard Shaw, absurdly, persuaded him to drop from the early editions. Or it can disturb like a movement from a late Beethoven quartet: read Chapter CIII, a tortuous, moving exercise in self-analysis ending with the cryptic sentence: 'Indeed, the truth was I did not like the "myself" I could see and hear.'

All books are of their time, and one generation's icons frequently become the next generation's footballs. 'A sonorous fake as a writer' is the verdict on Lawrence of one highly fashionable novelist of today. But against this hear these opinions. H. G. Wells wrote of *Seven Pillars*: 'It is a wonderful book. In my opinion it is the finest piece of prose that has been written in the English language for 150 years.' E. M. Forster wrote: 'I thought it a masterpiece'; but then added, 'To have said so would have been fatal.'

For the curious fact is that Lawrence would have agreed with his denigrators more than his admirers – indeed, perhaps only in his archaeological efforts and his mechanical work on speedboats some years later after his return to the RAF did he find any genuine self-satisfaction. The following statement expresses the view of his own writings from which he stubbornly refused to budge: 'What is the perversity which makes me, capable of doing many things in the world, wish only to do one thing, book-writing; and gives me no skill at it?' He wrote thus to Robert Graves in 1922, having decided that *Seven Pillars* had, as he put it, 'proved dud'.

By the time he became established at Clouds Hill, he was – for better or worse – beginning the process of getting *Seven Pillars* into print (with the aid of an expatriate American printer, Manning Pike, and a cadre of distinguished artists, including Augustus John, Eric Kennington, William Roberts, Paul Nash, Henry Lamb), and he had also written the vital chapters of a second book. Smaller in concept, earthier, far from Wagnerian, this was a distinctly avant-garde work: more minor Stravinsky or early William Walton. It was an account, compiled with stunning documentary precision and no self-conscious prose, of his first weeks in the RAF, while under basic training at Uxbridge. He was to call it *The Mint*, because at Uxbridge all recruits were hammered into identical shapes like coins. He pulled no punches in description or language, well aware that this would make the book unpublishable for a long time to come. He revealed an almost Gulag aspect of contemporary life (it has been compared to Solzhenitsyn's *One Day in the Life of Ivan Denisovich*) light years away from the experience of the literati who would form its first readership. He would add later chapters that were less immediately shocking, but even so the book would not appear in a generally available expurgated edition until 1955 and would not emerge as Lawrence wrote it until 1973. There are many who think this a greater, more classic work than *Seven Pillars*.

After *The Mint* he was to produce no other book apart from translations – the most notable of which was his widely admired *Odyssey* – so in a sense the would-be writer had virtually written himself out before he came to Clouds Hill. He would continue to write remarkable letters, and the view of some of his admirers is that he will live longest in literature through them. But he would never do other than tinker with the idea of another sustained literary work.

Clouds Hill, however, allowed him to craft, if not a book, a life. He had felt himself battered and hounded for too long. In a letter to Bernard Shaw in 1922 he had written – it is a statement both significant and moving – 'You see the war was, for us who were in it, an overwrought time, in which we lost our normal footing.' He had been much overwrought since. Clouds Hill was his way back to some kind of normal footing.

Lawrence was always a complex and would never be a happy man and Clouds Hill too must have had its dark times. Almost certainly some of the beatings to which he submitted himself in his later years took place here. But the mood and atmosphere of the place is positive, benign. He brought congenial fellow soldiers from the Camp there, and literary and other friends came to join the small, select company. 'What was Clouds Hill?' he wrote to Mrs Shaw after an evening of records and conversation in 1924: 'A sort of mixed grill, I fancy: but very good. Everybody is beginning to fall in love with it. The air of it is peaceful: and the fire burns so well.'

If the visitor senses a contented atmosphere there today, this was also the feeling of one of Lawrence's earliest guests, E. M. Forster – who was met by Lawrence and his motor-bike at nearby Wool station.

> He took me up through the bleak ungracious desert of Bovington Camp by a straight road which mounts slightly and then falls over a little dip into peacefulness and wildness and there was Clouds Hill. I liked the place at once. His friends were friendly to me, I felt easy and to feel easy was in T. E.'s eyes a great recommendation. We weren't to care as soon as we were inside the place. We weren't to worry about the world and the standards the world imposes.

A memoir by a former Tank Corps corporal, Alec Dixon, confirms the 'easy' mood of Lawrence's 'mixed grills':

> He presided over the company, settling arguments, patiently answering all manner of questions, feeding the gramophone, making tea, stoking the fire, and, by some magic of his own, managing without effort to keep everyone in good humour. There were many picnic meals (stuffed olives, salted almonds and Heinz baked beans were regular features) washed down with T. E.'s own blend of China tea. Some of us used chairs, others the floor, while T. E. always ate standing by the end of the wide oak mantelshelf which had been fitted at a height convenient for him.

The Greek motto over the cottage door, carved by Lawrence, conveys the same relaxing message: 'οὐ φροντὶς'. 'Wyworri?' was his translation of it, from the antics of an Athenian gentleman engaged to a merchant's daughter who stood on his head on the table at his pre-marriage feast and performed a leg-dance. 'You dance your marriage off,' said the outraged merchant who would now not become the said Athenian's father-in-law. 'Wyworri?' was the blithe reply. 'Herodotus tells the story so beautifully,' Lawrence wrote in a letter to Mrs Kennington, 'that I put the jape on the architrave. It means that nothing in Clouds Hill is to be a care upon its habitant. While I have it there shall be nothing exquisite or unique in it. Nothing to anchor me.'

Lawrence eventually changed from tenant to owner, and improved the property steadily over the years – though with his re-enlistment in the RAF in 1925 (following pleas on his behalf by Bernard Shaw and John Buchan and the personal intervention of the Prime Minister, Stanley Baldwin) he was often away from it for long periods.

The ground floor was initially full of lumber and firewood, but gradually it was transformed into what he called his book-room, a kind of study-bedroom furnished with a king-size bed and sleeping-bags, walled with his favourite volumes and with an armchair and reading-stand by the fire. The large upstairs room (scene of the said 'mixed grills') became a place of leather-chaired comfort under the lea of a massive E. M. Ginn gramophone – its horn like a ship's ventilator – which did greater justice than his earlier Columbia one to his vast and highly sophisticated record collection. There was a further leap forward when at 1.45 pm on 31 August 1933, driven by 'the smallest ram installed anywhere', water began to flow into the cottage at Clouds Hill. Soon he could enjoy the luxury of his own bath, the latter being supplied, aptly, by his former supply and ordnance officer at Aqaba.

Although the bookshelves now house photographs and drawings, and various pictures and mementoes have been imported, today's visitors see Clouds Hill much as it was when Lawrence declared it complete just a year before he died. On 18 May 1934 he wrote to Mrs Shaw:

> My cottage is finished, inside and out, so far as alien hands can finish it – and I feel rooted now, whenever I pass its door. Such a lovely little place, and so plain. It is ingenious, comfortable, bare and restful; and cheap to maintain.

Occasionally, if the weather is appropriate and the surrounding heath not tinder-dry, visitors will find another reminder of Lawrence's occupation – a wood fire burning in the grate of the book-room. They will also sense, if the air is still, how marvellously it diffuses its aroma around the whole grove. On such occasions it is almost possible to believe that the owner has just gone out for a while and will soon return. For Clouds Hill doesn't feel like a museum, but a house which still has its own life.

It was from Clouds Hill, some two months after his retirement from the RAF, that Lawrence rode off on his Brough motor-cycle on his last journey. He went down to the Camp to send a telegram and then set off back, riding up that 'straight road which mounts slightly and then falls over a little dip' as described above by E. M. Forster. It was just over that fatal dip, long obliterated by road improvements, that he had his accident, colliding with two errand boys on bicycles. He lay in a coma for six days and died on 19 May 1935, at the age of forty-six.

JOHN MILTON

CHALFONT ST GILES, BUCKINGHAMSHIRE

C. H. SISSON

John Milton's cottage at Chalfont St Giles is the only one of his successive residences that survives. When he went there, in July 1665, it must have been outside the village proper. Although there are now buildings on the opposite side of the road, it still stands at the bottom of a sweep of pasture, the downward slope of which is continued by the descending levels of the garden. It is a Tudor cottage from before the days when commuters began to invent such things, and must have been about a hundred years old when Milton moved in. He did not go to enjoy the country air. He went to avoid the Plague. Most of the best people thought that anywhere was better than London at that moment. The Court and many of the gentry departed and, as Pepys somewhat ironically reports, doctors whose patients had gone away and so 'left them free to choose'. The Bills of Mortality show the deaths from Plague to have been 267 in June, and by 7 September, 165: by the New Year it was virtually over, but Milton did not return to town for some months, although he was not a man to linger in the country as a matter of preference.

It was to his young friend Thomas Ellwood that Milton had turned so that 'he might go out of the city, for the safety of himself and his family'. The poet had been blind since 1650, and Ellwood was one of those who read to him. With his insatiable passion for books, and his knowledge of foreign languages, the demands he made on readers were exceptional. His daughters were not up to the job, and two of them were put to a trade; all three of them seem to have been thoroughly tired of their father, and the situation was complicated by the fact that they were the children of his first wife, and he was now on his third. Ellwood was a Quaker, closely connected with the Pennington family at Chalfont Grange, and the Grange was a centre for Quaker meetings from the surrounding neighbourhood. The rector of Chalfont St Giles, till 1661, had been Thomas Valentine, a famous Puritan; after the Restoration he had been turned out for nonconformity, as the clergy who stuck to the Prayer Book had been turned out under the Commonwealth. The cottage in which Milton took refuge still belonged to the only son of Colonel George

285

The bust of Milton in the cottage is a copy of the one in
Westminster Abbey by Rysbrack

Fleetwood, a local landowner who had been involved in the revolutionary committee which Buckinghamshire, like other counties, had enjoyed during the years of disaffection; he had also been a member of the Long Parliament, and one of the signatories of the King's death-warrant. One way and another the area was a natural retreat for a virulent anti-royalist.

The Milton who went to Chalfont in 1665 certainly did not pass for a famous poet. He had published a small volume of miscellaneous poems some twenty years before, and eight years before that *Comus, A Maske presented at Ludlow Castle*, when such things were still part of the courtly entertainments of the aristocracy. *Paradise Lost* was still unpublished, and neither *Paradise Regained* nor *Samson Agonistes* had been begun. Yet Milton was fifty-seven, a scholar of international repute, seasoned as a controversialist and, in the largely back-room job of Latin Secretary, as a public servant. 'He was much more admired abroade than at home,' the antiquary John Aubrey, who was twenty years his junior, assures us. 'Foreigners came to see him', and even to see 'the house and chamber where he was borne'. His public success had belonged to the time of the Commonwealth, and it is probable that the relatively large circulation of *Paradise Lost*, when the poem finally reached the public in 1667, was due rather to the sympathy of many of them for Milton's religious and political sentiments, than to any sudden leap in literary taste. Poets such as Dryden and Marvell certainly recognized his outstanding importance, in his life-time, but explicit widespread recognition had to await Addison's *Spectator* of 1712. Addison spoke as a Whig, and the Whigs for a stream of opinion which came from pre-Restoration sources as well as from the Revolution of 1689.

John Milton was born in Bread Street, in the City of London, on 9 December 1608. His father was of a good Oxfordshire family, his mother a London girl, the daughter of a merchant-tailor. The Oxfordshire grandfather is said to have been a stubborn Papist, who disinherited his son for changing his religion, in the general current of the times; one wonders whether something of this stubbornness did not descend to the poet, who, however, reserved it for different causes. The poet's father was a scrivener – a sort of solicitor who also offered financial services. He was no mere man of affairs but a musician and a friend of Henry Lawes, and altogether qualified to look after the interests of his sons, if the· care he gave their education is any indication. The young John was given a tutor, and was early acquainted with Greek and Latin. His appetite for work was abnormal; he sat up to midnight or beyond at his studies, and his father appointed a maid to sit up with the young gentleman. At the age of twelve he entered St Paul's School, where he spent five years, for four of which, it is interesting to reflect, no less a person than John Donne was Dean of the medieval cathedral which had not then been destroyed in the Great Fire. The boy must often have attended services at which the great man preached. In 1625 he entered Christ's College, Cambridge, already possessing a degree of scholarship unusual at any age. Life must have been harsh compared with the conditions he had known at home. There are stories of troubles at Cambridge, but the respectability and fastidiousness of his conduct are beyond doubt, as his nickname, 'The Lady of Christ's', suggests. The natural destination for a scholarly young man was the Church, but before leaving Cambridge in 1632 Milton had decided against this, without fixing on any other profession. His father had by now retired to the village of Horton, in Buckinghamshire, and seems to have been content for the young man to pursue his studies there, as he did until 1638, when his mother died. He then entered upon what might be regarded as the final stage of his education by making a continental journey which lasted some fifteen months. He conversed with the learned, in Paris and extensively in Italy. 'He was soon taken notice of by the most learned and ingenious of the Nobility, who caressed him with all the Honours and Civilities imaginable.' It had been his intention to go on to Sicily and even to Greece, but early in 1639 the news he received from England, 'that affairs there were tending towards a Civil War', made him decide that he should return, although his sense of public duty did not prevent him spending another two months in Rome on the way back.

Milton had no doubt known, from the first, where his sympathies lay in the struggle with the King, but he had no idea of taking arms. To Dr Johnson, and some others, it looks like something of an anti-climax that instead he took a lodging in St Bride's churchyard, and there 'undertook the Education and Instruction of his Sister's two Sons', one of them the Edward Phillips who became his biographer. Milton's addiction to study had not lessened with the years, and the variety of the

Milton's cottage, Chalfont St Giles

classical reading he shared with his pupils was such as 'in some measure increased his own knowledge'. His reading at this time included Hebrew, Caldee and Syriac, as well as French and Italian, of which he had long been a master. He soon moved to a 'good, handsome house in Aldersgate-street'. Here he was able to take more scholars, and started his long and immensely industrious course of controversy by producing tracts against prelacy. No doubt this was the sort of war work he had in mind as more suitable for himself than soldiering.

It was from this house in Aldersgate-street that, about Whitsuntide 1643, he took a journey into the country, 'nobody about him certainly knowing the reason', and came back married to a girl about half his age – Mary Powell, the daughter of a large and exuberant Royalist family. There is little evidence that Milton's judgement of practical affairs was better than might have been expected from a man who, at thirty-five, had done little but indulge himself with immense reading and with the conversation of those learned enough to have the privilege of discourse with him. It certainly does not look like that prudence for which he was noted, to marry into a family whose political views were clearly at the opposite pole from his own. It would hardly have been so, had he known the girl far better than he appears to have done. Anyway, she had been used to 'much Company and Joviality' and did not take to a 'Philosophical Life', which, according to Edward Phillips, was all she had at Aldersgate-street. A month later she had gone back to her family, and neither letters nor a foot-messenger could recover her. Milton, who at this stage might be described as little better than an intellectual, reacted by setting the world right as to the *Doctrine and Discipline of Divorce*. 'Indisposition, unfitness or contrariety of mind', he argued, might be proper grounds, and he made the points that 'woman was created for man and not man for woman', and that it is an 'injury' 'to be contended with in point of house-rule'. Johnson was surely right when he characterized Milton as 'one of those who could easily find arguments to justify inclination'. It was two years later that Mary Powell contrived to meet him where she could conveniently fall on her knees before him and ask his pardon – no doubt the only proper way for a disobedient wife to get a hearing from her lord. So the two lived together from 1645 till Mary's death in 1652, and had three children, unluckily all girls, so that there was no one who could benefit from their father's incomparable pedagogic attentions. There was a second marriage, with Catherine Woodcock, which lasted from 1656 to 1658 and ended with Catherine's death. His third wife, whom he married in 1663, survived him.

Milton thought that woman was made for obedience and man for rebellion (Johnson again). Certainly, after his return from his travels, he threw himself enthusiastically into what became the republican cause. His ecclesiastical iconoclasm took him, in the end, to regard sects and schisms as a sign of health. In the matter of civil government he was constant to the anti-royalist side, and indeed *Defensio pro Populo Anglicano*, his reply to the book in which a 'hired Frenchman', Salmasius, took the English people to task for the judicial murder of their King, achieved a *succès de scandale* throughout Europe and was publicly burnt in Paris and in Toulouse. No point now in arguing the cases advanced by the two sides in the Civil War: what can scarcely be denied is that, after the King's death in 1649, the revolutionary government went through the classic evolutions of such bodies, and parliament in the end gave way to the personal rule of a dictator. To this form of oppression Milton apparently had no objection. He did not shrink from flattering Oliver Cromwell:

> the whole national interest fell into your hands, and subsists only by your abilities. To your virtue, every man gives way ... nothing is more pleasing to God, or more agreeable to reason, than that the highest mind should have the sovereign power.

There are inconsistencies and absurdities enough here and there in Milton's views, and one can be put off by the egotism which directed so much of the course of his life. One cannot say of him, as one might of Shakespeare, that he is above having ideas, but there is nothing in him of the hawker of opinions. When the trap of his mind was opened, the flow that was released tapped profound sources he may truly be said to have shared with the great classical poets and with the Hebrew poets and prophets. Milton possessed his poetic gifts from very early years, yet he exercised them only intermittently, and certainly did not make the possession of them an excuse for evading his civil duties. When he wrote verse, the crotchets of opinion and controversy were demoted to a place below that of the demands of language and rhythms. His master in English poetry seems to have been Spenser, and if the works of his final period seem remote from that influence, the earlier poems leave no doubt of the fact. Yet one of the earliest, *On the Morning of Christ's Nativity*, written when he was only twenty-one, produces a sort of organ-blast not heard before in English poetry. The poems of the great period of production at Horton, when he had nothing to do but to indulge himself with his reading and, when it suited her, with his Muse, are of a different character from the solemn *Ode*, as are *L'Allegro* and *Il Penseroso*, which may slightly precede that 'interval of uninterrupted leisure'. The major work of the period was *Comus*, cool in temper and masterly in its versification. Something more like the voice of Milton's later work is heard in *Lycidas*, the elegy he wrote in 1637 for a friend 'unfortunately drown'd in his passage from Chester on the Irish Seas'. He had left his youthful poem on *The Passion* unfinished as 'above the yeers he had when he wrote it', and still, at twenty-eight, he began his elegy:

> Yet once more, O ye Laurels, and once more
> Ye Myrtles brown, with Ivy never sear,

Interior of Milton's cottage

> I come to pluck your Berries harsh and crude,
> And with forc'd fingers rude,
> Shatter your leaves before the mellowing year.

It was at once a confession of modesty and the confident promise of a man who was sensible that the great work was still to come.

It would perhaps have surprised Milton, at this stage, if he had known how far away it was – the other side not only of travel, but of marriage and children, employment which left him without leisure, absorbing and excruciating controversy, and blindness. The man who dictated *Paradise Lost* was certainly a different man from the idle scholar who had written *Comus*. The premonitions of the *Ode on the Morning of Christ's Nativity* were fulfilled in the voice which had found no less a subject than

> To justify the ways of God to Man

– a frontal attack on the whole theme of the Fall of Man and, incidentally, on the basic relations of man and woman. He had, so to speak, passed that way. Thomas Ellwood – himself a poet, but of the most pedestrian kind – was given the manuscript of *Paradise Lost* soon after he came to Chalfont. Milton 'called for' it, no doubt in the little study where the visitor is most tempted to imagine him, and perhaps in the peremptory tone which was certainly not unknown in his family circle. Ellwood was to take it away and 'return it to him with [his] judgement thereupon'. This request must have been a civility, thanks maybe for finding the cottage rather than submission to the Quaker's advice on creative writing. 'Thou hast said much here of "Paradise Lost", but what hast thou to say of "Paradise Found?"' Milton changed the subject, but later, back in London, he remembered the conversation and told Ellwood – surely again with an excess of literary courtesy – that he had put *Paradise Regained* into his head.

There is a sense in which the last work, *Samson Agonistes*, if not the peak of Milton's achievement, is in some sort the natural issue of his long development, for in it, more than in any other, he speaks for himself in a manner personal to a degree rare until much later times. The form of classical tragedy is, we know, something Milton had long considered working in. He had chosen the epic model for his major works, but reverted to his earlier idea at the end. One does not need any profound knowledge of his life, public and private, to identify the Old Testament hero with the poet:

> A little onward lend thy guiding hand
> To these dark steps, a little further on;
> For yonder bank hath choice of Sun or shade,
> There I am wont to sit ...

Where better imagine him in this role than in the lovely garden at Chalfont which he saw no more than Samson saw his place of respite in Gaza?

It is, at any rate, a perspective in which to consider Milton afresh. As one crosses the threshold of the cottage – not exactly the threshold Milton crossed, for the door seems to have been moved a little to one side – one comes into a small passage which is merely a partitioned-off part of the room which is known as Milton's study and which appears to have been his main living quarters in the house, except when he joined the family for meals in the kitchen next door. It was this general living-room into which, in accordance with a pattern common at the time, the front door formerly opened. Here and in the study the visitor is left to brood. The study, one wall of which is almost filled by a large fireplace, must certainly have been the centre of Milton's life at Chalfont. Inevitably, the small library collected since the Cottage Trust was set up in 1887 does not reflect the poet's vast reading, but it is appropriately evocative of his life and achievement. There are first editions of *Paradise Lost* and *Paradise Regained*, and of *Eikon Basilike* – the Royalist 'image of the King' which appeared a few months after the death of Charles I, and which Milton did his best to destroy. There are books representative of contemporary Quakers of the neighbourhood, and what can only be called an illustrative sample of translations of *Paradise Lost*. There is what was perhaps once a lock of Milton's hair, but is now only a wisp – the victim, no doubt, of depredations which, under the care of the Trust, have long been prevented.

Milton himself, at Chalfont, must have been looking back on a past of ferocious toil for the Commonwealth, a world in which the enlightenment he had preached had not come true. His public life had come to nothing. He was fortunate that the mood of the Restoration was in the main gentle and he never suffered anything that could be called oppression. Probably his dearest wish was that people should say, when the end came,

> Samson hath quit himself
> Like Samson and heroicly hath finish'd
> A life Heroic,

– not forgetting

> on his enemies
> Fully reveng'd.

This cannot be said to have been the position when he was buried in St Giles's, Cripplegate, in 1674, but he did his best. That year he still remembered that he had never had the portion due to him from his first wife's father, and so left it 'to the unkind children' he had had from her, who were to have no other benefit by his estate. But as Milton, in 1665, sought the sun or shade in the garden of his cottage, and regaled himself with the scent of herbs and flowers, or perhaps of a pig or two, if such down-to-earth inhabitants had not been extruded to make room for the poet, he could at least take some satisfaction in the completion of his great poem and perhaps in a faint adumbration of work still to be done.

As to the final critical question: Where should we place Milton now? the answer must be: Nowhere, unless we have first read him and much else besides. The time was when *Paradise Lost* was, for ordinary educated people, a 'good book' to set beside the Bible and *Pilgrim's Progress*. There was a time when the echoes of Latin constructions were reassuring rather than troubling, but it is over sixty years since the superbly educated Mr Eliot spoke of the 'Chinese stone-wall of Milton'. One might now venture to think of Chaucer, rather than Milton, as in second place to Shakespeare, but there is no other rival. He lives in his own isolation, and Wordsworth was being not flattering, but precise, when he addressed him in that sonnet of 1802:

> Thy soul was like a star, and dwelt apart:
> Thou hadst a voice whose sound was like the sea.

There is room for a new critical *entrée* into this lonely phenomenon. David Wright has made the illuminating comment that 'for all his Latinity and classical façade, Milton was the true precursor of the Romantics'. It is worth thinking about, whether you regard the news as good or bad.

WILLIAM MORRIS

KELMSCOTT MANOR, LECHLADE, GLOUCESTERSHIRE

PENELOPE FITZGERALD

William Morris (1834–96) was described by his daughter May as Artist, Writer, Socialist. 'Artist' implied 'mastercraftsman', and art, for Morris, came to mean pleasure in any kind of work in hand. (Both as a craft and as a business, Morris took up decoration, furnishing and stained glass around 1859, dyeing in 1875, weaving in 1878, printing in 1890.) He was also a good short-order cook, an observer of birds and weather, a moderately successful fisherman, a very successful Victorian businessman, the founder of the Society for the Protection of Ancient Buildings and at the same time a tireless fighter for an England totally different from the one he knew. From necessity he worked among the 'smoke-dried swindlers' of London. He rested – so far as he was capable of resting at all – at Kelmscott.

Kelmscott is in the south-west corner of Oxfordshire. On the other side of a stream it becomes Gloucestershire. This is the heart of the stone country, where, Morris said, 'every house must either be built, walls and roof, of grey stone, or be a blot on the landscape'. Local farmers who patched things up with corrugated iron drove him to furious despair. The manor (never really more than a farmhouse) stands two miles above Radcott Bridge on the upper Thames. A door in the garden wall opens on to a group of willows and the kind of river that Morris loved best – 'the smallness of the scale of everything, the short reaches and the speedy change of the banks give one a feeling of going somewhere, of coming to something strange, a feeling of adventure I have not felt in bigger waters'. In high summer, when at midday the rooks and even the doves are silent, the stream is the only voice in the meadowland. The manor, self-sufficient with its gabled barn and stone sheds, was built in the late sixteenth century, with seventeenth-century additions. Morris's faithful friend, the architect Philip Webb, judged that the masonry was 'really later than it looked to be', but it was difficult to be sure because tradition died so hard in the stone country. Morris himself wrote (in *Gossip about an Old House on the Upper*

Thames, 1895) that the house – 'not great at all, remember' – had 'grown up out of the soil and the lives of those that lived on it'. He tells us that he himself loved this place with 'a not unreasonable love, I think'. But how can love be reasonable?

Kelmscott Manor never belonged to him. In 1871, when he was 'looking about for a house for the wife and kids', he read a description of it in a house agent's list, went down to see it, and found it 'a heaven on earth', a phrase with particular meaning for Morris, who believed, with Ruskin, that 'there is no wealth but life' and no life beyond this one. He took a joint tenancy with the poet and painter Dante Gabriel Rossetti. Rossetti's nerves had been under increasing strain since the death of his wife, Elizabeth Siddal, from an overdose of laudanum. It was thought that a change of air (which, in the 1870s, seems to have been the doctors' favourite prescription) might help him. Indeed, although he was quite unused to the country, his health did, at first, improve among the willows and water-meadows and in the company of Jane Morris and her two little daughters. Morris, busy in London, was there much less often. The outcome was an ambiguous situation between Rossetti, Morris and Jane which has never been quite understood, not even at the time and by those who knew them best. All that can be said for certain is that Rossetti was obsessed with Jane's beauty and drew and painted her unceasingly, that the children, Jenny and May, showed no resentment but on the contrary pitied what they felt as his loneliness, that Jane was silent on the subject, and that Morris contained himself in patience. In spite of his frequent outbursts of rage at the stupidity of things and people, when doors would be kicked and books flew out of the window, there was a magnanimity in his nature, a largeness and noble generosity. It was his profound belief that every human being – men, women, and, as far as possible, children – should be free to choose their own life. 'Whatever is unhappy,' he wrote, 'is immoral.'

On the other hand, he longed for Rossetti to take himself off. 'Gabriel has set himself down as though he never meant to go away.' But the situation resolved itself. In the summer of 1874 Rossetti entered one of the darkest periods of his life, with delusions of horror and persecution, and he was taken to London, a sick man, in the charge of his doctor. This left Morris free to begin a new tenancy of Kelmscott, shared this time with his publisher, F. S. Ellis. Ellis, like Morris, was a lover of old books, but also of fishing and sailing and what Rossetti called 'bugging and blaspheming in a boat' across the spring floodwaters.

Neither of them did much to the house in the way of repairs or decoration. It was for holidays only, and you have to use your imagination to see it as it was, when it was no more, and no less, than that. The panelled room was always painted white, as it still is, but most of the beautiful things which are now on view (Rossetti's

The stream running through the grounds of Kelmscott Manor

Kelmscott Manor

Mrs Morris in a Blue Silk Dress among them) have been moved there since Morris's death. Again, most of the wallpapers and curtains are modern reprinting. What Morris asked for from Kelmscott was what he called its 'kindness' – a shelter from hot weather (which he hated), a precious sense of tradition, space for his daughters to 'lark about' and for himself, too, when an idea struck him, to pace up and down, and, outside, the 'delicious superabundance' of a small garden well tended through all four seasons. Given all this, it mattered little or nothing to him that the place was sketchily furnished, draughty, and damp, particularly when the floods were out. If you wanted to be comfortable, he said, you could always go to bed, and he

298

The Thames at Kelmscott

saw nothing inconvenient in the way the bedrooms opened out of one another. Meanwhile Mouse, the pony he brought back from his second journey to Iceland, was stabled in what is now the kitchen. Jane, writing to Wilfrid Scawen Blunt, called it a 'half-savage life'. It took years, she said, to get Morris to have a decent bookcase put in, 'several friends having complained of the dearth of books to read in the literary man's house'. Indeed, his dearest friend, the painter Burne-Jones, avoided, as far as possible, coming down there at all. Others, like Bernard Shaw, came, but refused flatly to go out fishing. Very few, however, failed to respond to Morris's unselfconscious welcome. At such times (as Yeats put it) he appeared at the same time helpless and triumphant, and was loved as a child is loved.

What did Kelmscott mean to him? To begin with, it was a place of birds and flowers – he even managed to persuade the Thames Conservancy Board not to cut back the wild flowers on the river banks. They are there for anyone to see in some of his most appealing designs – creeping bellflower, water forget-me-not, water avens, willow, snakeshead fritillary. 'Strawberry Thief' (1883) derives from the birds pecking away at the Kelmscott strawberry beds. (Morris, to the gardener's disgust, would never let them be driven off, and May Morris remembered that there were usually more birds than strawberries.) Secondly, the house itself, sober and moderate, soundly built with an economical use of the materials to hand, gave a promise of unity to his deeply divided personality. It was a home in a sense only possible in a cold climate, 'the heap of grey stones with a grey roof that we call a house northaway'. And it represented what he wanted (otherwise he would not have been Morris) for every other man and woman in his dreamed-of Society of Equals: 'dwellings which they could come to with pleasure, surroundings which would soothe and elevate them; reasonable labour, reasonable rest'.

That was his generous hope for the twentieth century. During his own lifetime he seems never to have got on very well with the villagers. They disapproved, at first, of the dashing presence of Rossetti in the household. Later there was trouble about a right of way. Morris himself felt a kind of resentful servility in the Oxfordshire farm labourers, which he tried in vain to dispel. Philip Comely, who worked at the manor, embarrassed him by constantly touching his hat 'as though by a trick of machinery'. In later years, however, May Morris took up quite naturally the role of lady of the manor. On Fridays she distributed soup from the brewhouse in the courtyard, and she taught the choir to sing 'Jerusalem' round the piano in the Green Room, girls in the front, boys and men at the back.

In 1872 Morris took it into his head, for the one and only time, to write a novel of contemporary life. Friends were discouraging, and it was never finished. The manuscript remained unpublished until 1982. But although when he wrote it he had only just begun his tenancy of Kelmscott, he gives a faithful picture, described almost as if in a trance, of the house and its river-meadows through the slow-moving days of high summer.

The two boys who are at the centre of the story are the sons of an Oxfordshire country parson. I have said that Morris's character was deeply divided, and John and Arthur represent two sides, as he saw them, of himself. Both are romantics, who see their own lives as 'stories going on', but John is for the open air, Arthur is the dreamer. John is at a crucial point of adolescence, behaving awkwardly, 'with that vague feeling of disappointment in life past yet hope of life to come'. His struggles to master himself are like Morris's own; so too is his remedy for depression. He sets off upriver with his fishing-rod until he reaches a point where

> the stream itself grew shallow and ran over gravel or pushed its way through beds of blue-flowered mouse-ear and horsemint and was bordered by willows instead of the harsh dark alders that hung over its black pools higher up.

(Anyone who cares to can still follow this path step by step from Radcott Bridge.) Then, at the end of the next reach, without looking, as if by instinct, his feet turned from the river onto a footpath which cut off the corner to a homestead lying at the foot of the slopes; the grey roofs showed among plenteous lime trees populous with rooks ... a paved footway led up to the house, and gave one the idea of a farmer and his family come home from church to the Sunday dinner.

The three gabled roofs are

finished with a stone ball threaded on an iron spike; the gable end of the main roof was windowless and covered all over with a great pear tree.

John has reached Kelmscott (called in the novel Leaser Farm). He hears the light footsteps of a girl coming along the wall side. This is Clara, and the beginning of John's love story, which was evidently going to turn, if Morris had ever finished his novel, into tragic disappointment. Clara will choose not John, but John's brother, leaving him to write a half-crazy letter:

If you are sure as you say you are that Clara loves you and that you love her heed nothing heed nobody but live your life through with her, crushing everything that comes in your way – everything –.

Soon after this the manuscript breaks off, but Morris never destroyed it. It survives as a witness of the unhappiest year of his marriage, and at the same time of his passion for Kelmscott, where John 'seemed to gather all the bliss of memory of many and many a summer's noon into this one'.

Twenty years later Morris was totally committed to practical socialism.

Intelligence enough to conceive, courage enough to will, power enough to compel ... and then, I say, the thing will be done.

Before he was sixty, however, he had given up, not his convictions, but his hope of seeing them realized in his lifetime. In 1889 he wrote *News from Nowhere*, publishing it in *The Commonweal*, a penny weekly which he edited for the Socialist League. In the first instalment (11 January 1890) he is shown going back from a League meeting, 'stewing discontentedly' in the hated new Underground Railway, to his house in Hammersmith. He wakes next morning to find himself fallen into the future. He is Guest – the guest of the hospitable, handsome Londoners of the twenty-first century, in an England without money, without competition, without politics, where the Houses of Parliament are only useful as a dung market. Fellowship has replaced mastery, and there is no need for law – an appeal to conscience is enough. Everyone shares in the joy of working with their hands, houses and markets look much as they did in the fourteenth century, and the weather, from beginning to end, is golden summer. All this looks like self-indulgence, but *News from Nowhere* is not a simple story. Although Guest feels a deep content, as though he were new-born, he disturbs the peace, making the inhabitants feel 'as if we were longing for something which we cannot have'. What they cannot have is unhappiness, the great motive power of poetry and ultimately of history, about which they understand so little. They have heard of it, but prefer, like children, to turn their backs on it. Guest knows that his position in Nowhere is unsure, and this is all the harder to bear because of his attraction to the young women who welcome him. These women are no longer the pale and remote Pre-Raphaelite creatures of Morris's early poetry. They are strong, sunburned, ready to work on the farm, to take an oar in a boat, or to make love. At the sight of one of them, the half-wild young Ellen, a child, it seems, of the earth and the weather, 'a sort of pang shot through me', the pang, that is, of someone who may make an old fool of himself.

Guest is rowed by his new friends up the Thames 130 miles from Hammersmith (a journey which Morris had made himself in 1880). Ellen comes with them, and the boats tie up at Kelmscott, among the fragrant hayfields. Then

> almost without my will my feet moved along the road they knew ... We crossed the road, and again almost without my will my hand raised the latch of a door in the wall, and we stood presently on a stone path which led up to the old house. The blackbirds were singing their loudest, the doves were cooing on the roof-ridge, the rooks in the high elm-trees beyond were garrulous among the new leaves, and the swifts wheeled whining about the gables. And the house itself was a fit guardian for all the beauty of this heart of summer.

Although in Nowhere the manor must necessarily belong to the whole community, Guest enters it alone with Ellen. They walk through the old hall, the tapestry room, then the attics, which,

> by the small size of the beds, and the litter of useless and disregarded matters, bunches of dying flowers, feathers of birds, shells of starlings' eggs, caddis worms in mugs, and the like – seemed to be inhabited for the time by children

– just as they had been when Jenny and May had slept there, although they were both grown women by now. Outside the house, Ellen cries out:

> How I love the earth, and the seasons, and weather, and all things that deal with it, and all that grows out of it, as this has done.

And Guest is too deeply moved to answer her. He has no place, even (or perhaps most of all) at Kelmscott. In fact, it is time for Nowhere to expel him from its consciousness. At the hay-harvest dinner he looks round at the company, but no one looks back at him.

> A pang shot through me, as of some disaster long expected and suddenly realized ...
> I turned to Ellen, and she *did* seem to recognize me for an instant; but her bright face turned sad directly, and she shook her head ... I felt lonely and sick at heart past the power of words to describe.

Morris's grave, by Philip Webb, in the churchyard at Kelmscott

As E. P. Thompson puts it, 'reality has entered the heart of the dream', always a dangerous process.

Morris was a natural story-teller. That, as a Victorian, was his birthright. He created a myth out of the solid old house which remained true to the past, but united it, through time and change, with the present and future. In Ruskin's words, 'you cannot make a myth unless you have something to make it of. You cannot tell a secret which you don't know.' And it is difficult to understand *News from Nowhere* without seeing Kelmscott and its stretch of river.

In 1895 Morris negotiated another lease from a new owner. It was for twenty years, which he evidently reckoned would see him out (he was sixty-two). His last visit was only a few months later, in the spring of 1896. 'And although you think I don't like music, I assure you the rooks and blackbirds have been a great consolation,' he wrote to Burne-Jones. By the autumn he was mortally ill, confined to his bedroom in London, longing for Kelmscott and for the sound of rain. He died on 3 October, and lies buried in the churchyard of St George's, at the north end of the village. Philip Webb, who had designed Morris's first house for him, was asked to design his grave. The carving on the gravestone, Webb explained, represents a 'slip of a tree' with growing branches, and at the same time Morris's own hands, as he had described them in the November Prologue of his *Earthly Paradise* – 'these outstretched feverish hands, this restless heart'. It is a memorial, in short, to a great man who had a sense of there always being more to do. Philip Webb knew Morris very well. In spite of this, Kelmscott Manor was and still is what Morris called it, 'a haven of rest'. In August 1888 (for example) he left a note there for the printer Emery Walker, who had been asked to stay. 'Look under the mat and you will find the house-key. Enter and be happy.'

ALEXANDER POPE

STANTON HARCOURT, OXFORDSHIRE
CHISWICK HOUSE, LONDON W4
POPE'S GROTTO, TWICKENHAM, MIDDLESEX

GAVIN EWART

It's not easy for a modern reader to enjoy Pope as he was once enjoyed. If you're going to get the best out of him, you must throw away some of the ideas about poets and poetry that have been floating around in Britain for the past century and a half. Poets are not necessarily inspired and tortured creatures with great souls, agonizing over their own private sorrows. Likewise, poetry itself is not concerned only with deep personal emotion.

The Romantic Movement of the early 1800s, with Wordsworth, Coleridge, Keats, Shelley and Byron as its foremost poets, very much spotlighted the poet as an isolated tragic actor. What, in Wordsworth's case, was called 'the egotistical sublime' became the most admired style, with mystical ideas about Nature. Byron's misanthropic rebel (the Corsair is a good example) was another model. Keats wrote his own tragic illness straight into his poems, with all the sadness of a man who knew that he would die of tuberculosis in the very near future. The world is a place

> ... where men sit and hear each other groan;
> Where palsy shakes a few, sad, last grey hairs,
> Where youth grows pale, and spectre-thin, and dies;

Keats nursed his own brother, until he died of the disease, and died himself when he was only twenty-six.

Now consider Pope. Keats thought of himself as practically a dwarf (he was 5 ft 2 in.) and unattractive to women because of this. Pope was even smaller (4 ft 6 in.) and suffered all his life from a congenital curvature of the spine, so that he was held upright only by a kind of complicated canvas corset. He is supposed to have contracted this tubercular condition from the milk of an infected wet-nurse. He himself described his life as 'this long disease'. After the middle of it, he could not

305

Eighteenth-century bust of Pope

dress or undress himself and was very often in pain: high fever, severe inflammation of the eyes, abdominal pain, headaches, numbness in the legs, respiratory problems, bad sight, colds, indigestion, piles. Yet he never complains in his verse. His personal sorrows are not among his subjects.

When Pope appears in person in his verse, the tone is light, as in 'A Farewell to London, in the Year 1715' – a verse letter to his friend the poet John Gay. Here is a brief extract:

> Dear, damn'd distracting town, farewell!
>   Thy fools no more I'll tease:
> This year in peace, ye critics, dwell,
>   Ye harlots, sleep at ease!

306

Why should I stay? Both parties rage;
    My vixen mistress squalls;
The wits in envious feuds engage;
    And Homer (damn him!) calls.

Why make I friendships with the great,
    When I no favour seek?
Or follow girls seven hours in eight?
    I need but once a week.

Pope was twenty-seven when he wrote this, on retiring to Binfield in Berkshire to begin work on his translation of *The Iliad*; and the harlots and the mistress of this lifelong valetudinarian needn't be taken too seriously – though friendship was always important to him. The point is that he didn't strike attitudes or shout defiance at Heaven, although his physical condition might have justified him in complaining.

The key to enjoyment of Pope's poetry is to appreciate its rational, straightforward statement. One of his very earliest poems is 'Ode on Solitude', a version of an ode by Horace:

Happy the man, whose wish and care
    A few paternal acres bound,
Content to breathe his native air
                In his own ground.

Whose herds with milk, whose fields with bread,
    Whose flocks supply him with attire,
Whose trees in summer yield him shade,
                In winter fire.

Blest, who can unconcern'dly find
    Hours, days, and years slide soft away,
In health of body, peace of mind,
                Quiet by day.

Sound sleep by night; study and ease,
    Together mix; sweet recreation:
And innocence, which most does please
                With meditation.

Thus let me live, unseen, unknown,
    Thus unlamented let me die,
Steal from the world, and not a stone
                Tell where I lie.

This poem is interesting because it shows how much he valued the independent life of a country gentleman (with all its opportunities of 'improving' a property). Pope's father was a linen-draper, though a rich and successful one, and Pope aspired to gentility.

His most famous achievement, in the history of English verse, was the perfection of what is known as 'the heroic couplet'. Many other poets, most notably Dryden, had written in this form. Pope regarded Dryden as a towering genius.. When he was a boy – and he can't have been more than twelve (Dryden died in 1700) – he had himself taken to the coffee-house that Dryden frequented, so that he could see the great man from a distance. Pope did this kind of writing so well that almost nobody has tried to do it since. It can be mock-heroic, as when dull poets are taken to task:

> While pensive poets painful vigils keep,
> Sleepless themselves, to give their readers sleep.

Or noble:

> Is there no bright reversion in the sky
> For those who greatly think, or bravely die?

But it almost always has the hint of an epigram about it:

> How happy is the blameless Vestal's lot?
> The world forgetting, by the world forgot.

Or else it is an outright epigram:

> 'Tis Education forms the common mind,
> Just as the twig is bent, the tree's inclin'd.

It is for this 'epigrammatic' style that Pope is admired today, and for his great satires: *The Rape of the Lock*, *The Dunciad*, *An Epistle to Dr Arbuthnot*, various other satirical Epistles, *An Essay on Man*, *An Essay on Criticism*. All are didactic, in a sense, and all largely quoted from in *The Oxford Book of Quotations*.

One line only is given from his translation of Homer:

> Welcome the coming, speed the parting guest.

Yet it was, as much as anything, for his translations of *The Iliad* and *The Odyssey* that he was famous in his lifetime. And it is not hard to see why. One of the notable things about Homer's style is his use of the extended simile, a detailed comparison of one thing with another. This was copied by Virgil in Latin and Milton in English. Here is Pope's translation of the lines from *The Iliad* where, in a very remarkable double simile, Homer compares and contrasts the behaviour of the silent Greeks and the noisy Trojans as they move towards one another in battle:

As when the winds, ascending by degrees,
First move the whitening surface of the seas,
The billows float in order to the shore,
The wave behind rolls on the wave before;
Till, with the growing storm, the deeps arise,
Foam o'er the rocks, and thunder to the skies.
So to the fight the thick battalions throng,
Shields urg'd on shields, and men drove men along.
Sedate and silent move the num'rous bands;
No sound, no whisper, but the Chief's commands,
Those only heard; with awe the rest obey,
As if some god had snatch'd their voice away.
Not so the Trojans, from their host ascends
A gen'ral shout that all the region rends.
As when the fleecy flocks unnumber'd stand
In wealthy folds, and wait the milker's hand,
The hollow vales incessant bleating fills,
The lambs reply from all the neighb'ring hills:
Such clamours rose from various nations round,
Mix'd was the murmur, and confus'd the sound.

Pope's Homer is nowadays neglected. Yet it can encompass the dramatic, in scenes of violent action – battle, shipwreck and the supernatural movement of rivers – even humour (one brief moment in *The Iliad* when he describes Priam's old companions sitting in the sun in Troy):

Chiefs, who no more in bloody fights engage,
But wise through time and narrative with age,
In summer-days like grasshoppers rejoice,
A bloodless race, that send a feeble voice.

The word 'narrative' invites us to remember the long-winded bores and dunces of his other poetry.

Pope himself, without boring, is a good 'narrative' writer. The account of how Odysseus outwits the giant Polyphemus in the land of the Cyclops is extremely telling. He can also reproduce the cruelty of Odysseus' revenge on the suitors, Melanthius and the slave-girls. There is nothing stilted or over-poetic in this. In its own way, the way of the eighteenth century, much of it *is* sublime.

Quite rightly, however, Pope is most famous as a satirical moralist. *The Dunciad* (his last poem) is full of dirty tricks, a sustained attack on all the poets, critics and booksellers (publishers in those days) that he considered to be no good. The paranoid critic Dennis, a man of talent, perhaps did (and perhaps didn't) deserve the caricature in the poem:

> But Appius reddens at each word you speak,
> And stares, tremendous! with a threatening eye,
> Like some fierce tyrant in old tapestry.

At any rate he responded by calling Pope 'a hunch-back'd toad', a Roman Catholic, a Jacobite and 'the very bow of the god of Love'.

How good were Aaron Hill and Colley Cibber? It's not easy to find verse by either nowadays; but Hill's 'Alone in an Inn at Southampton, April 25th, 1737' seems to me pretty good. Hill wrote opera libretti, and Cibber wrote plays that have not survived. As Laureate, his odes and other poems seem to have been execrable:

> Behold in ev'ry face, imperial Graces shine,
> All native to the race of George and Caroline.

Patience Strong verse, creep-like treatment of George II and his queen, the royal family as the holy family – all this followed his award of the Laureateship in 1730. Pope made him his king of dunces for such reasons, but also because Cibber told a scandalous story in which Pope, a 'merry Lord' and Cibber resorted to a brothel, and Cibber pulled Pope off a reclining harlot. The Lord complained that Cibber had 'spoiled the sport', to which Cibber replied, 'I have saved Homer!' (by saving his translator from venereal disease, presumably).

The Dunciad is an epic of the ludicrous, derived from Dryden's *MacFlecknoe*, a very similar put-down of rival authors, but it isn't Pope's greatest poem. That honour must be reserved for *The Rape of the Lock*. You can either call it light verse or you can call it marvellous poetry (Auden's view), and there's no doubt in my mind that it is one of the great poems of the English language.

The story was based on an actual happening. John Caryll, a Catholic gentleman who was a friend of Pope, asked him to write the poem. Robert Lord Petre had cut a lock of hair from the head of Arabella Fermor, a well-known beauty. As a result, there was bad feeling between the Petre and Fermor families. The poem was supposed, by making fun of the incident, to heal the breach. A first version appeared in 1712, and an enlarged one in 1714. It is beautifully written and, though light in tone, it makes some serious criticisms of human behaviour. The description of Belinda's morning toilet is, by implication, critical of feminine vanity:

> A heav'nly image in the glass appears,
> To that she bends, to that her eyes she rears;
> Th'inferior priestess, at her altar's side,
> Trembling, begins the sacred rites of pride.
> Unnumbered treasures ope at once, and here
> The various off'rings of the world appear;

Pope's Grotto, Twickenham

From each she nicely culls with curious toil,
And decks the goddess with the glitt'ring spoil.
This casket India's glowing gems unlocks,
And all Arabia breathes from yonder box.
The tortoise here and elephant unite,
Transformed to combs, the speckled and the white.
Here files of pins extend their shining rows,
Puffs, powders, patches, bibles, billet-doux.

311

The bibles are a nice touch. With its sustained elegance this passage parodies the arming of the hero before battle, as it might appear in an epic poem. The epigrams are rarer than in the poetic *Essays*, but they are there:

> Fair tresses man's imperial race insnare,
> And beauty draws us with a single hair.

With Queen Anne at Hampton Court Palace:

> Here thou, great Anna! whom three realms obey,
> Dost sometimes counsel take – and sometimes tea.

(Tea, in those days, was still pronounced 'tay'.) At evening

> The hungry judges soon the sentence sign,
> And wretches hang that jurymen may dine.

A harsh thought. And after it, one even more desolate:

> Oh! if to dance all night and dress all day
> Charm'd the small-pox, or chas'd old age away;
> Who would not scorn what housewife's cares produce,
> Or who would learn one earthly thing of use?

Long poems often have dull bits where the interest flags or the verse loses its gloss. This doesn't happen in *The Rape of the Lock*. Right to the very end, where Belinda's lock becomes a constellation – the fate of Callisto and other nymphs pursued by the gods of earth – the high standard is maintained.

Pope was remarkable as a pioneer in his own day. As the eighteenth century saw it, he purified and refined English poetry. The hectic qualities and what it regarded as the 'barbarism' of the Elizabethan playwrights and the Restoration satirists (such as Rochester) were no longer regarded as desirable. Instead, strong emotions were feared and mistrusted, and the tone of voice most admired was one of restraint and reason; no loose ends and no loss of control.

Interestingly enough, Pope was a pioneer in another respect. He was one of the first people to believe that by careful planning man could improve on Nature – Wordsworth later took exactly the opposite view. Pope was passionately dedicated to landscape gardening, as we now call it, controlling his surroundings in the same way that he controlled words. You could plant woods and plan avenues and vistas; even, if you had the money and the time, raise small hills and introduce ornamental lakes, or build a miniature Greek temple at a strategic point. In fact, like the poetry, this was a form of neo-classical art.

Among the places in England of particular interest to Pope scholars are the grotto of his villa at Twickenham; Chiswick House, the home of his friend and patron Lord Burlington; and the Tower at Stanton Harcourt, near Oxford, where he translated Homer. All that is now left of his villa in Cross Deep, by the Thames, is his famous grotto. After he died Lady Howe, who owned the house, got so fed up with people asking to see over it that in 1807 she tore it down. The present building, now St Catherine's convent, was built by a nineteenth-century tea merchant.

The grotto consists of two chambers, one on either side of a long underground passageway linking the river frontage with gardens on the other side of the Teddington road. There are seats in a central chamber, lit by a ceiling lamp, although only in very hot weather can it have been other than dank and cold. Chunks of volcanic stone, quartz, various ores, bits of petrified trees, and pieces of mirror line the walls and ceiling. In Pope's time water from a spring cascaded down the walls from 'Salient Spouts', reflected by the mirrors. At the garden end, at ground level, are large stone statues of two of Pope's much-loved dogs (all his dogs were Great Danes, and all called Bounce). At the end of the garden is a very small grotto, surmounted by a stone with a verse inscription by Pope, now only legible with difficulty.

From the time when he first lived there, in 1719, until his death, in 1744, Pope devoted himself to improving his 'elegant retreat' – 'a singular effort of art and taste', said Horace Walpole. Pope was an innovator. He more or less started the fashion for grottoes. His house was not a 'Great House' but a modest, though Palladian, country villa. It had no pretensions to being a 'stately home'. The rooms were full of portraits of his friends; Pope's great consolation was friendship. In the garden he had a vineyard, an orangery and beehives. He grew pineapples (then very rare), figs, French peas, broccoli, fennel and asparagus, in addition to the commoner vegetables, and even 'Jamaica strawberries'.

In the five acres he used landscaping to give an effect of depth and even mystery; avenues, paths, woods (in well-judged gradations of green) added to the effect. There were some quincunxes, groves, an amphitheatre, a 'wilderness', a bowling-green, a shell temple, three 'mounts' (each with a seat on top) and an obelisk dedicated to the memory of his mother, who died in 1732. This was inscribed:

> Ah Editha!
> Matrum Optima.
> Mulierum Amantissima.
> Vale

Let us now turn to Chiswick House in Burlington Lane. This great pioneer work of neo-classical architecture, built between 1727 and 1729, was designed by the 3rd Earl of Burlington (1694–1753), a friend and patron of Pope's. Burlington also

Chiswick House

supported artists and musicians (including Handel) as well as the poet John Gay and other writers.

From 1716 to 1719 Pope, with his mother and father, lived in a corner house nearby, in Chiswick Lane, now rebuilt as the Mawson Arms. Being only five miles from the centre of London, with access to its printers, publishers and booksellers, this location had advantages. It was also near Hampton Court, Queen Anne's

314

'summer palace', and many ladies and gentlemen of quality had houses in the neighbourhood.

Pope was born in London (2 Plough Court), but he lived at Binfield in Berkshire from 1700 until the move to Chiswick. At the age of twenty-eight he was already recognized as an outstanding poet. His friendship with Burlington was a genuine friendship, on equal terms.

Although Pope's own house in Chiswick has vanished entirely, the survival of Chiswick House itself is some compensation. The grounds are delightful, with a stretch of river spanned by a handsome stone hump-backed bridge. There are walks and vistas; an Ionic Temple, in front of which stands an obelisk in a small round lake; a Doric column; a Rustic House; various stone sphinxes; and a number of cedars of Lebanon, among the most beautiful trees in the world. The villa itself –

Pope's room in the tower at Stanton Harcourt

for Burlington thought of the house as a rural retreat such as a Roman nobleman might have owned – is extremely beautiful, both inside and out. The rooms, although there is no furniture to speak of, have been painted and contemporary paintings hang on the walls.

Stanton Harcourt Manor, built between 1380 and 1470, is one of the earliest unfortified manor houses in England, lying about six miles west of Oxford. The manor of Stanton became the property of the Harcourt family in the middle of the twelfth century, as part of the dowry of Isabel de Camville when she married Robert de Harcourt. The north side (the Hall, the Great and Little Parlours and the Chapel) has disappeared. Only the north-east corner of the Chapel (built in 1540) still stands – now known as 'Pope's Tower'.

The Harcourts were a distinguished family, and they lived in the house until 1688 (the year of Pope's birth). Elizabeth Harcourt then, on the death of her husband, Sir Philip, sold all the contents and allowed the house to fall into disrepair. Meanwhile, her stepson, Simon Harcourt, the 1st Viscount Harcourt and Lord Chancellor to Queen Anne, built himself a house three miles away at Cokethorpe, where the family lived until 1755. In that year a new house was begun at Nuneham Courtenay, using stone from the Stanton Harcourt building.

The octagonal Great Kitchen (in effect a gigantic oven) survives intact, as remarkable an example of this kind of building as the Abbot's Kitchen at Glastonbury. In the remains of the Old Gatehouse – now the only habitable part – there are a few fine family portraits and an outstanding portrait of a young man by Chardin. The top room in the tower was lent to Pope by Lord Harcourt in 1717–18, so that he could work on his translation of *The Iliad*. The chair on which he sat when he wrote has survived. It has a leather-padded circular back on which the poet, sitting the wrong way round, could rest his arms. In front of him then was a flat wooden table on which he could lay a book or writing paper. This saved his back from the strain of an ordinary chair. There is also a piece of red glass from a window on which Pope has scratched the words:

> In the year 1718
> I Alexander Pope
> finished here
> the fifth volume of Homer.

The stone staircase in the tower is now considered too dangerous for visitors; there are three rooms, the priest's living-room, his bedroom and the top one – with panelling of the period of Charles II – which was Pope's study.

In a letter to his close friend Martha Blount, in August 1718, Pope tells the story of John Hewet and Sarah Drew, rustic lovers killed by lightning in the harvest field and buried together in the graveyard of the church adjoining the manor. Both

316

Pope and Gay were touched by this, and persuaded Lord Harcourt to erect a monument over the grave, on which an epitaph by Pope was carved:

On Two Lovers Struck By Lightning

When Eastern lovers feed the funeral fire,
On the same pile the faithful pair expire:
Here pitying Heaven that virtue mutual found,
And blasted both, that it might neither wound.
Hearts so sincere th'Almighty saw well pleased,
Sent his own lightning, and the victims seized.

Lord Harcourt was afraid the villagers would not understand this. Pope wrote another version:

Think not, by rigorous judgment seized,
    A pair so faithful could expire;
Victims so pure Heaven saw well pleased,
    And snatch'd them in celestial fire.

Live well, and fear no sudden fate;
    When God calls Virtue to the grave,
Alike 'tis justice soon or late,
    Mercy alike to kill or save.

Virtue unmoved can hear the call,
    And face the flash that melts the ball.

Pope sent both versions (which seem to me equally deficient in poetic merit; the revised one is more of a moral injunction but the last line – an image from musketry? – is very awkward) to his caustic friend Lady Mary Wortley Montague, who replied, 'I must applaud your good nature in supposing that your pastoral lovers ... would have lived in everlasting joy and harmony.' Her own attempt ended:

For had they seen the next year's sun,
A beaten wife, and cuckold swain
Had jointly curs'd the marriage chain;
Now they are happy in their doom,
FOR POPE HATH WROTE UPON THEIR TOMB.

BEATRIX POTTER

HILL TOP, NEAR SAWREY, CUMBRIA

JANE GARDAM

'Hill Top, Sawrey? Oh, that's the house over in the trees.' I was asking my way of someone who said she was 'only a holiday-maker but remembered it from last year', and I wished that I had asked someone else. For Beatrix Potter country is surely not trees, but quintessential Lake District: purple mountains, sheets of silver water, whitewashed farms on distant fells.

But the holiday-maker was right. Skirting enormous, busy Windermere and the ice-cream eaters of Ambleside, a road turns south towards Hawkshead and another twists down from it to woods along the side of Esthwaite Water, shiny and speared with reed beds and very reminiscent of *The Tale of Mr Jeremy Fisher*. The country opens to meadows, grassy hills and clumps of woodland, and runs through the fertile village of Near Sawrey, which has huge trees in its gardens and azaleas and rhododendrons showering over its walls, as lush as Surrey. It is a tiny village and Beatrix Potter's house on the far side of it looks over fields with trees that stand in park-like clumps, then coppices, then woods that turn into the great sweep of Grizedale Forest that stretches for miles to the crags above Coniston. It is not majestic, Wordsworthian Lakeland, but what used to be called 'Lancashire in Westmorland', 'very pretty hilly country', Beatrix Potter called it, 'but not wild like Keswick or Ullswater'. In her journal she wrote, 'It is as pretty a little place as ever I lived in.'

Sawrey has always been protected by being rather off the track of the more dramatic lakes and it still keeps its inconsequential air of going nowhere in particular except the next village of Far Sawrey and the ferry to Bowness. It is even more protected from change now by being in National Trust heartland. The Trust has bought up as many houses in the village as it can, and Hill Top was left to it by Beatrix Potter herself. It is not altogether fanciful to think that there is something

Esthwaite Water

of a conspiracy to keep the village off the most popular tourist map (there is some anxiety about whether Hill Top is going to be able to stand up to the numbers of its visitors for ever), for there is no advertising at all. There is not one reference to it anywhere along the road from Hawkshead until you see a small old-fashioned signpost saying, only, 'Sawrey One Mile'.

And when we get there there is little to suggest we have arrived. A well-bred sign says, 'The home of Beatrix Potter', but it could easily be missed. The huge – and always packed – car-park for Hill Top is unobtrusive behind a stone wall and the splendid gift shop and ticket office are in local stone and so well built that they are almost invisible. One rather homemade-looking plaque on a wall says that this house has to do with *The Tale of Pigling Bland* (spelled wrong) and a water-colourish inn-sign painted above the Tower Bank Arms faintly shows it looking much as it did in *The Tale of Jemima Puddle-Duck*: but that is all.

Sawrey would still be recognizable to Beatrix Potter. The main street looks much the same as fifty years ago, though it is more prosperous and there is fresh paint about; and it is probably no longer safe for children to play in it. There are fewer apple trees, and there are new houses that have nothing to do with farming, but they sit well back, knowing their place, and there is only one real disaster.

The wonderful village shop of *The Tale of Ginger and Pickles* has gone, but it was old-fashioned long ago. There is a scoop taken out of the road outside Hill Top's garden gate for pausing visitors, but road-widening was beginning while Beatrix Potter was alive 'for the convenience', she said, 'of the worshippers of the internal combustion engine'. The last time I was there, outside the pub some dogs were conversing with each other on the triangle of grass, very like Beatrix's painting of her favourite sheep-dog, Kep, and the two silly foxhound puppies who ate all Jemima Puddle-Duck's eggs.

The view and the colours about Hill Top are unlikely, please God, ever to change and they still prove the accuracy of the lyrically beautiful paintings in the tales that they inspired – silvery greens, transparent golds, the tops of the hills rabbit-coloured in a hot summer, foxy-coloured with blobs of dark green in spring. In autumn they must be magnificent, but they are lovely at midsummer and in May are as various as any woods in the world, with pinks and pale oranges, sharp lemon-yellows, light-greens and silver and what is called 'copper' in the beeches and maples but is in fact warm rose-madder (the exact colour of Ovaltine!). All looks feathery and light, though the far woods are dense and dark, as one would expect of the home of the grubby night-wanderer, Tommy Brock, and his terrible acquaintance, Mr Tod.

When it rains in Sawrey, which is frequently and for long periods, these colours vanish like a light being switched off, but they change again startlingly in winter. Some of Beatrix's water-colours of the village under snow, the lamp-light splashing out from her parlour window on the ice-bound garden, or of sheep, yellowish-green, huddled under stone walls below the house and under a pewter sky, are as wonderful as anything she painted.

Beatrix Potter had known the Lake District for fourteen years before she came to Sawrey. Her hugely rich, puritanical and inordinately demanding parents, whose fortunes had been made in Lancashire cotton, liked to rent grandiose northern houses every summer for a three-month holiday, bringing with them a host of servants and Beatrix's succession of small animals, which seem to have been tolerated. (Peter Rabbit travelled a lot.) Mr Potter then would settle down to a summer of excellent photography, Beatrix to drawing and examining fungi in which she was beginning to be an authority. Bertram, her brother, painted and drove his sister about the lanes in a pony and trap. Goodness knows what Mrs Potter did, except perhaps rest from the gruelling daily round of calls in Kensington, where the family lived for most of the year, in gloomy style. 'My unloved home,' said Beatrix.

In 1896 the family came to stay at a fine house called Lakefield, which overlooked Esthwaite Water, and from there it was a short clip-clop for brother and sister to Sawrey's village street. There, behind the Tower Bank Arms (which it would have been hell-fire for Beatrix to enter: she was always a total abstainer), stood Hill Top Farm, hidden from the road, with good farm buildings below and a sheltering bank above. It was small, withdrawn, the home of a working tenant-farmer and his family, as it had been for years. Nine years later Beatrix bought it.

The family and the village thought this a great joke. Beatrix looked for all the world like the sort of overdressed, buttoned-up Kensington young lady that the Lake District was used to, for there is a long tradition of southern visitors (Wordsworth knew some) and a tradition in how to deal with them: one is welcoming, polite, watchful and never forgets they are foreign. They conceded that she had 'a bonny face', but she was tense, deeply frustrated, never quite well and was obviously dominated by the grim-looking urban parents who had instilled in her that it was her whole duty in life to look after them. She did not look like someone who would suddenly and with ferocious determination invest in property on her own account, elect to live and die among them as a Sawrey farmer and end up a respected judge of Herdwick sheep.

But she was nearer to the village than they knew. 'My brother and I were born in London,' she said, '. . . but our descent, our interest and our joy was in the north country'. And so was her way with money. Her books, almost all inspired by the north, were beginning to be very successful. With her royalties and a small legacy she not only bought Hill Top but moved out the tenant, built him an extension with a door through to the old farm so that his wife could look after her, and moved everyone back again. Almost at once she began to buy sheep, and in the new room she had built out at the back of the house she continued to paint and

A view of the village of Near Sawrey from Stoney Lane

write. She had recently had a great grief: a precarious engagement, opposed by her parents, to her publisher, Norman Warne, had ended in his sudden death, and to help get over it she threw herself into life at Sawrey with even more passion, yearning for it whenever she was away, furnishing it from farm sales, transforming its garden and transforming herself. The well-built but gawky, delicate-looking girl became in time the self-confident, stompingly healthy farmer fattening contentedly over the years, dressing in remarkable tweeds that grew greener and greener with age and were made from the wool of her own sheep: on her feet a pair of clogs and on her head in bad weather an old sack, in good weather often a rhubarb leaf against the sun. She never tried to disguise her southern, educated accent – the Sawrey people would have despised her if she had – and she did not, as is often supposed, try to preserve her new house in aspic as a typical Lakeland farmhouse. She adored it and it put its stamp on her, but she put her stamp on it too.

Nor was the house ever her real home. For years she was the dutiful daughter, going home to her parents in London whenever called to do so, and when at last

Hill Top, Near Sawrey

at forty-seven she married William Heelis, a local solicitor from Hawkshead, she bought another house in Sawrey that would be more suitable to her husband's ideas of comfort, and used Hill Top only for her work and secluded quiet. She sat in its porch arguing with her shepherd, Tom Storey, about farming, and she could always see it from her new windows across the village, where she died. And it was to Hill Top's kitchen that her husband brought her ashes wrapped in newspaper for Tom to scatter in a place known only to him.

Having gone to work on the alterations to the house, Beatrix attacked the garden, starting with the patch before the porch which was a scruffy, weedy place, very much for chickens. This she cleaned up and covered with chippings, which have not the suburban image in the north-west that they have elsewhere. A good farm-garden in Cumberland often has more creamy gravel about it than flowers – flowers not being a serious thing to farmers as 'there isn't the room'. From the old farmyard a long diagonal path runs down to a little white gate on the road – the gate over which Tom Kitten and his sisters peered at the three disgraceful geese who were

323

about to seize all their best clothes. On either side of this path Beatrix created two broad long borders, planting them with all she could find or acquire from cottage gardens when people were 'throwing out their rubbish in the autumn'. It was a big undertaking and she seems to have done it alone, cramming it with pinks, mignonette, foxgloves, lilies, sweet peas, ragged robin, ornamental thistles, delphiniums, big rose-bushes, nasturtiums, lilac, rosemary, sage, thyme, marigolds and purple cabbages. There is a patch of onions, the odd gooseberry bush and, along the wall, a vine. It all looks so simple but, unless you have grown up with this sort of gardening, it is not, and all you are apt to make is a mess. Beatrix's gift for it is to be seen in a visit to the house today where the beds have been carefully looked after, and also in the frontispiece to *The Tale of Tom Kitten*, painted eighty years ago, where Mrs Tabitha Twitchit marches her impossible children in disgrace between the border flowers on a dreamy, midsummer afternoon.

Against the house wall are wisterias, roses and lacquer-red fuchsias but the wall itself is not as pretty as what is on it, for Beatrix had the old stones rendered in gravelly grey – something the National Trust would not allow today. Opposite the tall slate porch with its pointed top, so often the frame for cats and kittens and the little dog Duchess – and for family photographs showing an older and older Beatrix – is the curly, green-painted metal gate that a great many visitors stop to look at with surprise, as if it belonged to them. This is the gate where Jemima Puddle-Duck made her great decision to fly away. The rhubarb-patch it leads to is still there, very little changed, with the two beehives in the niche in the stone wall behind it and the rows of strawberries, lettuces, onions and beans as straight as Mr McGregor's in *Peter Rabbit*. A McGregorish watering-can is always kept standing about on the wall, so authentic that we look for two long rabbit ears sticking out, though Peter was of course in Scotland and not at Sawrey for his dreadful adventure.

Below the rhubarb-patch is the farm, still tenanted and worked and smelling, as it should, very delicious. It is not open to the public, but its byres can still be seen standing in good nick. They are the buildings that Beatrix at last agreed to electrify – Hill Top was the last place in the village to have electric light – because she supposed 'the cows might like it'. Below the farm and to the side, the meadow rolls away with the patch of local wild-flowers Beatrix planted, including what she called 'the zig-zag clover', the leaf that the bumpkin Timmy Willy waved in farewell at his suave cousin, Johnny Town Mouse.

The farmhouse itself, if you turn from the green gate to look up at it, is not very remarkable under its slated roof, with the slightly makeshift slate porch and grey walls – windows pleasant enough, prettily proportioned with nice fat glazing-bars, but much like any other tenant farmhouse of perhaps the late eighteenth or early nineteenth century. The surprise comes when you go under the porch and push open the heavy oak door and step into a much mellower seventeenth-century world. The kitchen – or hall as it's called in Cumbria – is the biggest room in the house, with rich dark-oak panelling, black oak beams, deep oak window-seat and a floor of blue-black flagstones, smooth as moleskin. The furniture glows with years of beeswax polish – a solid table, a rocking-chair, all manner of other chairs (Beatrix loved chairs and drew and collected them wherever she went: the two Chippendales she found in the attic of her husband's solicitors' office), and a court-cupboard she found riven from a farm kitchen. It has the date 1667 carved on it (the same as my grandmother's over to the west. My grandmother's court-cupboard disappeared!) and was a great favourite. There is the grandfather clock we all know from *The Pie and the Patty Pan* ('I can't draw,' she said once, 'I can only copy') and the marvellous dresser from *The Tailor of Gloucester* and *The Tale of Samuel Whiskers*, where it is the back-drop for the fleeing rat Anna Maria with her stolen plate of dough that is to turn Tom Kitten into a roly-poly pudding. The old range – which Beatrix Potter removed and the National Trust has put back – burns bright with real logs ('I never saw such a good imitation fire,' I heard a visitor say) and is where Tom put his head up the chimney on what might well have been his last day on earth. The rag rug is the one on which he showered soot, and thereby saved his own life.

In one of the kitchen cupboards there is the hidden spiral stone staircase Beatrix found when she arrived ('This house would very much amuse children') but which is now blocked off. Outside the kitchen door is the true, probably newer staircase to the house, broad and easy and with a lovely carved banister and dark polished oak treads that, with the oak floorboards of the main landing and the three bedrooms round it, doesn't seem to show any sign of the hundreds of pairs of feet that pass over it four times a week. On the half-landing there is a dignified window, claret-coloured curtains and another grandfather clock that we feel we know in some larger and nobler house until we realize it is here that Tabitha Twitchit stood weeping for her son and she is, after all, only the height of a cat. Across the main landing – main is too grand a word, for everything at Hill Top is small – is Beatrix's bedroom, left exactly as she directed, with her Bible on a mahogany wash-stand beside her bed, pictures and ornaments and hand-stitched samplers in place and the two famous dolls, Lucinda and Jane from *The Tale of Two Bad Mice*, glaring from the oak bedding-chest. There is another comfortable window-seat here, where one can sit and be quiet between the surges of visitors and look at the oak four-poster bed that Beatrix picked up for twelve shillings and hung with green cotton damask curtains, embroidered by herself but never finished and whose stitches – it must be said – would not have satisfied the Tailor of Gloucester.

The other two bedrooms have been made into what Beatrix called the Treasure-Room and the Sitting-Room, full of mementoes and curios to do with the *Tales* – there is a complete set of miniature animals in bronze and a dolls' house rather

The kitchen range at Hill Top

like the one in *The Tale of Two Bad Mice*, full of clutter and including the original plates of plaster food that Hunca Munca and Tom Thumb bashed to bits with the fire-irons. There are some good paintings, trinkets, very nice china and valuable furniture – a square piano that looks rather dainty for a farm. In the room below the sitting-room, the parlour, there is a black and white Adam-style marble fireplace, very imposing, installed by Beatrix, lighter and more formally carved panelling and some lovely furniture and china including a set of spoon-backed chairs 'in the

French taste'. In a corner cupboard among other things is the coronation tea-pot (it has lost its lid) that Ribby poured from when she asked Duchess to tea in *The Pie and the Patty Pan* and on the wall hangs the Potter family's coat of arms. The parlour has a whiff, not – certainly not – of Kensington, but it must be admitted of Lancashire cotton.

At the back of the house, along a little corridor, is the New Room that once housed original Beatrix Potter manuscripts and paintings until the crowds became too dangerous for them, and here between 1905 and 1913 she produced seven of her best-loved books. The room was designed to accommodate her brother's huge paintings that hang in neo-classical panelling – an affectionate, sisterly act, for they are very gloomy. (Poor talented but alcoholic Bertram never had his sister's lightness of spirit.) There is a clutter of rather imposing furniture that looks as if it is there because there is nowhere else for it, and some facsimile letters from publishers lying about, including a letter of rejection from *Country Life*. The distinction of the room is the wonderful view of Stoney Lane – the silvery stone-walled lane that curves away behind the squat white chimney-pot wreathed in climbing roses in *The Tale of Samuel Whiskers*, and quite unchanged today.

This is all. A tiny house, stuffed with delicious and often very small things that have to be peered at and stepped round with care. The crowds shuffle by, talking in every language there is, four days of every week from April until November. At peak times they have to be limited, and there is anxiety about the floor-joists that have to be periodically examined to see if the floors can continue to take the strain. The ratio of visitors is still, interestingly, four to one in favour of adults, which might perhaps please Beatrix, who was never over-fond of children and knew comparatively few. I have noticed on all my later visits to Hill Top that parents tend to be rather impatient there with their own children ('I shouldn't bother with that,' I heard one mother say as a child picked up a fairy-book, 'it's rather advanced') as if Beatrix Potter was their own, not their children's property. I saw a number of children rather on the yawny side and hanging about on window-seats.

I even wonder if it is perhaps a mistake to take children to Hill Top at all, for everything and more that they see there is to be found in the *Tales*. The *Tales* are not altogether 'written for children'. They are Beatrix Potter's love poetry about the northern landscape and the creatures in it, and in some magic fashion children understand this and find the books more real than the everyday world. It is when the everyday world has taken charge and they have become parents themselves that they may need to go to the house.

Nevertheless, it was nice on my last visit to hear a small boy shout out as he sat making faces at the rhubarb-patch from Beatrix Potter's bedroom window, 'Oh look! There he is!' and we saw a small, artless-looking rabbit squeezing anxiously under the gate.

JOHN RUSKIN

BRANTWOOD, CONISTON, CUMBRIA

ROBERT HEWISON

On 1 October 1877, John Ruskin gave a lecture on the geology of the Lake District at the Friends' Meeting House in Kendal. His research was based on his visits to the Yewdale Crags above Coniston, which he could see from his study window at Brantwood. But geology was only the leading thread in a lecture that ranged through etymology, natural history, theology and social criticism in order to draw the moral that nature existed not to be exploited, but to be loved. All that needed to be known about the world could be discovered in the rocks and flora of Yewdale, if only they were studied in the right way.

It was a lesson that Ruskin had learned early, and one that had drawn him back to settle in the Lakes.

> I knew mountains long before I knew pictures; and these mountains of yours, before any other mountains. From this town, of Kendal, I went out, a child, to the first joyful excursions among the Cumberland lakes, which formed my love of landscape and of painting: and now, being an old man, I find myself more and more glad to return.

Ruskin was in fact only fifty-eight in 1877. He was contributing to the myth of the sage of Brantwood long before his death there in 1900. But he was also stating a simple truth about himself and his feelings towards the Lakeland landscape, feelings that can be recovered by any visitor to Brantwood today. Fascinating as it is, the house is less important than what you can see from its windows. Coniston Water is both frame and mirror for the heavy shoulders and blunt peak of the Old Man of Coniston, rising above the lake into a sky that can be serene in the morning, black and stormy at midday, and glow with colour at sunset. Ruskin, 'an old man', renamed the mountain 'Vecchio'; at Brantwood his moods were to change even

Brantwood

more violently than the landscape's, from storms of madness, to serenity, and then back again, closing at last in a long slow dusk.

Ruskin had been familiar since childhood with the surroundings that he acquired when he bought Brantwood in 1871. His father was a prosperous sherry merchant who in the summer months combined travelling for orders with the increasingly popular recreation of family tourism. Ruskin's earliest recorded memory, a recollection of Friar's Crag, above Derwent Water, is from his first visit to the Lake District in 1824 at the age of five and a half. (The spot is marked by a memorial to Ruskin, erected by Canon H. D. Rawnsley, whose reading of Ruskin inspired him to become one of the founders of the National Trust; appropriately the memorial stands on what was to be the National Trust's first Lake District property.) Ruskin's earliest published work, poems describing Derwent Water and Skiddaw, were the product of a second visit in 1826, and he and his parents came again in 1827 and 1830.

The Lake District appealed to the romantic and picturesque tastes of the early nineteenth century, a sensibility shaped by natural theology, articulated by the Lakeland poets, and given form by the paintings of Turner and other members of the English landscape school that the Ruskins admired. During their visit in 1830 the Ruskins saw Robert Southey at Crosthwaite, and Wordsworth in church at Rydal. The eleven-year-old Ruskin duly noted the fact in his *Iteriad*, a 2,310-line imitation of Wordsworth's *Excursion*.

Ruskin was storing up the childhood memories that he alluded to in his Kendal lecture; through the practice of observation, both by writing and drawing, he was laying the foundations of his career as a critic. Later, with the first long family tour on the continent in 1833, France, the Alps, Italy and the art galleries of Europe were opened up to his inquiring eye, an eye trained in these 'joyful excursions'.

The Lakes figure in Ruskin's first published criticism, a series of essays under the title *The Poetry of Architecture*, written in 1837 and 1838 when he was an undergraduate at Oxford. In the summer of 1837 he had returned with his parents to the Lake District, and was struck by the evident relationship between the landscape and the local vernacular architecture. In 'A Chapter on Chimneys' he illustrated Coniston Hall, with the mountain rising behind, a view he was to have daily when he came to live at Brantwood.

Ruskin visited the Lakes again in 1838, 1847 and 1848, but this latter visit was by no means a joyful excursion, for it was part of the disastrous honeymoon during which he failed to consummate his marriage to Effie Gray. By the 1850s he was a celebrity, as a result of his defence of Turner in *Modern Painters*, his championship of the Pre-Raphaelites and his praise of the Gothic in *The Seven Lamps of Architecture* and *The Stones of Venice*. But his friendship with Millais, who painted his portrait during a holiday with the couple at Glenfinlas in 1853, turned sour when Effie and

Millais fell in love with each other. Effie returned to her parents in 1854 and after Ruskin had had to endure the humiliation of an annulment on the grounds of his sexual impotence, she married Millais.

It was a different Ruskin who returned to the Lakes in 1867. He was a rich man, with a fortune inherited from his father in 1864. His reputation as an authority on painting and architecture stood even higher, a position confirmed when he was chosen as first Slade Professor of Art at Oxford in 1869. But he had extended his field to economics and social morality at large, where his critical views were controversial. For Ruskin, the gross materialism of the age was reflected in the changes he saw in the Lake District, where the picturesque tourism of his childhood had been replaced by railway excursions and plush holidays in new hotels.

He was also deeply troubled by his passion for Rose La Touche, a girl twenty-nine years his junior to whom he had proposed in 1866. She had asked him to wait three years for her answer, and her parents were now opposed to the relationship. Rose had already shown signs of the mental and physical illness that was to lead to her death in 1875. This love affair, consummated only in Ruskin's dreams, was to colour almost everything he thought or did.

In the summer of 1871 Ruskin was himself seriously ill. As he was recovering – and possibly taking consolation from childhood memories – he told his doctor, 'I feel I should get better if only I could lie down in Coniston water.' There then occurred one of those accidents of chance that Ruskin came to believe were more than accidental. He received a letter from the owner of Brantwood, asking him if he knew anybody who might be interested in buying the house. Without examining the property, Ruskin bought it for £1,500.

When he first visited the house on 12 September 1871, Ruskin found it 'a mere shed of rotten timber and loose stone'. It was more than a shed, but certainly much smaller than it is today. It had been built as an eight-room cottage in 1797, and extended by a further four rooms in 1830. In 1853 it was bought by the Chartist and radical pamphleteer William James Linton. Linton built an outhouse for his printing press, decorating the building with republican slogans, one of which can still be seen in the room in which he printed issues of *The English Republic* and *The Northern Tribune*.

Linton's second wife, Eliza Lynn, was a novelist, and wrote several books at Brantwood. When the Lintons returned to London from time to time, the house was let to the poet Gerald Massey during their absences. In 1862 the enclosure of the fells added six acres to the ten-acre estate, which consisted mainly of the steep wooded slopes behind the house, the 'brant' from which the house gets its name. In 1866 Linton emigrated to the United States, and again let the house, but he had left debts in Coniston, and it was these that decided him to sell. Ruskin had to spend a further £1,500 to make the place habitable, but that did not trouble

The Old Man of Coniston, from the turret at Brantwood

him, for he had acquired 'on the whole, the finest view I know in Cumberland or Lancashire'. He chose the first-floor room at the southern corner of the house as his bedroom, and ordered the construction of the little turret, to give him even better views of the landscape and the lake.

Ruskin did not move in until exactly a year later, on 12 September 1872. He still had rooms in Oxford, and a base in London at Herne Hill, in the Ruskins' first south London house which he had made over to his cousin Joan and her husband Arthur Severn. Joan had been his mother's companion until she married in 1871. Mrs Ruskin died shortly after he had bought Brantwood. Arthur was the son of Joseph Severn, who had nursed Keats in Rome, and was, like his father, a gentleman painter. For Joan and Arthur Severn, looking after Ruskin was to become a fulltime occupation, and his reputation became their chief investment.

Joan and Arthur helped Ruskin to move in, and the house was furnished partially from his London home. Ruskin was famously uninterested in interior decoration; he wrote that he took his visual pleasures 'from the sky or the fields, not from my walls, which might either be whitewashed, or painted like a harlequin jacket for aught I care'. His one gesture in that direction was to commission a wallpaper based on a detail in a painting in the National Gallery, the pattern on the sleeve of the officiating priest in Marco Marziale's *Circumcision*. The paper was used in his study on the ground floor, and the drawing-room next door. The original paper has disappeared, but in 1989 the rooms were repapered with a modern reconstruction. In 1872, at the time that the original wallpaper was being made, the house's stable block was demolished to make room for a lodge, designed by Ruskin for his servant Crawley, and a new coach house was built. All the building work at Brantwood was done by a Coniston builder, George Usher. When the coach house was damaged by fire in 1989, it was repaired by the same family firm.

The other major addition to the house in the 1870s was the new dining-room. The original dining-room, to the left of the front door, was too small and dark and once the new one was built became a second library and repository for Ruskin's ever-growing collections of books, manuscripts, pictures and minerals. The seven lancet windows of the new dining-room are said to recall Ruskin's praise of the Gothic in *The Seven Lamps of Architecture*. The room was hung with several of Ruskin's old masters, including the portrait of *Doge Andrea Gritti*, now in the National Gallery, believed by Ruskin to be by Titian, but which is now attributed to Catena. Most of Ruskin's pictures were sold off by the Severns after his death, and a copy of the 'Titian' by Ruskin's secretary, W. G. Collingwood, hangs in its place.

Above the sideboard hung three family portraits by James Northcote, his mother on the left, his father on the right, and Ruskin as a very small boy in the centre. This portrait was only returned to the house, with the help of the National Portrait Gallery, the National Heritage Memorial Fund and the National Art Collections Fund, after it turned up in a sale in 1987. It is now back beside Northcote's portrait of his mother, but the companion picture of his father is still untraced. Its place is taken by another portrait of John James Ruskin, by George Watson, which shows the dour Scots sherry merchant to have had romantic good looks as a young man.

The heart of the house was Ruskin's study, with a table near the fire for the winter and a desk at the further end of the room for the summer. In the spaces not taken up by fitted bookcases and mineral cabinets hung some of Ruskin's Turner water-colours, with more in his bedroom above. During the 1870s, from here, from lecture rooms in Oxford and elsewhere, and from hotel rooms on his continental journeys, Ruskin maintained a constant dialogue with the world, through private correspondence, letters to the press, collections of lectures, and most especially through *Fors Clavigera*, his monthly 'letters to the workmen and labourers of Great Britain', begun in 1871, and out of which developed his Utopian scheme for a reformed society, the Guild of St George.

At Brantwood, as elsewhere, it was Ruskin's habit to get up very early to write. Breakfast was at nine, and visitors would be the first to hear his latest work. The morning was occupied with letters, proof corrections, the packing and unpacking of parcels of books, minerals and drawings, ready for the midday post. Secretarial help was provided by assistants recruited from his classes at Oxford. James Reddie Anderson had led the student diggers (among them Oscar Wilde) who had taken part in Ruskin's road-building and drainage scheme at the village of Hinksey, outside Oxford. Anderson's cousin Sara became a key member of the Brantwood household. W. G. Collingwood, another Hinksey digger, eventually settled nearby, whence he kept a grim eye on the activities of the Severns, both before and after Ruskin's death. Collingwood published a biography of Ruskin in 1893. Another Oxford assistant, Alexander Wedderburn, became one of Ruskin's executors and under Joan Severn's supervision edited the monumental library edition of Ruskin's works in collaboration with E. T. Cook.

These young men and women, together with friends he had made in the neighbourhood, visitors on business to do with the Guild of St George, and guests drawn from his many contacts in the Victorian literary and political intelligentsia, made Brantwood in the 1870s a lively place. Ruskin did not join his guests for lunch, contenting himself with sherry and a biscuit. His afternoons were spent outdoors, chopping wood, cutting paths for the gardens he was extending around the house, or working on the small harbour that he and his assistants had dug to protect the rowing and sailing boats that were kept for recreation, and as a quicker means of getting to Coniston.

Indoors, Ruskin's favourite relaxation was chess. Dinner would be at six, and at eight tea was brought into the drawing-room. Ruskin liked to read aloud, most frequently from the novels of Sir Walter Scott, whose manuscripts he was collecting. *Jumping Jenny*, the boat designed for him by another assistant, Laurence Hilliard, which is still at Brantwood, is named after the brig in *Redgauntlet*. By ten, Ruskin was ready for bed, but he liked to end the evening, especially in later years, by being sung a sentimental lullaby or popular song.

Wherever Ruskin went his life was overshadowed by the death of Rose La Touche. He had taken part in spiritualist seances while she was alive, and after she died came to believe that there were ways in which she communicated with him from beyond the grave. He had been dangerously convinced of this while staying in Venice at Christmas in 1876, and had a similar experience at the same time the following year.

In February 1878 Ruskin broke down completely. He was at Brantwood, preparing notes for an exhibition of his collection of Turners to be held in London. The collection had been first formed with the sometimes grudging help of his father, and his thoughts were driven back to the loving yet frustrating relationship he had had with his parents. At the same time, his diary shows that his dreams were of the girl who had never visited Brantwood. He wrote in the introduction to his Turner catalogue:

> Morning breaks as I write, along those Coniston Fells, and the level mists, motionless, and grey beneath the rose of the moorlands, veil the lower woods, and the sleeping village, and the long lawns by the lake shore. Oh, that some one had but told me, in my youth, when all my heart seemed to be set on these colours and clouds, that appear for a little while and then vanish away, how little my love of them would serve me, when the silence of lawn and wood in the dews of the morning should be completed; and all my thoughts should be of those whom, by neither, I was to meet more!

Ruskin was feeling overcome by grief and frustration. Ten days later, during the night of 22 February, his mind gave way completely. He became convinced that the Devil was about to seize him, and stripped off his clothes, walking up and down his bedroom all night until dawn. Suddenly, by his own account, a black cat leaped at him. There was a struggle, and he threw it to the floor.

> Then, worn out with bodily fatigue, with walking and waiting and watching, my mind racked with ecstasy and anguish, my body benumbed with the bitter cold of a freezing February night, I threw myself upon the bed, all unconscious, and there I was found later on in the morning in a state of prostration and bereft of my senses.

This first, violent storm was brief, but others were to follow. In the intervals, Ruskin was able to resume his old life, to travel, to write, to lecture, and to continue his argument with the world in *Fors Clavigera*. But that argument was becoming increasingly bitter, for he saw the price of progress in the pollution from the blast furnaces at Barrow and Millom that stained the sky over Coniston. In *The Storm Cloud of the Nineteenth Century*, two lectures he gave in 1884, the 'plague wind' that he saw blowing through the air and through the souls of men became both a metaphor for the forces against which he was ranged, and a sign of the mental

A corner of Ruskin's study

anguish that he suffered. There were further attacks in 1881, 1882, 1885, 1886 and 1887. In periods of recovery he returned to work, but during the 1880s his grand schemes to reform the world were gradually reduced to pet projects at Brantwood. His proposals to drain the slopes of the Alps shrank to the construction of a reservoir and waterfall in the garden. His concern for the education and welfare of working men had to be limited to patronage of the Coniston Mechanics'

336

Institute. The reform of industry was confined to his encouragement of the production of 'Ruskin' lace, a craft still practised today. His views on educational reform were tried out on the children at Coniston school; his pleasure in innocent girlhood was sublimated in lavish teas for young visitors.

Ruskin's distressing and sometimes violent attacks changed his relationship with Joan Severn. At first the Severns had lived mainly in London, and Ruskin was master at Brantwood. But gradually the Severns became Ruskin's keepers, and in the 1880s the present top storey of the house was added to accommodate the Severns and their five children. In the 1890s the studio was built for Arthur. In 1885 Ruskin made a deed of gift that passed ownership of Brantwood itself to the Severns.

Both Ruskin and Joan knew that certain topics had to be avoided for the sake of his sanity, and she became increasingly watchful of what he wrote, and what visitors he had. For his part, in 1884 Ruskin gave up the monthly production of *Fors Clavigera* in order to produce instalments of an autobiography, *Praeterita*. The title is itself an allusion to the joyful excursions of childhood, and in his preface Ruskin firmly stated that he was 'passing in total silence things which I have no pleasure in reviewing'. Thus there is no mention of his marriage. But as the instalments progressed his sweetened narrative got closer and closer to his time with Rose. Joan feared both for his reputation and his mind. In 1889 she cut passages about Rose from what was to turn out to be the penultimate chapter of an unfinished work. Her fears were justified, for the previous December a deluded Ruskin had had to be escorted back from Paris and his last continental tour. After a final trip to Seascale, on the Cumbrian coast, where the last chapter of *Praeterita* was written, in June 1889 Ruskin returned to Brantwood, never to leave.

After another attack in the summer of 1889, Ruskin gradually lapsed into silence. There is a possibility that the silence was enforced, for Joan carefully monitored his visitors and conversation. When his publisher George Allen visited him in 1891 Allen complained afterwards that the 'old dragon sat opposite and never budged an inch'. Allen was an important figure to Joan, for over the years Ruskin had spent his original fortune, and the household had to depend on the income from his books. This was handsome, but she saw to it that Allen produced profitable editions of the early and popular works, while the disputatious relationship that Ruskin had enjoyed with his public through his later polemical writings was broken off. Ruskin was being made into a monument, even before he died.

In 1899, on the occasion of his eightieth birthday, there were many congratulatory addresses and telegrams. A small group of disciples, who knew him more by his books than by personal acquaintance, were allowed up to Brantwood, where the founder of the Birmingham Ruskin Society, J. H. Whitehouse, read an address.

Ruskin could utter only a few broken words in reply. The following winter there was influenza in Coniston, and Ruskin caught it from one of the servants. He died peacefully on 20 January 1900.

Ruskin was buried, as he wished, in Coniston churchyard. The funeral was the occasion for a gathering of Ruskin's friends and disciples, including those, like W. G. Collingwood and George Allen, who had latterly felt excluded from the Ruskin household by the Severns. J. H. Whitehouse was there, and he may then have foreseen what would happen to Brantwood now that 'the Master' was dead. While carefully guarding Ruskin's reputation, the Severns began to disperse his collections, and ignored his wishes that the house should be open to the public for thirty days a year.

As the Severns got rid of treasures to maintain their income, Whitehouse began to collect them. Joan died at Brantwood in 1924, and Arthur retreated to London, while the house fell into decay. When Arthur in turn died in 1931 the entire contents of the house were put up for sale in a tragic dispersal of books, drawings, letters and manuscripts. Whitehouse bought what he could, and in 1932 succeeded in buying the house itself, which he began to restore as a national memorial to one of the nineteenth century's greatest men.

Because of the dispersals that took place after Ruskin's death, a decay and decline that parallels the collapse in his reputation from the pinnacle achieved in the 1880s and 90s, everything you see in the house today is, in a sense, a reconstruction. It is a painstaking reassembly that is still going on, even as a new generation of Ruskin's readers are trying to reconstruct the truth of Ruskin's life and the real intentions of what he thought.

The sails of the little fleet that once sheltered in Brantwood harbour may have gone, replaced by those of today's windsurfers on Coniston Water, but through the windows of Ruskin's study the light and the landscape are unchanged. On 22 June 1876, Ruskin would have been at his summer desk when he wrote:

> I suppose few men now living have so earnestly felt − none certainly have so earnestly declared, that the beauty of nature is the blessedest and most necessary of lessons for men; and that all other efforts in education are futile till you have taught your people to love fields, birds, and flowers.

That is the lesson of Brantwood. But as always with Ruskin, there is an irony. Ruskin was writing to protest at the destruction of the Lakeland landscape by the building of railways, and the tourism they brought. The M6 and the English Tourist Board were yet to come.

VITA SACKVILLE-WEST

SISSINGHURST CASTLE, CRANBROOK, KENT
KNOLE, SEVENOAKS, KENT

U. A. FANTHORPE

I think perhaps Knole gets in the way always.

The two houses, Sissinghurst and Knole, seem to be conscious of each other, squinting across the small slice of Weald that divides them. Knole, with its famous panoply of seven courts, fifty-two staircases and 365 rooms, is clearly a man-made creature, though so old and strange that it seems to be sinking into the soil. It is guarded by ancient forms: the wild fallow-deer, which are actually tame enough to approach, hoping for food; and the witty literary leopards of the Sackvilles. These are the heraldic supporters of the Sackville coat of arms. They are to be found everywhere at Knole, from the roofs to the staircases; and also everywhere in the novels that touch on Knole, from *The Edwardians* to *Orlando*. Their grins suggest some special knowledge. The visitors, on a chilly May afternoon, don't know what to say:

'... on the lines of Hampton Court, really.'
'Were they much smaller in those days?'
'Nice, isn't it?'

And, from a lady on guard at the top of the Great Staircase:

'I call it Cyclone Corner. Sometimes I hide behind the door.'

Sissinghurst is quite different. There, it is the garden that is the point. The major hazard, even in an English May, is not the cold, nor the past, but other people. They are, of course, intensely respectable, moving reverently, academically along the beds, reflecting, in grave gardeners' voices, why it is that they have never succeeded with ... while She obviously did.

Vita Sackville-West's writing career divides itself between these two great places. Although she did some limited travel as Harold Nicolson's wife, it's really more characteristic of her that, while she was visiting him in Tehran, her mind was focused on *The Land*, that essentially English poem. But the love of her life was not

339

vaguely England; it was precisely Knole. 'I was never frightened at Knole,' she says, talking of her candlelit, exploring childhood. 'I loved it; and took it for granted that Knole loved me.' Perhaps love alone would have been enough to fuel her energies; but in fact to love was added a fierce sense of exile. As a child, she wrote endlessly: 'pretentious, quite uninteresting, pedantic, and all written at unflagging speed: the day after one was finished another would begin'. The stories were about Sackvilles, naturally: the 4th Duke, the 1st Earl, the 4th Earl, the 3rd Duke, the 6th Earl ... the subjects must have seemed infinite. Such a well-read child would have known about the sister-heiresses, Mary and Elizabeth, who when their younger brother was killed on the hunting field inherited the Sackville honours in turn. And this girl, surely, the only daughter of Lionel, 3rd Lord, grandson of Elizabeth, would do the same. But in fact, when the barony of Sackville was created for Mortimer Sackville-West, son of Elizabeth, in 1876, he was created a peer with limitation, in default of male issue, to his brothers. Since then, both property and title have been entailed. There was no future for Vita Sackville-West at Knole. 'I suppose my love for Knole has gone deeper than anything else in my life,' she wrote to Eddie Sackville-West, the male heir.

Her life divides sharply: the first thirty-six years (1892 to 1928, when her father died) are the ones in which Knole was in some way available to her; in the thirty-four years that followed, she created her own paradise, and could decide on her own heir. Not all this subsequent time was spent at Sissinghurst. Her first move was to Long Barn, only a couple of miles from Knole, where she began her gardening life. But the family moved at the prospect of having a chicken-farm in the neighbouring fields, and when Vita Sackville-West was shown Sissinghurst, she 'fell flat in love with it'. Like an offended lover, she turned her back on Knole for thirty years. The bitterness of her disinheritance reveals itself in her choice of phrase – it was the result of a 'technical fault': she was a woman.

Knole and the Sackvilles were responsible for her literary bent. The Sackvilles were not the hunting, wenching, riotous sort, nor the serious administrative. Apart from the 1st Earl of Dorset, who was Queen Elizabeth's last Lord Treasurer (Prime Minister), their honours were mostly of a mildly local kind: groom of the stole, Constable of Dover Castle, Colonel of the West Kent Militia, Warden of the Cinque Ports. They were melancholy; they were patrons; they wrote. The little girl on her own in the Sackville attics must have felt she was heir to Thomas Sackville, the 1st Earl, the great poet of the Induction of the *Mirror for Magistrates*; to the Lady Anne Clifford, wife of the 3rd Earl, whose diary she edited; to Charles, 6th Earl, Restoration poet and friend of Dryden, Pope, Prior, Wycherley, Rochester. And can any other aristocratic family in England boast of a Poets' Parlour? Here the

Sissinghurst garden

341

Knole

6th Earl entertained the many poets whom his own reputation, and his generosity as a patron, attracted from London. It is, says Vita Sackville-West, rich with memories. Though Knole itself was denied her, she must have felt that by writing she was following one of the great family traditions.

As might be expected from a woman in this position, she let the family and the house dominate her early prose works. Titles like *Knole and the Sackvilles*, *The Diary of the Lady Anne Clifford* and *The Edwardians* – such books make very clear the passion that can't be eradicated. *The Edwardians* is one of her most popular books, and one of the most personal. 'It is absolutely packed with the aristocracy,' she wrote to Virginia Woolf, whose *Orlando* had obviously provided a germ for it. 'Shall you like that?' Knole appears as itself, the great house Chevron. The heir to its magnificence is Sebastian, and his sister is Viola, Shakespearian twins who now in a liberating way represent the two natures, the two sexes, of herself.

All this is workmanlike stuff – she knew its qualities and its limitations. Virginia Woolf put it best:

Vita in the library at Sissinghurst, by Giselle Freunde

All about her is virginal, savage, patrician; and why she writes, which she does with complete competency and a pen of brass, is a puzzle to me. If I were she, I should merely stride, with eleven Elk hounds behind me, through my ancestral woods.

As she herself wrote to Prokosch, 'You ask which of my novels I prefer. I dislike them all.' It's only fair to note, however, that Virginia Woolf thought her long short story, *Seducers in Ecuador*, so good that she admitted to being jealous of it.

The biographies (*St Joan of Arc, La Grande Mademoiselle* and especially *Pepita*) have been properly and persistently admired. They are read not just as works of reference, but because the writer's feeling for these powerful, embattled women gives an extra imaginative dimension to the routine biographical facts. A new interest appears in the biography *Aphra Behn*. Aphra was a fellow-countrywoman, 'born under the green hill at Wye in Kent', but far more important, she was the first Englishwoman to earn her living by writing. Poet, dramatist, novelist, undercover agent, actress: there was a seamy side to her reputation which explains the forgetfulness of later centuries. But clearly for Vita Sackville-West this was a different, and essential, sort of ancestor. *All Passion Spent* has retained both its force and its popularity over the years. In its account of the finding of freedom and vocation at the end of a long life it is both a sad and a noble book. Leonard Woolf, its publisher, thought it the best of her novels. Her travel writing (*Passenger to Tehran* and *Twelve Days*), too, has lost none of its spirit. She was the right person at the right time for such work. In general, landscapes were not polluted, tribesmen were not westernized, visitors were not too knowing. And she had the catholic interests of the traditional English woman traveller, and what was particularly her own: the acute and imaginative ways of looking that she had practised in Kent were precisely appropriate for these new terrains. The English, since the time of Coryat, have been good at travel-writing; Vita Sackville-West follows in the English tradition.

But this is to leave out the poetry. The prose can be alien, remote in theme, aristocratic; the poetry is hard and definite, democratic, small in scale. It is doggedly rooted in Kent, and no doubt Vita Sackville-West's ancestors handed down as much love and understanding of the 'mild continuous epic of the soil' as they did of wine-coolers and stained glass.

What she needed was someone to say, 'Go more slowly. Mind the small things.' In poetry, she did. *The Land* is about the small things that make the infinite difference of the seasons, and about the traditional complicated one-man crafts that were in the process of dying out: bee-keeping, peddling, thatching, cider-making, ploughing. It's quite impossible to skate fast over something as detailed and overlooked as roadside wild-flowers:

> Wayside tramps, saucy and unafraid,
> Jack-by-the-hedge, Pickpocket, Ragged Robin,
> Small yellows and small scarlets, nowise strange,
> Nowise like aliens strayed,
> But English and robust,
> Fight tangled for their life, through grit and dust,
> Pushing their way with spring, when heifers range
> Uneasy up the lane, and as they go
> Tug at a passing mouthful, biting harsh.

This is good honest writing. She writes with passion and knowledge, and she goes, as she knew she must, slowly:

So my pedestrian measure gravely plods,
Telling a loutish life.

But there seems always to have been a touch of bad luck with good. Again, it was a matter of gender; could women write poetry? It had long been established that they couldn't, apart from exceptions like Elizabeth Barrett Browning and Emily Brontë, because of course physically they were unable to sustain the shocks of a classical education, and without a classical education one just couldn't write poetry. Vita Sackville-West, for all her privileges, had missed out on the classics, and she suffered the humiliation of being accused of copying Virgil's *Georgics*, which she had never read, when she was half-way through writing *The Land*.

A further stroke of bad luck was the timing of her poetic career. She was working at a time when the Georgian poets (and she was reckoned as one of them) were being described as 'bloodless'. *Prufrock and Other Observations* was published in 1917; then there was *The Waste Land* (1922), and Auden, Spender and Day Lewis in the wings. Vita Sackville-West was writing a traditional sort of poetry on traditional themes, and it was natural that she should feel inferior to these new, brilliant, different writers. Her popularity with readers must have made her feel inferior, too: good poets aren't popular, or so the critics seemed to suggest. She felt, she said in 1945, 'so out of touch with poetry as it is being written today ... It is just something left out of my make-up ... just a lack of interest in what must always be *temporary* things.' It made her gloomy about the future: 'Why, then, should it make me so unbearably happy to write poetry, when I know that it is all out of date rubbishy words that mean nothing at all to Ben's [her elder son's] generation? Will it ever mean anything to anyone's generation? I doubt it.' It was inevitable that the cosmopolitan, intellectual, urban poets of the twenties and thirties should make her work seem dated.

What happened, by a quirk of time, was that the poetry of the cosmopolitan, intellectual, etc. became the poetry of the establishment, taught in schools and universities; and the 'out of date rubbishy' became dear not particularly to expert poetry readers, but to those who cared about the issues (the environment, conservation, horticulture) that she cared for. A rather similar thing happened to A. E. Housman's poetry.

Most especially, with Vita Sackville-West, there are the gardeners. The countless reprintings of *The Land* and *The Garden* must often have been read and enjoyed by people who seldom read poetry. But this is poetry made safe by its subject-matter, and by traditional and therefore trustworthy use of rhyme. You can make quite a lot of poetry acceptable to wary readers if your subject and your style conform to their standards. Not that I think this poet was after such an effect; she simply wrote about what she loved, in a way that was familiar to her. When she is writing about

Entrance to the tower, Sissinghurst Castle

abstract themes, hers is a stiff sub-Victorian voice, whose ideas are knocked about by a 'poetic' vocabulary and syntax:

> Not always thus, for the resilient heart
> Thankfully lifts, the richer for that hour.
> Let but one gleam and promise of the sun
> Redly dissolve the mist . . .

and so on. But fortunately not always thus. As soon as the voice speaks of familiar, practical things it acquires point and verve:

> All's brown and red: the robin and the clods,
> And umber half-light of the potting-shed,
> The terra-cotta of the pots, the brown
> Sacking with its peculiar autumn smell.

I prefer *The Land* to *The Garden*, because *The Land* keeps its nose to the grindstone of Kent. *The Garden* was written throughout the Second World War, and such an immediate, important theme would naturally seem attractive to a writer. What seems attractive, though, is not necessarily what one can do best; and it's appropriate that *The Land*, under its fictional guise of *The Oak*, is in its unfinished state the persistent preoccupation of Orlando. *The Garden*, with its meditations on the quality of life in wartime, is like some of the prose works, a heroic move in the wrong direction.

'Out of date rubbishy' was her verdict on the poetry. Ironically, in a closely related field of interest, she was decidedly avant-garde. The work on Sissinghurst garden, in collaboration with her husband, Harold Nicolson, was adventurous, even provocative. She was in touch from the first with experimental gardeners like Gertrude Jekyll, Norah Lindsay, Lawrence Johnston, with suppliers like E. A. Bunyard, Colonel Hoare Gray and Hilda Murrell, with collectors like Clarence Elliott and Captain Collingwood Ingram. It was a time for thinking about the application to English gardens and English traditions of the immense discoveries of the Victorian plant-collectors, and Vita Sackville-West had the interests, the gifts and the funds to be among those in the lead in thinking through these problems.

A rather touching side-effect of her skill and reputation was the series of gardening articles for the *Observer* which she wrote, much against the grain, from 1946 to 1961. These, addressed to people with smaller or even no gardens, were always couched in a friendly tone, with not a scrap of *hauteur*. This sharing of her interests with readers led to some writing of great charm, as when she says:

Much as I love the chocolate look of the earth in winter, when spring comes back I always feel that I have not done enough, not nearly enough, to plant up the odd corners with little low things that will crawl about, keeping weeds away, and tucking themselves into chinks that would otherwise be devoid of interest or prettiness.

This has the kind of loving attentiveness that is characteristic of good gardening and of good writing. It also reminds me that the great English garden poets (Marvell and Pope, for instance) are famous for writing rather than for digging. Vita Sackville-West did all the hard jobs; as she wrote of a critic, in her column,

> I am not the armchair library fireside gardener he evidently expects, 'never having performed any single act of gardening' myself, and for the last forty years of my life I have broken my back, my finger-nails, and sometimes my heart, in the practical pursuit of my favourite occupation.

So she made up her mind to the renunciation of Knole, and instead turned Sissinghurst, with all the slurry and rubbish of a decayed farm, into a magic place. When I was there the air smelled of honey, curry and mown grass. Blackbirds, thrushes, robins, wrens and chaffinches were shouting; there was a rotary mower buzzing away at the farm beyond the Nuttery. The visitors were murmuring, like a litany, the sweet rural pedantry of flowers' names. The gardeners, as in the story of Cupid and Psyche, were invisible. It must have been like losing a whole Oxford college, said someone, apropos of Knole. But it is, perhaps, better to cultivate one's garden.

I have devoted more space to Vita Sackville-West's poetry than to her prose, because that seems to have been her priority. Her epitaph at Withyham, written by Nigel Nicolson, describes her plainly as 'V. Sackville-West CH, Poet'. I take it that, like all poets, she knew how to eliminate what didn't matter.

WALTER SCOTT

ABBOTSFORD, MELROSE, ROXBURGHSHIRE

A. N. WILSON

Abbotsford!
There is perhaps no writer's house more expressive of its occupant's literary personality. Indeed, one could say that Abbotsford was an extension of Scott's literary *œuvre* – an architectural Waverley novel, or a poem in stone of Border life and history. When we visit the houses of other writers, we might experience a greater or lesser excitement to know that this was the place where famous works of literature were composed. We might even, as when making our way up the wooded path of Yasnaya Polyana (the 'Bald Hills' of *War and Peace*), actually recognize it as a place which the author has depicted in one of his or her works. Nowhere, however, do we feel that a writer's whole artistic vision has been so consciously immortalized in architecture and furnishings. Also, in spite of later additions – most notably that of the chapel by Scott's grandson-in-law, who became a Roman Catholic – the house and library remain very much as they were in Scott's own lifetime, retaining his huge collection of books and antiquities. A further thing which makes Abbotsford a uniquely interesting house is that it was largely Scott's obsession with the place which led to his financial undoing. When Scott lost an immense fortune following the financial crash of 1826, he described Abbotsford as 'my Dalilah and so I have often termed it – and now the recollection of the extensive woods I have planted and the walks I have formed, from which strangers must derive both the pleasure and profit, will excite feelings likely to sober my gayest moments'. In fact, through an heroic effort of overwork, Scott managed to remake his fortune, pay off his debts, and die, a broken but independent man, in the house into which he had poured so much money and so much of his imaginative power.

Walter Scott was not a countryman by birth. His father was a Writer to the Signet in Edinburgh, and it was there that Scott was born in 1771. From early days, however, staying with his grandparents at Sandy-Knowe, Scott developed his profound knowledge and love of the Borders: their landscape, their ballad-tradition, and their history, in which his ancestors – Scotts and Rutherfords – played a

The north front of Abbotsford, which overlooks the Tweed

dramatic part. It was this part of the world which inspired his first best-selling poems, *The Lay of the Last Minstrel* and *Marmion*, and which enabled him – an Edinburgh lawyer like his father – to dream of making himself into a laird.

The period when he first began to be a literary success (and Scott was the first writer in history to make big money from his books and to be in modern terms a best-seller) coincided with his appointment as Sheriff of Selkirkshire, and he would take his family to spend the summer months in a rented house at Ashestiel; it was when the lease ran out on this that he decided to make the purchase of a farm, with adjoining land, known as Clarty Hole, and which he and his wife instantly renamed Abbotsford – because of its comparative proximity to the ancient abbey of Melrose. 'The farmhouse,' he wrote to a friend, 'was small and poor, with a common kail-yard on one flank and a staring barn on the other.' His imagination gradually transformed this place into the fantasy which his builders would one day realize. At first his ambitions were relatively modest:

> I intend building a small cottage here for my summer abode, being obliged by law, as well as induced by inclination, to make this country my residence for some months every year ... and I assure you we are not a little proud of being greeted as the laird and lady of Abbotsford.

Within three years, his 'cottage' had expanded considerably. The first architect, an Edinburgh man called William Stark to whom Scott entrusted his original plans, had died in 1813, and thereafter Scott employed the English architects Blore and Atkinson to carry out his innovative domestic designs. Although inspired by the Gothick tastes of an earlier English generation – notably that of Horace Walpole's Strawberry Hill – Scott had in mind for his cottage 'something more in the old fashioned Scotch stile which delighted in notch'd gable ends and all manner of bartizans'. We see how much his visual and his literary imagination went hand in hand because in 1814, the year that these plans for Abbotsford were being put into execution, he was writing his first novel, *Waverley*, with its descriptions of the medieval castle of Tully-Veolan and its 'high-steepled roofs and narrow gables ... the roof had some nondescript kind of projections called bartizans ∴.'

The more money he made (and by 1820, when he had written six of the Waverley novels, Scott was a very rich man indeed), the more he expanded his house and his estates. 'I have got a delightful plan for the addition of Abbotsford,' he wrote to his wife, 'which, I think, will make it complete, and furnish me with a handsome library, and you with a drawing-room and better bedroom, with good bedrooms for company etc. It will cost me a little hard work to meet the expense, but I have been a good while idle.' (Idle! He had written six novels, four very long poems, maintained a legal career as a Sheriff, and had a completely unstoppable life of social conviviality.) The rooms, which he had planned in this letter to his wife, were built and today they may be seen more or less as he conceived them.

To me, the most atmospheric room in the house is the study, a room pregnant with Scott's curious character. It is high-ceilinged (sixteen feet high) and measures about twenty feet by fourteen feet. It feels much smaller because it is so crowded with books, and because of the unusual arrangement of its doors. One door leads into a gallery from Scott's bedroom, and it was through this door that he would come, often before daybreak, lighting his own fire in the grate before scribbling off the statutory thousands of words which paid for the lordly fantasies which he entertained. It should not be forgotten that Scott kept the authorship of the anonymously published Waverley novels a closely guarded secret in those early

The armoury

days of publication; and that door in the gallery – vaguely reminiscent of concealed passages and priests' holes – is emblematic of Scott's secrecy. In Edinburgh, he wanted to be known as a convivial lawyer and antiquary who had written some highly acclaimed poems. In the country, he was proud to be a sheriff and a laird.

352

But the profession of novelist – the essentially middle-class avocation of Defoe, Richardson and Fielding – was something which he chose to keep hidden.

Scott himself freely spoke of his house as if it were one of his literary productions.

> What a romance of a house I am making which is to be neither castle or abbey (God forbid) but an old Scottish manor house … it is in the bravura style of building or, if you will, what a romance is in poetry or a melo-drama in modern theatricals.

The house therefore reflects the range (and quirkiness) of Scott's imagination and, by very virtue of its existence, it celebrates his commercial good fortune in being a best-seller. Like the houses of other *nouveau riche* people, Abbotsford has touches of vulgarity. Scott could not resist revealing to the world what a successful, prosperous and – here is the paradox – modern man he was. So the house had 'all mod cons', and was the first domestic building in Europe to be lit by gaslight.

The story of the installation of gaslight at Abbotsford is wittily conveyed by Scott's son-in-law, Lockhart, in his monumental biography. Scott had gas installed in 1823, together with all the latest gadgets – airbells, for example. Scott convinced himself that each newfangled device was not merely stylish, but more economical. 'In our new mansion we should have been ruined with spermaceti oil and wax-candles,' he said – not unabsurdly. Gas had everything to be said for it. 'There is no smell whatever,' he optimistically opined, before the system was introduced. 'It takes about five hours to fill the gasometer. I never saw an invention more completely satisfactory in the results.' Scott, who liked the theatre of social occasions, arranged for the lighting to be switched on one evening during dinner. 'In sitting down to table, in Autumn,' Lockhart recalled,

> no one observed that in each of the three chandeliers (one of them being of very great dimensions) there lurked a little tiny bead of red light. Dinner passed off, and the sun went down, and suddenly, at the turning of a screw, the room was filled with a gush of splendour worthy of the palace of Aladdin; but, as in the case of Aladdin, the old lamp would have been better in the upshot. Jewelry sparkled, but cheeks and lips looked cold and wan in the fierce illumination; and the eye was wearied, and the brow ached, if the sitting was at all protracted.

Lockhart even went on to speculate whether Scott's habit of sitting close to the gaslamp on his desk had hastened his demise.

The fact that Abbotsford – the 'romance' of Scott's dreams – was lit by the modern invention of gas is characteristic. Scott was deeply steeped in the past, but his achievement as an artist was to make the past accessible to his contemporaries; some would say, to reinvent the past for them. But he did much more than invent the historical novel as a literary form. He began a new way of looking at history itself – which had a profound effect upon thinkers and historians as well as upon

Bust of Scott, by Sir Francis Chantry, 1820

artists. His novels and verse romances assert what had either never occurred to historians of Gibbon's time, or did not interest them: viz. that history is full of human beings, in many respects comparable to ourselves, but also in noticeable aspects quite different. (For example, in the way that they dressed. It is astonishing to us how late the history of costume began. Eighteenth-century productions of Shakespeare were always in modern dress – Scott's generation were the first to try to reconstruct the costume of the past.)

Abbotsford, then, harked back to the past, but it also – in a way which true aesthetes would find distressing – looked forward to the future. It could, roughly speaking, be called the descendant of 'Scotch baronial' in style; but it is the ancestor, not merely of Balmoral and other great Victorian fantasy-houses of the kind, but also of the innumerable suburban and urban manifestations of Scotchery which invaded the English consciousness in the nineteenth century. This was partly, of course, because Scott was the favourite author of Queen Victoria and Prince Albert, so that his influence spread through them. But there is more truth than falsehood in the idea that whenever we see a Gothic town hall in some English industrial town, or a front door in a lower-middle-class suburb adorned, like some medieval abbey, with stained glass, or pub glass engraved with thistles, or biscuit tins emblazoned with tartan, we have Sir Walter to thank.

The River Tweed near Abbotsford

Purists, as I say, were profoundly shocked by this. John Ruskin, the great nineteenth-century aesthete, was brought up on a diet of Scott, Scott and more Scott. He and his father almost worshipped the laird of Abbotsford, and could hardly support the sorrow of having read aloud the last of the Waverley novels and knowing that there would be no more new Scott to read. (Many re-readings lay ahead, of course.) Scott, next to the Bible, was the biggest influence on Ruskin's imagination. In 1839, seven years after Scott's death, Ruskin made a visit to the house with a view to writing it up in a series called 'Homes of the Mighty'.

The house itself commences with a horrible-looking dungeon-keep, which rises full four feet above the level of the roof ... Next comes a large flat side of wall, in the middle of which, twenty feet from the ground, is built the actual wooden door of the old Tolbooth in Edinburgh, with lock, bars, and all, classically decorated with an architrave etc. ... The grand front is a splendid combination of the English baronial, the old Elizabethan, and the Melrose Gothic – a jumble of jagged and flanky towers, ending in chimneys and full of black slits with plaster mouldings, copied from Melrose, stuck all over it . . .

Ruskin was hideously disappointed. He was astonished, upon entering the house, to find that it was really quite small. For example, he found that the painted glass door opened 'into a hall about the size of a merchantman's cabin fitted up as if it were as large as the Louvre . . .' Most shocking of all, he found a replica of the arch in the cloisters at Melrose, an arch which, as Ruskin wrote, had been designed 'for raising the mind to the highest degree of religious emotion', being used by Scott as a . . . fireplace. My dear! 'This was to me the finishing touch,' added Ruskin,

> for it proved to me at once what without such proof not all the world could have convinced me of, that Scott, notwithstanding all his nonsense about moonlight at Melrose, had not the slightest feeling of the real beauty and application of Gothic architecture.

Ruskin's conception of what was or was not 'true Gothic' was better informed than Scott's, from a purely academic point of view, but was in its way no less personal, no less fanciful, and the passage is typical of his aesthetic intolerance. What Ruskin abominated, the sympathetic visitor to Abbotsford will find to love. It is not a house *pretending* to be a medieval abbey, nor a baronial castle. It is the house of an artist, and if Ruskin could only have viewed it more indulgently (or read Scott's books with more humour – as well as with the reverence and respect they deserve), he would have seen that Abbotsford was that new Waverley novel which he and his father so ardently wished they could read.

Like Scott's mind, the house is a wonderful mixture of contrarieties, crammed to overflowing with historical memorabilia. We enter the library, the finest room in the house and every last detail of which Scott planned or designed himself, and we find that it is both a repository of magnificent old books and furniture, and a treasure-house of 'relics'. It does not matter much whether we believe in the authenticity of them all – Rob Roy's purse, the pocket-book of Flora Macdonald, the lock of the Chevalier's hair – for these are the tangible and visible tokens of those historical events which Scott had made real in his writings. The hall is likewise crammed with historical mementoes, most of which recall the bloodiness of the human story, but all of which seem domesticated and tamed by Scott's own sunny and sane disposition. The murder of Archbishop Sharp triggers off the terrible series of events in *Old Mortality*, and in the hall at Abbotsford we find Sharp's basket grate sitting peacefully under the replica of the arch at Melrose which so distressed Ruskin. On the walls hang every variety of destructive instrument: cannon balls, said to have been used during the siege of Roxburgh Castle in 1464, the skull of

The reading desk in the library

Robert the Bruce, shields, targes, spears and pistols, each with some bloody tale to tell. Scott was better than any English-speaking novelist at depicting the destructive and irrational human propensity to violence. He neither despaired about it – as Nietzsche and Dostoevsky were to do later in the century; nor did he feel any Whig smugness about the possibility of human 'improvement'.

Abbotsford, which breathes the imaginative life of Scott, was also the death of him. If he had been content to live in his Edinburgh town house, and to put the considerable fortune he amassed from his writings into some solid form of investment, he might have lived ten years longer than he did. As it was, he put every penny he earned into his collection of antiquities, and into expanding the buildings and estates at Abbotsford, while recklessly placing the financial side of his writing life in the hands of his not always reliable publishers. When, in 1826, the London banks crashed, Scott discovered that he had in fact been running up huge debts, which he could barely hope to repay, and that he was ruined. His popularity in Scotland was such that, when he next appeared in the Court of Sessions in Edinburgh, friends pressed forward to assure him that they would set up some sort of fund to restore his fortunes and save Abbotsford for him. Scott's own personal liability, when the responsibilities of his printer and publishers had been taken out of the account, was something in the region of £130,000. Translate that into present-day figures and you have an almost unimaginable loss. It is the equivalent of many millions. His response to the offer of help from friends is justly famous in its heroism: 'My own right hand shall pay my debt.' For the next five years he worked at such a fever-pitch that, given his poor history of health, it was inevitable that it would kill him. Luckily for us, while he churned out the feeble novels of his later years, he also wrote what is arguably the most impressive book he ever penned, his journal, which he had begun, quite fortuitously, a few months before the crash occurred. 'The greatest figure he ever drew is in the journal,' John Buchan wrote, 'and it is the man Walter Scott.' Astute readers have compared it with the Book of Job 'with its accurate unexaggerated language of pain'. But we also find in the journal the voice which made Scott the best-loved conversationalist of his generation – anecdotal, self-mocking, gentle, and, even in his worst afflictions, fascinated by the world as it appeared to him through his vast reading, through gossip – at which he was an adept – and through the observation of his family and friends.

It was appropriate that Scott, after visits abroad to recover his strength – though in fact they only diminished it – should have died at Abbotsford. Before he died, he called Lockhart to his bedside and said, 'I may have but a minute to speak to you. My dear, be a good man – be virtuous – be religious. Nothing else will give you any comfort when you come to lie here.' When, the next afternoon, he died, his eldest son closed his eyes and kissed them. It was 21 September 1832. Through the open windows of the house, the family could hear, on that warm afternoon, the gentle murmur of his beloved Tweed.

Buchan applied to him Shakespeare's words that he was a 'man cast in the antique mould of humanity, equable, alert and gay', adding that such a man 'makes a light and a warmth around him'. It is not fanciful to say that those of strong personality leave their stamp on their houses. The receptive visitor to Abbotsford senses this light and warmth to this day. An aesthete would probably never see the point of the house, finding in it merely, as Henry James found in the English nineteenth-century novel, 'a treasure-house of detail, but an indifferent whole'. A moralist might reflect upon how little time Scott actually had to enjoy the place – seeing it as a monument to vainglory. Such an observer might think of the grandiose landowner in the parable, who said that he would pull down his barns and build greater ones, but to whom God replied, 'Thou fool – this night thy soul shall be required of thee.' What haunts the lover of Scott who has read his journal is that when Scott's soul was required of him, he was able to respond with such stoicism and courage. When I visit the place, I am reminded of all the hours of pleasure and illumination which his writings have afforded me; but above all I reflect upon the nobility and lovability of his character. So potently does Abbotsford retain the stamp of his personality, that I almost feel, in the library or the study, that if I turned to look about the room, I might see his lame, cheerful figure hobbling towards me with a welcome, and reminiscences of

> Old forgotten far-off things
> And battles long ago.

WILLIAM SHAKESPEARE

STRATFORD-UPON-AVON, WARWICKSHIRE

TIM PIGOTT-SMITH

Using a sixteenth-century Dutch code, a group of ingenious fanatics have proved to their own satisfaction that the inscription under Shakespeare's monument in Westminster Abbey reveals Francis Bacon to be the author of the plays. Marlowe died in 1593, but that doesn't stop the Marlovians; de Vere died in 1604, but that doesn't stop the Oxfordians. I have now performed in nearly twenty of the plays, and I think I recognize 'real Shakespeare'. I sense that certain words and sentiments are his rather than Marlowe's or Jonson's. But you don't need to have acted in his plays to know that they are not the products of the same mind as the essays of Bacon. However, when you combine the limited amount of factual information about Shakespeare himself with the essentially elusive nature of genius, it is inevitable that such theories abound. Where, then, do we look for him?

There is more to be found in and around his home town, Stratford-upon-Avon in Warwickshire, where I used to live, than you might expect. Although the town's present gloss of wealth owes much to the varied aspects of the Shakespeare industry, a great deal of its life continues now, as then, as though Shakespeare never existed – a fact of which some locals boast. The Stratford which the tourist does not see remains a market town, dominated by what cannot be missed – the river and church. The bridge was built by, and named after, Sir Hugh Clopton, nearly a hundred years before Shakespeare's time. It spanned a dangerous and muddy reach of river prone to flood, joining Felden to the south with Arden on its northern bank, where the wooden, thatched buildings housed a population of around two thousand. The pattern of the streets has altered little from the twelfth to the twentieth centuries, although in Shakespeare's day they were dung-laden. In the winter of 1962–3, the Avon iced over so completely that you could walk, talk and skate on it: it was reminiscent of the harsher winters of the Elizabethan era, although in 1962–3 no one went so far as to roast an ox on the ice.

Mary Arden's house, Wilmcote

Sheep Street – where I used to have tea with a friend in the magnificent Shrieves House – reminds us of what Stratford must have been like. The little paths that run through to Bridge Street, although packed with modern tourist shops in place of crowded courtyards housing the poor, convey something of the bustling intimacy of the narrow lanes of a small Elizabethan town, lined with slightly crooked squat houses. The boundaries of the town, then marked by elm trees, have been greatly extended over the centuries. The meadows bordering the river where Shakespeare walked were threatened in his time by the growing problem of enclosure; recent squabbles about building a sports centre and hotel there are a modern resurrection of the same problem.

You can savour the past more easily if you leave the town and stroll in the Welcombe hills. The Shakespeares came from a village on just such a hill – Snitterfield, a mile or so away. William eventually bought land there: he clearly had an eye for property. His mother, Mary Arden, who was a member of one of the leading families of the county, with pre-Conquest Saxon ancestors, also came

The interior of Mary Arden's house

from outside the town. Her father Robert's farm and home in the village of Wilmcote are quite grand.

There are people who will tell you that this house at Wilmcote is not Mary Arden's house, that the Birthplace is not the Birthplace: ignore them. The Shakespeare Birthplace Trust now administers all the properties in Stratford associated with Shakespeare, and devoted guides will tell you all you want to know: there is a joke that the guides at Mary Arden's house are so enthusiastic that they will tell you a great deal more. But I defy you to come away from this house without a picture of early Tudor life – or at least a certain aspect of it. Most of us are familiar with the small cramped stairways of these typically low, timbered buildings. On this farm the living accommodation is turned in on the yard, shunning the outside world, favouring the people who lived here in close proximity with their cattle.

When they fished up the yeomen's longbows from the *Mary Rose* a few years ago, there wasn't an archer in England strong enough to pull one to its full arc. The Tudors and Elizabethans were powerful men, and the low doorways suggest a shorter, tougher breed: men like John Shakespeare, William's father, who worked for Robert Arden.

The house is well supplied with historical clues such as the spooning-bench on which couples courted, suitably placed by the fireside. It is thought by some that the board or table at which the family ate doubled as a bed for an extra visitor (overturned to hide the grease) – a possible source of the expression 'bed and board'. It was a hard, grainy life, often lived in pain and always close to death. Mary Arden's house is deceptive; it shows the comfortable side of Elizabethan life.

An indication of the family's rank and reputation is the dovecote. The government rationed dovecotes among the better-off partly because of the potential crop damage, but also because doves produce guano, which was used in the making of gunpowder. In order to prevent explosives getting into the wrong hands, the authorities permitted only people of standing and assured loyalty to own dovecotes. On summer afternoons Mary must have brought young Will out here to enjoy the farm and countryside, for there is more than just the use of her maiden name in his idealized picture of life in the Forest of Arden:

> Under the greenwood tree
> Who loves to lie with me
> And tune his merry note
> Unto the sweet bird's throat.
> Come hither, come hither, come hither
>   Here shall ye see
>   No enemy
> But winter and rough weather
>
> (*As You Like It*, II: v)

363

The birdlife of the forest would have been prolific and, in the eyes of a curious child, wonderful and exciting. It is fitting that falconry is now one of the attractions of this atmospheric house:

> My falcon now is sharp and passing empty,
> And till she stoop she must not be full-gorg'd,
> For then she never looks upon her lure.
> (*The Taming of the Shrew*, IV: i)

As well as falcons, owls, kestrels, and eagles can be seen at Mary Arden's house today. Four hundred years ago some of these birds would have been similarly trained.

The Forest of Arden spread west then, almost as far as the few homesteads clustering together under the name of Shottery, where the Hathaways farmed fifty to ninety acres and lived in a twelve-roomed, timber-framed building – some cottage! When Richard Hathaway died in 1581, he left his daughter Anne, with a small dowry, to the care of her brother.

How much of Shakespeare himself can we find in what is now known as Anne Hathaway's cottage? The house itself is charming. There is a story-book, almost Victorian feel about it, which might be because Hathaways were farming it late into the nineteenth century. Stout-beamed, solid and snug, it catches well the yeoman's background. It is very different from the largesse of Mary Arden's house. The orchard beside the house is more conducive to thoughts of Shakespeare's courtship. Is this where Will the lover came,

> Sighing like furnace with a woeful ballad
> Made to his mistress' eyebrow.
> (*As You Like It*, II: vii)

It is frustrating that so little is really known, but we can stand amongst these trees, where William and Anne must have met, held hands and made vows, and imagine the course of their romance.

Let us return to Stratford, where Mary married John Shakespeare in 1557, exchanging her detached, comfortable, rural residence for a terraced house in Henley Street. Arden timber and Wilmcote stone were the only common features of Mary's much-changed accommodation, although John in fact owned two houses next door to each other, and used one for trading in gloves and wool.

John and Mary produced a good number of children, which was just as well, for their first two, who were daughters, died very young. William, born in 1564, was lucky to survive the summer plague, which carried off over 10 per cent of the town. Gilbert was born in 1566 and Joan, named after the couple's first-born and the only daughter to survive, in 1569. Richard arrived in 1574 and Edmund in

Anne Hathaway's cottage, Shottery

1580. He became an actor and followed William to theatre land but, sadly, fame and fortune eluded the baby of the family, who was only twenty-seven when he died in London, a few months after his bastard child.

In the song of the Owl and the Cuckoo at the end of *Love's Labours Lost*, where 'Milk comes frozen home in pail' and 'Dick the shepherd blows his nail' and 'Greasy Joan doth keel the pot', it is an irresistible thought that 'Greasy Joan' is William's sister. When William died in 1616, all but Joan had gone before him. She lived on in Henley Street for another thirty years. It was badly paved; there were ditches and even a stream – very different from the pedestrian precinct which now anaesthetizes it.

The Hathaway bedstead

The Birthplace is more of a tourist shrine than any of the other properties, which is a pity, because you really have to work hard to cut through the sheen of the present – the caring high polish, the meticulous presentation of the beds, the thoughtfully chosen furniture, and the desk from Will's school – to get an idea of what it must have been like.

Imagine the Shakespeares crammed into this tiny house in, say, 1574. It is a winter afternoon and darkening fast. Much against his mother's wishes, ten-year-old Will is next door with William Wedgewood, a bigamist who figures in *The Black Book of Warwick*. By trade he is a tailor and he should be cutting cloth; but his shears lie idly by as he entertains his avid young listener with dubious anecdotes. Eight-year-old Gilbert has been sent to fetch father John from his gloving to tend Mary, big with child, who is resting by the fire, patiently sticking cloves into an orange – a pomander to sweeten their bedroom. Five-year-old Joan is playing diabolo with her sickly younger sister, Ann. Outside, the street pongs, and inside, the rushes on the floor need changing; the newly lit candles, made from lamb's fat, fume and gutter; the fire is smoking, and the pot above it is steaming. The thatch is ageing and the cracks in the ceiling need mending. By the time John has finished work, and William has been parted from the 'wicked neighbour', there is no room to move or think. Forget the museum-like tranquillity of this lovingly preserved home; think 'mayhem'. Few of us would last more than ten minutes in there.

Nevertheless, I imagine that amid the daily chaos Mary would have insisted on order and sanity at mealtimes, one of the rituals of her old life that she was able to maintain; another age-old family ritual would have been the bedtime story. Perhaps William, being the best reader, chose a story from the family Bible. Maybe he made a story up. Might this be how his love affair with our language began? It is worth remembering that the culture then was primarily oral, and I picture him surrounded by the family, spinning yarns in the gutsy, sinuous language of Elizabethan England.

After William and Anne were married, it seems they joined the crush in Henley Street. Their wedding may have taken place under the dubious eye of John Frith, who was described in a survey made of the state of the ministry in Warwickshire in 1586 as 'an old priest and unsound in religion, he can neither preach nor read well. His chiefest trade is to cure hawks ...' He sounds like the model for Sir Oliver Martext in *As You Like It*. William Shakespeare's marriage licence, which was recorded in the Bishop of Worcester's Register on 27 November 1582, gave the bride's name as Anne Whately de Temple Grafton – not Anne Hathaway – a slip, it seems, made by the clerk of the consistory court at Worcester. John Frith was, at any rate in 1586, the vicar of Temple Grafton, a village five miles west of Stratford.

Were William and Anne virgins? Did the eighteen-year-old young man turn Anne's head, or did the unsupported woman who was eight years older deliberately get herself pregnant because she was confronting spinsterhood? It has been suggested that Anne's brothers forced William into marriage when the pregnancy was discovered, but such marriages were not rare in Elizabethan times. As with Shakespeare, every conceivable version of Anne Hathaway has been suggested: the shrew who needed taming; the bright lass who knew a good thing when she saw it, but refused to leave home for an actor's wanderings; the steady wife and mother who put up with years of lonely child-rearing, and was repaid by her husband's return home to share a comfortable old age with her. There are no rumours of faithlessness on her part, although there was plenty of opportunity, and any indiscretions could have been recorded and brought before the Bawdy Courts. We know they had three children, Susanna, born in 1583, and twins born less than two years later. But the truth of their relationship cannot be known.

Exactly when William left Anne and Stratford for the wide world is likewise uncertain, but we know he came back regularly. It was not uncommon for men to leave home in search of their calling, and William could have gone for good if he'd wanted to. As little is known about Shakespeare's own emotional life as about his relationship with Anne. While he was away from her, he could have been involved with both women and men. However, whilst writing keenly of the sensual pleasures of love, he often seems a man as much in love with the idea of love as one who is actually in love. The fact that he wrote about sexual jealousy proves nothing, although the sonnets, which are more personal, suggest that he was well acquainted with the green-eyed monster:

> Your shallowest help will hold me up afloat
> Whilst he upon your soundless deep doth ride.
> (80)

> So shall I live supposing thou art true . . .
> Thy looks with me, thy heart in other place.
> (93)

This is poetry not proof, but Shakespeare's emotions must be hiding somewhere in his work.

If we leave the Birthplace, stroll down towards the Clock Tower and turn into the High Street, we can follow the route that Will took to school. Four hundred years later, I used to make the same journey from our home in Shakespeare Street. It is frequently assumed that Shakespeare 'crept like snail unwillingly to school', because one of his many thousands of lines creates a hypothetical schoolboy who did so, but it seems more likely that a certain magpie thirst for whatever he could discover made William pretty nimble *en route* to his desk and horn book. You won't find much of Shakespeare at the old school. I would love to say that his ghost stalks the corridors, and that school folklore is rich in stories about him, but his name has moved off the register and on to the syllabus.

To celebrate the quatercentenary of his birth in 1964, our English master devised 'A Playing Day at Stratford', in which I was the leading actor of a touring company invited by Will's father to perform 'The Famous Victories of King Henry V' – a

Shakespeare's birthplace from the garden

popular Elizabethan chronicle – in Big School. In our play Will came to watch the visiting players with his father. 'The Famous Victories' is crude simplistic drama, better suited to boy actors than the more complex Hal and Henry plays which Shakespeare later crafted from them. When the performance was over, John Shakespeare thanked the players, paid them and bade them farewell. In the charged atmosphere that followed their departure, young William fell asleep on the empty stage, and prophetically dreamt his yet-to-be-written Henry delivering the famous Agincourt speech:

> This day is call'd the feast of Crispian ...
> This story shall the good man teach his son;
> And Crispin Crispian shall ne'er go by,
> From this day to the ending of the world,
> But we in it shall be remembered;
> We few, we happy few, we band of brothers.
> (Henry V, IV: iii)

369

The fact that we were performing in one of the original buildings of the old school, which Shakespeare had known as a boy, gave real edge to a piece of theatre which showed us the moment of Will's infatuation with the stage. It captured perfectly the spark that got a village lad from Stratford, where there was little theatre to speak of, to London, where a theatrical revolution was beginning. This moment was so true, it was almost as though Shakespeare was there, briefly, with us.

As an actor you bring your creative energies to bear on releasing someone else's words: you are in a way a medium. On a good night you feel as though you yourself are not there; on exceptional nights, you feel that the author is. In over twenty years of acting I have sensed a long-dead author's presence at a performance on just a few occasions. More than once I have sensed Shakespeare hovering in the final mystical moments of *Cymbeline* in which the old king of Britain blesses the outcome of the extraordinary story:

> Laud we the gods
> And let our crooked smokes climb to their nostrils
> From our bless'd altars. Publish we this peace
> To all our subjects . . . Never was a war did cease
> Ere bloody hands were washed with such a peace.
>
> (*Cymbeline*, V: v)

Shakespeare is described as sweet and gentle by his contemporaries, and the dulcet harmony of this incomprehensibly magical play seemed to conjure him up. I became convinced that Shakespeare must have played the part of Cymbeline himself. Minimal research reveals that he did indeed have a reputation for playing old kings.

Next to the school is a building which for me really does hold a ghost of Shakespeare. The Guild Chapel contains some medieval doomsday frescoes: these paintings – a mixture of Hieronymus Bosch and Stanley Spencer – were whitewashed out the year before William was born, for they were considered to be papist. By divine irony, it was the whitewash which preserved them for a later age, and my old art master, who devoted a lifetime to their study, taught us that one of the men who ordered them to be covered up was John Shakespeare, a member of Stratford Corporation. I get a very clear picture of John standing in the chapel and explaining to his son why it had been necessary to cover these images. I think William would have been troubled by the harsh simplicity of the ethic that led to their being blotted out, and they would never have been whitewashed from his young mind. Underneath the whitewash, the dead would always be climbing out of their graves:

> The graves stood tenantless and the sheeted dead
> Did squeak and gibber in the Roman streets.
>
> (*Hamlet*, I: i)

The garden at New Place, with the Guild Chapel on the left

Writers plunder whatever is available to them shamelessly, and in the same way that William scavenged for his plots, we can be sure that variations on his friends and acquaintances found their way into the plays. Justice Shallow is often thought to be a bit of writer's revenge. Dogberry, the hopeless constable in *Much Ado About Nothing*; Dull, the idiot constable in *Love's Labours Lost*; William, the gormless rustic in *As You Like It*; the red-nosed inn-keeper of Daventry and Will Squele, a Cotswold

371

man, who are both mentioned by Falstaff in *Henry IV (Part 1)*; all were real people. Falstaff himself, although he had his roots in Sir John Oldcastle of our 'Famous Victories', lived then and lives now in public houses all over England. Shakespeare did what Hamlet advises actors to do, and held a mirror up to nature.

But we cannot rely on the plays to tell us much about Shakespeare's own life or opinions. All attempts to deduce the facts end in conjecture. But perhaps not quite all: it is beyond dispute that Shakespeare was living at New Place at the time of his death, and it is reasonable to think that Dr Hall, Susanna's husband, would have walked round from Hall's Croft (worth a visit) to tend his ailing father-in-law. A Stratford search for Shakespeare should end at the site of his last home. When Shakespeare bought New Place in 1597, he was beginning to earn real money. It was the second-largest house in the town, and we can picture his hard-won gentleman's coat of arms carved defiantly into the lintel of the front door. There was only one other coat of arms in Stratford. The ageing Shakespeare could look out over his gardens, to a cottage which he owned on the other side of Chapel Lane, where a servant or gardener might have resided. There is nothing left but the foundations of New Place, and we don't even have a true picture of the house, although the measurements, which do survive, are impressive. In 1756 the Revd Francis Gastrell, who was then the owner, got so sick of people coming to look at the mulberry tree that Shakespeare was supposed to have planted in the garden that he cut it down; three years later, he destroyed the house too and the site is now gardens.

We can sit in these New Place gardens and collect our thoughts. As we look towards the Guild Chapel and the setting sun, as he must have done, we can ruminate on what sort of man he must have become. Everyone makes him in their own image. Some will find the Prospero figure who buried his craft and left London for family and gentry life away from the city; others will dismiss this as sentimental, and see the semi-retired writer, still dabbling in collaboration with Massinger or Fletcher. Some will find the property owner, still involved in deals all over Stratford and even in London; some may find the husband and father, who came back to spend time with Anne and look after his poor, sad daughter Judith, whose twin brother, Hamnet, had died at the age of eleven, and whose unhappy marriage to the unreliable vintner, Thomas Quiney, may have caused William distress in his last days. Some will find a Paracelsian, discussing herbs and medicines with Dr Hall; others will see only a simple gardener, tending his vines. The truth is somewhere within all these possibilities, and the fact is that we will never know. Sit in this garden, stroll through the hills outside the town, stand in the fields on the other side of the river opposite the church on a dark evening, and look for Shakespeare where he truly belongs – in the gardens, in the hills, and in the fields of our own imagination.

BERNARD SHAW

SHAW'S CORNER, AYOT ST LAWRENCE, HERTFORDSHIRE

MICHAEL HOLROYD

Bernard Shaw and Charlotte Payne-Townshend were in their early forties when they married in the summer of 1898. They had little in common except their determination never to marry. But Shaw was seriously ill. His proposal had taken the form of offering Charlotte widowhood.

The honeymoon developed into a year's convalescence, during which the relationship 'completely lost its inevitable preliminary character of a love affair'. Charlotte became GBS's nurse and for a time his secretary. She was, he boasted, 'a dragon'. She had a genius for worrying, registering his coughs and sneezes as a barometer registers the weather. Her mind ran largely on sickness and travel, diagnosing one, prescribing the other. A contest quickly developed between the two of them. 'I don't really like work,' Charlotte once admitted to Nancy Astor. But GBS liked nothing better, especially the sort of 'creative work', Charlotte complained, 'that pulls him to pieces'.

They lived in Charlotte's double-decker flat on the south corner of Adelphi Terrace, overlooking the Thames and Embankment Gardens. It was a quiet place to work and, left to himself, that is what Shaw would have done there. But Charlotte insisted on his getting plenty of 'air'. Sometimes she would rent a house in the Home Counties; at other times she would pack them both off to a hotel farther off. 'Oh, these holidays, these holidays,' he sighed.

A house in the country, they decided, would supply him with regular quantities of English air without the need to rush about. 'We are in the agonies of house-hunting,' Shaw wrote to H. G. Wells on 5 April 1904. 'Now is the time to produce an eligible residence if you have one handy.' Over two and a half years later they found the rectory at Ayot St Lawrence, not far from Wheathampstead in Hertfordshire. It was a magnificently situated but unremarkable late Victorian suburban villa. Here was a place about which they could agree: both of them disliked it. In terms of Shavian paradox this was an advantage, since Ayot would interfere neither with Charlotte's passion for travelling nor with Shaw's obsession with work. They had no intention of staying there long, though as things turned out they continued renting it for fourteen years and then, shortly after the First World War, bought it.

What had apparently predisposed Shaw in favour of the village was a tombstone in the churchyard inscribed in memory of a woman who had lived from 1825 to 1895. The inscription read: 'Her Time Was Short'. If the biblical term of three-score years and ten was reckoned short at Ayot, then this must surely be a fitting place for the future author of *Back to Methuselah* to inhabit.

It was to take the villagers a dozen years or more to accept him. They 'didn't attach much importance to Mr Shaw's literary fame', Edith Reeves (who lived next door) calculated. Almost no one had read his books or seen his plays, though they knew he was a notable figure. During the First World War he became so hated in Britain on account of his devastating pamphlet *Common Sense about the War* that he was sometimes prevented by the threat of violence from speaking in public. The popularity he had begun to accumulate with *Pygmalion* in 1913 was not to be recaptured until more than ten years later with *Saint Joan*. This swing in public esteem was modestly if eccentrically echoed at Ayot. 'The villagers all thought he was a rum one – a *very* rum one,' Edith Reeves reckoned, '... and it was not until 1915, during the terrible Hertfordshire blizzard, that the village in general got to know him more closely. He came out and worked hard with the other menfolk for days on end, sawing up trees which had been torn up by their roots and lay blocking the road.'

After this, the villagers began calling the rectory 'Shaw's Corner', and in time the collector of rates did so too. Near the end of his life, Shaw employed the blacksmith at Wheathampstead to work this title into a new wrought-iron gate – and had himself photographed peering through it. He was, said his housekeeper Mrs Laden, 'a prisoner in his own house'.

The red-bearded revolutionary writer who had so energetically promoted GBS as a world-wide publicity phenomenon was also this quietly mannered, fastidious gentleman who had chosen to live in a remote twelfth-century village the size of a pocket handkerchief, with two churches, one shop and no bus or train service, and where the last thing of real importance that had happened 'was, perhaps, the Flood'. People, he once told Mrs Laden, bothered him, and he had come to Ayot 'to hide away from them'. Even in the 1930s the village had no gas, no water supply, no delivery of newspapers and no electricity – the rectory itself used a private electrical generating plant. The agricultural community at Ayot St Lawrence seemed to have withstood centuries of improvement. It was, said Shaw, 'a very wonderful thing'.

Such a statement, by someone dedicated to social change, sounded puzzling, and helps to account for some villagers describing him admiringly as 'a real old

George Bernard Shaw

hypocrite', 'the greatest leg-puller the world has ever known' and 'Conservative by temperament'. In fact, many thoughts came initially to Shaw as jokes. He would tell the joke, then work out the meaning of it. His genius for comedy often obscured an emotional bleakness and intellectual pessimism as intense as that of Samuel Beckett – a whirling black expanse instead of a black hole. 'An Irishman has two eyes,' he once told a friend. One was for poetry, he explained, the other for reality. This is why, at his most serious, Shaw always seems to be winking: the eye for poetry is closed. Two experiences, both visual, had influenced his early years. The first was the sight of the Dublin slums 'with their shocking vital statistics and the perpetual gabble of its inhabitants'. The second was the view from a cottage at Dalkey, ten miles south of Dublin, which overlooked two great bays between Howth and Bray Head. Its natural beauty intoxicated the boy. 'The joy of it has remained all my life,' he was to write. But his childhood, he told Ellen Terry, had been 'rich only in dreams, frightful & loveless in realities'. Ireland represented to him a land of imagination, dreams and emotions. Coming to London at the age of twenty he turned his back on dreaming and, through his literary and political work in England, sought to make the realities of life less frightful. To his dentist in Welwyn Garden City, Shaw wrote: 'Far from contrasting our occupations I often compare them. I spend my life cutting out carious material from people's minds and replacing it with such gold as I possess. It is a painful process and you can hear them screaming all through the Press.' His humour was a form of anaesthetic, but the quality of the gold he supplied for replacement had been diminished by years of emotional self-denial. There was nothing of Dalkey at Ayot. This deliberate eradication of beauty reflected a banishment of the inner life of the emotions by one who created at Shaw's Corner something of the imprisonment that St Joan describes as a form of death. But a latent part of him continued to supply a subversive and fantastical sub-text to his plays. 'Joey the Joker', as Mrs Patrick Campbell called him, loved to trip up GBS the prophet.

One play in particular derives from Ayot St Lawrence: *Village Wooing*. This 'Comediettina for Two Voices in Three Conversations' is one of Shaw's most delightful pieces for the stage, through which runs a curiously regretful and self-revealing undercurrent. On 15 December 1932 Charlotte had persuaded him to embark with her on the *Empress of Britain* for a world cruise, and while they were in the Sunda Strait Shaw began his play almost as an act of rebellion. He had developed the habit of labelling his people with a sequence of letters of the alphabet, from A onwards for the males, and Z backwards for the females. In *Village Wooing* he needed only two main letters, A and Z, which he retained as codenames for the characters. 'I do not see myself as the Man,' he told Lillah McCarthy. 'He is intended as a posthumous portrait of Lytton Strachey.' But A is as much Lytton Strachey as Marchbanks was De Quincey in *Candida* or Tanner the frock-coated Marxist H. M. Hyndman in *Man and Superman*: all use other men to camouflage a Shavian self-portrait. As for Z, she is not Charlotte but someone who lived down the road from them at Ayot: the village postmistress, Jisbella Lyth.

Mrs Lyth was a widow. She had started her career as a kennel-maid, then travelled round the world and returned to England, where in 1931 she and her husband took over the post office at Ayot. But almost immediately he died of a heart attack in the garden. Shaw and Charlotte came to visit the widow, and she told them her story. 'Oh! What a glorious death to die,' GBS complimented her. 'I hope I die like that in my garden underneath the stars.' 'Yes sir,' Mrs Lyth replied, 'but not at fifty-four, surely?' On leaving, Shaw said, 'I hope we shall have you here in Ayot for many years.'

And they did. 'Mr Shaw wrote personally to me for every batch of stamps he needed,' Mrs Lyth recorded over twenty years later.

> He wrote every request in his own hand, addressed the envelopes himself, and had them delivered to me by hand – five or six pounds' worth each time, approximately once a month – not £100 worth at a time, as he could have done ... he was able to combine his artistic nature, his genius if you like, with being an ordinary man as well – at least, that's how I found him. I've sold almost all those letters by now, of course – I believe he meant them to be a sort of legacy to me.

It is this relationship that is transformed by Shaw's imagination into *Village Wooing*. The play contains, in miniature form, many Shavian themes and obsessions including the phonetics from *Pygmalion*, the Life Force of *Man and Superman* and the sense of literary futility engulfing *Heartbreak House*. It is a tribute to Jisbella Lyth's awareness of the 'ordinary man' concealed within the GBS framework. But she did not like the play much. It was not very exciting and it lacked, she thought, suspense. Shaw's hairdresser, too, didn't think much of him as a dramatist. Ayot was a microcosm of Britain, with all the ordinary dullness and romantic suppositions that Shaw said he had been sent into the world to stamp on in thick boots.

On a small scale, he made suggestions for the improvement of Ayot, including the quelling of a local rubbish dump; pressing the Ministry of Transport for a bus service and a fast new road from the new schoolhouse to St Peter's church; the replacement of two obsolete old cottages without sanitation or water supply by a couple of modern 'gadgeted pre-fabs'; and the erection in the church meadow of a 'glorious' eighty-foot colonnaded water-tower that would stand as an ornament to the village. 'I believe it was meant to be funny,' pronounced Mrs Harding, wife of the licensee of the Brocket Arms, 'and we were all very serious.'

Such local jousting gave GBS a chance of demonstrating 'How to Quarrel Properly', which was the subject of a talk he delivered at the local Women's Institute. With his immaculately preserved Dublin accent, he had, as one resident put it, 'a funny way of expressing himself sometimes'. When invited to present a prize at the village school for the best-conducted boy or girl, he responded with the alternative idea of starting a rival prize 'for the worst-conducted boy or girl and we will watch their careers and then find out which really turns out best'. This proposal was not taken up. On another occasion, following a visit to South Africa, he suggested that all villagers should dance to the hymns in church 'as the black people do', and add to their repertoire such songs as 'O, You Must Be a Lover of the Lord'. It was disconcerting, too, for the local chemist to be urged to 'try out' some of his own bottles of medicines on himself so that his customers could see how they worked: or, when greeting Shaw in the street with a 'How are you?' to be answered with: 'At my age, Sir, you are either well or dead.'

The hat-stand at Shaw's Corner

He had a funny way, too, of dressing: a Norfolk jacket, knee breeches, brown shoes, wide-brimmed hat and cape. For wood-chopping, to the delight of children, he appeared helmeted. In the street, clipping his hedge, he was often spotted wearing a battered panama hat, a darned tussore suit, white shirt and a collar and tie of conflicting shades of beige. A bright macintosh illuminated him at night.

He was at his most 'ordinary' with children and animals. 'He always stopped and spoke to my little dog, Judy,' said Mrs Hinton to whom he did not speak much. 'He always talked to my children as an equal, so they liked him and looked upon him as a favourite uncle.' Each year he sent the headmistress of the school at Ayot a cheque to be spent on sweets. She would pass the money over to the village shop and the children were allowed to get their sweets, without paying, to the maximum of a shilling each.

With adults and neighbours he seemed on his guard. 'He wouldn't, or couldn't, let himself go. I felt he was shy,' one of them observed. The local landowner Captain Lionel Ames, whose 'outlook on life was completely opposed to his on almost everything', acknowledged that Shaw 'made you believe you were the most clever guy. He was a most charming person.' The Conservative Party agent for the district, who received Shavian sermons on socialism, thought him 'friendly and unassuming, yet at the same time as remote as God'. He was less god-like with less grand people. 'He would mix with the poorest people in the village as well as with the "top ten",' said Albert Bedford.

Those who knew him best were his and Charlotte's staff: Henry and Clara Higgs, head gardener and housekeeper; Fred Drury, the assistant gardener; Margaret Cashin, the parlourmaid; and Fred Day, chauffeur. The Higgses worked for the Shaws for over forty years and 'never had a cross word'. Being childless themselves, Charlotte and GBS treated a few special friends – T. E. Lawrence, Harley Granville-Barker – as surrogate children; and, in their fashion, the Higgses belonged to this category. 'Mrs Shaw looked upon my wife almost as a daughter,' Henry Higgs said; 'they were like a father and mother to us.' GBS inscribed one of his books for them: 'To Henry and Clara Higgs, who have had a very important part in my life's work, as without their friendly services I should not have had time to write my books and plays nor had any comfort in my daily life.' This sensitive statement of fact is echoed on the tombstone he erected to them in Windlesham cemetery: 'For many years they kept his house and garden at Ayot Saint Lawrence in the County of Hertfordshire thereby setting him free to do the work he was fitted for.' He was, however, criticized by the local stonemason for ending his sentence with a preposition.

Fred Drury's most persistent memory is of the Shaws walking round their garden by a special route one mile long. 'It gave him exercise without the need for going outside the gates.' Each time the Shaws passed the house they put a pebble on one of the windowsills to mark the number of circuits they had completed: then they would walk the other way round removing the pebbles. Several balanced miles were achieved in this way. Fred Drury used to watch them from the flower-beds, wondering what they were talking about, and concluding that it was Mrs Shaw who *made* Mr Shaw. 'She used to help him a lot with his work. Theirs was that sort of marriage.' Shaw himself didn't notice the flowers. Of the large red poppies at the end of the garden he merely inquired whether the seeds were poisonous ('We must get a packet and send them off to Hitler'). He was more interested in his fruit than flowers – especially the strawberry bed. 'He loved strawberries and cream,' Fred Drury explained. He enjoyed bonfires too, tackled the log-sawing with great gusto and collected acorns which he sent in seven-pound bags to Sidney

Webb. 'Pruning with the secateurs was his chief interest,' Fred Drury noticed. '... He always had his notebook with him.'

Margaret Cashin remembered Shaw as a tidy man. 'He always put chairs back in place, and his pyjamas on his bed in his room, neatly folded.' He was particular about his appearance and held himself absolutely straight – 'proud of his person and figure' he was. He changed for the evening meal 'regardless of whether anyone was coming to see him or not' and was full of unsuspected kindnesses. She often came upon him slipping money into envelopes. He paid for her trips back to Ireland and lent her his Rolls for her wedding which was grand.

Fred Day, the chauffeur, had the most adventurous time. When he came to the Shaws in 1919, GBS was still a fiery motor-cyclist, eager to 'ginger-up' his two-stroke machine, which was frequently bucking him off and landing on top of him. He knew all about these machines except how to ride them. Mrs Shaw was rather nervous of the car and preferred to sit on the back seat which GBS had specially upholstered for her, sealed from draughts and fitted with a heater. She, on the other hand, designed a front seat for him with a small cushion at his head 'which enabled him to sit bolt upright'. Shaw would take the wheel in the mornings, Day in the afternoons. 'It was a very anxious time for me,' Day acknowledged. 'I was fully occupied trying to keep him out of trouble.' Cars travelling in the opposite direction were a particular hazard. They often bumped. Shaw's most frequent mistake was to put his foot hard on the accelerator instead of the brake. He didn't drive much after 1937 (when he was eighty-one). He had, Day noticed, a Bohemian streak in him and, if Mrs Shaw was not with them, might pick up a tramp and give him a lift and some money.

Nothing disturbed Shaw's disciplined rhythm of work. 'I had either to write under all circumstances or not to write at all,' he explained; 'and I have retained this independence of external amenities to this day. A very considerable part of my plays have been written in railway carriages between King's Cross and Hatfield.' At Ayot he worked at the bottom of the garden in his revolving hut, furnished like a monk's cell (and sometimes mistaken for a tool-shed) with its desk, chair and bunk. Since this office was two minutes' walk from the house, Charlotte was able with perfect honesty to inform callers that her husband was 'out'.

He was up and ready for work before eight each morning, but latterly took a couple of hours over lunch, a silent meal (except, sometimes, for the radio) during which he went through his letters. There followed a siesta of an hour and a half, which started off with a book and ended, rather guiltily, with a nap. Then more work and, in the evenings, he would listen again to the radio, play the piano and sing to Charlotte. He was the last to bed, and liked to go into the garden to examine the stars, sometimes still singing. Then, forgetting to lock up, he wandered upstairs shortly before midnight.

Shaw's writing hut

He seemed to enjoy the air-raids at the beginning of the Second World War and treated them as firework displays. Perhaps behind this light-heartedness, as with the characters at the end of *Heartbreak House*, there was a wish to end it all. Charlotte was growing increasingly ill and felt 'buried' at Ayot. She seemed to have tumbled into old age. 'Charlotte's *osteritis deformans* is incurable,' Shaw wrote; 'she is often in pain, and moves about very slowly & not far.' He had placed the piano at the bottom of the stairs and would play to her, singing arias from operas and Irish airs he'd heard his mother sing, while Charlotte lay in bed. On 12 September 1943, aged eighty-six, she died. Shaw wrote to their old friend Sidney Webb:

> Her long illness had changed her greatly, and was very distressing in some ways (she was troubled with hallucinations) but at the end the distresses cleared off; and her last hours were happy. As she lies now she is not a crippled old woman; she is just like she was in her first youth. The change is inexpressibly touching . . .

The Shavian armour which had twinkled so brightly for so long was suddenly pierced. He had barricaded himself against grief, not because he was incapable of that feeling but rather because he knew too well its power to capsize him. Sometimes in public, he could not prevent himself from crying. A bookseller nearby noticed that for the next two or three years 'he seemed extraordinarily "caved in" ... He looked very sad. I did not think he was capable of such emotional feeling, but he showed it quite obviously.'

He fought this enemy, grief, with every Shavian contrivance. Though he looked very sad, he continued to speak very cheerily. His jokes were, people felt, sometimes in the worst taste – as if grief has anything to do with taste. Charlotte's death, he said, had been a great loss: a great *financial* loss as he had been obliged to pay tremendous death duties on the money she had left him. Money took an increasing hold on his imagination. Some people pointed to this as fresh evidence of his sham socialism; others found confirmation in it of his meanness. Only those who had lived at Ayot many years and remembered that it was Shaw who had put the Vitaglass into the school to improve the children's health, and Shaw who had largely restored the church roof, renovated the organ and meticulously supported the local tradespeople, could now put his fears of bankruptcy into a truer perspective.

'If you're after my money, you'd better see Mrs Laden – she'll probably give you some,' Shaw told a party of carol singers one Christmas. Mrs Laden, who was a trained nurse, had originally come to look after Charlotte during her last illness, and to some extent she took Charlotte's place. Shaw had resolved to add nothing to his weight, yet had developed an extremely sweet tooth. He could eat chocolate like a schoolboy. Mrs Laden seldom saw him 'without a large chunk of cake in his hand', and sometimes caught him in the evenings seated with a bowl of sugar or jar of honey in his lap.

Mrs Laden guarded him devotedly, keeping reporters, photographers and tourists at a distance. But a group of eccentrics had closed in on him, ruthlessly competing with one another for hand-outs of money and the spotlight of reflected fame. 'It always amazed me the way in which certain people could take advantage of Shaw,' said his doctor. 'It seemed to me that he was surrounded by people who really took the most terrible advantage of his good nature.' Shaw watched them with amusement and some anguish: it was little more than he had expected. He completed his will. He could hardly wait to be dead.

In September 1950 Mrs Laden went for a short holiday to Scotland and Margaret Cashin Jones, Shaw's old parlourmaid, returned to look after him. No sooner had she gone and it was dark than he set out with his secateurs, fell and broke his thigh. Margaret heard him blowing the whistle he carried for emergencies. 'I ran out into the garden and found him on the ground. I had him sitting on my knees for fifteen minutes.'

'If I survive this I shall be immortal,' he told a doctor at the Luton and Dunstable General Hospital. He was in great pain, but came well out of a first operation, and refused a second. 'I'm in *Hell* here,' he told a visitor.

At the beginning of October he was released from the hospital so that he could end his days at Ayot. What he called 'this damned vitality of mine' kept him alive another month. Up to the time of his accident he had continued to absorb himself in work. His last work had been *Rhyming Picture Guide to Ayot St Lawrence*, an endearing pamphlet of execrable photos and verses. Now he was unable to work at all and looked a different person, 'as though he had shed his skin', one of his neighbours said, 'as some animals do'. He was a skeleton. 'It was pitiful to see him the last time I cut his hair,' his barber, Mr Knight, remembered. '. . . Formerly he enjoyed having his hair cut, but that last time he was completely miserable. I don't know how I got through it. He was a changed man – like a child.' But he still held on to his good manners, his battery of jokes: though hardly able to eat, he took care to compliment Mrs Laden on her cooking and was alert enough to detect the Scotch whisky she had surreptitiously spooned into his soup.

'Shaw's last days were an agony for me,' Mrs Laden recalled. The house was encircled by reporters as egregious as the journalist reporting the death of Dubedat in *The Doctor's Dilemma*. Shaw had asked everyone not to try to prolong his life. On Tuesday 31 October he spoke his last words: 'I am going to die.' His temperature rose to 108, he went into a coma and just before five o'clock on the morning of 2 November 1950 he died. 'When he was dead he looked wonderful – quite different,' Mrs Laden said; 'clear of complexion and with a sort of whimsical smile on his face, as though he had had the last laugh.'

PHILIP SIDNEY

PENSHURST PLACE, KENT

―――――

KENNETH BAKER

In 1586 Elizabeth, Queen of England for nearly thirty years, very reluctantly and for the first time in her reign, dispatched an English army to fight in Holland. The purpose was to prevent the Netherlands from being overwhelmed by Philip II's Spanish army – an immediate threat to England's security. It was an amateurish expedition led by the Queen's prime courtier, the handsome Earl of Leicester, who was the only Englishman she might have married. But he was already fifty years old, overweight, and not up to the complexities of the task that confronted him. He had let Elizabeth down before by marrying secretly. He was to disappoint her again in the Netherlands.

The English army, on a foggy September day, tried to intercept a Spanish force which was seeking to relieve the town of Zutphen. The fog lifted and the two forces found that they were virtually face to face. But the Spanish heavily outnumbered the English. One of the officers, Sir Philip Sidney, experiencing his first skirmish, gave his steel thigh-pieces to another officer – a fatal act of generosity. The English troops advanced to heavy musketry fire. One ball hit Sidney about two inches above his knee and shattered his thigh bone. The story is told by his old school-friend and biographer, Sir Fulke Greville:

> In which sad progress, passing along by the rest of the Army, where his Uncle the Generall was, and being thirstie with excess of bleeding, he called for drink, which was presently brought him; but as he was putting the bottle to his mouth, he saw a poor Souldier carryed along, who had eaten his last at the same Feast, gastly casting up his eyes at the bottle. Which Sir Philip perceiving, took it from his head, before he drank, and delivered it to the poor man, with these words, 'Thy necessity is yet greater than mine.' And when he had pledged this poor souldier, he was presently carried to Arnheim.

The chestnut roof in the Great Hall

He died eleven days later. Fulke Greville had not fought at Zutphen, and his account of this episode, which is the only one that exists, was written many years later. However, there is no reason to suppose that it was invented. None of those who had fought in the battle contradicted his story. Indeed, the incident reinforces one of Sidney's well-known qualities, namely his generosity to others. In the months that Sidney was in the Netherlands there were several recorded incidents where he spent a great deal of trouble and money, which he could not afford, not only on training and equipment for his soldiers but also on their welfare.

England mourned his death, and early the following year he was the first commoner to be given a state funeral. It was a great affair, with hundreds of troops and horses leading his coffin through the narrow, winding London streets to old St Paul's. Carried proudly before it was his armour, his weapons and his helmet, surmounted by his heraldic emblem – a porcupine – which can still be seen at Penshurst today. So remarkable was his procession that John Aubrey, writing a hundred years later, remembered that as a child he had a toy which was a large cut-out model of this procession which stretched all round the room and could ingeniously be made to move.

Sidney's death became one of the most celebrated episodes in English warfare. It epitomized the Elizabethan concept of chivalry – the prince-like figure setting aside his own suffering on seeing one of his own men in even greater distress. It inspired generations of soldiers and writers. For instance, one of General Gordon's biographers said, 'He was as unselfish as Sidney'; and in the First World War Sir Henry Newbolt, writing after Julian Grenfell's death, said, 'However we suffer, we have seen the England of our dreams – the Black Prince, and James Audley, and Philip Sidney . . . all the company of the High Order of Knighthood.'

There is no doubt that Sidney had a capacity to inspire and win the devotion and love of others. When Fulke Greville composed his own epitaph for his tomb forty years later, all he wanted inscribed was 'Servant to Queen Elizabeth, Counsellor to King James, Friend to Sir Philip Sidney'.

Sidney came from a great family. On his mother's side his grandfather, the Duke of Northumberland, had ruled England under the young Edward VI. His father, Sir Henry Sidney, was President of the Council of Wales and Lord Deputy of Ireland. His two uncles were among the leading nobles at Court – the Earls of Warwick and Leicester – and for some years young Philip was their heir. His godfather, after whom he was named, was Philip II of Spain. Sidney was to die fighting his soldiers; on receiving the news, Philip noted: 'He was my godson.'

The family home of the Sidneys was Penshurst Place, which lies twenty miles south of London – a day's journey by horse in the sixteenth century. It was far enough away to be lost in the countryside of Kent, but close enough to be in contact with the life of the Court. It is a spreading and romantic house which has

The Great Hall, Penshurst

at its centre a high, medieval hall where the gentry of Edward III's time foregathered, where Edward IV stayed and which Henry VIII visited.

Sidney grew up at Penshurst Place, but at the age of ten he was sent to Shrewsbury School, which Camden called 'the best-filled school in England'. Elizabethan schooling was a hard business – the boys at Shrewsbury studied from 6.00 am to 5.30 pm in the summer and from 7.00 am to 4.30 pm in the winter. When he first went to school, his father wrote, 'Be humble and obedient to your master, for unless you frame yourself to obey others, yea and feel in yourself what obedience is, you will never be able to teach others how to obey you.'

From Shrewsbury he went to Christ Church, Oxford, and then at the age of seventeen he was sent on a continental tour which lasted for three years. While in Paris, in 1572, he had to take shelter in the embassy during the famous St Bartholomew's Day Massacre in which several thousand Protestants were killed by

Sidney's funeral helmet

Catholics. It was an experience which reinforced his own devotion to the Protestant cause.

On his return to England in 1576, he spent some time at Court, playing the part of diplomat and courtier. He also engaged in the elaborate jousting tournaments which revived the cult of medieval England. Proud of his horsemanship, he boasted of it in one of his sonnets:

> Having this day my horse, my hand, my lance
> Guided so well, that I obtained the prize,
> Both by the judgement of the English eyes,
> And of some sent from that sweet enemy France.

Like many other courtiers he overspent himself on handsome armour, fine horses, expensive equipment: Renaissance grandeur.

In 1580 he fell out of favour with the queen when, in support of his uncle Leicester, he sent her a letter setting out the reasons why she should not marry the Duke d'Alençon. The word went out and he slipped away from the Court, only returning some two years later, when as a symbol of his submission he presented the queen with a whip encrusted with jewels.

If he had been only a minor courtier, one would have little reason to remember him. But he was much more – a scholar, a poet and a patron of the arts, a man of genius. On his continental tour he had met many scholars and artists in France, Germany, Italy and the Low Countries, and had already aroused great expectations.

In all these countries, the arts were enjoying a renewal, a great flowering of creativity that was stimulated and sustained by the patronage of nobles and royal families. On his return, Sidney became one of the leading figures in the English Renaissance. He was the centre of a group of talented writers and poets – Fulke Greville, Edward Dyer and Edmund Spenser. They met at Penshurst and at Wilton, the home of his sister, Mary. On the continent, culture and civilization were centred in the courts and in the cities; in England it flourished at Court and in the great country houses such as Penshurst, Wilton, Knole, Hardwick and Longleat. Much of the writing and poetry was pastoral, and the greatest flower of the English Renaissance came from a quite small country town, Stratford-upon-Avon.

Sidney's group wrote poems and plays as well as translating the Psalms into verse. They supported other artists and musicians. Not much good verse had been written in English for a century or more, so there was a great opportunity to experiment in metres, rhythms and new verse-forms. Sidney was early inspired to write: '"Fool," said my Muse to me, "Look in thy heart and write."' He had the ambition to create a literature which could compare with Italian or French, and himself set models and standards in verse and prose. He wrote a prime work of literary criticism in English, *The Art of Poesy*, emphasizing the high moral purpose of poetry. It was to elevate, and not just divert and entertain. But he did not practise what he preached, for his own poetry is some of the most passionate and sensual love-poetry in the English language.

While he was absent from Court in 1580, he wrote a prose pastoral romance entitled *Arcadia*. This work of fiction is set in pre-Christian Greece. It tells of the adventures of two princes driven on by passion – there are disguises, deceptions, love potions, seduction and the threat of execution for adultery. There are also subtle political messages, for one of the main characters is an old king whose authority is challenged. Sidney's devotion to Elizabeth fluctuated according to whether he was in favour or not. *Arcadia* became very popular in the seventeenth century. Although it is scarcely read today, Virginia Woolf believed that it contained 'all the seeds of English fiction'. Sidney included some poems in it as well as his most celebrated song, 'My true love hath my heart'.

In 1582, some four years before his death and just one year before his own marriage, he wrote a sequence of over a hundred love sonnets addressed to Stella. The subject of the poems was, in fact, Penelope Devereux, the beautiful, vivacious sister of the Earl of Essex, Elizabeth's ill-fated last favourite. Some years earlier, Sidney might have married Penelope, but she was then too young; in 1581 she was married off against her will to the wealthy Lord Rich. She detested him and was later to leave him for the more intelligent Charles Blount, Lord Mountjoy.

These poems are the first great sequence of sonnets in the English language. They are so much more inspiring and vigorous than anything of the sort that had been written before. They were not published until after Sidney's death, but they circulated among the literary coteries of late Elizabethan England. They had a profound effect upon the development of English poetry and particularly upon a whole series of sonnet-sequences by other writers who followed in Sidney's footsteps.

No one really knows to this day whether Philip Sidney and Penelope Devereux were lovers – there is no firm evidence, no letter, no memoir, no indiscreet comment from a friend. It is probably unlikely as Sidney was above all an idealist and a moralist. But just read the poems: they are passionate and intellectual, intensely true to Sidney himself. They range from frustrated and unrequited love to ardent outpourings and sensual allusions. Can all this be an intellectual exercise by a refined scholar, critic and patron of the arts? Or did it derive from the experience of a handsome, brave courtier in his late twenties who was soon going to have to marry a mere sixteen-year-old in order to restore his personal finances? Well, everyone will have to make up his own mind. But no one can doubt the plain eroticism with which Sidney ended one of his sonnets:

> Yet let this thought thy tigrish courage pass:
> That I perhaps am somewhat kin to thee;
> Since in thine arms, if learn'd fame truth hath spread,
> Thou bear'st the arrow, I the arrow head.

There was no possibility of marriage and in 1583 he married Frances Walsingham, daughter of Queen Elizabeth's Secretary of State. This was a political marriage which had the added consolation that his father-in-law paid off his debts of £1,500 and allowed the couple to live in his own house.

Sidney is chiefly remembered for his sonnets. They are complex, full of conceits, metaphysical in language. The words he wrote all those centuries ago still remain vibrant and memorable today:

> My true love hath my heart, and I have his,
> By just exchange, one for the other giv'n.
> I hold his dear, and mine he cannot miss:
> There never was a better bargain driv'n.
> His heart in me, keeps me and him in one,
> My heart in him, his thoughts and senses guides:
> He loves my heart, for once it was his own:
> I cherish his, because in me it bides.

His heart his wound received from my sight:
My heart was wounded, with his wounded heart,
For as from me, on him his hurt did light,
So still me thought in me his hurt did smart:
 Both equal hurt, in this change sought our bliss:
 My true love hath my heart and I have his.

One of his descendants, Lord De L'Isle, who died in 1991, was himself a distinguished soldier, winning the VC. He, too, loved Penshurst, restoring much of the house and laying out an elaborate series of gardens. In one of these he placed a memorial to his first wife bearing a phrase from Catullus, 'Mutuis Animis Amante Amantur', which echoes one of Sidney's sonnets:

They love with equal spirit – and are loved.

THE SITWELLS

RENISHAW HALL, NEAR SHEFFIELD, S. YORKSHIRE
WOOD END, SCARBOROUGH, N. YORKSHIRE
WESTON HALL, TOWCESTER, NORTHAMPTONSHIRE

SARAH BRADFORD

The three Sitwells, Edith (1887–1964), Osbert (1892–1969), and Sacheverell (1897–1988), were a twentieth-century literary and social phenomenon. They made an impact on their age which was out of proportion to the purely literary qualities of their work, and their reputations have subsequently suffered.

Their star burned brightest in the decade after the First World War when they were the impresarios of the avant-garde in all the arts, the major preceptors of the post-war generation. D. H. Lawrence said of them that they taught young England how to be young. As style-setters and standard-bearers in the war against the Philistines, they were heroes to a new generation of dandy writers. They stood for modernism as against the consensus culture of Edwardian England, for French and American poetry against the traditionalist Augustan poets who then ruled the poetic roost, for Picasso whom Sacheverell early marked down as the greatest genius of the century, and for Modigliani, Diaghilev, Bakst, Cocteau, Stravinsky. They patronized Wyndham Lewis, William Walton, Pavel Tchelitchev. They preached the gospel of aestheticism and the importance of architecture to a generation which included Cyril Connolly, Harold Acton, Evelyn Waugh and John Betjeman. Anthony Powell wrote of them:

> The great thing about the Sitwells was that they believed, however idiosyncratically, that the arts were to be enjoyed; not doled out like medicine for the good of people's social or political health. Their phalanx impeded a wholesale takeover by the pedantic, the doctrinaire, the 'committed'; assailants by whom the arts are also eternally menaced.

As individual artists they had considerable talent which deserves a measured judgement. Edith, principally because of her extraordinary personality, wit and

A wing of Renishaw Hall from the garden

power of self-presentation, is the best-known of the three. Her early poetry was innovative in its deployment of syncopated jazz rhythms in *Façade* (1923). A sense of despair about twentieth-century civilization and the human condition underlay her later work, *Gold Coast Customs* (1929) and *Street Songs* (1942). Osbert's early poems, bitingly satirical, as in *Church Parade* or *Mrs Kinfoot*, are his best; in *Tales My Father Taught Me* and elsewhere he has created out of Sir George Sitwell one of the great comic characters of English literature. His five-volume autobiography *Left Hand! Right Hand!* was his most successful and popular achievement. Rich, discursive, anecdotal and powerfully evocative, written as Osbert sat cold and despairing in wartime Renishaw, it is a baroque family monument. Sacheverell was considered by his peers the most gifted of the trio; Eliot described him as having 'unusual poetic merit'. Although often difficult to read, he is immensely skilful in his use of rhythm. His 'garden' poetry has been compared with that of Marvell; in another vein, 'Agamemnon's Tomb' in *Canons of Giant Art* is one of the finest poems on the subject of death written this century. His literary output has been too prolific and diverse for his own good, but he is capable of passages of extreme beauty when dealing with the intensity of a sensory experience, as in *All Summer in a Day* (1926) and in his last autobiographical work, *For Want of the Golden City* (1973). Lastly, he had a sensitive and authoritative eye which enabled him to identify new or unusual trends in art and aesthetics. *Southern Baroque Art* (1924) changed the taste of subsequent generations; *British Artists and Craftsmen* and *Conversation Pieces* initiated a reappraisal of their subjects and a romantic interest in British art exemplified by Waugh and Betjeman. The same qualities illuminate his travel books such as *Roumanian Journey* (1937). His biography of Liszt remains one of the best available in English.

Few writers have been more influenced by their family circumstances and physical surroundings than the Sitwells. Their peculiar family relationships, the houses in which they lived, the ancestry which sustained them provided motivation as well as inspiration in their literary careers. Their father, Sir George Sitwell, was a man of talent, taste, and originality with a penetrating financial ability, but he was also a tyrannical, even machiavellian, husband and father. Their mother, Lady Ida, stylish, irresponsible, sensual, extravagant, provided the counterpoint to him. Renishaw Hall, the Sitwells' ancestral home in Derbyshire, haunted their literary imagination, appearing again and again in Edith and Sacheverell's poetry and in Osbert's monumental autobiography. This extraordinary house with its long crenellated façade, poised on the scarp of a Derbyshire hill, symbolized for them an enclosed childhood of close companionship and heightened sensory perceptions, a magical ambience in which the past seemed as close as the present, where mundane considerations were of small importance compared with beauty and style.

Sitwells had lived in the neighbourhood of Renishaw since the thirteenth century.

The first mention of them was Simon Cytewel, named as the son and heir of Walter de Boys who had died in 1301 on pilgrimage to the Holy Land. Renishaw was founded on minerals; the nucleus of the present house was built in the early seventeenth century with money derived from the nearby Eckington ironworks by a Cavalier ancestor, George Sitwell, and by the end of the seventeenth century the Sitwells were the world's largest manufacturers of iron nails. By the eighteenth, however, they were transformed from ironmasters into sporting squires with large estates and fortunes to support them. The curiously named Sitwell Sitwell who succeeded at the beginning of the nineteenth century was famous throughout Derbyshire for his fighting cocks, thoroughbred racehorses and pack of harriers. He built a magnificent stable block for his horses, a Gothic temple and an archway on the drive, then added a splendid new dining-room and in 1808 a ballroom in which he gave a ball for the Prince Regent, receiving a baronetcy from the prince in return. Forty years later his son, Sir George Sitwell, lost his fortune in the collapse of a Sheffield bank and soon after his death debt forced the sale of much of the estate and the contents of the house. Renishaw remained half-empty and deserted for a generation until the discovery of rich seams of coal under the park in the 1870s. Sir George Sitwell, father of the trio, inheriting a considerable fortune after a long minority, began the restoration of the house. He installed the massive oak staircase in the hall, acquired Italian Old Masters and ornate furniture, including vast beds with elaborate hangings surmounted by dusty plumes, and masterminded the landscaping of the garden on the south side of the house, with its Italianate terracing, hedges and baroque statuary.

The Renishaw which the Sitwell children knew was essentially Sir George's creation. Despite its romantic aspects, it was cold, dark (there was no electric light) and at night positively frightening. It was haunted, one wing being left unused because of the aggressive nature of its ghosts. The spirits of the past, most of them highly malevolent, who had had free rein when the house was deserted, did not give up their dominion without a struggle. One impertinent phantom had the temerity to slap Sir George's face, and Edith used to warn visitors to hug the wall when going up or down the great staircase as the ghosts might try and push them over the banisters. Other apparitions were gentler: the sad, damp ghost of a drowned eighteenth-century boy was renowned for waking ladies with cold kisses from the grave; and another spirit played the harp 'and all kinds of tricks' in the young William Walton's bedroom. Raymond Mortimer, guilty of some unspecified offence against the Sitwells, was punished by being put into the 'most blood-curdling' of the haunted bedrooms. 'He was duly frightened,' Sacheverell gleefully reported to his wife in August 1925.

The 'melancholy and even sinister' atmosphere, as Anthony Powell described it, has largely vanished. The ghosts were exorcised by Edith and again by Sir Reresby

Detail of one of the Brussels tapestries
in the ballroom at Renishaw

Sitwell, the present owner, and the house has been redecorated by the present Lady Sitwell. The main rooms, however, remain much as they were. The core of the house, the hall with its great stone fireplace and the library leading off it, retains the seventeenth-century ceilings of the original house and much of the old furniture, although the Pipers which decorate the walls were commissioned in the 1940s by Osbert during his residence there. The charming portrait of the Sitwell children painted in 1787 by John Singleton Copley still hangs in the dining-room. Sacheverell wrote that in the darkest days of his childhood it had seemed like a beacon of hope and a message of reassurance from his ancestors. From a literary point of view the objects which had the greatest influence on the three Sitwells were the five magnificent Brussels tapestries in the drawing-room and ballroom. Sacheverell wrote of their 'world of Indian suavity and opulence ... elephants and black slaves, bell-hung pagodas and clipped hornbeams ... clouds tacking like sailing ships ...

terraces with pots of orange trees ... and continual fountain jets'. They inspired Osbert and Sacheverell's love of the baroque and their exotic imagery appeared constantly in both Edith and Sacheverell's poetry. The tapestries featured as an important part of Sitwell iconography in the Sargent family group orchestrated by Sir George in the spring of 1900 and in the magical photographs by Cecil Beaton of the family at Renishaw in the 1920s.

Renishaw's air of 'sad magnificence' formed the perfect backdrop for the 'Peacockian household' of the eccentric, remote Sir George (known to his children as 'Ginger'); his equally odd wife, Lady Ida, who was the protagonist of a spectacular family scandal which resulted in her imprisonment in Holloway; their extraordinary servants with whom, according to Evelyn Waugh, they lived on terms of 'feudal familiarity', and their remarkable children. The Sitwells provided an annual spectacular for their circle at the August house-parties held there in the 1920s and 30s when Evelyn Waugh, Anthony Powell, Peter Quennell, Arthur Waley and Beryl de Zoete, Constant Lambert, William Walton, Gerald Berners, Robert Byron, Cecil Beaton, Stephen Tennant and Siegfried Sassoon would be summoned to be amused by the guerrilla warfare between 'Ginger' and his children, the scenes caused by Lady Ida, the jokes, the plots and the huffs, the antics of the ghosts and the servants, and the delicious food provided by chefs from the Ritz.

Renishaw was essential to the Sitwell mythology, a part of their image. 'Tall, fair, attenuated courtiers from a medieval tapestry,' Anthony Powell called them. 'We all have the remote air of a legend,' Edith wrote in *Colonel Fantock*, describing how she and her brothers walked in the 'sweet and ancient gardens' like 'shy gazelles Among the music of the thin flower-bells ...' The terraced gardens, the wilderness below, the tall chimney-stacks and golden August cornfields beyond with the stone keep of Bolsover on the far horizon, form the opening paragraph of Osbert's *Left Hand: Right Hand*. Sacheverell's feeling for nature, the strength of his poetry, began in the Derbyshire woods round Renishaw where he wandered as a child in the hot Augusts and misty Septembers and which he recalled in his Proustian early autobiography, *All Summer in a Day*.

Until the First World War, however, the Sitwells lived principally at Scarborough, then an elegant resort for county families on the Yorkshire coast. Edith was born there, at her grandmother's house, Wood End, a golden stone building of the 1830s in sober classical style which is now the Natural History Museum, and Sacheverell a stone's throw away at 5 Belvoir Terrace, a double-fronted, pilastered limestone terrace house then inhabited by his parents. The whole area, known as the Crescent, was a family enclave; the Sitwells' maternal grandparents, the Earl and Countess of Londesborough, owned a summer house there next but one to Wood End, Londesborough Lodge, now council offices. The Londesboroughs were 'swells', extremely rich and with royal connections. Lady Ida's mother, the Countess of

The conservatory at Wood End looking across the valley in Scarborough

Londesborough, was the daughter of the 7th Duke of Beaufort, thus claiming the Plantagenet blood which fascinated Edith. Her father, the 1st Earl, was a munificent figure who reigned as virtual king of Scarborough during his sojourns there, supporting Cricket Week and the Regatta out of his own pocket. Osbert was born in London but spent most of his childhood and adolescence in Scarborough, principally at Wood End, where his parents lived until they migrated to Italy in 1925. In the early years Wood End was dominated by the children's paternal grandmother, Louisa, Lady Sitwell, a shrewd, soft-spoken lady of iron will and adamant religious conviction with a great love for animals and flowers. The principal feature of the house was her conservatory, connecting what used to be the drawing-room with the library, added by Sir George in imitation of the library at Renishaw. It was filled with orchids and exotic plants and lit by Chinese lanterns; the tropical birds which fluttered among its palms became a recurrent theme in Edith and Sacheverell's poetry.

Some effort of the imagination is required to recreate Wood End as it was in the Sitwells' childhood. The house is not much changed architecturally, but natural history specimens in cases take precedence over Sitwelliana. There are echoes of Renishaw in the library with its Jacobean-style plasterwork ceiling and stone fireplace, and in the dining-room there is a collection of paintings: a water-colour of Lady Sitwell's conservatory, a depiction of the ceremonial arrival in Scarborough of Sir George and Lady Ida after their London wedding, a gouache by Max Beerbohm of Osbert and Sacheverell with parrots on their wrists, dated 1923, and two John Pipers of the Grand Hotel and the South Bay, and of Wood End from the garden aspect.

Scarborough was the constant in the early lives of the children, the place of their first impressions, of street cries, of strange figures in the streets, like the man who mewed like a cat, a world of dramatic natural forces. As they lay in their beds in the cabin-like upper rooms of Wood End, the wind tore in across the North Sea in the winter months flattening the bare black trees above the curving bay, a savage contrast with the cosy bourgeois world behind the lace curtains of the terraced houses on the cliff. Sacheverell's tutor, Major Brockwell, was the original of Edith's *Colonel Fantock* and of Osbert's Major Viburne; the diminutive, delicate and mysterious Miss Lloyd, who gave them delicious teas and cultivated miniature exotic gardens in glass cases, appears as Miss Morgan in Sacheverell's *All Summer in a Day*. The huge ornate Grand Hotel, projecting like an ocean liner above the foreshore, the rows of pierrots' booths on the sands, the hot glare of municipal flowerbeds on the cliff, were a part of their landscape. Osbert wrote about the town in *Triple Fugue* and in his first *roman à clef*, *Before the Bombardment*, which described Scarborough as it was in the years before the German bombardment in December 1914 virtually ended its existence as an elegant resort. Sacheverell referred to it constantly in all his autobiographical works; the title of his first book of poetry, *The People's Palace*, published in 1918 at the age of twenty, was inspired by the popular underground amusement arcade behind the beach at Scarborough. 'My journeys,' he wrote in *For Want of the Golden City*, 'brought me to many different parts of the world [but] I could as well say that each and every one of them has started and had its end upon the Scarborough sands. It was there, scrambling upon the rocks, that I first began to think, and hear and see.'

Weston Hall, a seventeenth-century manor house set in the unspoilt rolling fields of Northamptonshire, came to the Sitwells by marriage or descent over two hundred years from 1714 when Sir John Blencowe bought the lease of a small farmhouse for his daughter, Susanna Jennens, and seven years later presented her with the freehold as a Valentine present. Subsequent generations improved the house, adding

The view from Sacheverell's study at Weston Hall. The photograph on the desk shows him sitting at this window

the fine drawing-room and hall. Over the years, possessions acquired by the various families accumulated there, many of the owners being wealthy widows.

When Sir George Sitwell first saw the house in 1922 on the death of his aunt, Lady Hanmer, it was a treasure trove: lacquer cabinets commissioned in Paris by an early eighteenth-century ancestor who had made a fortune in the Levant trade; miniatures by Cosway and drawings by Ingres; a portrait of Henrietta Maria by Van Dyck; and a pair of tiny kid gloves rolled up in two halves of a walnut shell, given by Pauline Borghese to the romantic Colonel Hely-Hutchinson, Sacheverell's great-grandfather. (Hely-Hutchinson died at Weston in 1874. Before his death he could be heard groaning with pain from old wounds acquired at Waterloo, a historical connection which fascinated Sacheverell.) The colonel apart, the house has always had a particularly feminine atmosphere, having been inherited by generations of women, who have left their mark in an abundance of needlework and a wonderful bed embroidered by Susanna Jennens. Other treasures include

400

feather pictures, needlework and jewellery boxes, books of household receipts and a very fine collection of eighteenth-century clothes worn by the gentlemen of the family.

After Sacheverell's marriage in 1925 to Georgia Doble, a vivacious and beautiful Canadian, and the birth of their eldest son, Reresby, in 1927, they moved into Weston. There they created their own atmosphere, a particular blend of society and talent, gossip, serious talk and music. Patrick Leigh Fermor called it 'a marvellous haven' from his wartime barracks:

> Arriving from the freezing squalor of the Guards Depot to the luxury, civilization, charm and fun of Weston was like going to heaven ... The house was full of books and pictures and a great charm floated in the air, enhanced by the logs and sometimes a liquid heated in a spoon on the hearth, which gave off a delicious aromatic smell. The house was full of delights and surprises, unconventional pictures and books and objects, scattered among the inherited stuff of a country house ... chests of beautiful eighteenth-century clothes, miraculously intact and carefully looked after, laid away by Sachie's Heber relations.

It was to be Sacheverell's home for half a century. It was here that he did most of his work, sitting at a table in his first-floor study, with its view up the lawn to the trees on the horizon but seeing, perhaps, in his mind golden baroque churches, red oriental temples or some dazzling gilded and painted rococo interior. Weston provided the essential requisite for a writer – peace. For Sacheverell, whose garden poetry was perhaps the most lasting part of his work, the Arcadian atmosphere of a country manor house close to the earth and its seasons gave him precisely the setting and inspiration he needed. Working always under financial pressure he wrote travel books, books on art and architecture, birds and flowers, contributions to journals and magazines, volumes of autobiographical fantasy. However, he considered himself primarily a poet. In his last years at Weston he continued to write poetry, publishing it in slim volumes which he had privately printed at the nearby town of Brackley and sent to his friends.

His study is kept as it was when he worked there surrounded by his favourite drawings and prints. Many of the Weston possessions are still in the house, with the addition of modern works like the portraits of Sacheverell by Graham Sutherland and Derek Hill, and of Edith by Pavel Tchelitchev and Wyndham Lewis. Sacheverell and Edith are both buried, with their mother, Lady Ida, in a small rustic cemetery in the neighbouring village of Weedon Lois.

The Sitwells' houses reflect their particular world in which the past was always present, peculiarly English and yet at the same time exotic. Nothing quite explains how the lines of sporting squires culminated in the extraordinary twentieth-century literary trio, but the physical landscape which shaped them provides a clue.

LAURENCE STERNE

SHANDY HALL, COXWOLD, N. YORKSHIRE

MALCOLM BRADBURY

Today there is no doubt at all that Laurence Sterne is one of the very greatest of the English novelists. Yet he produced only two works of fiction, and one of them was spawned by the other. On the other hand, the first of those novels was nine volumes long, and so open-ended and comprehensive in its many stories, opinions and playful inventions that some critics doubt whether it was a novel ('though written in prose and by way of being called a novel,' wrote Virginia Woolf, the book 'adopts from the start a different attitude ... There, one sees, is poetry changing easily and naturally into prose, prose into poetry') and others wonder whether he actually finished the book at all, or whether it finished him. The author describes his work in its closing pages as a 'cock-and-bull story' ('And one of the best of its kind, I ever heard'), and so it is. But the critics, writers and readers of our own time would doubtless call it the first truly modern novel, and it is that too.

The book is, of course, *The Life and Opinions of Tristram Shandy, Gentleman*, the great book of Sterne's life. He followed it with the delightful, far less scabrous and teasing *A Sentimental Journey through France and Italy* (1768), which was also never properly finished. Its assumed author is Parson Yorick, who is one of the characters from *Tristram Shandy*. It was also the name that Sterne took out of the novel and gave to himself, even publishing his own sermons under that title. Like so many English writers of the time, Sterne was a clergyman. Like so many English writers, he was actually born in Ireland, in 1713 in Clonmel, in the south. But his father was an army ensign from a Yorkshire family who died in service when Sterne was still a schoolboy. Sterne therefore came under the often unwilling patronage of his family, who had many connections with the Anglican Church. His great-grandfather had been Archbishop of York, and sometime Master of Jesus College, Cambridge.

St Michael's church, Coxwold

An uncle sent him to school in Halifax; a cousin sent him to Cambridge. Then another uncle, who held church office at York Minster, arranged for him the living of Sutton-on-the-Forest, which is to the north of York and on the fringe of the Hambledon Hills. And he also acquired, from a marriage that was not happy in any other way, the benefice of nearby Stillington.

So Sterne became a clergyman, though a somewhat mischievous one. But he was also a Yorkshireman, and it is clear that the region has much to do with his literary identity. *Tristram Shandy* is set in the lovely North Riding, and the assumed name of Parson Yorick is based on a triple pun – the Danish court jester, the skull in *Hamlet* ('Alas, poor Yorick') and the parson from York (which was formerly Jorvik). Sterne may share with Swift, and indeed with Joyce and Beckett, an Irish humour, but he was undoubtedly a writer from the region he lived in. When he dedicated later editions of his by now famous book to the Secretary of State, William Pitt, he declared that it was written

> in a bye corner of the kingdom, and in a retired thatched house, where I live in a constant endeavour to fence against the infirmities of ill health, and other evils of life, by mirth; being firmly persuaded that every time a man smiles, – but much more so, when he laughs, it adds something to this Fragment of Life.

Indeed the book's peculiar comic humour – what Kurt Vonnegut would call 'gallows humour' – is one reason why it seems so modern a novel, a work of a dark, mortal comedy that uses the play of the mind as a survival mechanism, making it the true antecedent of modern works by Joyce and Beckett, and also Nabokov and Borges. The other reason is that the book can fairly be called the first true anti-novel in the British tradition. It was written, of course, close to the beginnings of the novel form in Britain, at a time when the novel could truly be described as novel. Daniel Defoe, Samuel Richardson, Henry Fielding and Tobias Smollett can be called the founding fathers of British fiction, and they invented its major forms: the realist and mercantile report, the sentimental romance, the novel of comic social and moral adventure, the picaresque epic. Then there is Sterne, who wrote under different influences: Cervantes, Rabelais, the association theories of John Locke. His work is seemingly chaotic, and invents a strange and chaotic self as author. His cock-and-bull story methods subvert all the key conventions of the newly developing genre, subjecting them to teasing, self-questioning and experiment, so giving us the tradition of the anti-novel.

When *Tristram Shandy* first appeared, it caused a sensation, for its teasing and its bawdy, and because it was hard to believe a clergyman could have written such a novel, eccentric and often outrageous work. 'Nothing odd will do long, *Tristram Shandy* did not last,' said Doctor Johnson; but it did. It has remained a sensation and an influence ever since. It linked the British novel to European literature (it

Sterne's study at Shandy Hall

was much admired in France) and has been especially important for the experimental writers of the Modern and the Postmodern age, who have seen it their task to reconstruct the generic character of fiction in tune with the twentieth-century world. There is scarcely a serious novelist of our time who has not made some acknowledgement to it, and if the complex and lively history of the English novel is indeed born out of a small body of works written in the early and middle eighteenth century, there is no doubt who among these great predecessors is

405

the most mischievous, the most experimental, the most outrageous, the most monumentally unmonumental – or, we might say, the most modern. Sterne's quirky and deeply learned book did more than startle and upturn the conventions, literary and moral, of his day: it created an attitude *to* the conventions – that they are there to be challenged – which lasts into the era of what we now call 'meta-fiction'.

This is because it is a work of extraordinary play. Most of the novels of Sterne's own age of the novel start, very reasonably, with the birth of the hero, and then tell of his adventures in direct narrative order until they reach a dramatic conclusion. Sterne elects to start not with the birth but with the conception of the hero (hero? well, small hero, says Sterne) and then tell of, well, whatever ... his opinions, his chatter, his disorder, his hobby-horses, by the method of what Mr Shandy calls 'transverse zig-zaggery'. And perhaps Tristram is really no sort of hero at all, for his is in every sense a botched conception, his parents being far more concerned with their monthly winding of the clock than they are with the procreative process, his doctor making a spectacular incompetence of his fictionally very delayed and extended birth. Indeed Tristram is a clear case – and the allusion is definitely intended – of *post coitum tristis*.

If Tristram's is indeed a botched conception, it therefore seems very appropriate that the book he offers to write for us will also be a botched conception, in its own chosen way. After all, as Tristram says, he does all things 'out of rule', even though he clearly knows what the rule is. In the various drawings and squiggles with which he decorates the book (along with marbled or blank pages, or a black one when Parson Yorick dies (though not for long)) he shows us the proper narrative line he ought to follow – and then the crazy line he somehow has followed, by his own special laws of association. He is the writer claiming fictional freedom – freedom to have his chapters in the wrong order, the preface in the middle, the freedom to digress, upturn, change narrators, go back. Having written much of the book, he can claim it is now about to begin, for 'I have but been clearing the ground to raise the building – and such a building do I foresee it will turn out, as never was planned, and as never was executed since Adam.' If Sterne is averse to beginning the book, he had even more aversion to the notion of ending it (which is why some critics say he never did). For the work refuses that logic of endings that normally confer meaning and shape on narratives, and so it keeps us in the eternal middle of things. Indeed, for Sterne, always sickly, the one real ending was the mortal one, the ending we seek to defer by telling ourselves stories. Long before Roland Barthes, Sterne believed in the Death of the Author – but also in his birth, as a thinking consciousness seeking to claim an original relation to his reader.

When Sterne began to write *Tristram Shandy* in 1759, he was, as his dedication says, indeed an obscure, middle-aged and sickly parson living in a 'bye corner of the kingdom'. His marriage was unhappy, his wife half insane and under medical

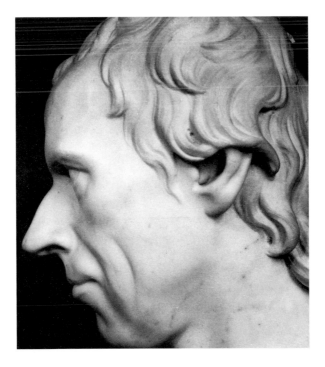

Bust of Sterne, by Joseph Nollekens

care, he was worried about his tuberculous ill-health, and he indeed wrote it as a comic prop against infirmity and misfortune. He was also involved in the bitter controversy among the clerics of the Minster Yard, and had won some notoriety for intervening in a church quarrel by publishing the satirical and offensive *A Political Romance*, which was burned. *Tristram Shandy* was originally intended to continue the spirit of satire, but as he wrote it turned into a deeper and more painful spirit of comedy. He wrote it at speed: two volumes appeared in 1760, two more in 1761, and two more in 1762. Within a year of the appearance of the first two volumes, Sterne was the talk of London. He was presented at court, and his sermons attracted large audiences. He was painted by Reynolds, illustrated by Hogarth, had his bust done by Joseph Nollekens. He became known for his quirky and teasing temper, and so did his characters – Tristram, Parson Yorick, Walter Shandy, Uncle Toby, Dr Slop, the Widow Wadman – who regularly appeared in the prints and drawings of the day.

Sterne enjoyed the adulation, frankly admitting that he wrote not to be fed, but to be famous. When he travelled to France for two years, he found the same adulation there. He continued with *Tristram Shandy*, though ill-health as well as fame began to slow him down. Volumes 7 and 8 of what was now a best-selling serial appeared in 1765, and the ninth and final part in 1767. A year later he published *A Sentimental Journey*, the product of yet another European tour. His ill-health defeated him at last, and he died a few days after its publication, on 18 March 1768, in London. However, his adventures were far from over, and his choice of pseudonym continued to be appropriate, for he was to have an extraordinary exhumatory history. Two days after his death, his grave in the cemetery of St George's, Hanover Square, in Bayswater, was snatched, and his body taken to Cambridge for use in anatomy lessons. The skull was trepanned, and it is said that one of the witnesses fainted, recognizing that it was Sterne's. It seems that the remains were promptly and secretly returned to the grave. There they stayed until the 1960s, when the graveyard was deconsecrated for property redevelopment.

Shandy Hall from the garden

408

Sterne's skull and bones were recovered, and in a series of further misadventures were returned to Yorkshire, to Sterne's final parish of Coxwold, the true home of *Tristram Shandy*.

Coxwold is a delightful North Yorkshire village, eighteen miles north of York, set just on the rise into the impressive Hambledon Hills, with a view over to the ruins of Byland Abbey, and Castle Howard (lately featured on television as Evelyn Waugh's Brideshead) not far away. Sterne's connection with the village occurred just as his novel began to appear and his fame began. His friend and patron the Earl Fauconberg lived at the great house nearby, Newburgh Priory, and when the parson in the village died he offered Sterne the living, as 'perpetual curate'. Sterne loved the village, calling it 'a sweet retirement in comparison with Sutton'. There was, though, one problem: at the time there was no official parsonage there. Sterne, however, was already beginning to find wealth from his novel (he earned a substantial £250 for the copyright of the first two volumes, the same sum for the next two, and even the same sum again for his sermons). He had no difficulty in renting for £12 a year from his patron an ancient, fine if ungrand low stone house at the very top of the village, and setting about its improvement. He and his friends were soon calling it 'Shandy Castle' or 'Shandy Hall'.

It is said that 'shandy' is the local dialect word for 'crazy', though other wise sources say it means rather 'odd' or 'unpredictable' (a Yorkshireman myself, I have to confess I have never heard the word in use). But from all we know of Sterne, both from reports of his life and the very spirit of his writings, we can understand why the name attracted him, and why he used it both for his fictional and his real house, which gradually became almost indistinguishable. And if it suggests the eccentric character of the novel, that eccentricity was to pass into the house where he continued to write it – the house affecting the book just as the book affected the house. It was not his only residence; he was also a Prebend of York Minster and had a house in the Minster Yard. But Coxwold was what he called his 'philosophical retreat', and the place where he was happiest; as he told his friends, 'I am happy as a prince, at Coxwold – and I wish you could see in how princely a manner I live!'

Recent restoration work on the house done in the 1960s, when it was being transformed into a living museum for the author, revealed that, appropriately enough, it had almost certainly been the priest's house of the village in the Middle Ages. Built around 1430, as an open-halled timber frame house, it was altered in the seventeenth century, being cased in a brick façade and divided into rooms. However, behind panelling some fine Christian wall painting was discovered, suggesting that there had been an oratory there. Probably Sterne did not know that, but in any case he was a good eighteenth-century gentleman who believed in 'improvements', and Shandy Hall was to become, like the house in the novel, like the novel itself now being written there, his folly. Just as in the book he wanted to construct a building such as never was planned and never executed since Adam, so he clearly decided to invest the same Yorick-like spirit into the house itself.

Here, then, in the 'delicious retreat' where he retired from the pressure of his fame, his travels, and indeed later on his wife, who settled in France, he organized for himself a small and confortable study, and, often writing through the night, he worked away on the ever extending saga of *Tristram Shandy*, and on the warmer *Sentimental Journey*. The house began to acquire the spirit of Shandyism and become part of the imaginative topography of the novel. He made substantial and curious alterations, and in 1767 he employed a York architect, John Carr, to build out a quirkily unproportionate Georgian front on the garden side, at odds with the rest of the low ancient house but decidedly in the spirit of Shandyism.

By now Sterne, separated from his wife, had developed a sentimental – for all his Rabelaisianism he was always sentimental – attachment to a young woman, Eliza Draper. There were many problems. He was a clergyman, and a married man, and she had a husband in the East India Company in Bombay. The relationship was sufficiently public for Daniel Draper to summon his wife back to India, but Sterne and Eliza continued their friendship in letters and his *Journal to Eliza*, and in Shandy Hall itself. He imagined her living in Coxwold with him, and he fancifully reconstructed part of the house for her to live in. He built her an upstairs apartment, 'a sweet sitting room', added Adam-style fireplaces, some highly practical appurtenances like a good wine cellar, and awaited her arrival. Eliza was, he said, his 'wife elect', but she never came to Shandy Hall, though his memorial to the relationship remains in the building itself.

Sterne's building fever also extended to the church where he was the incumbent – the ancient church of St Michael, across the road and down towards the centre of the village. It is a large and noble church for such a community, clearly indicating the importance of Newburgh Priory and the Fauconberg family, originally the Belayses, whose grand and glorious tombs, one by Grinling Gibbons, fill the chancel. Indeed, being in an area of important ecclesiastical settlement (this part of Yorkshire is filled with dissolved abbeys and crumbling priories), it is a church of great distinction, with a remarkable horseshoe altar rail and box pews. But as a result of his great popularity the church could scarcely accommodate those who came to hear him preach, and he rearranged the pews 'something in the form of a cathedral' so that all could hear him. His Shandyan influence is even more present in the churchyard. On the south wall of the church, looking across the fields, are to be found not one but two memorial stones to him, both in the rumbustious spirit of the novel. One is from two freemasons who wished to include him in their order, and each shows a different date of death.

Sterne was, of course, much remembered, and his influence in the village continued long after his death and continues to the present. In 1968, the bicentennial year of his death, I was present at a decidedly curious ceremony held in the fine interior of St Michael's church. The University of York had joined with the Laurence Sterne Trust, newly formed to rescue Shandy Hall from a state of ruinous neglect, in the holding of an international conference on the great author and his work. The event was attended by critics and writers from all over the world, as well as many clerics and prebends. We had gathered on the appointed day not only to praise Sterne but, we thought, to bury him. For Kenneth Monkman, the Chairman of the Sterne Trust, had been instrumental in delaying building on the now deconsecrated graveyard in Bayswater where Sterne's remaining remains were buried, which was being developed by a property company, and had applied to the Diocese of London to investigate the site. Now we hoped the remains would be recovered and reinterred in the churchyard Sterne knew so well.

Alas, poor Yorick! It was not to be. The memorial service went ahead, with a sermon by the Chancellor of York Minster, the Revd Canon Reginald Cant. A case of port donated by Croft's, a firm founded by Sterne's great friend Stephen Croft of Stillington, also went missing, having been entrusted to British Rail. The Diocese of London continued to dally, but a year later the dig at last took place. Sterne's skull and a few bones were identified, with the help of the Nollekens bust. On Sunday 8 June 1969, at Coxwold, another reburial service was held, with a full church and another sermon by Dr Cant. The port had arrived, and was drunk to acclamation, and Sterne's remains were at last buried in the place it was thought he would most like to be. Or the skull was; the remaining bones presumably are still in London, beneath the product of a rebuilding fever that he would have understood so well.

As for the house where Sterne conceived and completed most of his fiction, and made the spirit of Shandyism survive both in words and in architecture, that too has since had a complicated history. Not long after his death it ceased to be a parsonage, when in 1805 a later rector took charge of the nearby Grammar School, another fine Coxwold building. Shandy Hall reverted to being a farmhouse, was then divided into cottages, then became empty and fell into severe neglect. So, by the time we visited it for the bicentennial celebration, it was in a sad and sorry state – its floors had rotted, the bedroom ceilings had fallen in, the stone roof was in danger of total collapse, the garden was overgrown. The fact that it survives at all today (the architects consulted could only advise that the whole thing be pulled down) is almost entirely due to the efforts of two latter-day Sterneans, Kenneth and Julia Monkman, who determined to start on its restoration.

Kenneth Monkman, who has rightly been called the finest of the Sterne scholars, became Sterne-obsessed when he worked for the *Yorkshire Evening News* and one day in 1936 picked up *Tristram Shandy*. Thereafter, though working for the BBC for twenty-nine years, he became one of the great bibliographers of the author and a remarkable collector of Sterneana. He, who had first visited Shandy Hall in 1938, returned in 1963 with his wife, when they were appalled by what they saw. The house was ruinous, and ought, they were told, to be rebuilt from scratch. Instead they approached the Wombwell family, the contemporary owners of Newburgh Priory, set up a Laurence Sterne Trust, and raised an appeal. Henry Moore donated a sculpture, and the modern Yorkshire novelist J. B. Priestley wrote a charming appeal document called 'The Saving of Shandy Hall' – which is itself now a collectors' item.

In one way at least, the disastrous condition of the house was to prove its good fortune. The restoration, begun in 1968, took five years (Shandy Hall was opened to the public by Frank Muir in 1973), but most of the major features from Sterne's own time survived. What did not could be accurately reconstructed. The Monkmans devoted themselves entirely to the restoration, and worked with love, dedication and ·perfect taste on the rebuilding, redecoration and refurnishing of the house. Julia Monkman also set to work to revive the charming eighteenth-century garden. They were finally able to move in and to become the curators, showing visitors around personally. With absolute justice they can claim to have restored Shandy Hall not just as one of the oldest but as the most unspoiled home of any of the great English writers.

Perhaps what is equally remarkable is that the farming village of Coxwold itself has also remained almost entirely unspoiled, and must, except for an inevitable process of gentrification, be much as it was in Sterne's time. What has preserved it perhaps is its distance from York (quite a long commute, though it must have been far worse for Sterne himself), its position just off the conventional tourist routes (for this part of the world is also James Herriot country), and the protection that comes from the fact that this is, like a good many rural Yorkshire settlements, a true and well-kept estate village. If you approach it from the York side, you first pass Newburgh Priory, with its fine lake and grounds, and come to the broad and upsloping village street, with neat Yorkshire stone-built, white-windowed cottages, the almhouses on one side, the excellent and hospitable inn, the Fauconberg Arms, on the other. The street is quiet, the houses, greens and cobbled verges beautifully kept. At the very top of the village, where the road leads out of it, there is Shandy Hall on the right, with its neat and narrow front garden and great stone chimney, now looking in admirable shape under the care of the Monkmans, and open to the public.

The Monkmans have indeed restored it so affectionately and well that they have virtually recreated the atmosphere of the house as it was when Sterne passed his days there. At the same time they have made it a first-class monument to his work and achievement. Many of the rooms are left much as Sterne had them: Eliza's 'sweet sitting room', Sterne's small study, the carefully coloured panelling and the furniture and furnishings, many of which have direct Sterne associations. Kenneth Monkman's own lifetime of collecting Sterneana is reflected there too. He has given his collection of fifty years on loan to the house, and been able not only to reconstruct Sterne's small study but to fill it again with the books he would have known and used.

Part of the collection has already been secured permanently for Shandy Hall, and the rest must soon be, for it is as significant as the building itself – a bookish memorial to one of the most widely (and sometimes wildly) learned of eighteenth-century writers. Among this remarkable and invaluable collection is an original King James Bible, and the works of many of Sterne's favourite authors and contemporaries, Montaigne and Locke, Cervantes and Rabelais. There are more first and lifetime editions of Sterne's widely translated works than exist anywhere else. There are many of his letters and manuscripts, and long runs of the various York newspapers for which he wrote at intervals. There are also first and early fine-bound editions of works by all his major eighteenth-century contemporaries, and a comprehensive library of Sterne biography, criticism and bibliography. Added to this is an extraordinary collection of Sterneana. This includes many of the popular prints – some by Hogarth, Rowlandson and Cruickshank – that illustrated Sterne's work in the days when Parson Yorick, the Widow Wadman, Corporal Trim and the house itself became widely famous. There are also more modern representations of Sterne and the lasting legend he created – a painting by Frith, etchings by Angelica Kauffmann.

The collection includes two famous visual images of Sterne and his impish features, which fascinated the people of his time and added to his fame as an eccentric. One is a print of Sterne by Joshua Reynolds; the other, in pride of place, is the lifesize white marble bust by Joseph Nollekens. This depicts a peculiarly small head, and copies of it became a popular household item; it was also the means of identifying Sterne's skull when it was disturbed, for Nollekens worked by calibrating the heads of his subjects. It is this collection (quite unusual in the preserved home of a writer) which has made Shandy Hall into not only a site for interested tourists but a place of pilgrimage for the many loving Sterne scholars. It is therefore excellent news that the University of York, which has always taken an interest in the reconstruction of the house, and in 1990 awarded Kenneth Monkman an honorary degree for his achievement, has decided to place the house under its protection. It now intends to establish there a Centre for Sterne Studies, to encourage further research into the life and writings of this everlasting author, and also to maintain it as a centre for all interested visitors.

There is something enormously gratifying about the fact that the house that Sterne himself reconstructed – turning it, in effect, into his own eighteenth-century

413

literary folly – has been reconstructed with love for a second time. This time it has been done in the accurate spirit of modern restoration, by two people whose own intense enthusiasm and devotion have brought back to life a strange, original building that, without their intervention, would undoubtedly have collapsed into ruin. There is now a new appeal in train, to secure the rest of the precious Monkman Collection permanently for the house, and so maintain what they have singlehandedly, or rather doublehandedly done, as well as to develop the study centre. It is not only the scholars and the expert Sterneans who ought to feel grateful to the Monkmans. For they were always right in their fundamental idea – that nothing could better bring back the spirit of Shandyism to life than the reconstruction of his house.

As Professor Jacques Berthoud of the University of York elegantly put it, in the citation for the award of Monkman's honorary degree:

> every text, as we call books today, once had its local habitation, and every textual persona shelters a human being who once lived and died. So even casual visitors to Coxwold may be lured into reversing the usual order of things and discover the work through the life.

Monkman himself, over eighty but still despite some recent ill-health the ideal guide to the place, quotes Lamartine:

> The place which a great man has inhabited and preferred, has always seemed to me the truest and most appealing relic of himself: a kind of material manifestation of his genius – a living and sensible commentary on his life, actions, and thoughts.

Some houses are built like fictions, and are even built *of* fictions. Shandy Hall is just such a house, and that is why there is no better way to come to know the spirit of Sterne than by visiting it.

ROBERT LOUIS STEVENSON

LADY STAIR'S HOUSE, EDINBURGH

CLAIRE HARMAN

Of all Scotland's famous authors, Robert Louis Stevenson remains the most elusive to the literary pilgrim. No house where he lived is open to the public – indeed, he never had a home of his own in his native country. Condemned to follow his ailing chest into warmer weather, he spent his adult life travelling, in France, America and the Pacific, where he settled for the last five years of his life in Samoa, in a wooden house called Vailima, 'very like a bandstand in a German beer-garden'.

On his four hundred acres sloping towards Mount Vaea, draped in the shadows of foreign trees, Stevenson wrote some of his most Scots books, *Catriona*, *Ballads*, *Weir of Hermiston* and the autobiographical *Record of a Family of Engineers*. *The Master of Ballantrae* was partly written on board ship in the South Seas. Stevenson's letters of this period to his old crony Charles Baxter are heavy with nostalgia for their drunken student larks in the brothels and shebeens of Edinburgh's Old Town. But Stevenson's feelings about the city of his birth were nicely mixed. His last visit to Edinburgh was for his father's funeral in 1887, which he was subsequently unable to attend, 'one of the vilest climates under heaven' having its usual effect on his lungs. He wrote in *Edinburgh: Picturesque Notes*:

> For all who love shelter and the blessings of the sun, who hate dark weather and perpetual tilting against squalls, there could scarcely be found a more unhomely and harassing place of residence, and yet the place establishes an interest in people's hearts: go where they will, they will find no city of the same distinction; go where they will, they will take a pride in their old home.

Much of Stevenson's pride in Edinburgh derived from his family's eminence as engineers and inventors there. Within two generations they had risen from Glasgow and obscurity to the top of the Edinburgh professional class, models of all that was

17 Heriot Row

respectable, hard-working and God-fearing. The family moved from Howard Place (where Stevenson was born in 1850) to Inverleith Terrace, then to 17 Heriot Row, increasingly impressive addresses within the 'draughty parallelograms' of Edinburgh's Georgian New Town. But Stevenson's heart was not in this solidly bourgeois existence; he preferred the gutter on the Lothian Road where he and Baxter loitered in their days as law students together. Dispossession had a sort of glamour for Stevenson – who was said to 'gloat over discomforts' – and he developed a powerful affinity 'like a transmigration of souls' with the poet Robert Fergusson, who died in the city Bedlam in 1774. 'Ah! what bonds we have,' wrote Stevenson,

> born in the same city; both sickly, both pestered, one nearly to madness, one to the madhouse, with a damnatory creed; both seeing the stars and the dawn, and wearing shoe-leather down the same closes, where our common ancestors clashed in their armour, rusty or bright.

Stevenson's identification with the city's most neglected writer was strangely persistent; in the last year of his life, it still rankled with him that so little had been done for his 'unhappy predecessor in the causey of Auld Reekie'. Burns had erected a monument to Fergusson in the Canongate churchyard in 1787, and Stevenson nagged Baxter to have the stone repaired and a new inscription added to include Stevenson's own name, though not too large or prominent as to seem presumptuous.

This request was never carried out, and the only prominent memorial to Stevenson in Edinburgh is the huge brass replica of an engraving of him in the Moray Aisle of St Giles Cathedral (in the original he was holding a cigarette – here it is a pen). Stevenson was a bohemian, a traveller; he died young, many thousands of miles away. It is hardly surprising there is so little to see of him here in Edinburgh: the bits and pieces which Stevenson's mother, Margaret, brought back with her from the South Seas, and the things left by Stevenson's nurse and his friend Lord Guthrie constitute the only public collection of Stevensonia this side of the Atlantic. They are housed in the Burns, Scott and Stevenson museum at Lady Stair's House, in a close just off the Lawnmarket.

The fact that neither Burns, Scott nor Stevenson ever had any connection with Lady Stair's House does away with any hankering after the spirit of place. Indefatigably vertical, like everything else on the Mound, Lady Stair's House is a renovated seventeenth-century building which was presented to the city of Edinburgh for museum use by Lord Rosebery in 1907. The disconnection between the house and its contents makes it at times seem more a monument to the condition of being relict rather than a monument to three great writers. Things that once led a useful life in a cottage in Ayrshire, a mansion in the Borders or a verandah in Samoa have a long, cold career ahead of them as relics, and in a way have already lost their real connection with their famous owners merely by surviving.

This is less noticeable in the cases of Burns and Scott than in that of Stevenson, who has so little else to memorialize him. Scott hardly needs Lady Stair's House – he has Abbotsford, that most effective self-memorial left by any author, and half of Edinburgh is named after him, including the railway station. The decision to build a monument to Scott was taken at a public meeting only two weeks after his death in 1832, and displays in the museum show how keen the subsequent competition was. The winning entry, famously huge and elaborate, dominates Princes Street Gardens, looking like a grounded cathedral spire. Scott is Edinburgh's favourite son, born in the College Wynd in 1771, and living for much of his youth in George Square. A pane of glass from that house with 'Walter Sc' scratched on it is in the museum now, and his rocking-horse, with the left foot-rest higher than the right on account of the boy's lameness. Its seat is stuffed with legal documents from his father's business as a Writer to the Signet, Scott's own first profession.

Scott never suffered from lack of admirers. At the age of six he was described as 'the most extraordinary genius of a boy', and the museum is well supplied with locks of his hair, all cut from the living head, including one cut 'on the night he left for Malta' in 1831. This, and the last portrait of Scott, done in Naples by a Mrs Auldjo, are relics of his convalescent travels in the vain hope of a return to health following his financial collapse in 1826. Scott had left too many of his affairs tied up with his publisher Ballantyne, and they both suffered huge losses when the London banks fell that year. The story of how Scott won back by his pen more than £117,000 is justly famous. He saved Abbotsford by a huge effort, but ruined himself. Two life-size figures in wax, arranged in a 'period set' of contemporary furniture in the museum, depict Scott and Ballantyne at a happier period of their acquaintance, musing over a manuscript, ideals of author and publisher. And at the top of the building is the printing press on which Ballantyne produced the Waverley Novels, the compact engine which took Scott around the world.

The meeting between Burns and Scott in the Sciences Club in Edinburgh, when Scott was about sixteen and Burns twenty-eight, has been a boon to biographers. We have only one side of it – Scott's – and his description is as hagiographical as anything written subsequently about himself: '[Burns's] eyes were large and glowed (I say literally glowed) when he spoke with such feeling and interest. I never saw such eyes in a human head.' A plaster cast of the top half of Burns's skull, taken when his wife was buried in the same grave thirty-eight years after his death, bears out Scott's impression that the poet had an exceptionally large head: 'I think his countenance was more massive than it looks in any of his portraits. I would have taken the poet, had I not known what he was, as a very sagacious country farmer of the old Scotch school.' In the collection at Lady Stair's House, only one portrait of Burns, in a farmer's hat and painted by Peter Taylor, really represents this aspect of him. The engravings of Burns in Sibbald's Circulating Library, and of his inauguration as Poet Laureate of the Canongate Freemasons' Lodge, are reminders of a man who did not necessarily think of himself as a provincial, as is the diploma awarding him honorary membership of the Royal Company of Archers, a select and aristocratic group.

Burns's statement that the muse found him at the plough-tail is frequently depicted literally, sometimes with the 'wee sleekit mouse' thrown in for good measure, and Burns looking as demure as an Annunciation. The famous picture by Hardie of the Sciences Club meeting itself is by no means free of quasi-religious overtones. Yet the relics of Burns in the cases beneath these pictures are pleasingly ordinary: a snuff-mull, a quaich, a lustre jug, and the sword-stick and land-surveying chain he used in his work as an excise officer. Unlike Scott, he was never much in the way of gathering gear. One of the oddest exhibits in the whole museum is an enamelled marble apple, a simple thing, like a toy, which Burns gave to Jean

Brackenridge on her marriage to his brother Gilbert. Whatever the significance or not of this gift, it is now suspended above a velvet-covered mount by means of wire and string, too precious, perhaps, to be held by anything but air.

It would have seemed very marvellous to Stevenson to be memorialized in the same place as the national heroes Burns and Scott. He seems far removed from them in both time and type, though he was born only eighteen years after Scott's death. His separateness is acknowledged in the location of the Stevenson Collection in the semi-basement of Lady Stair's House, where there is a series of wall-displays, with reproductions of the many photographs in the museum's collection, and plenty of biographical information.

Stevenson was only reluctantly a man of property. The building of Vailima, which he referred to sardonically as 'Abbotsford' or sometimes 'Sub-priorsford', became a necessity for his South Seas clan: his wife, Fanny, her children, her grandchild and Stevenson's widowed mother, Margaret, as well as a retinue of servants, though nothing could have been less like Scott's grand home than the Stevenson bandstand, as an early visitor noted fastidiously – 'A pervasive atmosphere of dirt seemed to hang round it, and the squalor was like a railroad navvy's board hut.' After Stevenson's death in 1894, and Fanny's eventual removal to California, the belongings were dispersed, beaching up eventually at museums in Monterey and Silverado. The collection at Lady Stair's House is eclectic, to say the least, treasures and blatant facsimiles all mixed up together: a kaleidoscope, a rag book, a school prize, Skelt's sheets for Juvenile Drama, a golf ball, a tartan sash – all overseen by the portrait of Stevenson's beloved hell-fire nurse, Alison Cunningham. Too many of the exhibits are traps for our attentiveness: cigarette papers 'of the kind used by', a pap boat bought, not used, by Stevenson, an anonymous umbrella and, strangest of all, a small pair of scissors dug up in the garden at the Stevensons' rented cottage at Swanston which 'may have been used by young Stevenson to cut out the paper characters for his toy theatres and then lost in the garden' – an ingenious bit of wishful-thinking, and, like everything else in the semi-basement, a lament for the absence of Stevenson.

The second of the two rooms contains objects and pictures mostly from Stevenson's years in the Pacific, including the strangely coloured paintings done by Count Nieri on his visit to Vailima in 1892. In one of the cases is an order Stevenson sent to an Edinburgh bookseller which he had incorrectly dated 6 December 1894, a date which in the end he never reached, dying suddenly on 3 December, not of the tuberculosis which threatened him for forty years, but of a brain haemorrhage. The ring he was wearing is here, a tortoiseshell band with his Samoan name, Tusitala, 'teller of tales', inlaid in silver. A sailing cap and a pair of his boots are also on display. Perhaps it is not the pens, chairs and desks of writers that are as eloquent as their boots. When Stevenson had collapsed and lay dying, his stepson Lloyd Osbourne removed his boots, remembering as he did so that Stevenson had often spoken about wanting to die in them. But who knows which pair this is?

It was in an attempt to furnish Lloyd with something to do that Stevenson bought the camera which documented his travels in the Pacific and life at Vailima so thoroughly. The photographs show those boots on the living man, that cap in his hand, the thinness of his arms under the sleeve. 'How could anyone write books with arms like these?' exclaimed the doctor attending the death-bed. There is an enlargement of the famous group photograph taken (not by Lloyd) of the household on the steps of Vailima, illustrating very clearly the contrasts between the life they had left behind in high-Victorian Europe and the Polynesian idyll they hoped to embrace. In a corner of the room is the tiny hand-press on which Lloyd printed the Davos Press booklets (another of Stevenson's diversions for him), and across from that the heavily carved cabinet which stood in Stevenson's bedroom at Heriot Row, made by Deacon Brodie, an Edinburgh character who fascinated Stevenson and about whom he wrote a play in collaboration with W. E. Henley. By day Brodie was a cabinet-maker and member of the town council; by night a

Stevenson's boots

420

The type still stored in the museum at Lady Stair's House
was used in the printing of Scott's novels

common criminal. He seemed to Stevenson a personification of the doubleness which he saw in the very town itself:

> Half a capital and half a country town, the whole city leads a double existence; it has long trances of the one and flashes of the other; like the King of the Black Isles, it is half alive and half a monumental marble.

A small booklet, sporadically available, invites tourists to go on the 'Robert Louis Stevenson Heritage Trail', which is made up of four sites: Swanston; Colinton Manse, where Stevenson's grandfather was minister and which was virtually a second home to the writer during his childhood; Heriot Row; and the Hawes Inn, South Queensferry, where Stevenson used to stay on canoeing expeditions, and which features in the kidnapping scenes in *Kidnapped*. Two buses and a twenty-minute walk will show you the baffle of trees around Swanston Cottage; Colinton is similarly cloaked in decent privacy, and Heriot Row says PRIVATE HOUSE NOT A MUSEUM. For years there was a museum at Stevenson's birthplace in Howard Place, but that too is in private hands now. None of this has to be a disappointment; more may be lost than gained when a writer's house is preserved artificially. In the case of Heriot Row, which is owned by a Stevenson devotee, Lady Dunpark, its likeness to Stevenson's old home may well be all the greater for not being poked over. Stevenson is a writer who recreates rather than reproduces in his works the places that were important to him. His long absences may have encouraged him to favour fantastic, romantic and historical themes when writing about Scotland – his works about the South Seas are noticeably topical and contemporary. So a walk on the Pentlands may tell you as much or as little as there is to tell, or to Glencorse church, which Stevenson thought he might haunt, the Lothian Road, Drummond Road, or the pub sign at the corner of Lawnmarket and Bank Street, which depicts Deacon Brodie, good man on one side, rogue on the other – a reminder that the Edinburgh Stevenson knew was one of lawyers and doctors, drinkers and prostitutes, Burke and Hare, and, obliquely, Jekyll and Hyde.

But after a day on the 'Trail', perhaps a surer way to remember Stevenson is in the weather that blew him away. It is permanently open to the public, and the best place to find it is on the bridge which connects the Old Town with the New, 'that windiest spot, or high altar, in this northern temple of the winds'. As you lean over, you can recall Stevenson doing just the same, watching the trains steam out of Waverley station, longing to get away, and longing for home.

DYLAN THOMAS

THE BOAT HOUSE, LAUGHARNE, DYFED

GLYN JONES

On the afternoon of Whit Monday, 1934, Dylan Thomas was walking purposefully down a steep grassy path which would bring him, within half a mile, to Black Scar, a marshy headland jutting out into the broad tidal estuary of the River Tâf, in rural Carmarthenshire. The weather was splendid, warm and sunny, and the countryside around, and the farms, Sunday-silent, and the whole scene seemingly deserted. Dylan was staying at the time with relatives in Blaencwm, Llangain, a couple of cottages off the Carmarthen–Llanstephan road, a few hundred yards from what was to become later, surely, the most famous farmhouse in Wales – Fern Hill. He had called for his companion, the present writer, in the village of Llanstephan, and the two, intending an afternoon visit to Laugharne, had walked the three or so miles across the broad headland of Lord's Park, the promontory in Carmarthen Bay separating the mouth of the Tâf from that of the Towy (in Welsh, Tywi); they proceeded through an undulating countryside of considerable although unspectacular charm and then, from a rise in the road, the two were able to see, below them, the almost mile-wide waters of the Tâf where it entered Carmarthen Bay. They aimed to cross the lake-like river by ferry-boat from the jut of Black Scar, summoning the ferryman from the far shore by tolling a bell, the bell-rope of which hung down from the roof of the tiny church-like building to which their path out across the marsh had led them. As they stood in that desolate and romantic spot, awaiting, the 'palavers of birds' loud in their ears, the arrival of Jack Roberts the ferryman and his boat, they were able to see, at the water's edge, at the foot of the red cliffs opposite, two isolated white cottages. One of the remote dwellings belonged to Jack and his remarkable family. The other was the 'seashaken house/On a breakneck of rocks' which was to be Dylan's home for the last four years of his life – the Boat House. The view of it thus, in the tranquillity of bright sunshine, from the other side of the sandbanked estuary of the Tâf, was, I believe, his first

423

Dylan Thomas's writing shack

sighting of the dwelling that, by his presence in it, he was later to make world-famous.

Dylan was at that time approaching twenty, a small, slight young man of very attractive appearance, not markedly unlike the Augustus John portraits, well-dressed, clothes-conscious, very far removed from the 'walrus' and 'rag-doll' images of later descriptions of his appearance – his own and other people's. His fair hair was plentiful and curling, his skin clear, his large brown eyes luminous and expressive. The wit, the responsiveness, the fun, the endless inventiveness of his conversation were already among the charms of his presence and companionship. His life seemed relatively tranquil; he would appear to have been in one of what he called his 'turbulent doldrums' – he was certainly not yet, as he described himself with despairing humour towards the end of his troubled life, 'a manacled rhetorician with a wet trombone, up to his blower in crabs'.

By then, 1934, Dylan had, as a schoolboy and a newspaper reporter in Swansea, already written in his notebooks a very large number of his poems, perhaps hundreds, including, in one form or another, many that were later to make him famous, poems like 'The Hunchback in the Park', 'And death shall have no dominion', 'Light breaks where no sun shines', 'The force that through the green fuse drives the flower' and 'After the funeral'. But he was still as a poet virtually unknown to the general and even to the poetry-reading public; in spite of that prolific youthful outpouring very little of his work had as yet appeared in print, only a handful of poems in such prestigious periodicals as the *Listener* and the *Adelphi*. His first volume, the block-busting *18 Poems*, did not appear until later in 1934.

'The strangest town in Wales,' Dylan wrote of Laugharne about this time. Whether it struck him then as a desirable place to live in, as a place, as he wrote later, he loved 'beyond all places in Wales', is of course impossible to say. He was not the first literary person to find the town attractive enough to live in. The poet Edward Thomas was at one time an inhabitant, and the novelists Charles Morgan and Hilda Vaughan once occupied a dwelling not far from the Boat House; Richard Hughes, who was elected to the town's ancient office of Portreeve, lived for many years from 1934 with his family in the house adjoining Laugharne Castle. Although well within the borders of Wales, Laugharne (pronounced Larn; in Welsh Talacharn) became, because of England's historic policy of establishing settlements of Flemings, Normans and English along the South Wales coast, very largely English in speech in that Welsh-speaking area of Wales. It was also, of course, as were Swansea and New Quay, near the sea, on an estuary, and Dylan, like his yellow-haired namesake in the *Mabinogion*, seemed always prepared to make, if not for the sea, at least for the shore. Again, it was near, indeed it was part of, his 'country heaven', that area of rural South Wales where, or about which, he had already written some of his

Dylan Thomas, by Augustus John

best poems and about which he was later to write 'Fern Hill', 'Poem in October' and 'Over Sir John's Hill'. Well-known stories like 'The Peaches' and 'A Visit to Grandpa's' and many of his successful broadcasts are also about this area, and the later *Under Milk Wood*, whether a portrait of Laugharne or not, we can be certain would have been a very different work had he never lived in the town. However, another four years were to pass after 1934 before Dylan was to take up residence in Laugharne, and then that residence was not the Boat House.

Laugharne, 'out of the route of the general traveller', as one writer has it, is well south of the great arterial roads running from the English border to the farthest western tip of South Wales; and its centuries-long isolation has probably been an important element in the unchanging quality of its institutions and the conservatism of its lifestyle. The place has been described as a village that thinks it is a town, but it certainly has a charter which was granted to the citizens by Guy de Brian, the local Norman land-grabber, as long ago as 1307. Even today its affairs are rather quaintly administered by an elected Portreeve, who wears (as a visible acknowledgement of a one-time important industry of the town – cockle-gathering) a sort of mayoral chain made of golden cockleshells. He has the support of two

426

common Attorneys, a Recorder, four Constables, a Bailiff and a Foreman with a Grand Jury. There are also in the constitution hereditary Freemen or Burgesses who inherit land in or near the township. The fortnightly meetings of the Grand Jury begin with traditional *O, yes, O, yes*-ing from the Bailiff and end with his *God save the Queen*-ing. If the occupations mentioned in *Under Milk Wood* reflect the ways in which Laugharne people earn a living, then they work as farmer, shopkeeper, cobbler, schoolteacher, postman, publican, milkman, undertaker, policeman, baker, butcher, dressmaker, guesthouse-keeper and so on. The pluralist Mr Waldo, who was of course a native of Pembroke, not of Laugharne, falls outside any neat classification, being rabbitcatcher, quack, barber, herbalist and catdoctor.

The road to Laugharne – Jack Roberts is long dead, his summoning bell silent and his ferry no longer in operation – leaves the main Carmarthen–Haverfordwest road at the left turn in the country town of St Clears (Sanclêr) and runs for three or four miles through undulating farmland southward, more or less parallel with the winding River Tâf, entering Laugharne itself alongside the set-back thirteenth-century church of St Martin. There, up on the hillside burial ground behind the ancient church, is Dylan's grave, marked, not by any memorial in stone (that, since 1983, has been in Westminster Abbey), but by a simple white wooden cross. This graveyard, like the Boat House, has become, over the years, a place of pilgrimage for lovers of Dylan's work and, alas, also of larceny for exploiters of his fame.

Laugharne's main street, King Street, consisting of cottages, a variety of shops and some rather elegant Georgian houses (Laugharne was at one time a place of posh retirement) is broad and pleasant and flanked with pollarded elms (or are they, as Dylan thought, cherries?). It descends past the famous Brown's Hotel, past the striking white tower of the ancient Town Hall (and ancient gaol), past the school, past the entrance to the Boat House lane, and eventually, at the bottom of a short steep hill, to the open space of what is called the Grist, on one side of which is a rather un-beachlike beach, and the sea. Here one sees at the water's edge, set in a landscape once painted by Turner, the considerable bulk of Laugharne Castle, a picturesque ruin facing, as in some romantic stage set, the open sea. This stronghold has of course changed hands several times in its long history and was once in the possession of Sir John Perrot, a reputed illegitimate son of Henry VIII. It was he who gave his name to nearby Sir John's Hill, about which Dylan wrote one of his most famous poems. Looking back from the foreshore up the river, past the castle and back along the estuary, one sees in the distance, at the foot of the cliffs, the white rear elevation of the Boat House. Laugharne is a small place and no landmark there is far from any other landmark.

Dylan first came to live in Laugharne, as was said, in 1938. He was by this time a published author with two highly esteemed books, namely *18 Poems* and *Twenty-five Poems*, to his credit. Also he was married to Caitlin, née Macnamara, a gifted

427

beauty of Irish-French descent. The two occupied a rented cottage named (not by them) Eros, in Gosport Street, at the far end of the town from the Boat House, beyond the castle and the beach and out on the Pendine road to the west. After a few months they moved into the larger Sea View, a house rising tall among its neighbours, isolated-looking, although nearer the town centre than Eros, rather like a subject painted by the late Christopher Wood. Here the young couple's bohemianism of dress and behaviour appeared to their conservative small-town neighbours strange and became a subject of remark: and here also were entertained some of Dylan's earliest literary friends, including Vernon Watkins, the Swansea poet, and Henry Treece, one of the first critics of his work.

The idyll, if indeed idyll it was, did not last. The next year, 1939, the Second World War broke out and the Thomases, who appear never to have owned a house, a cottage or even a flat of their own – when Dylan claimed, in 1951, to be selling the Boat House it was not his to sell – began their moving from place to place, staying with friends and relatives, a lifestyle that was to characterize their existence for the next ten years – to Swansea, to Blaencwm, to Caitlin's mother in Blashford, to New Quay where they were nearly murdered, back to Laugharne as guests at the home of Richard Hughes, to Oxford as the tenants of Mrs A. J. P. Taylor, the wife of the well-known historian. But by 1949, the war over, Dylan, and probably more so Caitlin, who had given birth to a son, Llewelyn, in 1939 and a daughter, Aeronwy, in 1943, seem to have wished for a place of permanence for their family. This Dylan, through the extraordinary generosity of Mrs Taylor, found in 1949 in the Boat House, purchased by her for £3,000. Here he was to live until his death four years later.

The building of boats was at one time a flourishing craft along the South Wales coast and the Boat House, occupying a site some distance from the town centre and standing beside what was once the town harbour of Laugharne, is so called because its last-century occupant was such a craftsman, a shipwright. To reach it from the main street of Laugharne, one coming into the town from St Clears in the north would pass St Martin's church and, further along, still on one's left, the unmistakable landmark of Dylan's favourite pub, Brown's Hotel; then, at the end of the block, within a very short distance of the pub, one would turn left into Victoria Street. Victoria Street bends left into Cliff Road which is really the beginning of what is now known, officially, as the sign there indicates, as Dylan's Walk. This is a long, straightish, narrowish path along the cliff top, with protective railings on one's right and the estuary far below and on one's left woodland rising above a containing wall. From this path, used daily by Dylan on his walks to and from town, one looks eventually directly down on the slate roof and into the chimneys of the Boat House below – it is the gable end of the house that faces the cliff – except that the chimneys appear now to have been capped. A narrow stepped

The Boat House, Laugharne

path leads off from Dylan's Walk downwards through a small garden to the front door of the white Boat House. That front elevation of the cottage is similar to the façades of countless farmhouses (although not the remarkable Fern Hill) in that part of Wales – a door central, a window on each side of it and three bedroom windows in a row on the first floor, very much as in a child's drawing. Since the house is built on a sloping site the rear elevation, facing a kind of extensive paved yard or patio, has an additional pair of rooms at the back. The building is small – Dylan called it 'very small' – and not one of its rooms could be described as spacious. One unusual feature is a black wooden verandah that runs round two sides of the building.

The poet who came, perhaps hopefully, to live in this house in early May of 1949, the man the Laugharne people saw sitting in Brown's, or the Cross House Inn, or the Corporation Arms, or walking their streets perhaps on his way to visit his parents who already lived opposite Brown's, in one of the nice houses on King Street, this man was naturally a very different figure from the young writer who had visited their town some fifteen years earlier. After years of worry, uncertainty, improvidence, the 'capital punishment' (as he called his life in London), long gone were the good looks, the trim figure, the brief attempts to look 'poetic'. Dylan had by now become stouter and, allowing for his frequent self-disparagement and the comic extravagance of his language, 'a shabby barrel', 'a red, blubber face' on a 'ballooning body'. But in many ways he remained unchanged; in spite of the mounting anxieties of his condition and the endless crises of his life at the Boat House, financial, literary, marital, his warmth, his humour and his ability to charm remained undiminished.

Much was to happen to him in this new home. Within months of moving in a third child, Colm, a son, was born. The year of his death, 1953, saw the deaths, before his own, of his father and his sister. His best-selling *Collected Poems 1934–1952* appeared to great critical acclaim in 1953. Paradoxically perhaps, four events of much importance in Dylan's life at the Boat House took him away from it, namely his trips to America. Having published four volumes of poetry before his *Collected Poems* appeared, as well as the autobiographical short stories in *Portrait of the Artist as a Young Dog*, he was becoming an increasingly well-known literary figure; indeed he was famous, his work held in high regard by almost everyone of any consequence in the English literary establishment and he himself known personally to many of them – T. S. Eliot, Stephen Spender, W. H. Auden, Roy Campbell, Louis MacNeice, William Empson, Edith Sitwell. With increasing reputation came increasing financial rewards, if not more secure solvency. During the war years, working in London, he had produced a considerable amount of material for radio and he had also written several scripts for the Strand Film Company and the Ministry of Information. He was the well-known possessor of a marvellously rich voice, resonant and expressive, which he used to tremendous effect always in the reading of his own work and usually in the reading of the poetry of others. All these public activities, achievements and involvements had helped to increase his already high reputation as a poet. His work began to be known in America. He had hoped for some years before coming to live in the Boat House that this development in his career might take place. Now, perhaps the difficulties which beset him in his new home increased his desire to bring about a visit there. In 1949 he was invited to America to read his poems by a man who was to become his friend and who later visited him in the Boat House – John Malcolm Brinnin, the Director of a Poetry Centre in New York. Early in 1950 Dylan flew to America on his first visit.

In his letter of thanks to Mrs Taylor for her generosity over the Boat House, Dylan says, 'Here I am happy and writing' and '... this place I love and where I want to live and where I can work and where I have started work (my own) already'. But as time passed, very soon in fact, the inadequacies of the Boat House as a family dwelling ('only we would live in it') came in for criticism and for Laugharne itself he had a very rude anatomical comparison. 'The water pipes have burst & the house is flooded, etc. etc.,' he writes to a friend in America, 'And the etceteras are almost worse than the rest.' He claims that the rats have invaded the place and the rat-man, 'unfortunately for my peace of mind', he writes, 'has only one arm'. The Laugharne weather he found hard to endure and he complains about the 'grey perpetual rain' and the 'flat, dull day with grey rain oozing like self-pity'. 'I am sick of Laugharne,' he wrote in April 1951. 'It has rained here since last June.' Caitlin, he claims, 'in the general hell of sickness, children, excruciating worry, the eternal yellow grey drizzle outside', has developed 'her own slowly accumulated loathing for the place in which we live'.

Allowing for the extravagance, often humorous, of Dylan's language in some of his letters and his constant desire to please and entertain the friends he was writing to, one cannot but conclude that life at the Boat House was sometimes far from tranquil. At best it would appear to have been a place of loving and harmonious interludes. Disagreements, conflict, violence even, verbal and physical, from time to time took place between Dylan and Caitlin. Caitlin wished her husband to be a poet, writing poetry, not a clown or a performer or an entertainer. She was passionate, strong-minded and outspoken and Dylan must often have been, like another writing Thomas, 'ill to live wi''. He had of course no steady job and so had no steady income. He earned from time to time good money, more, it is said, than some of the people approached to support him financially; but he was feckless, improvident, wasteful. He fell alarmingly into debt. In spite of the efforts of people like Brinnin and his agent David Higham, his debts, he said, 'mount every day nightmarishly'. He owed local tradesmen money and he talked of bailiffs moving in and summonses on the way. The question of his poetry reading visits to America occasioned sharp conflict, Caitlin complaining that Dylan wished to go merely for 'flattery, idleness and infidelity' and he countering that his purpose was 'appreciation, dramatic work and friends'. However, his second tour, when he was accompanied by Caitlin, took place in 1952 and his third and his disastrous fourth in 1953. It was during his fourth visit that, following a bout of suicidal drinking, he died in New York in his fortieth year.

While living out his harassed life at the Boat House, a sanctuary from his mounting troubles was at hand and readily available. A family called Cowan had occupied the Boat House after the First World War and a Miss Cowan, the daughter, became the owner of a sort of primitive motor car, a quaint two-cylinder DKW, made in Germany, which, having no reverse gear, had always to be manhandled backwards. To house this droll vehicle a wooden garage was built beside what is now Dylan's Walk, just above the Boat House, 'the structure springing out from the cliff face', one local tells us, 'and supported at its remote end on steel pipes from the garden below'. Above the front door of that now blue-painted structure a board has been fixed bearing the words – 'In this building Dylan Thomas wrote many of his famous works seeking inspiration from the panoramic view of the estuary.' Perhaps the 'many', considering the whole volume of Dylan's poetry, is a slight exaggeration; six poems were probably written here and also perhaps the bulk of the preposterous and utterly convincing 'play for radio', *Under Milk Wood*, at which he worked, off and on, for many years. But certainly it was here that Dylan spent his afternoons alone, working, writing. A tiny incident recalls for me the strictness, the ferocity almost, with which he guarded his privacy in this place. I had made arrangements to see him and I was taken, by the path from the back of the Boat House, up to the garage, by Aeronwy, then a little girl. Her light tap at the garage door was answered promptly by a very loud and very cross shout from within – 'Go away.' Explanations followed and the garage door was opened on a smiling and apologetic Dylan.

The garage door has now had a sheet of glass inserted into it so that the visitor can view the interior while the door remains locked. The inside is sparsely furnished, undecorated, containing a plain wooden table, a stove, a couple of kitchen chairs and a few pictures, photos of writers cut out of periodicals stuck on the wooden walls. At the far end a double casement window opens out over the estuary below and beyond it, over Welsh-speaking Wales, at a good swathe of his 'country heaven'. The low green hills rising above the opposite river bank are dairy farmland, one farm to be seen there being Pentowyn, where the aunt featured in 'The Peaches' and 'After the funeral', Ann Jones of Fern Hill, had once farmed with her husband, the bibulous Jim. On the top of one of the hills opposite stands Llanybri church, perhaps the church with its 'horns through mist' in 'Poem in October', although that church only ever had one horn or spire and that has now been taken down. In the chapel graveyard of Llanybri are the graves of both Jim and the doting Ann. To the right of the window is Sir John's Hill and 'Over Sir John's Hill', we are told, was the first poem Dylan wrote after moving into the Boat House in 1949. It is a poem that for me has a small puzzle, three in fact. The river flowing past the Boat House, past Dylan's workroom and then on below Sir John's Hill and into Carmarthen Bay, Dylan appears to be calling the Towy. It is in fact the Tâf, which is, strangely, not mentioned in the poem.

To return to the words on the board outside the workroom. 'Seeking inspiration from the panoramic view of the estuary' is surely correct. What supplied Dylan with the imagery in some of his best poems was the surrounding countryside. Much of his vocabulary is rural, pastoral, rather than urban. It is true that even in his first volume, *18 Poems*, he employs words associated with an urban culture, with modern life, with science, the sort of Audenish vocabulary that was in the 1930s beginning to become poetically fashionable; words like 'girdered', 'chemic', 'gunman', 'acid', 'galactic', 'neural', 'synthetic' and so on. But in all the great lyrics – 'Light breaks where no sun shines', 'The force that through the green fuse', 'Especially when the October wind', 'This bread I break', 'After the funeral', 'In My Craft', 'Poem on his birthday', 'Do not go gentle', 'And death shall have no dominion', 'Fern Hill', 'The Hunchback in the Park', 'Poem in October' – Dylan employs largely a vocabulary which is traditional, even in a sense old-fashioned. It was his gifted and original use of it that gave to a seemingly old or out-worn vocabulary a new life, an explosive freshness and beauty. Dylan in his maturity appeared never to have had any strongly held political, religious or social convictions. The excellence of his poetry does not seem to me to arise primarily from the urgency of his thoughts and his emotions as a man, or in original response to the events and the circumstances of the world around him; rather it arises from his passionate concern with the nature of the medium he is employing, that is, language, words, and the metrical constraints he has decided to place upon himself. A true poet, Dylan was more interested in perceptions and texture than in ideas.

HORACE WALPOLE

STRAWBERRY HILL, TWICKENHAM, MIDDLESEX

JOHN HARRIS

First the man, from an entertaining self-portrait:

Imagine the Rev. Seward's surprise when he visited Ragley Park in 1758 and observed the astonishing and peculiar behaviour of what turned out to be a fellow guest ... Strolling about the house, he saw me first sitting on the pavement of the lumber room with Louis, all over cobwebs and dirt and mortar; then found me in his own room on a ladder writing on a picture: and half an hour afterwards lying on the grass in the court with the dogs and the children, in my slippers and without my hat. He had some doubts whether I was the painter or the factotum of the family; but you would have died at his surprise when he saw me walk into dinner dressed and sit by Lady Hertford. Lord Lyttleton was there, and the conversation turned on literature: finding me not quite ignorant added to the parson's wonder; but he could not contain himself any longer, when after dinner he saw me go romps and jumping with the two boys; he broke out to my Lady Hertford, and begged to know what sort of man I really was, for he had never met with anything of the kind.

This is all entirely in character with Walpole, who acted out so much and was so conscious of an audience, as he was in his writings. What is sadly missing for us is his speech. General Fitzwilliam said that it was 'like a shooting star or like Uriel, gliding on a sunbeam', and George Hardinge remarked that 'he talked as he wrote, and one left him, at least I did, fatigued, though charmed with his enlivening sallies'. His effect upon everyone was emotional. All this from a man of shortish stature, with a long pallid face, and delicate tapering fingers, themselves acting out a scene. Strawberry Hill was Horace's private theatre.

Strawberry would seem to have been deliberately constructed as an antithesis of his father's (Sir Robert Walpole's) lifestyle at his great Palladian mansion of Houghton in Norfolk, a place that Horace found unlovable. Even when he became

The Gallery, Strawberry Hill

435

3rd Earl of Orford in 1791 as 'the poorest peer in England', he rarely went there. He would have preferred to have died at Strawberry, but when he was so ill in 1797 it was too cold and he was brought up to London to the family house in Arlington Street. No doubt as he left Strawberry for the last time, he could look back and admit that it was a self-indulgent attempt at a self-portrait. Few houses anywhere have been so penetrated by the personality and spirit of their owners, but then few houses have been so presented to society almost as a public relations exercise.

There may have been cause and effect between the task of writing the *Aedes Walpolianae* or *A Description of the Collection of Pictures at Houghton in Norfolk*, published in 1747, and the decision to acquire a place in the country. The *Aedes* had been compiled off and on over the years when Walpole wanted to escape from 'those mountains of roast beef out of whom streamed gravy' that were his father's friends. The manuscript was probably finished in the precincts of Windsor Castle, when he rented a house for the summer of 1746. Its preparation may have urged him to possess his own house, make a collection, amass a library, and catalogue. In any case, the mania for writing had infected him, and despite being a 'Friend of London' as Thomas Gray described him, he yearned for a peaceful place to write and entertain.

Not even the loquacious Walpole gives us a clue as to his real intentions when in 1747 he rented a small cottage built in 1698 and standing in five acres just beyond Twickenham. The 'enamelled meadows with filigree hedges' sloped gently to the Thames three hundred yards away. In 1748 the competent but tame William Robinson added a small extension, 'before', as Walpole admits, 'there was any design of farther improvements to the house'. This was the 'cot' that moved Etheldreda, Lady Townshend to cry profanely, 'Lord God! Jesus! what a house,' when she saw it early in 1750. However, Walpole had already declared his intentions to George Montagu on 28 September 1749: 'Did I tell you that I have found a text in Deuteronomy to authorize my future battlements: when thou buildest a new house, then shalt thou make a battlement for thy roof.' Much later in the preface to his *Description* of the villa he admits that he does not intend to 'defend by argument a small capricious house ... built to please my own taste, and in some degree to realize my own visions'.

The origins of Strawberry may lie in a house that Walpole could not have omitted to see when he stayed at Windsor, and refers to when he wrote to Lord Strafford on 13 June 1781, railing against the chinoiserie or 'Sharwadgi' style, confessing that he had preached 'so effectually' against its use that 'every pagoda' of its founder Dicky Bateman had taken 'the veil'. Dicky was the Hon. Richard Bateman of Grove House, Old Windsor, a cottage of about Strawberry's original size that had grown between *c.* 1731 and 1741 and had acquired a Chinese façade, and perhaps a Gothic one. In view of Walpole's long acquaintance with Dicky, his delight in his gardens ('a Kingdom of flowers') and his fascination with Dicky's curious and antiquarian collections (that added much to Strawberry after his death), this 'half Gothick, half Attic, half Chinese and completely fribble house' must have exerted a powerful effect. Its ambience was very much Strawberry in miniature. Indeed, later both Richard Bentley and J. H. Muntz worked there after their dismissal from Strawberry. Certainly, such a house must have remained in Walpole's subconscious.

Strawberry has long been fêted as the first house planned upon irregular principles. This is not so. As Clive Wainwright has convincingly demonstrated, when Walpole rebuilt his cottage with its south and east fronts and their bows all off centre, this asymmetry was determined by the structure of the existing cottage and the hugging proximity of the wall to the Teddington–Hampton road. Irregularity became more and more evident as the house grew in its *ad hoc* manner based upon no predetermined plan. Far more influential was the realization that just as there were principles and precedents for composing neo-Palladian or neo-classical interiors, so this archaeological principle could be applied to Gothic invention. As Walpole wrote, Strawberry was based upon 'Specimens of Gothic architecture, as collected from standards in cathedrals and chapel-tombs and shewing how they may be applied to chimney-pieces, ceilings, windows, balustrades, loggias etc.'. This required much library work and, of course, an able and amiable companion in the venture. So he formed a Committee of Taste with his connoisseur and antiquarian friend John Chute (1701–76) and Richard Bentley (1708–82), who has been rightly described by Howard Colvin as a Georgian Rex Whistler. In this Walpole was acting as the amateur. The first task of the committee was to enlarge the cottage and encase it totally in Gothic, without, it must be added, any idea of how Strawberry might develop in later years.

The work was finished by the end of 1755, and the Gothic precedents were as rigorously applied as anything taken from Desgodetz by Lord Burlington for his Palladian villa at Chiswick. So the chimney-piece in the Little Parlour was designed by Bentley from the tomb of Thomas Ruthall in Westminster Abbey, the arches in the Library bookcases were from the side door to the choir from Dugdale's Old St Paul's, and the chimney-piece there imitated from the Earl of Cornwall's tomb in the abbey. Yet whatever may have been translated from abbey or cathedral, the translation was not without judgement and taste.

Something must be said about Walpole's collection. This can be judged by the illustrated *Description* of 1784 and the famous sale catalogue of 1842. Although he has sometimes been compared to William Beckford, this is unjust to the latter, for the exalted artistic quality of his works of art and furniture were not to be found at Strawberry. Walpole would make an arrangement of varied pieces of china of

Strawberry Hill

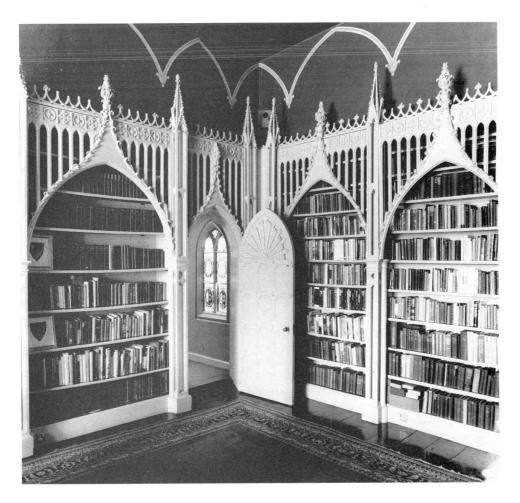

The Library

no particular rarity, seeing his things as a consciously composed pattern in relation to comfortable furniture. The curiosity value was high, and in this he was in line of descent from those who assembled cabinets of curiosities in the Renaissance. There is undoubtedly a relationship between the collecting and the growth of the house, although the evidence of purchase is lacking. In the enlarged cottage of 1755 furniture and objects were crammed in, with more than seven hundred pieces of china in the China Room and twenty-two pictures and prints in the Great Parlour. Yet as we examine the views of the interiors, there is order, as if Walpole's eye determined all. Long hours must have been spent on the arranging, judging one thing against another, one colour beside others, and the effect of papers, stuffs, floor coverings and, importantly, the quality of light, especially light filtering through stained glass. Walpole saw Gothic as a pictorial affair, and there is evidence to suggest that the interiors were conceived as pictorial compositions. In this Bentley's drawings, highly theatric in presentation, are in contrast to Chute's more authentic but linear style.

But this is anticipating the whole. In 1757 the accounts refer to the 'new Bedchamber towards the road'. This was in a two-storey block adjacent to the north entrance. There was a cloister on the ground floor, and the bedroom became famous as the Holbein Room, with its 'oil paper by Vertue from the original drawings', a chimney-piece by Bentley after the Warnham tomb in Canterbury, and a strangely Moorish-looking screen copied from choir gates at Rouen. In matters of planning, the new works are, again, clearly *ad hoc*. This leaves one perplexed, as if Walpole was unable to solve the problems of odd and inconvenient juxtapositions of spaces. It was all very amateur.

On 24 May 1760 Walpole wrote to Mann, 'I am flounced again into building – a round tower, gallery, cloister, chapel, all starting up.' In fact, the accounts refer to digging the foundations of the gallery in June 1761, its building in 1762, its ceiling and decoration in 1763, and finishings the following year. The new five-bay extension to the north had a cloister open to the lawns and a fifty-six-foot gallery above. Windows were divided by buttresses and the parapet battlemented. There is a puzzling resemblance to the river façade of the neighbouring Radnor House, which was built in the 1740s. Chute designed the exterior, then worked on the interior, first with Bentley, then, after Bentley fell out with Walpole, with Thomas Pitt (later Lord Camelford), another amateur who replaced Bentley on the committee and who 'drew Gothic with taste'. What Thomas Gray described as 'all Gothicism, and gold, and crimson, and looking-glass' was composed from the fan-vaulting of the side aisles in Henry VII's Chapel at Westminster, the north door of St Albans and the Bouchier tomb at Canterbury. William Vile's side-tables were loaded with various antiquities and were *en suite* with chairs and stools. The effect must have been dazzling, especially with the bright-crimson Norwich damask.

Beyond this gallery, via a vestibule, was the Round Room in the Round Tower, for which (perhaps surprisingly) in 1766 Robert Adam designed the 'Cosmati'-style chimney-piece, based upon the tomb of Edward the Confessor, and provided the decorative trim. This room was not finished until 1771. Off the vestibule towards the road Walpole conceived a room planned as a square in a quatrefoil covered by a fan-vaulted canopy. This was first called the Chapel, later the Tribune, and sometimes the Cabinet. Again, the effects of light were important. A star of yellow glass as an oculus in the vault threw 'a golden gloom over the room'. What started off as as an intended chapel was soon secularized when Walpole made it into a treasure cabinet of rare and exquisite objects. Finally came the Beauclerk Tower tucked in between the Round Tower and the north face of the Tribune. By now

Chute was dead, Pitt had gone elsewhere and the committee had been disbanded. In a sense this last addition marked a watershed, for it was a transition between the *ad hoc* approach of the committee of amatéurs and the professionalism of a different stamp of designer, in this case James Essex. If 1776 saw the completion of Strawberry as a physical entity, Walpole had also by then run his innovative race, and sensed it. The unillustrated *Description* of 1774 is really the moment when Walpole saw everything ready for public view.

By concentrating upon the house and its interior, the garden may be forgotten. In reply to a facetious comment by Mann in 1753 that he supposed the garden would also be Gothic, Walpole wrote:

> Gothic is merely architecture, and as one has a satisfaction of imprinting the gloomth of abbeys and cathedrals on one's house, so one's garden, on the contrary, is to be nothing but *riant*, and the gaiety of nature.

Although Walpole's gardening taste has been associated with that of Capability Brown ('Madame Nature' as Walpole called him), it was closer to the gardenesque tradition of rococo informality and compartition. Throughout the peripheral walk around pastures and lawn were appealing incidents, such as a Po Yang pool and borders of annuals, cascades and rills in a wood, the screened Prior's Garden full of flowers, or Bentley's huge Shell Bench. Indeed, with the lilacs, tulips, jonquils, acacias and syringas, Strawberry was as much a 'Kingdom of flowers' as Bateman's Old Windsor. The Thatched Brick Cottage could have been designed by Adam in 1765. Adorned with *treillage* and *agréments* from Paris, for a while it served as Kirgate's Printing House. There was the Chapel in the Wood, based upon Bishop Audley's tomb in Salisbury, and the Offices, first designed by Essex before his death in 1784, but redesigned by James Wyatt and built in 1791.

Strawberry Hill, inside as well as out, and of course its owner, cannot be assessed without mention of the consequences of the printing press, set up in 1757. Just as Walpole sought Gothic precedents for his architecture, so it pleased him that the Earls of Worcester and Rivers had been patrons of Caxton. The catalyst had been the pleasure experienced in preparing Bentley's *Designs for Six Poems* by Gay in 1753. At first printers came and went, but after 1765 the industrious Thomas Kirgate was printer and typographer of all Walpole's works.

Walpole was forty before he wrote for publication, and the real spur was his press and his personal printer. Now the stage was set for an extension of that early achievement of the *Aedes Walpolianae*; for Walpole as scribbler, cataloguer, anecdotist, memorialist, novelist and the author of his own guide to his house. It was natural to him to write at Strawberry, to see what he had written through the press (except for the explosive *Memoirs!*), and even to keep a Journal of the Printing House.

A corridor, Strawberry Hill

His first work appeared in April 1758, and was an immediate success: *A Catalogue of the Royal and Noble Authors of England, with Lists of their Works.* The style is conversational, as if dictated into a machine, and in this was like much of his writing, for he so often wrote as he spoke. Few books of the time were more readable, 'an entertainment worthy of a Roman epicure', as Lord Macaulay put it; or as Walpole himself wrote, something 'calculated for the closets of the *idle* and *inquisitive*'. Walpole drew upon his own library of these royal and noble authors, and immersed himself in an antiquarian dream of reliving their lives. Today we may recognize the triteness and bigotry of many of Walpole's opinions, as his essay on Bacon demonstrates, but there was nothing like these essays at the time, and he was, in his words, 'a door keeper at the Temple of Fame'.

He could not have imagined the furore of criticism and praise which was to

442

follow, and although his immediate reaction was never to put pen to paper again, hardly had the clamour died down than he was scribbling away for his *Fugitive Pieces in Verse and Prose*, a medley of mostly minor articles, essays and poems that appeared the same year. We can sense Walpole realizing the power of his pen with his Printing House at hand. He never had to plead his cause with a publisher.

It was natural that he should catalogue his own collection, and in 1760 *A Catalogue of the Pictures and Drawings in the Holbein Chamber* was printed; but he must have sensed the pace of the growing collection, and nothing more was produced until the unillustrated *Description of Strawberry Hill* in a small limited edition in 1774. He was constantly adding to his own copy in pen, and a shorter version was printed for the servants to guide visitors. An amplified *Description* was published with many fine illustrations in 1784. It is a model of the desire to inform, educate and enthuse, from which many a compiler of modern country-house guides could learn much.

This educating zeal was triumphantly expressed when Walpole took from his library the thirty-nine rough notebooks compiled by George Vertue over a lifetime of inquiry and observation. Walpole titled his five volumes *Anecdotes of Painting in England*, and they appeared between 1762 and 1771. Today no one would dispute the words of Lionel Cust in 1914 that they 'laid the foundations for an historical study of the Fine Arts in England, which to this day has proved the chief authority for reference upon this subject'. Lapses of judgement there may be, but Walpole's wide-ranging, eminently readable texts are still of paramount interest, not least for their observations on architects and insights into his own Gothic motivation.

It is very difficult to single out any work printed at Strawberry that does not reflect in some way Walpole's interests as incarnated by the house, but perhaps one does more than any other: *The Castle of Otranto*, printed in 1765 as translated by William Marshall 'from the original Italian of Onuphrio Muralto, Canon of the Church of St Nicholas, at Otranto'. So successful was it that Walpole had to confess authorship; and in a second Strawberry edition in 1811, he admitted that 'it was an attempt to blend the two kinds of romance, the ancient and the modern'. It was, he says, inspired by a dream of 'a gigantic hand in armour', no doubt similar to the armour that decorated the walls of his staircase. His master was Shakespeare, his castle, of course, Strawberry. It is extraordinary that there were twenty-one editions, including ones in Dublin, Paris, Amsterdam, Berlin and Parma, before 1800, and in this century alone there have been more than that number again. It is the most significant and compelling of all the early Gothic novels and is wonderfully constructed, so that the reader is transfixed by the text, moving from one exciting event to the next: from horrible trap-doors, clanking knights, persons stepping out of portraits, to frightening exposures, and the huge helmet with sable plumes that falls from heaven to crush the fifteen-year-old heir to Otranto. Walpole claims to have written it as a relief from the boredom of politics, but it is also a powerful criticism of the insipidity of the modern novel as represented by Richardson, or of the coarsenesses of Fielding and Smollett. It cannot be disassociated from a blank-verse tragedy called *The Mysterious Mother* that Walpole wrote in 1768, with its 'horrid' descriptions of double incest and much more that shocked the blue-stockings of his day. As Byron said in 1821, Walpole was the 'author of the first romance and of the last tragedy of our language, and surely worthy of a higher place than any living writer, be he who he may'.

All this is but a small part of his literary output, among which must be mentioned the *Memoirs* that Walpole ordered to be sealed from prying eyes until 1810. What is so compelling about the total literary achievement is how Strawberry is central to it all.

Strawberry was being built from 1748 to 1792. It became the most famous house in England. Visitors clamoured to see it, and better still to catch a glimpse of its owner. Yet curiously few illustrations were ever published for popular consumption, not even by the ubiquitous John Britton. The mystery that surrounded Strawberry was not unlike that surrounding Fonthill, and like Fonthill when the great sales occurred, Strawberry was opened up to public curiosity in 1842. But there was a decline in Strawberry's popularity around 1790; it belonged to an earlier era, and the later employment of James Essex and James Wyatt is significant. When Walpole saw Wyatt's Lee Priory (of *c.* 1785) he sighed that this 'child of Strawberry' was 'prettier than the parent', wistfully confessing that

> neither Mr Bentley nor my workmen had studied the science, and I was always too desultory and impatient to consider that I should please myself more by allowing time, than by hurrying my plans into execution before they were ripe. My house therefore is but a sketch by beginners.

And later he wrote to Mary Berry that his interiors were 'more the works of fancy than of imitation'.

Today we might describe Walpole as an amateur, designing his own house with an amanuensis, just as the 9th Earl of Pembroke acted with Roger Morris as architect. He would be scathing of the modern historians who labour for their doctorates, myopically motif-mongering Strawberry's fabric. Of them the ghost of Walpole might write acid memorials, scratching away with his pen in his library, the Thames Gothic-framed in the view, his dog at his feet: this most literary of men in one of the most literary houses in England.

IZAAK WALTON

SHALLOWFORD, NEAR STAFFORD

DAVID PROFUMO

In my experience, visiting shrines, like meeting heroes, can be a disappointing business, but Izaak Walton's cottage at Shallowford is exactly what one might expect. A modest, timber-framed building, tucked away by a little river, its rural seclusion would be complete were it not for the Manchester Intercity trains which whistle past the end of its garden; indeed, it was a spark from a steam-engine which, earlier this century, set fire to the thatch and caused so much damage.

On the day I visited it, the roof was being rethatched at great expense by the Stafford borough council (which now administers the cottage) and preparations were afoot for the annual garden party to celebrate Walton's putative birthday, 9 August. Walton was born in Staffordshire in 1593, and was fairly well known during his long life as what we would nowadays term a biographer. Yet thousands of admirers have made pilgrimages to this spot – the first Visitors' Book, dated 1924, records parties from as far away as Peiping, China – because of a little book about fishing which he first published in 1653. He would have been astounded.

Tradition has it that he was born at 62 Eastgate Street, Stafford, on a site now occupied by a police station. I have always preferred the theory that he was actually born in this cottage, which is why he purchased it in later life, but we simply do not know; ironically, for one of the first English biographers, details of his early life are obscure. His father, Gervase, was a 'tippler' or tavern-keeper, who died when Walton was four. His mother, Anne, married another tippler the following year, and the next we know of Izaak is that he was apprenticed to his brother-in-law, Thomas Grinsell, a prosperous draper in London, sometime between 1608 and 1613. He was made a Free Brother of the prestigious City Company of Ironmongers in 1618, and became a mercer in Chancery Lane.

Although Walton appears to have received little in the way of formal education, he seems to have enjoyed a minor reputation as a poet in his youth. He associated with leading writers like Donne, Jonson and Drayton, as well as Sir Francis Bacon,

the philosopher and former Lord Chancellor. Through his first marriage, to Rachel Floud, he was introduced to the descendants of Thomas Cranmer, and during his life he numbered many distinguished clerics among his acquaintances. There must have been something exceptional in the character of this untutored linen-draper which made him attractive to many of the intellectuals of his day. I suspect it was a combination of innate curiosity and a willingness to listen.

He prospered in trade, though his personal life must have been sad; Rachel died in 1640 and each of their seven children before her. In 1646 he married Anne Ken and they had two children who survived, Anne and Isaac. During the 1650s Walton began to acquire interests in Staffordshire property, including Halfhead Farm, on which his cottage was situated.

During the turbulent years of the Civil War and the Interregnum, Walton was involved in covert activities in support of the Royalist and Anglican causes; after the crippling defeat of their forces at Worcester in 1651, he retrieved an item of the Garter regalia called the Lesser George, conveyed it to the Royalist Colonel Blague (then a prisoner in the Tower) and thus helped its restoration to the exiled Prince Charles. In 1660 he became steward to his reinstated friend Dr George Morley, Bishop of Worcester and then of Winchester, and often stayed with him, his son (who became Canon at Salisbury) and his son-in-law, Dr William Hawkins, Prebendary at Salisbury.

Izaak Walton died on 15 December 1683 in Winchester and was buried in Prior Silkstead's chapel at the cathedral during a great frost. In his will, which was sealed with a ring given him by Donne depicting Christ crucified upon the anchor of Hope, he left two houses in London, a farm near Winchester, and his property at Shallowford. The latter was to pass to his son, or to the borough if Isaac did not marry before the age of forty-one. In the event it went to the town, as did a charitable provision 'to buie coles for some pore people ... in the last weik of Janewary or on every first weik in Febrewary ... the hardest and most pinching times'. His inventory also records the item 'Fishing Tackle and other Lumber – £10'. One can only speculate what this tackle would be worth today; apart from being the most famous fisherman who ever lived (and the sport enjoys a following of many millions world-wide), Walton's *The Compleat Angler* is one of the most reprinted books in the history of the English language.

Visitors to Shallowford can see a wide collection of Waltonian editions, along with displays illustrating the history of angling, the life of the author and the history of the cottage itself. While none of Walton's own tackle or furniture remains there, the interior preserves the ambience of his period. Originally two dwellings with separate entrances and twin chimney-stacks (the northern one being timber-framed),

Dovedale, where Walton used to fish

the cottage, with its large inglenook fireplace, remains modest – and as such it is a fitting shrine to an unassuming man.

It was probably Donne who introduced Walton to Sir Henry Wotton, the poet and former ambassador who was created Provost of Eton College in 1624. Although he had a first-class intellect, Wotton was a procrastinator when it came to writing. Amongst his numerous projects were a 'Life' of Donne, and a book about his recreational passion, which was angling. When he died in 1639 his projected tribute to Donne was unwritten, and his friend had to complete it in some haste. Thus it was that, at the age of forty-seven, Walton made his literary debut. His *Life of Donne* was the first of five Lives he published. His other subjects were Wotton himself, the Anglican apologist Richard Hooker, George Herbert and Bishop Sanderson. They were to be the cornerstones of his contemporary reputation.

The importance of these works is twofold. They demonstrate that Walton was no mere rustic revivalist who happened to write a book about rural pursuits that has endured as a period piece. They are significant contributions to the biographical form which was then in its infancy, and, in the case of Donne and Wotton, Walton's accounts are the closest original sources.

While they are by no means as dishevelled as the charming *Brief Lives* of his contemporary John Aubrey, Walton's accounts are undeniably idiosyncratic. He was more interested in character than the accurate recording of events, and tended to select the facts which suited his argument. It was his avowed intention to commemorate those aspects of his subjects which would present exemplary patterns to posterity. An example of this is his concentration on Donne's pious later life to the exclusion of his rakish earlier poems and lifestyle. His approach owes much to the seventeenth-century tradition of the 'character' sketch, in which the personality was filleted out from the storyline.

But of course these works are not his main claim to fame. It is time to turn to *The Compleat Angler* and to sing its proper praises. This is not as simple a task as one might assume, because Walton has been ill-served by the most well-meaning of his admirers; his reputation has been hijacked by piscatorial sentimentalists (and I write as an angler of some thirty years' devotion), and those who prefer to see him as a yokel rather than an artist. Another problem is that many of those who express opinions about the book have never actually read it. In fact, there is little trouble involved, for it is one of the most readable works of prose ever to have been published. In keeping with its intention of being 'a Recreation of a Recreation', it delights and entertains as much as it instructs and speculates. But there is more to it than meets the casual eye.

When the first edition appeared in 1653, it was an unprepossessing little octavo, bound in down-market sheepskin, suitable for popping into the pocket. It was published anonymously and cost eighteen pence. Today a first edition would cost you thousands of pounds. There have been more than 450 editions, and it has attracted some of the foremost editors, illustrators and printers in history. It has been parodied, abridged, praised, abominated and translated like few other works; it was even disastrously dramatized by a certain Charles Dance in 1839. Its standing diminished after its author's death, but it was revived in 1759 and has not been out of print since. Johnson (who is erroneously credited with a disparaging aphorism about angling being a matter of a pole with a worm at one end and a fool at the other) admired the book, knew many of its passages by heart and cited it in his *Dictionary* for everything from 'Brandling' to 'Culverkey'.

It went through five editions during Walton's lifetime, but it is generally referred to in its 1676 state. What happens is this: three protagonists – Venator (a hunter), Auceps (a falconer) and Piscator (an angler, generally held to be a personification of Walton himself) meet at Tottenham Hill one Mayday and start to debate the relative qualities of their passionate pursuits. The Angler and the Hunter, who becomes his pupil, proceed toward the River Lea at Ware, Hertfordshire, and spend five days laying siege to a variety of fish, enjoying songs during the evenings with the locals.

On the face of it, this is none too promising. Yet to generations of anglers this book has become a kind of bible, and its author been dubbed the patron saint of angling. The heyday of the Waltonian religion belongs to the early part of the last century, when his book was collared by the Romantics. Wordsworth addressed two sonnets to him; his characterization of Walton as a 'meek, thankful Soul' was typical of the way the book was classified as the work of an innocent genius whose spirit had triumphed over circumstance. In fact, Walton was a self-made man who mixed (if not exactly as an equal) with the great and good of his day.

There were detractors of his reputation, of course, including Byron, who labelled fishing 'the cursedest, coldest and the stupidest of sports'. He objected to the cruelty he perceived in the *Angler*, but it is interesting to consider his letter of 7 September 1814 in which he writes, 'I have caught a great many perch and some carp ...' Other objections concerned the extent to which Walton had borrowed from previous books on the subject – for there were many – the foremost written by the Cromwellian trooper Richard Franck, who sneered at Walton's politics in his *Northern Memoirs* (1658) and accused him of plagiarism, 'wherewith he stuffs his indigested octavo'. In fact, Walton acknowledges most of his sources, from Gesner to the influential *Arte of Angling* by William Samuel, and only the very dedicated scholar now consults Franck.

The truth about the *Angler* is that it is one of the most attractive of the thousands of books written on the subject. It is in many ways not original in its information,

Walton's cottage at Shallowford

but it demonstrates a passionate commitment to an inherently egalitarian pursuit. Angling has never been the preserve of princes, the sport of kings or the privilege of gentry. This is an important aspect of Walton's book.

We should consider the times in which it was written. Apart from the author's own domestic unhappiness, he and those who thought like him were facing a world turned upside down. A few years before the *Angler* appeared, the monarch had been executed. Many of Walton's friends were dispossessed clerics or Royalists who had fled from the cities during the regime of the Insurrectionists. *The Compleat Angler* opens its action on Mayday – an occasion for traditional fun and games, quite apart from any piscatorial considerations. In this respect it might be read as a subversive work.

450

A clue is to be found in the retirement theme which the book so carefully promotes. Unlike the country-house poems in whose tradition Jonson and Marvell wrote, Walton's book extols a communal pastime which has nothing to do with the husbandry of a private estate. His anglers meet on relatively equal terms, and the emphasis is on fellowship and thrift. The idyllic countryside he depicts was consciously presented, even then, as a thing of the past, a vanished order of Albion, belonging to a more innocent Elizabethan age. But this apparent nostalgia served a purpose beyond mere escapism. It was, in its way, a political statement.

To the outlawed Royalists and members of the Episcopalian community seeking refuge in the countryside, their compulsory retirement from city life was a form of isolation which Walton sought to enhance as sane and restorative. His idyll was written partly as a consolation to them, and partly as an antidote to the noisy world of the metropolis. The *Angler* can be read as a spell against turmoil and as a source-book of solace and hope. It is interesting that Gilbert Sheldon, the unofficial caretaker of the Anglican Church (and later its Archbishop), was himself a renowned angler – Walton alludes to his prowess with barbel – and that in the discreet letters Sheldon exchanged during this period with his circle of correspondents, there is much mention of the 'Brotherhood of the Angle' as a kind of punning code for the Anglican Church. This echoes Walton's insistence on the Christian aspects of the sport.

But the reason for its immortal fame is that the *Angler* is a book of quirky delights, partly an anthology of previous writings (it contains some three dozen poems and songs, as well as music and exceptional illustrations) and partly a repository of proverbs, natural lore, devotional allusions and fishy wonders. We read of tadpoles strangling pike, the medicinal value of carp-stones and how to concoct minnow-tansies. The writing is fresh and lively even today. Here is his encomium on the humble bleak: 'A Fish that is ever in motion, and therefore called by some the River-Swallow ... his back is of a pleasant sad or Sea-water-green, his belly white and shining as the Mountain-snow ...' One should not sentimentalize the image of Walton, but it is worth considering whether there is not still some merit in his homespun philosophy of 'Study to be Quiet'.

GILBERT WHITE

THE WAKES, SELBORNE, HAMPSHIRE

RICHARD MABEY

Are houses always vital influences in their occupants' lives, shaping and registering what goes on inside? Sometimes, I think, they function as little more than rudimentary moorings. Gilbert White, eighteenth-century clergyman and author of the best-known natural history book in the English language, lived in the same house (the Wakes) in the Hampshire village of Selborne for all but the first eight of his seventy-three years, and used it as casually as an old coat. It was convenient, cosy, loved as a matter of habit, but in the end more or less taken for granted. Despite forty years of writing journals and letters which are remarkable for their acute sense of place, he scarcely acknowledges his home base. Yet much of the important business of his life was carried on inside the Wakes. Somewhere upstairs – perhaps overlooking the stable-yard with its nesting house-martins, or looking out across the garden to the louring beechwoods – was the study where, for eighteen years, he conjured with the slow-growing manuscript of *The Natural History of Selborne*. Somewhere in the small T-shaped house were enough rooms to accommodate the vast numbers of relatives and friends that the bachelor curate entertained, and whose regular increase he logged contentedly among his gardening notes:

> Mrs Edmund White brought to bed of a boy, who has encreased the number of my nephews & nieces to 56. One polyanth-stalk produced 47 pips or blossoms.

For all this industry and bustle, the impression White gives of the Wakes is not so much of a home as an enthusiast's *pied à terre*. Sometimes it is an observatory or laboratory, sometimes a natural history curiosity in its own right, a *hybernaculum* (White's latinism for an animal's winter quarters) fascinating because of its responses to Selborne's turbulent weather. But mostly it was simply an anchor for a life lived

Selborne from the Hanger

453

somewhere else. Gilbert made no secret of where his heartland was. When he commissioned the Swiss artist Hieronymus Grimm to prepare illustrations for *The Natural History*, most were of the tangle of woods and tracks and sunken streams that made up the parish landscape. There were just two distant glimpses of the Wakes. They are nearly identical views, taken from the foot of the Hanger, the steep beechwood that rises to the west of the village. In the foreground are the Wakes' out-fields ('the Park') where the hay has just been cut and raked. Beyond the tall field-trees, the two-storey east wing of the Wakes is just visible, with White himself out in front, a tiny, self-effacing figure leaning on a stick.

One of the few heartfelt references he makes to the house in his writings is taken from a similar vantage point. When he was about twenty-five, and exiled on family business to the inhospitable flatlands of Cambridgeshire, he composed a nostalgic poem about his 'native spot' entitled 'The Invitation to Selborne'. The Wakes appears in the final stanza, glimpsed again from the Hanger, a green refuge in a wooded vale:

> Now climb the steep, drop now your eye below;
> Where round the verdurous village orchards blow;
> There, like a picture, lies my lowly seat
> A rural, shelter'd unobserv'd retreat.

Two centuries later, the Wakes still has an incidental, happenstance look, and has become something of a monument to the venerable architectural tradition of *extension*. What was a modest vernacular dwelling in the eighteenth century has been encrusted like a hermit crab with outgrowths and elaborations in half a dozen disparate styles. Seen from Gilbert's own viewpoint, on top of the Hanger, it is hard to credit it is a single house.

To the left (or north-west) is the 'billiard room' wing, built in a rather severe Tudor revival style in 1903 by Andrew Pears (who also added downstairs bay windows at this end of the house, and a second storey). To its right is the library built by Professor Thomas Bell, Professor of Zoology at King's College, London, and a White scholar, who lived in the house between 1844 and 1880. On the extreme right is the replacement dining, kitchen and servants' block put up soon after Gilbert's death by his brother Benjamin. Marooned in the middle of all these additions is the original cottage, a simple three-unit dwelling built from local malmstone sometime about 1500, and named after one of its early owners, a Mr Wake.

The house passed to the White family thanks to the foresight of Gilbert's grandfather (also Gilbert), who was vicar of Selborne from 1681 until his death in 1728. He bought the property as a security for his wife Rebekah, and when he died, she and her two unmarried daughters took up residence almost immediately –

an easy move since the Wakes lies just a hundred yards across the street from the vicarage. The daughters were married the following year, and Rebekah, finding herself with an empty house, invited her son John and his growing family to move in.

Gilbert, then nine years old, was John's eldest child, and already had five brothers and sisters. By 1733 eleven people were crammed into the Wakes. It was probably a cheerful enough atmosphere, especially for the six youngest Whites, who were then all under eight. But Gilbert was five years older than his oldest brother, Thomas, and must have become used to spending time by himself, especially in the Wakes' grounds and the countryside beyond. His father, John, had begun to replan the garden, but he seems to have been a withdrawn and inadequate character, and can't have been much company or help in the household.

Gilbert went to school in Basingstoke, then to Oriel College, Oxford, to study theology, and was finally ordained in 1746. But because the living of Selborne was with Magdalen College, not Oriel, he was never able to become rector of the village to which he was so emotionally attached. With no great conviction he took up official posts at Oxford and successions of temporary curacies in the Hampshire area. But his heart remained in Selborne, and increasingly his time was absorbed by a growing fascination with the natural world. The garden that his father had started became, in effect, his first field laboratory, and by 1751 he was recording his energetic work there in a journal he called the *Garden Kalendar*.

The garden he developed became a place which was both functional and floriferous. In borders underneath the dining-room windows he planted out crocuses and crown imperials, and wild plants transplanted from the Hanger. In the eastern half of the garden he built a south-facing fruit wall, and finished its coping with stones taken from Selborne's ruined medieval priory. (Parts of the wall still survive, and bear a plaque inscribed 'GW 1761'.) His orchard and kitchen garden took shape on a naturally raised mound known as Baker's Hill in the south-east of the garden, and were filled with more than forty different varieties of vegetable. He grew artichokes, white broccoli, marrowfat peas, scorzonera, skirret, squashes, and species like maize, wild rice and potatoes that had not long been introduced to this country.

But his greatest energy was reserved for what he referred to rather grandly as his 'melon ground'. Melons held a particular fascination for eighteenth-century growers, and in many ways seemed to symbolize contemporary attitudes towards the whole business of gardening. They were exotic, Gothic, and repaid technical ingenuity with huge productivity. Gilbert's hot-bed (also on Baker's Hill) was forty-five feet long, and had some thirty cart-loads of dung applied to it annually. And each year, as he went through the rituals of preparing the ground and nursing these temperamental fruits through to harvest, Gilbert seemed to become locked

The Wakes

in a personal struggle with the vagaries of the eighteenth-century climate. He built a thatched 'earth-house' to prepare and protect high quality mould for the fruits, devised ways of damping down the bed when it became over-heated, and built a sophisticated ventilation system for those melons that were in glass or oiled-paper frames.

There were more contrivances among the hedges and meadow grass of the park, where Gilbert had set down a series of follies and conceits: oil jars on nine-foot-tall pedestals, obelisks, an early bird-hide with a still-surviving brick walkway leading to it from the Wakes. In this he was following the fashion set by landscapers like William Kent. But some of his ornaments were so preposterous that they could well have been intended as landscaping parodies or puns. In May 1756 he cut a vista through the tall hedges in the out-fields, and ranged six gates so that they would be seen as receding images, terminating in a twelve-foot high figure of Hercules, painted on a board. Gilbert's life-long friend and correspondent, John

456

Mulso, confessed that he was overwhelmed by the growing elaboration of Gilbert's estate, and caught exactly the right note of tongue-in-cheek appreciation:

> You see me with my hand over my Brows & retiring to the prescribed Distance, I wave my head about, & take them in with a critical Survey ...

The serious point behind Gilbert's advanced gardening and landscape experiments is that they were all explorations of one of the central conundrums of the Age of Enlightenment: what was the proper relation between nature and humankind, and where should the line be drawn between productive wildness and disciplined culture?

In the end Gilbert, in his garden as in his writing, swept the whole notion of such a division aside – or at least underground. In 1761, the same year that he built the fruit-wall, he began work on the most significant architectural feature of the Wakes – the ha-ha between the garden and the park. He recorded the details meticulously in his Journal:

> Jan 24: Long the mason finish'd the dry wall of the Haha in the new garden, which is built of blue rags, so massy, that it is supposed to contain double the Quantity of stone usual in such walls. Several stones reach into the bank 20 inches. The wall was intended to be 4 feet 7 & an half high: but the labourers in sinking the ditch on inclining ground mistook the level, especially at the angle: so that at that part to bring it to a level it is 5 feet 8 inch: high, & 4 feet 6 inch: at the ends: an excellent fence against the mead, & so well fast'ned into the clay bank, that it looks likely to stand a long while.

The ha-ha was an ingenious device consisting of a ditch and sunken wall between garden and outlying farmland or pasture. It was intended to act as a boundary and keep cattle out of the flower and vegetable beds without interrupting the view. Ideally, it provided a way of visually (and to some degree philosophically) merging the garden with the wilder countryside. For White it meant an uninterrupted vista sweeping all the way from his neat borders to the hillside beeches, those 'most lovely of all forest trees'. This prospect of the Hanger must have had a lasting influence on Gilbert's attitudes towards landscape. It is constantly in view, and rises steeply 300 feet above the village, reducing the daylight of those who live in its shadow by up to three hours. (In 1792, the year before his death, Gilbert rather poignantly notes the February day when he 'began to drink tea by day light'.) But it was also a wild wood, full of ferns and orchids, where swallows and martins hawked for insects in the late summer, and where he once watched 'near 40 ravens playing about ... all day'. And rising like an intricate green parapet just a couple of hundred yards from the Wakes, it must have been a continual reminder that the vitality of nature lay in intimate detail and close-up, not in vague and grandiose vistas.

Despite all this outdoor enterprise, Gilbert undertook only one significant building project inside the Wakes. Inspired by his brother Harry's extensions in nearby Fyfield, he planned to create more space for visitors to the Wakes by building what he called his Great Parlour. Work began on 6 June 1777, and continued throughout the autumn. It was a considerable room, 23 feet long, 18 feet wide and 12 feet 3 inches high. Gilbert logged the progress of tiling, floor-laying and plastering in his *Naturalist's Journal* – and the times that work was held up by the weather. But by the New Year it was largely a matter of letting the room dry out, giving yet another opportunity for White the naturalist to take over from White the home improver. The plasterer, he believed, had skimped his work

> by improvidently mixing wood-ashes with the morter: because the alcaline salts of the wood will be very long before they will be dry at all; & will be apt to relax, & turn moist again when foggy damp weather returns.

On 28 January 1778 he notes:

> Frost comes in a doors ... Little shining particles of ice appear on the ceiling, cornice, & walls of my great parlor: the vapor condensed on the plaster is frozen in spite of frequent fires in the chimney. I now set a chafing dish of clearburnt charcoal in the room on the floor.

Fortunately there were drying winds throughout February, and the room was soon well aired. As the days grew longer, Gilbert allowed himself some satisfaction at the alignment of the room, and noted that 'the sun at setting shines into the E: corner'. The fittings and furnishings chosen for the room were lavish. The chimney-piece was '23 foot 7 in. of superfishal [sic] white and veined Italian marble'; there was a large looking-glass (costing £9.19s) and the room was finished with a 'fine stout large Turkey carpet' and 'flock sattin' wallpaper in light brown with a coloured border (debited in G.W.'s accounts at £9.15s). That summer, Gilbert's favourite niece, Molly, declared the parlour 'one of the pleasantest rooms I ever was in'. It continued, as far as one can tell, to play that role until the end of Gilbert's life.

The most recent act in the history of the Wakes began when the last private owner died in 1953. The following year an appeal was launched in *The Times* for funds to enable the house and grounds to be endowed as a memorial to Gilbert White. Sadly the appeal failed to raise sufficient money, and the Wakes was saved only because of a link-up between the White appeal and relatives of the Antarctic explorer, Captain Lawrence Oates, who were seeking a home for the family's memorabilia. The result was the successful, albeit incongruous, purchase and endowment of the Wakes in 1955 as a museum and library jointly devoted to White and Oates. In the years that followed the White museum became a focal point for a good deal of active natural history work, which culminated in the establishment of an educational Field Studies Centre in the old stableyard.

But more recently, influenced by the current fashion for 'heritage' restoration, there have been moves to redecorate the interior of the Wakes in eighteenth-century style. White's old bedroom has been opened up and furnished with a facsimile eighteenth-century bed. The Great Parlour is being restored to its original dimensions by the use of curtains, and there has been much repainting in contemporary colours and general tidying-up. Eventually the Field Studies Centre will be moved elsewhere in the village so that nothing compromises the historic profile of the building. The result is a clean, elegant and, in academic terms, 'authentic' interior, but one which feels quite lifeless. It is certainly hard to detect any echo of the busy curate, naturalist, host and countryman whose life and example is the only reason the house is of any interest, and whose attitude towards house decoration is summed up by the occasion he used hair-clippings from his dog Rover in 'plaster for ceilings'. ('His coat weighed four ounces. The N:E: wind makes Rover shrink.')

There is only the Hanger, that 'vast hill' that dominates the view through almost every window, to remind one that the important thing about the Wakes was not its bricks and mortar, but its position, and its role in the continuing experiment which White made out of his daily life. This architecturally unexceptional building would have been a splendid site to challenge contemporary fads, and interpret conservation not as a kind of historical mime, but as a tribute to the guiding spirit of a place. The Wakes would then have become a naturalists' haven again, crammed as it was two centuries ago with books, plants, insects, and inquisitive children gazing at swallows over the Hanger and young house-crickets swarming about the hearth.

VIRGINIA WOOLF

MONK'S HOUSE, RODMELL, E. SUSSEX

JEANETTE WINTERSON

I do not know whether pilgrimages to the shrines of famous men ought not to be condemned as sentimental journeys. It is better to read Carlyle in your own study chair than to visit the sound-proof room and pore over the manuscripts at Chelsea. I should be inclined to set an examination on Frederick the Great in place of an entrance fee; only, in that case, the house would soon have to be shut up. The curiosity is only legitimate when the house of a great writer or the country in which it is set adds something to our understanding of the books.

So began Virginia Woolf in her first piece of work to be accepted for publication. Her account of her pilgrimage to the Brontë home at Haworth appeared in the *Guardian* just before Christmas 1904.

It had been an eventful year; Virginia's father, Sir Leslie Stephen, had died after nine years of being cared for by his daughters, Vanessa and Virginia. Like most Victorian patriarchs, Sir Leslie assumed that after the death of his wife, the girls of the house would bury their lives in his. The boys, Thoby and Adrian, were expected to do as they pleased. There is no doubt that Virginia and Vanessa loved their father, but during his lifetime they were both painfully aware of how impossible it was to explore their own considerable talents, Virginia as a writer, Vanessa as a painter. In the third volume of Virginia's diary, her entry for Wednesday 28 November 1928 begins:

> Father's birthday. He would have been 96 today: and could have been 96 like other people one has known; but mercifully was not. His life would have entirely ended mine. What would have happened? No writing, no books; – inconceivable.

After his death, the Stephen children shut up the gloomy house at Hyde Park Gate and set themselves up in splendid freedom in Gordon Square. Here, in the closing months of 1904, they dined with Leonard Woolf, Thoby's friend from Cambridge.

Monk's House, Rodmell

Woolf was about to leave for Ceylon and a career in the Civil Service. It was almost seven years before he saw Virginia again and he returned to England with the express purpose of marrying her.

Virginia Stephen and Leonard Woolf were married in May 1912. She was thirty, he was thirty-two. Virginia's nephew and biographer Quentin Bell has called it 'the wisest decision of her life'. We may safely conclude that it was, too, the wisest decision of Leonard's.

They were well suited in temperament and ambition: both were absolutely committed to their work and neither worried very much about the everyday niceties of middle-class life. They were determined to live cheaply, although this did not include giving up the lease on Asheham House in the South Downs. They both enjoyed the Sussex countryside, and after Vanessa and her husband Clive Bell took the lease on Charleston Farmhouse nearby, the Woolfs hoped to find somewhere permanent of their own.

461

The sale was on Tuesday. I don't suppose many spaces of five minutes in the course of my life have been so packed with sensation ... the room at the White Hart was crowded. I looked at every face, and in particular every coat and skirt, for signs of opulence, and was cheered to discover none. But then, I thought, getting Leonard into line, does *he* look as if he had £800 in his pocket?

The hammer finally fell in their favour, and on a hot July afternoon in 1919 the Woolfs became the owners of Monk's House, Virginia 'purple in the face' and 'Leonard trembling like a reed'. They had paid £700.

What did it matter that Monk's House had no mains water? That it had neither gas nor electricity? The garden, about three-quarters of an acre at that time, was filled with mature fruit trees and brazen clumps of untamed flowers. There were vegetables set out in neat rows, canes of peas and beans, and in keeping with an orthodox tradition of gardening, yellow marigolds in between the cabbages. Virginia was especially delighted with the crowd of ramshackle outbuildings, one of which eventually became her study, although not 'a palace of comfort' until 1929.

Comfort was never very important to the Woolfs, and the visitor to Rodmell might be surprised by the simplicity of the furnishings and the very basic nature of the amenities. A hot water range and an oil-fired cooking stove were fitted after some years, but we know that the rough tiled kitchen floor ran with water when it rained. Rubber boots were highly valued by Virginia. When the Woolfs built their extension in 1929, they never quite managed to knock a door through into the main house, and so, for the rest of her life, Virginia trudged out through the kitchen door and off to bed. This night-time ritual was mirrored by the regular morning tramp to her study. For Virginia, the solitary hours of work and sleep were emphasized by a physical departure from the sociable comfort of Leonard and their friends. Since she could have chosen to both work and sleep in the main house, had she wished, it is worth asking what this cutting away gave her.

Most clearly, it gave her at least twelve out of every twenty-four hours alone. She slept, breakfasted on her usual egg, then went out through the garden to her study from about 9.30 am till 1.00 pm. In the afternoon she walked, often by herself, for an hour or two, criss-crossing the flats and down to the River Ouse.

It is a solitary picture, warmed by tea with Leonard and the evenings spent reading or listening to music by the fire. But it is the solitary picture to which we return. There is a particular intensity of concentration, unlike any other kind that I know, which is the living, breathing atmosphere of a writer and which can only come about when one is absolutely alone. There can be no shuffling in the hall or rustling in the next room. The sweet companionship of the beloved is not welcome. Especially not the sweet companionship of the beloved's typewriter. In those days there was no such thing as the discreet keyboard.

And so, Leonard scratched and clattered in the house and Virginia scratched

View of the garden

and clattered in her shed. Her divorce from domesticity while she worked was more vital to her than it ever was to Leonard, partly because of the difference in their sexes. We have to imagine, in Virginia, the young woman growing up in Hyde Park Gate, someone endlessly frustrated by the lack of privacy in that house. A developing writer without a room of her own, without even a desk that she didn't have to share. She talks of curling inside an armchair with a heap of books and willing herself invisible. But she was a girl, not a boy, and although Sir Leslie admired his clever daughter, he did not value her time. Again and again she was disturbed. She tells us, too, that the narrow confines of her bed were not her own; her half-brother George Duckworth was only too willing to slip in and cuddle his poor motherless 'sister'. Not odd then that Virginia Woolf, as soon as she was able, needed to mark out very determinedly the space for her work and the space for her dreams.

Her bedroom is the most interesting room on show at Rodmell (and there are only three and a half, plus the study, open). It is full of Virginia. First and foremost, her green paint. A sort of eggshell dog-kennel green seems to have been her passion on a grand scale and she was deeply hurt when all her friends continually made fun of this. It seems that she forced it on Leonard in the living-room and it has been re-matched in her bedroom. I rather like it and the sense that it meant so much to her. Here is a genius, an exquisite writer who knew the pitch of colours as assuredly as Van Gogh, burying her nose in a tin of green paint. We find one another in the little things.

It's a small room, sparsely furnished, a single bed, a chest of drawers, a table and chair. It has the feel of a den, with two large, low windows looking out, but so shaded by foliage that it would be tricky to look in. In the centre of the main wall is the fireplace, its surround tiled and painted by Vanessa Bell for her sister in 1930. A small boat sails towards a lighthouse. It can only be a recognition of one of Virginia's best books, *To the Lighthouse*, published by the Hogarth Press in 1927. The story doesn't matter, for Virginia was never very interested in plot. Her method was to properly convey the workings of the mind as it is charged by impressions, logical thought, unpredictable emotions, and ordinary things like the weather and one's friends. All this happens at once in the mind, but how to show it without becoming incoherent or contrived? The proper achievement of Virginia Woolf is that she was able to do this and still write poetically and still be readable. Her colleagues in similar experiments, James Joyce, Gertrude Stein, e. e. cummings (*The Enormous Room*), are now mainly read only by other writers and academics. Virginia Woolf's gift was more magnificent than theirs because she knew how to communicate. Snob that she was, she nonetheless wanted a fairly wide audience for her work, and she was never too grand to speak at working men's institutes, women's guilds or to eager undergraduates at the newly founded women's colleges.

The Woolfs were committed socialists, and Leonard spent all of his life working and writing politically, but it was not only a social conscience that made Virginia want to communicate. While she and Leonard really believed that good writing could make a difference, and accordingly founded the Hogarth Press, she was specifically concerned with developing the novel form. She wanted to unshackle language.

This determination was entirely different from that of James Joyce, whose manuscript *Ulysses* Virginia Woolf read in 1918. It is characteristic of Joyce that he felt that the Hogarth Press should devote all its resources to his cause. He was not concerned with either developing language or communicating; he wanted to bring language to a dead halt, to finish off the novel once he had smashed it up. Both

Virginia Woolf and her friend Katherine Mansfield (the only writer whose style Woolf envied) felt that there was something important about *Ulysses*; neither of them agreed with another friend and frequent visitor to Monk's House, T. S. Eliot, that the novel was a masterpiece. Virginia held the sensible view that great works of art should not be boring.

Standing quietly in the little bedroom at Monk's House, it is possible to reflect, as Virginia often did, on the turning points of her career. She was gleeful over her successes, wounded by her failures, everything coming to her vividly, painfully. She thought in colour.

If *Jacob's Room* (1922) marked out Virginia Woolf as an original voice and *To the Lighthouse* confirmed her genius, it was *Orlando* (1928) which brought her a far larger readership than anything before. She dashed the book off in a few months as a plaything and a love-gift to her friend and sometime inamorata, Vita Sackville-West. Vita, aristocratic and wayward and a more popular writer than Virginia, was married to the diplomat Harold Nicolson, with whom she lived at Sissinghurst Castle, Kent. Her marriage never interfered with her passion for women and Virginia was just one of a string of romantic friendships. Underneath this froth, which pretty much evaporated on both sides after about a year, was real affection. Virginia loved Vita for her abundance, her fecundity and a generosity of spirit that seemed to make room for life.

> She shines in the grocer's shop in Sevenoaks with a candlelit radiance, stalking on legs like Beech trees, pink, glowing, grape clustered, pearl hung.

Virginia was hooked, but she was still able to say that Vita wrote with 'a pen of brass'.

Orlando is an experimental novel that hoodwinked the public into thinking it was not. The public, wherever you find them, have a great antipathy to anything experimental. It worries them. *Orlando* has a heroine who changes sex, who travels through time. The style is dizzy with effect. There is no care for social realism or for sticking to a story. When Virginia gets bored with one track, she switches to another. Her language is as acrobatic as ever. But she got away with it. The public didn't even seem to mind that the early editions had photographs of Vita in various disguises.

Orlando is the right place to start for anyone beginning Virginia Woolf. Here it is possible to get comfortable with her method without having to work too hard. She never thought of reading as a passive act, and those who complain about how difficult she is are often suffering from a surfeit of the fast-food school of writing, where everything can be swallowed in five minutes and forgotten about.

If you care about Virginia Woolf's work, then the focus of your interest at Monk's House will probably be her study. Sadly this is the most disappointing room and

Bust of Virgina Woolf, by Stephen Tomlin　　　*Bust of Leonard Woolf, by Charlotte Hewer*

yields nothing of the atmosphere of her writing life. It was enlarged after Virginia's suicide in 1941 and used by Leonard's new friend and fairly constant companion, the artist, Trekkie Ritchie. Thus, you will be propelled into a dull antechamber to stare through a piece of glass into the original study. Her desk is there, and her blue writing paper and one or two other bits and pieces, but she is long gone. The sense of someone else having taken over that space is all too pervasive. Here is the writer behind glass, mummified, invented. I found it horribly depressing.

The only thing to do, when you have ogled into the goldfish bowl and dutifully noted the photograph display in the antechamber, is to go and stand in the garden and look at the view. To see what she saw. If you concentrate, then gradually the present will fade and the day trippers will fade, and you, with the peas and beans on your right and a pear tree beside you, will be able to narrow your eyes across the flats and catch the distant wind of the river under its sentry of trees. How often she saw this view; saw it every time she raised her eyes from her writing block, saw it and never saw, as the mind can do when wrapped in thought. But it was what she wanted, that long flat stretch with no man-made interruption to qualify her gaze.

It was to be the last thing she saw. On 28 March 1941, she sat in her study writing two letters; one to Leonard and one to Vanessa. Some time in the middle of the morning, she slipped them on to the mantelpiece in the house, then taking her stick, she walked as she usually did, through the garden, through the fields and down to the river. She put a heavy stone into her pocket and drowned herself.

It's a long way from the garden to the river and she had to walk every step of it. There was time to reconsider. It is true that she had suffered from mental instability throughout her life and that she had tried to kill herself many years before, but those times were always accompanied by raving and dislocation. She had not gone over the edge on the day of her death but she feared she had reached that edge again and that this time she would not recover.

Her letters to Leonard and Vanessa are sane, full of love and responsibility. I think that for her suicide was a rational decision and a brave one. She, who could imagine everything, could not imagine putting those she loved through another bout of madness.

In 1941 it seemed certain that Hitler would invade England. The Woolfs, who had permanently removed themselves to Rodmell to escape the Blitz, were only four miles from the coast and the steady procession of German bombers. More than once a hail of bullets drove them out of the garden. Leonard, as a Jew, had very specific things to worry about, while Vanessa at Charleston was billeting soldiers, trying to work, and involving herself in the war effort. What room was there for Virginia's madness and how would they have cared for her? She needed peace, proper food and vigilant medical attention, all in short supply.

This was the outer picture, oppressive enough for a thicker skin than hers, while the inner picture was one of depression and uncertainty after finishing her last novel, *Between the Acts*. She was exhausted. Under such circumstances, was she wrong to take her life into her own hands while she still could?

When the Woolfs moved to Monk's House, two elm trees stood side by side in the garden and these were immediately christened Leonard and Virginia. Her ashes were buried beneath one of them, but a great storm brought it down in 1943. It was about then that Leonard really did begin to lead a new life, spending more and more time at Monk's House and altering it according to his taste. Virginia never saw the long conservatory that now greets the visitor before he or she can pass through the door. I think it is fair to conclude that the Monk's House available to us is far more Leonard's house than it is Virginia's. Not even her books are on sale. Just a few postcards.

It doesn't matter. It's a funny occupation, wandering from room to room, hoping to catch something of the dead. We're superstitious to believe that a chair or a writing desk will yield up a vital clue, a new insight. The more we stare, the less we see. But we go on staring, perhaps to look death in the face, perhaps to persuade ourselves that nothing really passes away.

> I know that Virginia will not come across the garden from the lodge, and yet I look in that direction for her. I know that she is drowned and yet I listen for her to come in at the door. I know that it is the last page and yet I turn it over. There is no limit to one's own stupidity and selfishness. (Leonard Woolf, 28 March 1941)

WILLIAM WORDSWORTH

COCKERMOUTH, CUMBRIA
DOVE COTTAGE, GRASMERE, CUMBRIA
RYDAL MOUNT, AMBLESIDE, CUMBRIA

MELVYN BRAGG

William Wordsworth never owned any of the houses he lived in. The Lake District is littered with homes the poet inhabited; houses were planned and leased, but none was bought. That in itself is no small irony in the life of the most hearth-bound of English poets, a compulsive home maker, a man for whom home ground was sacred and essential.

If any place in England is the literary property of one man, then that property is Cumbria and that man is William Wordsworth. It seems very much as it should be that by words alone he enjoys ownership; in everything else he is a tenant, which tallies with the notion of the Romantic poet and with our knowledge, through his work, of the unbounded nature of his hold on the whole district, which became the paradigm for the whole of nature.

His sensitivity to place was profound. Yet, despite his search for security, something prevented him from investing in any of the houses he occupied. Lack of money in the earlier years and lack of need as good houses came on to the market to be leased are some of the mundane reasons for his refusal to purchase. Nevertheless, one senses that his poetry could not be tied down and needed freedom.

Homes figure in his life and work insistently. Few writers can equal the compulsive nature of his passion for place; but at the centre was the household. Wordsworth's domestic joys and tragedies have been well chronicled: there can be few more striking instances and even fewer more striking accounts of conjugal bliss, brotherly love and parental solicitude. His family was usually an extended one, further increased by friends who longed to be adopted, and the houses in which these lives intertwined were in turn interwoven not only with his own life but with his imagination. Wordsworth was a wanderer who sought out nature in order to bring it home: a perpetual traveller whose day's end was most often spent by his own fireside.

It is possible to draw from each of the houses he inhabited some clarifying notion

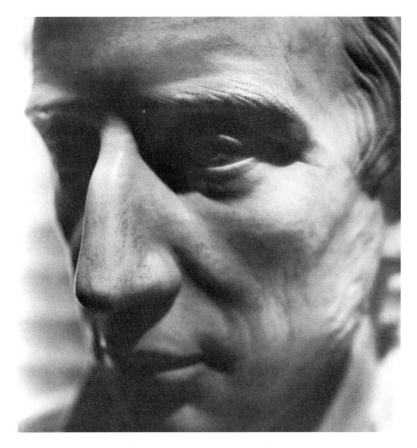

*Bust of Wordsworth, by Sir Francis Chantry, in the
Wordsworth Museum at Grasmere*

about that specific stage in the poet's work: the grand design of the Cockermouth house, signalling the amplitude and classical learning of childhood; the snug security and charm of Ann Tyson's cottage, where he stayed while at school at Hawkshead; Racedown and Alfoxden were stopping-places for the temporary exile; Dove Cottage, the haven and breeding ground for the adult poet's future; Allan Bank and the rectory in Grasmere, places of loss and pain; Rydal Mount, the culmination of his achievement.

His birthplace in the market town of Cockermouth is now called Wordsworth House. He was born in 1770, the second of five remarkable children. Richard the eldest, born in 1768, became an attorney; Dorothy, born in 1771, was one of the greatest diarists of any age; John, 1772, became the Commander of the ill-fated *The Earl of Abergavenny*; and Christopher, born in 1774, became Master of Trinity College, Cambridge. All the children were born in the same house.

Wordsworth's birthplace, Cockermouth

Their father was John, son of Richard Wordsworth, a lawyer from Yorkshire who became agent to Sir James Lowther. John, too, was a lawyer, and he also acted as agent to Sir James Lowther, a post which gave him a splendid house and bequeathed to his family years of unnecessary misery through the long withholding of monies owed by Sir James the 5th Baronet, created Earl of Lonsdale in 1794. Lowther himself was heir to scarcely imaginable wealth – land and, more especially, colossal profits from mineral mining and trading rights in west Cumberland; rights which he plundered and profits which he never re-invested in the land from which they derived. He boasted of owning nine Members of Parliament who did his bidding. He was described by a contemporary as 'truly a mad man, though too rich to be confined'. He built for his agent what remains the most imposing building in Cockermouth's main street. Pevsner called it 'quite a swagger house for such a town' and apparently the Wordsworths lived in it rent free. Nine windows wide at the front, with a garden that leads to the River Derwent, it appears an unlikely birthplace for a poet of plain men, humble creatures and modest pursuits.

Yet Wordsworth's connection with the local gentry can be underplayed. He always belonged to it and it supported him in cash and kind on several crucial occasions. There was also a nexus of culture, a grouping of remarkable families (the Christians, the Hutchinsons, the Daltons and others) in the Cockermouth district at that time and Wordsworth's expectations would have been tuned and perhaps directed by this. Nor is the connection with the Lowther family to be undervalued. To have direct access to the 'Emperor of Cumbria' – however feared – was rare. To be the object of his injustice after their father's death – the Croesian earl owed and refused to pay several years' wages – was a serious but educative threat to his family. To make up with the Lonsdales later, as Wordsworth did (he dedicated the *Excursion* to the then Earl), was a significant act of social reparation and intellectual accommodation. The big house in Cockermouth's main street, a town mansion then and now, stands for more than has been allowed. For everyone has virtually ignored the house and followed Wordsworth himself straight into the garden which borders the River Derwent. He took them there with some of his most seductive lines in *The Prelude* (1805–6):

> When, having left his mountains, to the towers
> Of Cockermouth that beauteous river came,
> Behind my father's house he passed, close by,
> Along the margin of our terrace walk.
> He was a playmate whom we dearly loved.
> Oh, many a time have I, a five years' child,
> A naked boy, in one delightful rill,
> A little mill-race severed from his stream,
> Made one long bathing of a summer's day,
> Basked in the sun, and plunged, and basked again
> Alternate, all a summer's day, or coursed
> Over the sandy fields, leaping through groves
> Of yellow groundsel; or when crag and hill,
> The woods, and distant Skiddaw's lofty height,
> Were bronzed with a deep radiance, stood alone
> Beneath the sky, as if I had been born
> On Indian plains, and from my mother's hut
> Had run abroad in wantonness, to sport
> A naked savage, in the thunder shower.
>
> Fair seed-time had my soul, and I grew up
> Fostered alike by beauty and by fear:
> Much favoured in my birthplace, and no less
> In that beloved vale to which, ere long,
> I was transplanted ...

472

The back of the birthplace seen across the Derwent

The small fields across the river are now largely occupied by a children's playground and new housing, but the Derwent still flows fast and clear, the pebbled walk is in place, the back of the house still retains the higgledy piggledy look so very much in contrast with the show front of a Lowther home.

Cockermouth is recorded by the poet almost entirely in terms of ravishment: 'Fair seed-time had my soul'. He attended a couple of gentle schools there. His father 'set him very early to learn portions of the best English poets by heart'. The deep affinity with his sister Dorothy dates from that time:

> The Blessing of my later years
> Was with me when a boy;
> She gave me eyes, she gave me ears,

473

And humble cares, and delicate fears,
A heart, the fountain of sweet tears,
And love, and thought and joy.

When he was eight his mother died and the family split up; the Cockermouth idyll was over, but was forever revisited for its visionary gleam in a childhood 'fostered alike by beauty and by fear'.

The interior of the house itself is altogether different, importantly different from the life as portrayed by Wordsworth. There is no wildness of a young savage here. Though there have been some later alterations, panelling removed, chimney-pieces added, and though the furnishing is not that which surrounded the knee high poet, there is more than enough about the place to give a firm impression of his first habitation. The rooms – dining-room, drawing-room, parlour – are grand, elegant and orderly. It is not difficult to recapture a place in which the parents occupied the larger rooms, the children marshalled and conducted by an ample cluster of servants. The language would be formal, though possibly heavily accented northern 'Upstairs', and broad Cumbrian, full of ancient dialect words and usages (but very strong on grammar) 'Downstairs'. There would be talk about the mad Sir James and gossip about the latest consequences of poor harvests, family misfortunes and malnutrition. Amid all this the children would be ferried as in a safe boat on a rough lake. The architectonic grandeur of the home is echoed throughout Wordsworth's life in the spaciousness of his more ambitious poetry. The great structure of *The Prelude* begins behind the gentleman's façade in Cockermouth. It is tempting to see the outdoors as an escape or at least a desired alternative, freedom from confinement, sensation not sublimation, action not manners.

The feature I most enjoy about the Cockermouth house is its plethora of window seats. From them you can see the Fells beyond the main street. In Dove Cottage at Grasmere, the hardest thing to imagine now is the clear view across to the lake, which has been blocked off by a Victorian development. Everything else about Dove Cottage is so resonant that the imagination need make little effort. Of course we know it housed not only Wordsworth but also Coleridge and was later rented by de Quincey. It took in Scott and Southey, saw the determined manifesto of the poet's life and work, bred great poetry, great prose and children. There is the landscaped mountain garden, the water from the well, the home-made candles, the chill buttery, the children's bedroom papered with pages of *The Times*, the miracle of accommodation – at one stage six adults, three children, guests, and five dogs were living in the few cabined rooms ... Perhaps it is this very accumulation of poetry and family in such a space which is at the centre of its identities. Or maybe it is because it was originally built as a pub, with old ships' timbers shaped for floorboards, the rooms snug for travellers and celebrants, that it still carries the

Dove Cottage from the garden

essence of hospitality with it. It could be the small rooms, hugging each other like an affectionate family. But it appears to lack anything to harm or overawe or threaten with pain or misery.

There are surprises. For someone who claimed to live as frugally as a hermit, Wordsworth, we discover, was willing to pay extra tax for extra windows, take the newspapers (at a price twice that of a day's wage for local labour) and indulge in tea, then 15 shillings a pound – say £50 in today's money. There was a servant, part-time but well worked. And although Walter Scott was so disgusted with a Wordsworth breakfast that he nipped off to the local hotel to enjoy a decent meal, the Wordsworths themselves seem to have eaten what would be regarded today as an exemplary diet.

Dove Cottage is a house of words and, above all, the words of a brother and a sister. It was at least as much Dorothy's house as that of her brother. And empathy and mutual devotion seemed to find its perfect setting in the former Dove and

475

A room in Dove Cottage which Dorothy lined with newspapers to keep out the damp

Olive Branch pub. The intensity of her observations and his perceptions, together with the stimulation of Coleridge, made Wordsworth the poet he became. His tribute to her giving him eyes and ears, humble cares and delicate fears appears to have been a sober and accurate acknowledgement of a truth in his life.

William and Dorothy arrived at the cottage at the end of 1799. The decision to return to the Lakes coincided with or confirmed his decision to strike out as a poet and a poet of destiny. In the first *Prelude* (1798–9), he had already outlined the way in which he had been chosen and prepared for the greater task ahead. In the poems written just before that, while in Germany with Dorothy, he had shown the brilliance and moving simplicity that his lyrical gifts could command. He came back to Grasmere well armed.

He had a great deal to prove. Almost thirty, he had no worldly prospects, a very small literary output (the *Lyrical Ballads* had come out in 1798, finding friends but making no immediate literary sensation), a bare but sufficient income which still threatened to break down in the face of unexpected demands, forcing calls on the charity of his friends or brothers; a man at the very end of youth with a great deal to achieve. At Dove Cottage he wrote 'Michael'; 'Ode: Intimations of Immortality'; 'Resolution and Independence'; several of his best-remembered short poems and the longer *Prelude*. Dove Cottage was a workshop.

John, the beloved naval brother, came to Grasmere and declared himself in love with it. Coleridge was persuaded north to join his friend and continue, as planned, to give and receive inspiration, encouragement and thought on the great purpose of writing poetry. Quite soon the house would welcome Mary Hutchinson as Wordsworth's wife, whom he had first met as a child in Cockermouth.

Dove Cottage is now flanked by a fine bookshop and backed by an excellent museum whose permanent collection is an intoxicating complement to the cottage. And of all the seats, that outside in the poet's summer-house still offers the best view of the landscapes and the man himself.

Rydal Mount was Wordsworth's final house. Between the cottage, which they left in 1808, and the Mount, where they went in 1813, were Allan Bank and the Old Vicarage, both in Grasmere Vale; smoking chimneys and general structural misery drove them from Allan Bank into the vicarage in 1811. There were then five children. Two years later there were only three; Mary's health and spirits were badly depleted; Wordsworth was financially overstretched and he needed to regain a reputation under siege by the *Edinburgh Review*. There was the terrific quarrel with Coleridge over an alleged act of betrayal of their friendship by Wordsworth. The move to Rydal Mount was seen as a relief all round. Seven of them went there: William, Mary, her sister Sara, Dorothy and the three surviving children, John, Dora and William. The adults were to live in the house for the rest of their lives.

In 1813 Wordsworth gained a reasonable financial income through his appointment as Distributor of Stamps in Westmorland, a situation obtained for him by Lord Lonsdale. This staunched the financial wounds and helped him to make a comfortable middle-class home for himself and his six dependants. He had brought some ease and eventually greater consolation to Mary and the house was, Dorothy declared, 'the nicest place in the world for children'. Although grandly situated and named, it was in truth a cobbled-together job, a farm cottage heaped up into a small country villa, nestling on the fells overlooking Rydal Water. From here he launched *The Excursion* in 1814, his great cannonade against his critics and the press, which would rally his admirers and make his fortune. It was a terrible, hurtful flop. There is a connection between the flop, the tax gathering job, the return of the Lonsdale connection and Rydal Mount. Byron led the younger poets' sniggering at Wordsworth 'being agreeable' . . . 'at dinner at Lord Lonsdale's'. Was this the revolutionary poet, the poet of common men and ordinary language, the democrat and idealistic leader?

> Just for a handful of silver he left us
> Just for a riband to stick in his coat.

Browning's opening lines in 'The Lost Leader' were cruel, but they expressed a view which has held sway among many serious critics ever since: that Wordsworth sold out. This coincided with the opening line of the *Edinburgh Review*'s comment on *The Excursion*: 'This will never do.' The responsibilities of domestic life, the distress of family bereavement, the difficulties of a financial shortfall – these are all admitted. But

> Bliss was it in that dawn to be alive,
> But to be young was very heaven!

– the poet of those lines has never been forgiven by some for what is seen as his disastrous move back into the establishment.

The explanation is more complicated and more interesting than that. It involves the long secret of the unpublished *Prelude*; the dreadful illness and exhausting nursing of Dorothy; and the by no means ignoble attempt to continue to develop a philosophical, then a religious tone fit for and fitted to the times. But there is some truth in the crude accusation too. The best way to see it is not as a betrayal of his youthful idealism, but as a return to his natural middle-class estate.

Rydal Mount has none of the external style of the Cockermouth house but inside it is the house of his parents' son. It is very like the house of a third-generation lawyer. And with another title a Wordsworth is still an agent for Lord Lonsdale. Rydal Mount is nothing like as grand as Cockermouth, but the aspiration is there, the example is clear. Just as Dove Cottage is the archetypal dwelling of a poet, Rydal Mount is the archetypal home of a local gentleman.

What is of great interest indoors is the memorabilia. The chairs in the dining-room worked by Mary, Sara and Dorothy; the Haydon portrait; and the statuette of the curious child in the drawing-room. Dorothy's bedroom is the most poignant and intriguing room in the house, not only because of her terrible illnesses at Rydal but because this space seems peculiarly resonant; quite simply, it is easier to imagine her here than anywhere else, except for Dove Cottage, where she inhabits all the rooms.

The glory of Rydal is in the garden, extended by Wordsworth but originally constructed by previous owners in the eighteenth century. Wordsworth's theories of landscape gardens were meticulously applied, which makes it a cunning arrangement of terraces and prospects – and of course there had to be his composing area, the famous terraces or gravel paths which aided and accompanied his composition.

The last thirty-seven years of Wordsworth's life are the most mysterious of all, and yet Rydal Mount gives few of the immediate clues that one can find when visiting the house in Cockermouth or Dove Cottage. Perhaps he became too public in Rydal, part of one of the sites of the relentlessly fashionable Lake District.

At the door of the house you can pick up a guide in any one of thirty-four languages, including Punjabi, Turkish, Persian, Chinese, Urdu and Esperanto. Rydal Mount appears a house without secrets, the domestic diagram of the achieved life. Yet a strategy is needed to take off the bland bandage and uncover what is too often dismissed as Wordsworth's arthritic surrender. Somewhere in or around Rydal Mount there must be the unexplored site of his struggle to remain a poet. Or is Rydal Mount only what it seems? Certainly the least of the houses; certainly the most in need of an idea, a truth more comprehensive than the accepted notion of intellectual stagnation, political betrayal and increasing moral pomposity. In that sense, it is the most puzzling of the houses of the poet who owned none he lived in.

W. B. YEATS

THOOR BALLYLEE, GORT, GALWAY

SEAMUS HEANEY

'What do you think of our address – Thoor Ballylee?' W. B. Yeats wrote to Olivia Shakespeare in 1922. 'Thoor is the Irish for tower and it will keep people from suspecting us of modern gothic and a deer park. I think the harsh sound of "Thoor" amends the softness of the rest.' Nowadays, those words – *Thoor Ballylee* – appear in bold lettering on the Irish Tourist Board's signpost, although it is unlikely that motorists on that particular stretch of road between Galway and Gort will ponder the phonetics of the name with the care and judiciousness of the tower's most famous tenant. A little further along the road towards Gort, on the right-hand side of the highway, another sign points past a modern estate into a long avenue of lime trees, leading towards the lakes and woods of Coole demesne, and to the site of Lady Gregory's mansion, Coole Park. The foundations of the mansion are all of it that remains, and they are buried under a raised level of greensward, the house itself having been vandalized in the 1930s and destroyed in the 1940s. The estate is currently managed by the Irish Forestry Board.

Visitors to these sites nowadays cannot fail to realize how successful Yeats has been in his ambition to make the places symbols of his work, 'plainly visible to the passer-by'. And yet, in spite of his devotion to tradition and stability, W. B. Yeats never did make a permanent home for himself and his family in any one chosen spot. It is true that he deliberately associated his life and work with Ireland, and that from the beginning of his career the west of Ireland was a vital imaginative backdrop for much of his writing, yet the majority of his days were lived at addresses in other places – Dublin, London, Oxford, Italy. Indeed, in a typically stirring and affirmative phrase, Yeats once boasted that he had no house but friendship, and the claim has a great deal of truth in it. Even the houses which figure most significantly in his *Collected Poems* – Coole Park and Thoor Ballylee – are not so much domestic situations as emblems of vocation and commitment. They were

Thoor Ballylee

481

symbols before they were amenities, and what they symbolized were the values and possibilities of culture, poetry, inheritance and love.

Yeats might equally have claimed to have had no home other than the country of Ireland as he had re-imagined it, transfigured by otherworldly presences, bathed in the associations of legendary heroes and happenings. Yeats lived, in other words, as much in the imagined place as in the topographical place, and the poetry he wrote has subsequently coloured the way we see his favoured landscapes: certain lake-shores, hillsides, skyscapes and mountains are now as unshakeably associated with his name as the battlements of his Norman tower at Ballylee. A century has passed since he brewed the special literary atmosphere he named 'the Celtic Twilight', and the actual country has undergone much political, economic and environmental change, but it nevertheless continues to retain a certain glamour and promise because of the poet's romantic effort. His whole *œuvre* is intended to act as a reminder of a previous, luminous, visionary Ireland that he passionately conceived of, impervious to change and irrespective of modernity.

In a way, therefore, it is possible to think of the whole of Ireland as 'Yeats Country', although the term is conventionally reserved for the solitary landscapes of County Sligo. Yeats knew this area as a schoolboy and a young man when he spent his annual summer holidays with his mother's and father's relatives. In fact, it would make more sense to think of Sligo as the '*Young* Yeats Country', because the older poet was powerfully involved with his second landscape, barer and greyer and farther to the south, in County Galway.

This countryside lay on the edge of the Burren, and spoke of the historical rather than the mythological realities. Here centuries of conquest and settlement, dispossession and displacement, were inscribed in the walled estates, unroofed cottages, Norman keeps and ruined abbeys, and here too the landmarks of a new era – the era of Irish independence – began to appear in the early 1920s in the shape of burnt-out mansions and celebrated sites of ambush. Any consideration of 'Yeats Country' must take account of this darker region on the psychic and cultural map, and set its evidence of destructive historical process against the visionary joys of the world seen through 'the collar bone of a hare'.

It is also worth noting that although Yeats was born in Dublin in 1865 in a semi-detached villa on Sandymount Avenue (it has a plaque but is not open to the public) and lived in town houses for the greater part of his life, the settings of his poems rarely reflect this. Dublin figures occasionally in his early mature verse as the domain of 'unmannerly' demagogues and acquisitive businessmen, and once (in 'Easter 1916') it is presented favourably as the locus of a great apotheosis in which the leaders of the Easter Rising are 'changed utterly' from being players in 'the casual comedy' of political squabbling into being a part of the 'terrible beauty' of heroic tragedy; but apart from these occasions, and Dublin's association with

William Butler Yeats

great patriotic names like Jonathan Swift or Wolfe Tone, the capital city held little imaginative appeal for the poet.

This lack of identification with the city of his birth was obviously due in part to the interrupted life he led there as the eldest child of an impoverished genteel family who were always on the move. He may have been born in the place but he did not grow up belonging to it. Yeats's father, John Butler Yeats, was an energetic but impractical parent, a man who abandoned a career as a barrister in order to devote himself to becoming a portrait painter. During the first two decades of the poet's life, this vigorous but unsuccessful figure shuttled wife and children to and fro across the Irish Sea, from one rented accommodation to the next, until they settled in London in 1888, in the relatively secure circumstances of Bedford Park. But Yeats's disinclination to make poetry out of his urban places was also deeply sanctioned by the Romantic tradition to which he always faithfully adhered, so his literary formation reinforced his ancestral connections to ensure that Sligo would be his 'land of heart's desire'.

At school in London, among children of the English professional classes, or walking in the parks and avenues of the suburbs, the young Yeats was acutely aware of his Irishness, and must have realized the bitter truth of his Sligo grandfather's warning that there (in England) he would be 'nobody' while here (in

Ireland) he was 'somebody'. The early chapters of his *Autobiographies* describe the circumstances of this divided life, the upshot of which was his epoch-making bid to integrate himself into the Irish literary movement and to found a poetic self upon the grounds of an Ireland that existed as much in his emotional being as in the actual scenes and contours of the countryside itself. This country of the mind was the one to which he returned summer by summer throughout his schooldays, and for many years after that. It lay between the mountain of Knocknarea to the south of Sligo Bay and the sterner promontory of Ben Bulben to the north, the former associated with Queen Maeve, the mythic queen of Connacht, and the latter with Fionn McCool and the heroes of the legendary Fianna; it formed a prospect of glens, lakes, harbours, islands and towns which would command his imagination throughout his life and would subsequently lay claim to his body after his death. Indeed, given that the fame of Yeats's grave in Drumcliff churchyard is far greater than that of the house in which he was born, his epitaph could well be revised to read 'In my end is my beginning': both his mother's and his father's families hailed from this region, and the site where he chose to be buried is deliberately situated between the symbolically maternal bosom of Maeve's Cairn on Knocknarea and the long patriarchal shadow cast by the more imposing cliff-faces of Ben Bulben.

In the Yeats household, however, cliffs were associated with mother rather than with father. When the poet was born, John Butler Yeats boasted that by marriage with the Pollexfens he had given a tongue to the sea-cliffs. Susan Yeats was indeed a withdrawn, unassertive presence, but her father's family, the Pollexfens, were turbulent, passionate and taciturn, in great contrast to the brilliantly talkative Yeatses. Susan's mother's people, on the other hand, were notably sociable and easygoing, and it was to these amiable Middletons rather than to the more eccentric Pollexfens that the young poet owed his first encounter with the country people of Sligo. When he stayed with the Middletons at Rosses Point, he would visit the cottages of fishermen and hear stories of ghosts and fairies, changelings and revenants, stories with an otherworldly dimension that would eventually pervade his own writing. His first major long poem, *The Wanderings of Oisin* (1889), and scores of his early short lyrics, such as 'The Stolen Child', share this haunted, inviting atmosphere: the names of local places like Sleuth Wood and Glencar and Rosses get translated into the remote and airy idiom of the fairy speakers:

Where the wandering water gushes
From the hills above Glen-Car,
In pools among the rushes
That scarce could bathe a star,

Glencar Waterfall

485

> We seek for slumbering trout
> And whispering in their ears
> Give them unquiet dreams.

Yeats's most famous Sligo poem, however, is entirely without fairies. 'The Lake Isle of Innisfree' is not only a universally known title, it is a place to be visited on Lough Gill, although the actual place will mean less than it should to the visitor who has not internalized the hankering nostalgic melody of the poet's lines. The poem was born out of an emotional nexus which combined traces of an early childhood adventure when he spent a night in the open on the shores of the lake with other memories of the homesickness he knew as a schoolboy in London; but the literary influence of Henry David Thoreau's *Walden* is also present, as is the powerful cadence of biblical prose, in that the opening line echoes the Prodigal Son's declaration at the end of his exile, 'I will arise and go to my father':

> I will arise and go now, and go to Innisfree,
> And a small cabin build there, of clay and wattles made:
> Nine bean-rows will I have there, a hive for the honey-bee,
> And live alone in the bee-loud glade.

The wandering rhythm of these lines owes something to the airs of Irish folksong which Yeats also heard in Sligo, a rhythm which makes its presence felt in other poems like 'Down by the Salley Gardens' and 'Red Hanrahan's Song about Ireland'. The countryside which these poems reflect, however, is much less ethereal, less bathed in languid atmospheres, more recognizably subject to the actual weather of the western Irish seaboard:

> The old brown thorn-trees break in two high over Cummen Strand,
> Under a bitter black wind that blows from the left-hand;
> Our courage breaks like an old tree in a black wind and dies,
> But we have hidden in our hearts the flame out of the eyes
> Of Cathleen, the daughter of Houlihan.

There is a certain coldness and hardness about these lines which represent the way Yeats's poems continued to develop over the years, away from what he called 'longing and complaint' towards 'insight and knowledge'. That knowledge would grow to include not only the fairyland wisdom of 'The Fiddler of Dooney' –

> . . . the good are always the merry,
> Save by an evil chance,
> And the merry love the fiddle,
> And the merry love to dance

– it would widen beyond those early poetic limits to include the doomed fates of the Anglo-Irish Ascendancy in the aftermath of Irish Independence. The Yeats of the late, great phase, for example, would be as tender towards the vanished culture of Lissadell, the home of the aristocratic Gore-Booths, as he had previously been towards the vanished folk beliefs of their humblest tenants. This Georgian mansion (built in 1840) was to become as much a part of the Yeats country as Dooney Rock or Drumcliff church:

> The light of evening, Lissadell,
> Great windows, open to the south,
> Two girls in silk kimonos, both
> Beautiful, one a gazelle.

Yeats had visited Constance and Eva Gore-Booth when he was a young man, long before Constance became the Countess Markievicz, and a heroine of the Easter Rising. He had been on the edge of that horse-riding, Big House society from the beginning, but it was not until the late 1890s that he was finally and fully admitted to the Ascendancy's way of life.

This eventually took place in the hospitable circumstances of Lady Gregory's home at Coole Park. Lady Gregory's milieu was admirable to him because it kept in place a 'dream of the noble and the beggarman' – the possibility of a traditional society in which hierarchy and tradition would remain benignly and mutually supportive. In fact, Yeats's suppression of the Dublin side of his experience represents a definite anti-modern, anti-democratic disposition in his sensibility, and this aspect of his work remains the obverse of his generous celebration of the positive side of life at Coole Park, its patronage and creativity and the dedication to cultural renewal which characterized the whole endeavour of Lady Gregory herself:

> Here, traveller, scholar, poet, take your stand
> When all those rooms and passages are gone,
> When nettles wave upon a shapeless mound
> And saplings root among the broken stone,
> And dedicate – eyes bent upon the ground,
> Back turned upon the brightness of the sun
> And all the sensuality of the shade –
> A moment's memory to that laurelled head.

This concluding stanza of 'Coole Park 1929' and the testimony of other poems such as 'The Wild Swans at Coole', 'Upon a House Shaken by the Land Agitation' and 'Coole Park and Ballylee 1932' constitute a powerful reminder of the central significance of Coole not only in Yeats's development as a poet, but in the history of modern Irish culture as a whole. The great figures of the literary revival, including the novelist George Moore and the dramatists J. M. Synge and Sean O'Casey, were all drawn to the place and were in part directed towards a unified purpose by the influence of Lady Gregory; and the physical evidence of all this is to be seen to this day in the shape of their initials, carved into the autograph tree in the walled garden of the estate.

It has often been observed that Coole gave Yeats delusions of aristocratic grandeur at a moment when he should have been concerned about the establishment of Irish democracy, and this is undoubtedly the case. He was susceptible to a certain foolish entrancement with 'carriage folk' (as George Moore called them) and was too ready to conflate the philanthropy of one good Galway landlord with the patronage of dukes in Renaissance Italy. This was what W. H. Auden meant when he called Yeats 'silly', but it was a silliness that went hand in hand with a totally commendable desire for the establishment in Ireland of a civilization that would be spiritually and materially enhancing for everyone. Yeats believed that the scientific philosophies and technological advances of the nineteenth century were ultimately destructive of any beatific possibility realizing itself in human society, and his reactionary predilections should be understood in the light of this visionary yearning, which never deserted him.

In fact, Yeats's need to promulgate his belief in the value of courtesy, ceremony, heroic steadfastness and harmonious decorum came to a climax at a time when the world was experiencing a traumatic breakdown of these ways in large historical convulsions extending from the trenches of the First World War to the revolutionary turmoil on the squares of Moscow. It was just at this moment that Yeats proceeded to 'set a powerful emblem up' in the shape of his restored Norman tower at Ballylee. The fact that the purchase of the building was in one way a domestic event – the place was a present of sorts for his new wife, George Hyde-Lees, whom he married in October 1917 – in no way diminished the tower's potency as a symbol within his imagination. For the remaining two decades of his life, Thoor Ballylee would persist as an enabling and amplifying poetic force.

It was in the course of an early visit to the Coole region in the 1890s (described in the essay 'Dust Hath Dimmed Helen's Eye') that Yeats first saw the edifice which would take on such fabulous significance in the years to come. That it was situated in Ballylee, that Ballylee had been the home of a famous beauty called Mary Hynes, that Mary Hynes had been made radiant in the Irish imagination by the words of the blind wandering poet Anthony Raftery – all that was marvellous and important.

But equally important was the fact that the tower was part of the Gregory Estate, that in 1916 it was being sold off by the Congested Districts Board (one effect 'upon a house shaken by the land agitation') and that the poet was able to buy the whole thing – an aristocrat's castle with a peasant's cottage symbolically attached –

for £35. It was the first home that Yeats personally owned and everything about it was resonant: it had been built as a Norman fortification in the thirteenth or fourteenth century, its ownership descended through the great family of the de Burgos, and it had been registered in *The Booke of Connaught* at the end of the sixteenth century. Inevitably, it retained an aura of past magnificence, and sponsored a haughty attitude and a high tragic style.

In a paper written to mark the tower's second restoration (by the Irish Tourist Board) in 1965, Mary Hanley documented the preparations and negotiations which surrounded the building and furnishing of the new dwelling. Her researches show that from the start Yeats's letters were informed with a large sense of occasion: the whole business was undertaken like a ceremonious action, and his relations with builders and architects were conducted in a heightened tone, as if he were a Renaissance Pope commissioning masters. A boozy professor of architecture becomes a 'man of genius'. The adjective 'great' begins to repeat itself like a mantra. Here he is, writing to John Quinn on 23 July 1918:

> We are surrounded with plans. This morning designs arrived from the drunken man of genius Scott, for two beds. The war is improving the work, for, being unable to import anything, we have bought the whole contents of an old mill – great beams and three inch planks and old paving stones; and the local carpenter and mason and blacksmith are at work for us. On a great stone beside the door will be inscribed the lines:
>
> > I, the poet William Yeats
> > With common sedge and broken slates
> > And smithy work from the Gort forge
> > Restored this tower for my wife George;
> > And on my heirs I lay a curse
> > If they should alter for the worse
> > From fashion or an empty mind
> > What Raftery built and Scott designed.

As it turned out, these lines were revised and a different version of the poem appears on the plaque beside the door. At the time, however, everything was a flurry of action, with Scott designing what his employer designated 'great' chairs and tables, and 'great' elmwood beds, and ceilings which would be painted with magical stars and angles, some of which are still to be seen in the restored castle. For a castle it was and 'castle' Yeats inclined to call it, as in the following letter to his father on 16 July 1919. By now his wife and young family had been able to move in but the passage conjures up not so much a family home as an Homeric chamber: the word 'hall', for example, gradually gives the place the amplitude of Thomas Moore's legendary Tara:

I am writing in the great ground floor of the castle – pleasantest room I have yet seen, a great wide window opening over the river and a round arched door leading to the thatched hall. There is a stone floor and a stone-roofed entrance-hall with the door to a winding stair to left and then a larger thatched hall, beyond which is a cottage and a kitchen. In the thatched hall imagine a great copper hanging lantern (which is, however, not there but will be I hope, next week). I am writing at a great trestle table which George keeps covered with wild flowers.

Three years passed between Yeats's purchase of the tower in 1916 and the summer of 1919 when he and George moved in; but even then, the residence was never to be permanent. Thoor Ballylee functioned as a kind of summer home, occupied occasionally by the family between 1919 and 1928, after which date they ceased to visit altogether. By then, Yeats's health was beginning to fail. Moreover, in 1928, the volume of poems entitled *The Tower* appeared and its sequel, *The Winding Stair*, had been conceived. The tower had finally entered so deeply into the prophetic strains of his voice that it could be invoked without being inhabited. He no longer needed to live in it since he had attained a state in which he lived *by* it.

Still, to call it a summer home is really slightly off the mark, since it is now obvious that the tower's first function was not domestic. It became one of the poet's 'singing schools', one of the soul's 'monuments of its own magnificence'. His other addresses were necessary shelters but Ballylee was a sacramental site, an outward sign of an inner grace. The grace here was poetry and the lonely tower was the poet's sign. Within it, he was within his own mind. The posture of the building corresponded to the posture he wanted to attain. The stone in all its obstinacy and stillness, the plumb drop and unshakeable profile of the keep made the actual building stones into touchstones for the kind of work he would aspire to. And that work would have to be a holding action in the face of old age, death and the disintegration of the old European civilization which he perceived in its decline.

One of the first functions of a poem, after all, is to satisfy a need in the poet. The achievement of a definite form and the utterance of a self-given music have a justifying effect within his or her life. And if the horizons inside which that life is being lived are menacing, the need for the steadying gift of finished art becomes all the more urgent. And so, it is in the light of just such a constantly flickering horizon of violence and breakdown that we must read the tower poems and much else of Yeats's work at this period.

The Easter Rising had occurred in Dublin a few months before his negotiations with the Congested Districts Board in 1916. The Battle of the Somme was fought that summer also. The Russian Revolution broke out in 1917. From 1919 onwards, the War of Independence was in full swing in Ireland, and between 1922 and 1923, the Civil War got close enough to Ballylee for the builder Raftery to get shot, the

The winding stair

491

bridge outside the tower to get blown up and for the mind of this most public-spirited of poets to be darkened by a sense of personal danger and civic collapse.

So it is no wonder that the plough was now set deeper into the emotional ground than ever before. If refuge within a medieval keep had given Yeats intimations of a new authoritativeness, the authoritativeness would not be credible to him until the poems were there to prove it, poems like ramparts built to show that he had survived the onslaught of menacing circumstances. Thrown back within a final personal ring of defence, he was forced into single combat with old age and with history, and he employed as weapons only those things which lay most adjacent to his hand or most indelibly inside his mind. In these circumstances, therefore, the ancient physical defences of the tower became analogues for the psychic fortifications he was determined to construct in his art.

For example, 'My House', the second poem in 'Meditations in Time of Civil War', begins and accumulates its force as a pile-up of nouns wrested from the air and placed like builder's blocks in a course of stonework. There are thirteen lines of dense affirmative word-chunks which convey a feeling of block-built strength, of gathered, battened-down, self-absorbed power:

> An ancient bridge, and a more ancient tower,
> A farmhouse that is sheltered by its wall,
> An acre of stony ground,
> Where the symbolic rose can break in flower,
> Old ragged elms, old thorns innumerable,
> The sound of the rain or sound
> Of every wind that blows;
> The stilted water-hen
> Crossing stream again
> Scared by the splashing of a dozen cows;
>
> A winding stair, a chamber arched with stone,
> A grey stone fireplace with an open hearth,
> A candle and written page.

This poem and the sequence of which it forms a part, and the other great sequence entitled 'Nineteen Hundred and Nineteen', are all ultimately about artistic faith, about trusting images and emblems, about holding fast, living in a fastness, fastening the mind upon the certain tragedy of one's extinction but still refusing, even in the face of that extinction, to cede the value of what Yeats calls elsewhere 'the spiritual intellect's great work'. The tower functioned as a concrete equivalent of that spiritual force.

In the title poem of *The Tower* volume, therefore, Thoor Ballylee is not just picturesque, nor is it simply emblematical of the menaced splendours of Anglo-Irish cultural heritage. It is rather a podium from which the solitary spirit's voice can be projected. In the third section of this poem, the tower's stoniness is communicated by the hard, clean-chiselled edges of the verse-form; its head-clearing airiness is present in the rise and enjambement of the three-stressed line. Inevitably, the tower continues to affiliate Yeats with the values of the Anglo-Irish Ascendancy and casts him as its self-appointed panegyrist. But it also marks an original space where utterance and being are potentially synonymous. This section of 'The Tower' so strives to transcend its personal and historical occasion that it reminds one of the exultation and absolutism of another tower-dwelling visionary, the German poet Rainer Maria Rilke. It was Rilke who declared in one of his sonnets to Orpheus that *Gesang ist Dasein*: singing is being, or song is reality – phrases that could easily stand as epigraph to Yeats's superb peroration:

> Now shall I make my soul,
> Compelling it to study
> In a learned school
> Till the wreck of body,
> Slow decay of blood,
> Testy delirium
> Or dull decrepitude,
> Or what worse evil come –
> The death of friends, or death
> Of every brilliant eye
> That made a catch in the breath –
> Seem but the clouds of the sky
> When the horizon fades;
> Or a bird's sleepy cry
> Among the deepening shades.

When he quartered himself and his poetry in Thoor Ballylee, Yeats was backed into an extreme existential position. He was being compelled by his years and his times to perceive himself as a solitary protagonist out in the mortal arena, and suddenly, in that needy space, a tower ascended. Yet by now that tower is as deep inside our hearing as the temple which Rilke (in another sonnet) imagines the god Orpheus building inside the listening consciousness of the creatures. Indeed, that sense of a temple inside our hearing, of an undeniable acoustic architecture, of the firmness and in-placeness and undislodgeableness of poetic form, that is one of Yeats's great gifts to our century; and his power to achieve it was due in no small measure to his purchase of an old Norman castle in Ballylee, a place that was nowhere until he wrote it into a second existence within his poems.

Ben Bulben from the churchyard at Drumcliff, Sligo, where Yeats is buried

Yeats's final home in Ireland was to be a house called Riverdale, at Rathfarnham, on the outskirts of Dublin. Even so, he and his wife continued to move around during the last years of his life, often for the sake of his health, and they were actually staying in the south of France when the poet died in January 1939. But all through the late poetry, Sligo and Ballylee continued to call him back. One of the greatest of his *Last Poems*, 'The Man and the Echo', is set in a glen called Alt, on the side of Knocknarea, and the poem which he was revising on his deathbed was the defiant and undaunted 'The Black Tower'. By then he must have been confident that he had indeed succeeded in 'rooting his mythology in earth'. Certainly the words of his most celebrated late poem ring out with pride and an utter trust in his ultimate earthly dwelling 'Under Ben Bulben':

Under bare Ben Bulben's head
In Drumcliff churchyard Yeats is laid.
An ancestor was rector there
Long years ago; a church stands near,
By the road an ancient cross.
No marble, no conventional phrase;
On limestone quarried near the spot
By his command these words are cut:

> *Cast a cold eye*
> *On life, on death.*
> *Horseman, pass by!*

LIST OF CONTRIBUTORS

Mary Archer was educated at Cheltenham Ladies' College, St Anne's College, Oxford, and Imperial College, London. She was Official Fellow and College Lecturer in Chemistry at Newnham College, Cambridge, and Lector in Chemistry at Trinity College from 1976 to 1986. She is married to Jeffrey Archer and their family home is the Old Vicarage, Grantchester.

Kenneth Baker has been a Member of Parliament since 1968 and has served in the governments of Edward Heath, Margaret Thatcher and John Major. He has been Environment Secretary, Education Secretary, Party Chairman and Home Secretary. He has edited four anthologies of poetry, including *The Faber Book of English History in Verse* and a collection of parodies called *Unauthorised Versions*.

A. L. Barker, FRSL, is the author of ten novels and nine collections of short stories and novellas.

Ronald Blythe is one of the editors of the New Wessex edition of *The Works of Thomas Hardy*, and also the editor of the Penguin Classics edition of *Far from the Madding Crowd*. He is an essayist, short-story writer, poet and critic, and his work includes *Akenfield*, *Divine Landscapes*, *The View in Winter* and *From the Headlands*.

Vernon Bogdanor is a Reader in Government and Fellow of Brasenose College, Oxford. He has written widely on historical and constitutional topics, and is at present preparing a book on 'The New British Constitution'.

Malcolm Bradbury is a novelist, critic, television dramatist and Professor of American Studies at the University of East Anglia. His novels include *Eating People is Wrong*, *The History Man*, *Rates of Exchange* and *Doctor Criminale*. His critical books include *The Modern World: Ten Great Writers* and *The Modern American Novel*.

Sarah Bradford was educated at St Mary's Convent, Shaftesbury, and Lady Margaret Hall, Oxford. Her books include *The Englishman's Wine: The Story of Port*, a classic on the subject; *Cesare Borgia*, inspiration for the BBC television series *The Borgias*; *Disraeli*, *Princess Grace* and *George VI*; and a biography of Sacheverell Sitwell, *Splendours and Miseries*.

497

Melvyn Bragg was born in Cumbria in 1939. He is Controller of Arts at London Weekend Television and editor and presenter of the *South Bank Show*. His novels include *For Want of a Nail, The Maid of Buttermere* and *A Time to Dance*; his non-fiction books include *Laurence Olivier* and *The Life of Richard Burton*.

Malcolm Brown was a BBC TV documentary producer from 1960 to 1986. He is co-author of *A Touch of Genius: The Life of T. E. Lawrence*; editor of *The Letters of T. E. Lawrence* and of *Secret Despatches of Arabia, and Other Writings by T. E. Lawrence*. He is also author of *Tommy Goes to War*, co-author of *Christmas Truce*, and author/editor of *The Imperial War Museum Book of the First World War*.

Ian Campbell is Professor of Scottish and Victorian Literature at the University of Edinburgh. He has published extensively on the Carlyles, and is one of the editors of the Duke-Edinburgh edition of the *Collected Letters of Thomas and Jane Welsh Carlyle*.

Thomas Crawford, Hon. Reader in English at the University of Aberdeen, is author of *Burns: A Study of the Poems and Songs, Society and the Lyric* and *Boswell, Burns and the French Revolution*, as well as of many articles on Scottish literature. He is at present editing the correspondence between Boswell and the Revd W. J. Temple for the Yale Editions of the Private Papers of James Boswell.

Anthony Cronin's most recent works include *The End of the Modern World*, a sequence of poems; and *No Laughing Matter: The Life and Times of Flann O'Brien*. For the past five years he has been cultural and artistic adviser to the Irish Prime Minister.

Margaret Drabble was born in Sheffield in 1939 and is the author of twelve novels, from *A Summer Birdcage* in 1963 to *The Gates of Ivory* in 1991. She is also the editor of the fifth edition of *The Oxford Companion to English Literature*.

Douglas Dunn's books of poems include *Elegies, Selected Poems* and *Northlight*. He has also edited *Scotland: An Anthology* and *The Faber Book of Twentieth-Century Scottish Poetry*. He is a Professor in the English Department of the University of St Andrews.

Gavin Ewart, the veteran British poet, born in London of Scottish descent in 1916, has published two main collections: *The Collected Ewart 1933–1980* and *Collected Poems 1980–1990*. He is also the editor of *The Penguin Book of Light Verse*. In 1991 he was awarded the Michael Braude Award for Light Verse by the American Academy and Institute of Arts and Letters.

U. A. Fanthorpe was born in Kent, educated at Oxford, and lives in Gloucestershire. She has been employed as a teacher (head of English at Cheltenham Ladies' College) and also, in the heady 1970s, as a receptionist (Burden Neurological Hospital, Bristol). Her publications are *Side Effects, Standing To, Voices Off, A Watching Brief, Neck Verse* and *Selected Poems*.

498

Penelope Fitzgerald was born in Lincoln, brought up in Sussex and London, and educated at Somerville College, Oxford. She is a member of the William Morris Society, and her first book was a biography of the painter Edward Burne-Jones. Her novel *Offshore* won the Booker Prize in 1979, and her last two novels, *The Beginning of Spring* and *The Gate of Angels*, were both on the Booker short-list.

Sibylla Jane Flower is the biographer of Edward Bulwer Lytton and the author of books and articles on British architecture, history and literature.

Michael Foot became a Labour Member of Parliament in 1945, representing the Devonport division of Plymouth until 1955. In 1960 he was elected for the Ebbw Vale constituency and retained this seat until he retired from parliament in 1992. He was leader of the Labour Party from 1980 to 1983. He has written extensively on Jonathan Swift, William Hazlitt and Lord Byron. Among his books, which include various essays on these subjects, are *The Pen and the Sword, Aneurin Bevan, Debts of Honour, Another Heart and Other Pulses, Loyalists and Loners* and *Politics of Paradise*.

Rebecca Fraser is the author of a recent biography of Charlotte Brontë. She is presently at work on a new biography of another nineteenth-century figure, Florence Nightingale. She is a contributing editor to *Vogue* magazine and reviews books for various newspapers.

Jane Gardam has a Yorkshire and Cumbrian background and her short stories, *The Hollow Land*, about life in north Westmorland, won the Whitbread Children's Book of the Year Award in 1981. Her other books include *A Long Way from Verona, Bilgewater, Crusoe's Daughter* and *The Queen of the Tambourine* which won the Whitbread Novel of the Year Award in 1992.

John Grigg was born in 1924 and educated at Eton and Oxford. He was the editor of the *National and English Review* from 1954 to 1960; a columnist for the *Guardian* from 1960 to 1970, and is now on the staff of *The Times*. He is the author of *Two Anglican Essays*; *The Young Lloyd George*; *Lloyd George, the People's Champion* (Whitbread Prize); *Lloyd George: From Peace to War* (Wolfson Prize); *Nancy Astor, Portrait of a Pioneer*; *1943, the Victory that Never Was*. He was Chairman of the London Library from 1985 to 1991.

Claire Harman won the John Llewelyn Rhys prize in 1990 for her biography of Sylvia Townsend Warner, whose diaries she is editing for publication.

John Harris has written many books on architecture and garden history. He is an international authority on architectural drawings and the founder of RIBA's Heinz Gallery. Since retirement he has devoted his time to the International Confederation of Architectural Museums, of which he is Hon. Life President.

Alethea Hayter, whose books include *Mrs Browning, A Sultry Month, Opium and the Romantic Imagination, Horatio's Version* and *A Voyage in Vain*, joined the editorial staff of *Country Life* on leaving Oxford, had a wartime job in Gibraltar, Bermuda and Trinidad, and subsequently worked for the British Council in Athens, Paris and Brussels. FRSL 1962, OBE 1970.

Seamus Heaney was born in Northern Ireland in 1939 and has made his home in the Irish Republic since 1972. A resident of Dublin, he teaches one semester each year at Harvard University and is also the current holder of the Professorship of Poetry at Oxford University. His *New Selected Poems* appeared in 1990, and he has since published a volume of poems, *Seeing Things* (1991), and a version of Sophocles' *Philoctetes* entitled *The Cure at Troy* (1990).

Robert Hewison has written a number of books on Ruskin, among them *John Ruskin: The Argument of the Eye* and *Ruskin and Venice*. He has published a three-volume history of the arts in Britain since 1939, and the cultural critiques *The Heritage Industry* and *Future Tense*. He has broadcast regularly on BBC Radio 3, and has written on the arts for the *Sunday Times* since 1981.

Richard Hoggart has been Professor of Modern Literature and Director at the Centre for Contemporary Cultural Studies, University of Birmingham; Assistant Director-General, UNESCO; and Warden of Goldsmiths' College, University of London. His books include *Auden, The Uses of Literacy, Speaking to Each Other, An English Temper, Life and Times* (3 vols.).

Michael Holroyd was born in 1935. He has written biographies of Hugh Kingsmill, Lytton Strachey, Augustus John and Bernard Shaw, and with Robert Skidelsky edited William Gerhardie's *God's Fifth Column*. He has been Chairman of the Society of Authors and President of English PEN.

P. D. James (Baroness James of Holland Park, OBE) was born in Oxford in 1920 and educated at Cambridge High School for Girls. She has published thirteen novels, eleven of which are traditional detective stories. She is a Governor of the BBC, a former member of the Arts Council of Great Britain and former Chairman of its Literature Advisory Council. She has been Chairman of the Society of Authors, and in 1987 chaired the judging panel for the Booker Prize for Fiction.

Glyn Jones was born in Merthyr Tydfil, Glamorganshire, in 1905. He is a novelist, short-story writer, poet, critic, translator and the author of *The Dragon Has Two Tongues*, an account of Welshmen writing in English, which contains a long essay on Dylan Thomas.

Alan Judd is the biographer of Ford Madox Ford, for which he won the 1991 Heinemann Award. His other works are novels: *A Breed of Heroes* (Royal Society of Literature Award), *Short of Glory, The Noonday Devil, Tango* and *The Devil's Own Work* (Guardian Fiction Prize).

Richard Mabey is a writer with a particular interest in countryside and natural history subjects. His life of Gilbert White won the 1986 Whitbread Award for biography and his other books include *The Flowering of Britain, The Common Ground* and his 'landscape auto-biography', *Home Country*.

Kate Marsh has worked for *The Times Literary Supplement*, Curtis Brown Ltd and the Arts Council of Great Britain. She is now working as a freelance editor.

Philip Mason spent twenty years in the Indian Civil Service, in which he was both a District Officer and Joint Secretary in the Defence Department of the Government of India. He retired in 1947 and wrote a number of books, including *The Men Who Ruled India, A Matter of Honour* and *Kipling: The Glass, the Shadow and the Fire*.

Elizabeth Mavor has written several novels (one of which, *Green Equinox*, was shortlisted for the Booker Prize), a biography of the Duchess of Kingston and *The Ladies of Llangollen*. She has edited a number of journals, including those of Fanny Kemble, Katherine Wilmot and *The Grand Tour of William Beckford*.

Michael Neve teaches the History of the Life Sciences and the History of Psychiatry at University College London and the Wellcome Institute, London. In 1989 he edited, with Janet Browne, *The Voyage of the Beagle* for Penguin Classics.

Tim Pigott-Smith is a graduate of the Bristol University Drama Department and the Bristol Old Vic Theatre School. He has worked extensively in regional theatre, played leading roles with the RSC and the National Theatre, in the West End and on Broadway. He has recently combined his acting career with that of director and artistic director. He is a frequent broadcaster who is internationally known for his work on television. His book *Out of India* was published in 1985.

Peter Porter is an Australian poet who has lived in England since 1951. In 1974 he presented a BBC Television programme in the series *Writers' Houses* on Newstead Abbey. He has made selections of Byron's verse and written critical articles on it. His books of poetry include *Collected Poems, The Automatic Oracle, Possible Worlds* and *The Choir of Babel*.

David Profumo was born in 1955 and educated at Magdalen College, Oxford, and King's College, London. His first novel, *Sea Music*, won the Geoffrey Faber Memorial Prize in 1989, and his second, *The Weather in Iceland*, appears in 1993. He was co-editor of *The Magic Wheel*, an anthology of fishing in literature.

Anthony Quinton (Lord Quinton) taught philosophy in Oxford until becoming President of Trinity College there (1978–87) and then Chairman of the British Library Board (1985–90). His chief publications are *The Nature of Things, Utilitarian Ethics* and *Thoughts and Thinkers*.

James Runcie is a television producer who specializes in making documentary films on literary subjects. He is also a freelance journalist and writes regularly for the *Daily Telegraph*.

C. H. Sisson was born in Bristol in 1914 and educated there and in France and Germany. He has in his time served as a sergeant in India and as an Under Secretary in Whitehall. He is a poet, translator, and critic. His books include *Collected Poems*, translations of Dante, Lucretius and Virgil, and *In Two Minds* and *English Perspectives* (essays).

Frances Spalding is an art historian and biographer. She is the author of *British Art since 1900* and *The Dictionary of Twentieth Century British Painters and Sculptors*, as well as biographies of Roger Fry, Vanessa Bell and the poet Stevie Smith. Her most recent book was *Dance Till the Stars Come Down: A Life of John Minton*. She is now at work on a biography of Duncan Grant and is the current editor of the *Charleston Magazine*.

Ann Thwaite has published a number of children's books and three biographies: *Waiting for the Party: the life of Frances Hodgson Burnett*; *Edmund Gosse: A Literary Landscape*, which won the Duff Cooper Prize; and *A. A. Milne: His Life*, which was the Whitbread Biography of the Year. She lives in a mill-house in Norfolk with her husband, Anthony Thwaite. *The Brilliant Career of Winnie-the-Pooh* was published in 1992.

Claire Tomalin is the author of biographies of Mary Wollstonecraft, Shelley and Katherine Mansfield, as well as *The Invisible Woman: The Story of Nelly Ternan and Charles Dickens* (winner of the James Tait Black and Hawthornden prizes and the NCR Book Award). She has been literary editor of the *New Statesman* and the *Sunday Times*, and is a frequent reviewer and broadcaster.

Jenny Uglow is Editorial Director of The Hogarth Press at Chatto and Windus. Her own books include *The Macmillan Biographical Dictionary of Women*, *George Eliot* and *Elizabeth Gaskell: A Habit of Stories*.

John Wain, poet, novelist, short-story writer, dramatist (particularly for radio), literary and social critic, biographer and autobiographer, was born in Stoke-on-Trent, Staffordshire, and has lived most of his adult life in Oxford while maintaining Staffordshire roots. His literary output, up to 1986, is detailed in David Gerard's *John Wain: A Bibliography*. From 1973 to 1978 he held the Chair of Poetry at Oxford University. He was awarded the CBE in 1984.

Harland Walshaw and **Peter Burton** contributed many of the photographs to the famous Shell Guides to the English counties, edited by John Piper and John Betjeman. Most recently they have worked closely with Henry Thorold on *Cathedrals, Abbeys & Priories* and *Ruined Abbeys*, and with Mark Girouard on *The English Town* and *Town & Country*.

A. N. Wilson's study of Sir Walter Scott, *The Laird of Abbotsford*, was published in 1980 and was awarded the John Llewellyn Rhys Prize. He has written twelve novels and biographies of Tolstoy, Milton and C. S. Lewis.

Jeanette Winterson is the author of *Oranges are Not the Only Fruit*, *The Passion*, *Sexing the Cherry* and *Written on the Body*. Her current work includes commissions for stage and screen.

GAZETTEER

Please check opening times and admission charges before setting out. It is advisable to verify all important details such as the extent of facilities for disabled visitors. Only properties where the house is accessible show the Disabled symbol (**Dis**), but often the gardens are accessible although the house is not.

The following symbols have been used to denote certain facilities or services:

P	Car parking	**C**	Café
G	Gardens	**L**	Lunches
S	Shop	**T**	Teas
Bk	Bookshop	**D**	Dogs accepted on a leash
Mu	Museum collection	**Dis**	Facilities for disabled visitors
Ma	Manuscript collection	**BR**	British Rail station
Sp	Special exhibitions	**LU**	London Underground station

Jane Austen

Jane Austen's House, Chawton, Alton, Hampshire GU34 1SD
Tel: (0420) 83262
Contact: Miss Jean Bowden
Owned by the Jane Austen Memorial Trust
Open Apr–Oct daily; Nov, Dec & Mar, Wed–Sun; Jan–Feb, weekends only. Closed 25 & 26 Dec.
Coach parties accepted with advance notice
Short introductory talk to groups
P G Bk Mu Dis
Off A31, 1m SW of Alton
BR Alton, $1\frac{3}{4}$m NE

J. M. Barrie

Barrie's Birthplace, 9 Brechin Road, Kirriemuir, Angus DD8 4BX

Tel: (0575) 72646
Contact: Mrs Karen Gilmour
Owned by the National Trust for Scotland
Open Easter weekend; May–Sep daily
Guided tours by arrangement
Mu T
On A926 in Kirriemuir, 6m NW of Forfar

Bloomsbury Group

Charleston Farmhouse, Firle, Nr Lewes, East Sussex BN8 6LL
Tel: (0323) 811626
Contact: Christopher Naylor (Director)
Owned by private trust
Open Apr–Oct (afternoons only), Wed, Thur, Sat, Sun, Bank Hol Mon & some summer Fri; Jul–Aug every Fri
Coach parties accepted by special appointment only
Guided tours, exc. Sun & Bank Hol Mon; summer school; festival

P G S Bk Mu Sp
Off A27, 6m E of Lewes
BR Lewes, 6m W; Berwick, 2m E

James Boswell

Auchinleck House, by Ochiltree, Ayrshire
  KA18 2LR
Tel: (0620) 842757
Contact: John Clare at the Scottish
  Historic Buildings Trust
Owned by the above
Exterior may be viewed
Open by appointment (house unfurnished
  at present)
Off A76 or A70, 5m S of Mauchline
BR Auchinleck, 3m E; Ayr, 15m W

The Boswell Museum, in mortuary chapel
  behind parish church, Auchinleck,
  Ayrshire
Tel: (0290) 20931
Contact: Mrs Chrissie Wilson, 88 Main
  Street, Auchinleck
Open by appointment
Mu
On A76
BR Auchinleck; Ayr, 14m W

The Brontës

Brontë Parsonage Museum, Haworth,
  Keighley, West Yorkshire BD22 8DR
Tel: (0535) 642323
Contact: Jane Sellars (Director)
Owned by the Brontë Society
Open all year daily, exc. Christmas & mid
  Jan–mid Feb
Coach parties accepted with advance
  notice
Lectures by arrangement; some weekend
  courses; audio-visual presentations for
  pre-booked groups only; library by
  appointment only
P G S Mu Ma Sp Dis
8m W of Bradford and 3m S of Keighley
BR Haworth

Rupert Brooke

The Old Vicarage, Grantchester,
  Cambridge CB3 9ND
The house is privately owned and is not
  open to the public

Edward Bulwer Lytton

Knebworth House, Knebworth, nr
  Stevenage, Hertfordshire SG3 6TY
Tel: (0438) 812661
Contact: Liz Wagstaff (Curator)
In private ownership
Open Apr–May, weekends & Bank Hols;
  end May–beginning Sep, daily; rest of
  Sep, weekends. Booked parties by
  appointment end Mar–Sep. Closed
  Mon exc. Bank Hols
Coach parties accepted with advance
  notice
Regular guided tours; specialized tours;
  guided tours by arrangement during
  closed period; audio-visual presentations
P G S Mu C L T D (only in Park)
Off A1 (M) signposted from J7 (Stevenage
  South)
BR Stevenage, 2m N

John Bunyan

Elstow Moot Hall, Church End, Elstow,
  Bedford, Bedfordshire
Tel: (0234) 228330
Contact: Sally Wileman (Cultural &
  Community Services Assistant)
Owned by Bedfordshire County Council
Open Apr–Oct, Tue–Sun & Bank Hol
  Mon. Groups by appointment at other
  times
Coach parties accepted
Guided tours by arrangement
P S Bk Mu Ma Sp
Off A6, 2m S of Bedford
BR Bedford, 2m N

Bunyan Meeting Church and Museum,
Mill Street, Bedford, Bedfordshire
MK40 3EU
Tel: (0234) 358870/358075
Contact: A. F. Cirket (Curator),
　71 Curlew Crescent, Bedford
Owned by Bunyan Meeting Church
Open: Museum, Apr–Oct, Tue–Sat, 2–
　4pm; Church, all year, exc. Sun, Mon &
　Bank Hols, 10am–4pm
In town centre
BR Bedford

Houghton House, Nr Ampthill,
　Bedfordshire
Tel: 071–973 3569
Contact: Richard Gray (Regional
　Presentation Manager)
Owned by English Heritage
Open all year at any reasonable time
Ruins, but site display on house's history
P D Dis
Off A418, 1m NE of Ampthill, 8m S of
　Bedford
BR Bedford, 8m N

Robert Burns

Burns Cottage, Alloway, Ayr KA7 4PY
Tel: (0292) 41215
Contact: John Manson
Owned by private trust
Open all year daily, exc. Sun in winter
Coach parties accepted
Guided tours by arrangement; education
　facilities
P G S Bk Mu Ma Sp L T D Dis
Off A719, 2m S of Ayr
BR Ayr, 2m N

Burns House, Burns Street, Dumfries,
　Dumfries and Galloway DG1 2PS
Tel: (0387) 55297
Contact: Dumfries Museums
Owned by Nithsdale District Council
Open Apr–Sep daily; Oct–Mar, Tue–Sat
Mu Ma
BR Dumfries

Ellisland Farm, Nr Dumfries, Dumfries
　and Galloway DG2 0RP
Tel: (038 774) 426
Contact: Mr & Mrs James Irving
　(Caretakers)
Owned by private trust
Open throughout the year at all reasonable
　times
Groups by appointment
P Mu Ma D
Off A76, 6m NW of Dumfries
BR Dumfries, 6m NW

Lord Byron

Newstead Abbey, Linby, Nottinghamshire
　NG15 8GE
Tel: (0623) 793557
Contact: Pamela Wood (Keeper) or Haidee
　Jackson (Assistant Keeper)
Owned by Nottingham City Council
Open Apr–Sep daily; by written
　appointment in winter
Grounds open all year, daily, exc. last Fri
　in Nov
Coach parties accepted
Guides on duty to answer questions;
　evening and winter guided tours by
　appointment; occasional lectures; audio-
　visual presentations
P G S Mu Ma L T
Off A60, 12m N of Nottingham

Thomas and Jane Carlyle

Carlyle's House, 24 Cheyne Row, London
　SW3 5HL
Tel: (0494) 528051
Contact: Anthea Palmer (Assistant Historic
　Buildings Representative, Thames and
　Chilterns Region)
Owned by the National Trust
Open Apr–Oct, Wed–Sun & Bank Hol
　Mon; closed Good Fri
Guided tours by arrangement
Mu
Off Cheyne Walk between Battersea and

Albert Bridges, or off Oakley Street
LU Sloane Square

Thomas Carlyle's Birthplace, Ecclefechan, Lockerbie, Dumfries and Galloway DG11 3DG
Tel: (0576) 300666
Contact: Mrs Nancy Walter
Owned by the National Trust for Scotland
Open Apr–Oct daily
Guided tours by arrangement
P Mu Ma
Off A74, 5½m SE of Lockerbie
BR Lockerbie, 5½m NW

Jane Welsh Carlyle Museum, Lodge Street, Haddington, E. Lothian EH41 4EE
Tel: (062 082) 3738
Contact: Mrs Pamela Roberts (Organizer, Lamp of Lothian Trust)
Owned by private trust
Open Apr–Sep, Wed–Sat
Coach parties accepted with advance notice
Regular guided tours and by arrangement
P G Mu
Off A1, 17m E of Edinburgh
BR Edinburgh

Winston Churchill

Chartwell, Westerham, Kent TN16 1PS
Tel: (0732) 866368
Contact: Mrs J. Broom (Administrator)
Owned by the National Trust
House, garden and studio open Apr–Oct daily, exc. Mon & Fri; open Bank Hol Mon, but closed following Tue. House only also open Mar & Nov, Sat, Sun & Wed
Coach parties accepted with advance notice
Guided tours by arrangement
P G S Mu L T Dis
Off B2026, 2m S of Westerham
BR Oxted, 5m W

William Cobbett

Willmer House, Museum of Farnham, 38 West Street, Farnham, Surrey GU9 7DX
Tel: (0252) 715094
Contact: Mrs Anne Jones (Curator)
Owned by Waverley Borough Council
Open all year, Tue–Sat
Coach parties accepted with advance notice
Guided tours by arrangement
G S Mu Sp Dis
Off A31
BR Farnham

Samuel Taylor Coleridge

Coleridge Cottage, 35 Lime Street, Nether Stowey, Bridgwater, Somerset TA5 1NQ
Tel: (0747) 840224
Contact: John McVerry (Assistant Historic Buildings Representative, Wessex Region)
Owned by the National Trust
Open Apr–Oct, Tue–Thur & Sun; by written application to custodian in winter
Mu
Off A39, 8m W of Bridgwater
BR Bridgwater, 8m E

William Cowper

Cowper and Newton Museum, Orchard Side, Market Place, Olney, Buckinghamshire MK46 4AJ
Tel: (0234) 711516
Contact: Doreen Osborne (Curator)
Owned by private trust
Open mid Feb–Nov, Tue–Sat & Bank Hols, exc. Good Fri
Coach parties accepted with advance notice
Introductory talks on Cowper; costume gallery; lace exhibition

P G Mu Ma (by prior arrangement)
On A509, 6m N of M1 J14

Charles Darwin

Darwin Museum, Down House, Luxted
 Road, Downe, nr Farnborough, Kent
 BR6 7JT
Tel: (0689) 859119
Contact: Solene Morris (Curator)
Owned by private trust
Open Jan & Mar–mid Dec, Wed–Sun &
 Bank Hol Mon
Groups by appointment only
Coach parties accepted with advance
 notice
P G S Bk Mu Dis
Off A233, 7m S of Bromley
BR Bromley South, 5m NE (then 146
 bus)

Charles Dickens

Dickens House Museum, 48 Doughty
 Street, London WC1N 2LF
Tel: 071–405 2127; Fax: 071–831 5175
Contact: Dr David Parker (Curator)
Owned by private trust
Open all year daily, exc. Sun, Bank Hols &
 Christmas week
Coach parties accepted
Guided tours, lectures and research
 facilities by arrangement; library and
 photographic collection
G S Bk Mu Ma Sp
LU Russell Square

Charles Dickens Birthplace Museum, 393
 Old Commercial Road, Portsmouth,
 Hampshire PO1 4QL
Tel: (0705) 827261
Contact: Rosalinda Hardiman (Keeper of
 Art)
Owned by Portsmouth City Council
Open Mar-Oct daily
S Mu
Off M275, in Portsmouth town centre

BR Portsmouth & Southsea

Bleak House Museum, Fort Road,
 Broadstairs, Kent CT10 1HD
Tel: (0843) 862224
Contact: L. A. Longhi (Curator/Owner)
In private ownership
Open Mar-Nov daily
Coach parties accepted
Guided tours by arrangement
G S Bk Mu D Dis
In centre of Broadstairs, near harbour
BR Broadstairs

Gad's Hill Place, Gad's Hill School,
 Higham, Nr Rochester, Kent ME3 7PA
Tel: (0474) 822366
Contact: Mrs A. Everitt (Headmistress)
Owned by charitable trust
Open during Rochester Dickens Festival
 in May & Dec. At other times after
 school hours or by arrangement at
 weekends
Coach parties accepted with advance
 notice
Special 'all-in' tours including bus ride and
 refreshments during Festival; lectures
 periodically
P G
On A226, 2m N of Rochester
BR Higham, $1\frac{1}{2}$ E; Rochester, 3 m S

Benjamin Disraeli

Hughenden Manor, High Wycombe,
 Buckinghamshire HP14 4LA
Tel: (0494) 528051
Contact: Anthea Palmer (Assistant Historic
 Buildings Representative, Thames and
 Chilterns Region)
Owned by the National Trust
Open Apr–Oct, Wed–Sun & Bank Hol
 Mon (but closed Good Fri); also open
 in Mar, Sat & Sun
Coach parties accepted on Wed–Fri with
 advance notice
Guided tours by arrangement

P G S Mu Dis
Off A4128, 1½m N of High Wycombe
BR High Wycombe, 1½m S

George Eliot

Arbury Hall, Nuneaton, Warwickshire
   CV10 7PT
Tel: (0203) 382804
Contact: Major W. D. Morris-Barker
   (Administrator)
Owned by the Viscount Daventry
Open Apr-Sep, Sun & Bank Hol Mon only
Private parties by appointment on most
   days
Coach parties accepted
Regular guided tours
Corporate hospitality functions
P G S Mu Ma Sp C L T D Dis
Off B4102, 2m SW of Nuneaton
BR Nuneaton, 2m NE

Elizabeth Gaskell

Tabley House, Knutsford, Cheshire WA16
   OHB
Tel: (0565) 750151
Contact: Peter Startup (Administrator)
Public Rooms managed by the Tabley
   House Collection Trust
Owned by the Victoria University of
   Manchester
Open Apr–Oct, Thur–Sun & Bank Hol
   Mon
Coach parties accepted with advance
   notice
Guided tours by arrangement
P S Mu T Dis
Off A5033, 1m W of Knutsford
BR Knutsford, 1m E

Tatton Park, Knutsford, Cheshire WA16
   6QN
Tel: (0565) 654822
Contact: David Hardman (Marketing
   Manager)
Owned by the National Trust (financed

and managed by Cheshire County
   Council)
House open Apr–Sep, Tue–Sun; Oct, Sat–
   Sun. Grounds open Apr–Oct daily;
   Nov–Mar, Tue–Sun
Coach parties accepted
Regular guided tours of Old Hall.
   Education facilities: lectures and
   weekend courses in gardening and art.
   Events every weekend
P G S Bk Mu C L T D Dis
Just off M6 J19 or M56 J7; off A50, 2m
   N of Knutsford
BR Knutsford, 2m S

Thomas Hardy

Hardy's Cottage, Higher Bockhampton,
   Nr Dorchester, Dorset DT2 8QJ
Tel: (0747) 840224
Contact: John McVerry (Assistant Historic
   Buildings Representative, Wessex
   Region)
Owned by the National Trust
Gardens only open Apr–Oct daily, exc.
   Tue. House by prior appointment with
   custodian
Coach parties accepted with advance
   notice
G Bk
Off A35, 3m NE of Dorchester
BR Dorchester, 3m SW

Max Gate, Dorchester, Dorset DT1 2AA
Tel: (0305) 262538
Contact: The tenants
Owned by the National Trust
Open by prior written appointment to
   bona-fide scholars and members of
   literary societies
BR Dorchester

Henry James

Lamb House, West Street, Rye, East
   Sussex TN31 7ES
Tel: (0892) 890651
Contact: Peter Battrick

(Regional Public Affairs Manager, Kent
and East Sussex Region)
Owned by the National Trust
Open Apr–Oct, Wed & Sat
G
Off A259
BR Rye

Samuel Johnson

Samuel Johnson Birthplace Museum,
Breadmarket Street, Lichfield,
Staffordshire WS13 6LG
Tel: (0543) 264972
Contact: Dr G. Nicholls (Curator)
Owned by Lichfield City Council
Open all year daily, exc. Christmas & New
Year Bank Hols
Coach parties accepted with advance
notice
Guided tours by arrangement; lectures and
audio-visual presentations
S Bk Mu Ma
BR Lichfield

Dr Johnson's House, 17 Gough Square,
London EC4A 3DE
Tel: 071–353 3745
Contact: Margaret Eliot (Curator)
Owned by private trust
Open all year daily, exc. Sun & Bank Hols
Coach parties accepted with advance
notice
Mu Ma
BR Blackfriars
LU Temple, Blackfriars, Chancery Lane

James Joyce

James Joyce Tower, Sandycove, Co.
Dublin
Tel: 0001–2809 265/2808 571
Contact: Curator
Owned by Dublin Tourism (Regional
Tourism Organization)
Open May–Sep; Oct–Apr by appointment

Coach parties accepted with advance
notice
Guided tours by arrangement
Bk Mu Dis
1m SE of Dun Laoghaire, off coast road
to Sandycove

John Keats

Keats House, Wentworth Place, Keats
Grove, Hampstead, London NW3
2RR
Tel: 071–435 2062
Contact: Mrs C. M. Gee (Curator)
Owned by London Borough of Camden
Open all year daily
Coach parties accepted
Guided tours by arrangement; lectures
S Bk Mu Ma
BR Hampstead Heath
LU Hampstead

Rudyard Kipling

Bateman's, Burwash, Etchingham, East
Sussex TN19 7DS
Tel: (0435) 882302
Contact: David Fox (Administrator)
Owned by the National Trust
Open Apr–Oct daily, exc. Thur & Fri, but
open Good Fri
Coach parties accepted with advance
notice
Working watermill
P G S L T
Off A265, $\frac{1}{2}$m S of Burwash
BR Etchingham, 3m E

D. H. Lawrence

D. H. Lawrence Birthplace Museum, 8A
Victoria Street, Eastwood, Nottingham,
Nottinghamshire NG16 3AW
Tel: (0773) 763312

Contact: Mrs Jane Lillystone
  (Museum Manager)
Owned by Broxtowe Borough Council
Open all year daily, exc. Christmas & New
  Year
Coach parties accepted with advance
  notice
Regular guided tours; audio-visual
  presentations
S Mu
Off A610, 7m NW of M1 J26
BR Nottingham

The Breach House, 28 Garden Road,
  Eastwood, Nottingham,
  Nottinghamshire NG16 3FW
Tel: (0773) 719786
Contact: Mr Lawrence Wright
Privately owned, but the house is available
  for lettings. Enquiries at the Birthplace
  Museum or from Blake's Holidays Ltd
  (0603 783221)
Open all year by appointment
Off A610, 7m NW of M1 J26
BR Nottingham

T. E. Lawrence

Clouds Hill, nr Wareham, Dorset BH20
  7NQ
Tel: (0747) 840224
Contact: John McVerry (Assistant Historic
  Buildings Representative, Wessex
  Region)
Owned by the National Trust
Open Apr–Oct daily, exc. Mon, Tue &
  Sat, but open Bank Hol Mon; Nov–
  Mar, Sun only
P D
Off A352, 1m N of Bovington Camp
BR Wool, 3m S

John Milton

Milton's Cottage, Deanway, Chalfont St
  Giles, Buckinghamshire HP8 4JH
Tel: (0494) 872313

Contact: T. G. May (Curator)
Owned by private trust
Open Mar–Oct, Tue–Sun & Bank Hol
  Mon
Coach parties accepted with advance
  notice
Short informative talk by Curator
P G S Mu Dis
$\frac{1}{2}$m W of A413
BR Gerrards Cross
LU Chalfont and Latimer, 4m N

William Morris

Kelmscott Manor, Kelmscott, nr Lechlade,
  Gloucestershire GL7 3HJ
Tel: (0367) 252486
Contact: Mr & Mrs D. Chapman
Owned by the Society of Antiquaries of
  London
Open Apr–Sept, Wed; also open Thur,
  Fri & some Sats for group visits by prior
  arrangement
P G S C
Off B4449, 3m E of Lechlade

William Morris Gallery, Lloyd Park, Forest
  Road, Walthamstow, London E17 4PP
Tel: 081–527 3782
Contact: Assistant Keeper
Owned by the London Borough of
  Waltham Forest
Open all year, Tue–Sat & first Sun of each
  month
Coach parties accepted with advance
  notice
William Morris lived in this house for eight
  years as a child, and it contains a large
  permanent exhibition of his work
Guided tours by arrangement
G S Bk Mu Ma Sp Dis
Off A503 and A112
LU/BR Walthamstow Central, then bus
  from bus park (Terminus C) down Hoe
  Street to the Bell Corner. Turn left into
  Forest Road and cross over to Lloyd
  Park

Alexander Pope

The Manor House, Stanton Harcourt, nr
 Witney, Oxfordshire OX8 1RJ
Tel: (0865) 881928
Contact: The Hon Mrs Gascoigne
In private ownership
Open Apr–Sep, irregular Thurs & Suns, &
 Bank Hol Mons, or by appointment
Coach parties accepted with advance
 notice
P G T D Dis
Off B4449, 9m W of Oxford, 5m SE of
 Witney

Chiswick House, Burlington Lane,
 Chiswick, London W4 2RP
Tel: 081–348 1286
Contact: Regional Presentation Manager
Owned by English Heritage
Open all year daily, exc. Christmas Eve &
 Christmas Day
Coach parties accepted with advance
 notice
Guided tours by arrangement
P G S Bk C D (only grounds)
Off Hogarth Roundabout between A4 and
 A316
BR Chiswick, $\frac{1}{2}$m SW
LU Turnham Green (then E3 bus)

Pope's Grotto, Pope's Villa, Cross Deep,
 Twickenham, Middlesex TW1 4QJ
Tel: 081–892 5633
Contact: St Catherine's Convent
In private ownership
Open by appointment Sat afternoons only
Entrance through the front door marked
 'Pope's Villa' in the main building
Off A310
BR Strawberry Hill, $\frac{1}{2}$m SW

Beatrix Potter

Hill Top, Near Sawrey, Hawkshead,
 Ambleside, Cumbria LA22 0LF
Tel: (053 94) 36269
Contact: Mike Hemming (Administrator)

Owned by the National Trust
Open Apr–Oct daily, exc. Thur & Fri, but
 open Good Fri
Coach parties accepted with advance
 notice
P G S
On B5285, 2m S of Hawkshead in hamlet
 of Near Sawrey, behind the Tower Bank
 Arms
BR Windermere, 6m NE

John Ruskin

Brantwood, Coniston, Cumbria LA21
 8AD
Tel: (05394) 41396
Contact: Bruce Hanson (Manager)
Owned by private trust
Open mid Mar–mid Nov daily; mid Nov–
 mid Mar, Wed–Sun
Coach parties accepted with advance
 notice
Guided tours by arrangement; lectures,
 video presentations; nature walks
P G S Bk Mu Sp L T Dis
Off B5285, $2\frac{1}{2}$m SE of Coniston on eastern
 shore of Coniston Water
Regular boat services from Coniston Pier
 to Brantwood

Vita Sackville-West

Sissinghurst Castle, Sissinghurst,
 Cranbrook, Kent TN17 2AB
Tel: (0892) 890651
Contact: Peter Battrick
 (Regional Public Affairs Manager, Kent
 and East Sussex Region)
Owned by the National Trust
Open Apr–mid Oct daily, exc. Mon
Coach parties accepted with advance
 notice
P G S Bk L T
Off A262, 1m E of Sissinghurst village
BR Staplehurst, 6m N

Knole, Sevenoaks, Kent TN15 0RP

Tel: (0732) 450608
Contact: Mr Fred Downer (Administrator)
Owned by the National Trust
Open Apr–Oct, Wed–Sun & Bank Hols, exc. Thur mornings
Coach parties accepted
Guided tours on Thur only for prebooked parties
P G S Mu C L T D (only in park) **Dis**
Off A225, 1½m SE of Sevenoaks
BR Sevenoaks, 1½m NW

Walter Scott

Abbotsford, Melrose, Roxburghshire TD6 9BQ
Tel: (0896) 2043
Contact: Mrs P. Maxwell-Scott (Owner)
In private ownership
Open mid Mar–Oct daily
Coach parties accepted
Regular guided tours
P G S Bk Mu T Dis
Off B6360, 2m W of Melrose

William Shakespeare

Shakespeare's Birthplace, Henley Street, Stratford-upon-Avon, Warwickshire CV37 6QW
Tel: (0789) 204016
Contact: Mr Roger Pringle (Director)
Owned by Shakespeare Birthplace Trust
Open all year daily, exc. Christmas, New Year and Good Fri
Coach parties accepted
Regular guided tours, lectures, weekend courses, audio-visual presentations
G S Bk Mu Ma Sp Dis
BR Stratford-upon-Avon

Mary Arden's House, Featherbed Lane, Wilmcote, Stratford-upon-Avon, Warwickshire CV37 0ER
Tel: (0789) 204016
Contact: Mr Roger Pringle (Director)
Owned by Shakespeare Birthplace Trust

Open all year daily, exc. Sun mornings 28 Oct–24 Mar, Christmas, New Year & Good Fri
Falconry flying displays daily; working blacksmith; occasional other craft demonstrations
Coach parties accepted
Regular guided tours
P G S Mu Sp L T Dis
Off A3400, 3½m NW of Stratford-upon-Avon
BR Wilmcote, ½m E

Anne Hathaway's Cottage, Cottage Lane, Shottery, Stratford-upon-Avon, Warwickshire CV37 9HH
Tel: (0789) 204016
Contact: Mr Roger Pringle (Director)
Owned by Shakespeare Birthplace Trust
Open all year daily, exc. Christmas, New Year & Good Fri
Coach parties accepted
Regular guided tours
P G S Bk L T
Off A439, 1¼m W of Stratford-upon-Avon
BR Stratford-upon-Avon, 1¼m E

Hall's Croft, Old Town, Stratford-upon-Avon, Warwickshire CV37 6BG
Tel: (0789) 204016
Contact: Mr Roger Pringle (Director)
Owned by Shakespeare Birthplace Trust
Open all year daily, exc. Sun mornings 28 Oct–24 Mar, Christmas, New Year & Good Fri
Coach parties accepted
Regular guided tours
G S Mu L T Dis
BR Stratford-upon-Avon

New Place/Nash's House, Chapel Street, Stratford-upon-Avon, Warwickshire CV37 6EP
Tel: (0789) 204016
Contact: Mr Roger Pringle (Director)
Owned by Shakespeare Birthplace Trust
Open all year daily, exc. Sun mornings 28 Oct–24 Mar, Christmas, New Year & Good Fri
Coach parties accepted

Regular guided tours
G Mu Dis
BR Stratford-upon-Avon

Bernard Shaw

Shaw's Corner, Ayot St Lawrence, nr
 Welwyn, Hertfordshire AL6 9BX
Tel: (0494) 528051
Contact: Anthea Palmer (Assistant Historic
 Buildings Representative, Thames and
 Chilterns Region)
Owned by the National Trust
Open Apr–Oct, Wed–Sun & Bank Hol
 Mon; Mar & Nov, parties by written
 appointment
Coach parties accepted with advance
 notice
Guided tours by arrangement
P G Mu Dis
Off B653, 2m NE of Wheathampstead; at
 SW end of Ayot St Lawrence
BR Welwyn, 5m E

Philip Sidney

Penshurst Place, Penshurst, nr Tonbridge,
 Kent TN11 8DG
Tel: (0892) 870307
Contact: Adrian Gilpin (Business Manager)
In private ownership
Open Mar–Oct daily
Coach parties accepted
Guided tours by arrangement
P G S Mu Sp L T
On B2176, 7m W of Tonbridge
BR Tonbridge, 7m W

The Sitwells

Renishaw Hall, Renishaw, nr Sheffield,
 S31 9WB
Tel: (071) 262 3939/(0246) 432042
Contact: Sir Reresby Sitwell
In private ownership

Open Apr–Sept by written application to
 Sir Reresby Sitwell
Gardens open Easter Mon & every Sun
 May–Jul
Guided tours given by the owner
Off A616 from M1 J30, 2m
BR Chesterfield 6m SW

Wood End, The Crescent, Scarborough,
 North Yorkshire YO11 2PW
Tel: (0723) 367326
Contact: C. I. Massey (Senior Museums
 Officer)
Owned by Scarborough Borough Council
Open all year, Tue–Sat & Bank Hol. Mon;
 end May–end Sep, also open Sun
Guided tours by arrangement
P Dis
Near town centre, 5 mins walk from
 railway station
BR Scarborough

Weston Hall, Towcester,
 Northamptonshire NN12 8PU
Tel: 029 576 8212 Fax: 029 576 8352
Contact: Mr Francis Sitwell
In private ownership
Open for group visits Apr–Oct by written
 application to Mr Francis Sitwell
Guided tours given by owner
Arrangements for refreshments can be
 made in advance
Off B4525, 10m NE of Banbury and 8m
 W of Towcester
BR Banbury, 12m SW

Laurence Sterne

Shandy Hall, Coxwold, North Yorkshire
 YO6 4AD
Tel: (034 76) 465
Contact: Mrs J. Monkman (Curator)
Owned by registered charity (the L. Sterne
 Trust)
Open June–Sep, Wed & Sun; other times
 by arrangement with Curator
Coach parties by appointment only
Regular guided tours and guided tours by
 arrangement

P G S Bk Mu Sp
Off A19, 10m SE of Thirsk, 20m N of
York

Robert Louis Stevenson

Lady Stair's House, Lady Stair's Close,
Lawnmarket, Edinburgh, Lothian EH1
2PA
Tel: 031–225 2424
Contact: Elaine Finnie (Assistant Keeper
of Social History)
Owned by Edinburgh District Council
Open all year daily, exc. Sun (unless during
Edinburgh Festival); closed Christmas &
New Year
Coach parties accepted with advance
notice
S Bk Mu Ma
Off the Royal Mile
BR Edinburgh Waverley Station

Dylan Thomas

Dylan Thomas Boat House, Dylan's Walk,
Laugharne, Dyfed SA33 4SD
Tel: (0267) 234567 ext. 221
Contact: Colin James (Head of Tourism &
Marketing)
Owned by Carmarthen District Council
Open all year
Parties and school tours by appointment
Coach parties accepted with advance
notice
Guided tours by arrangement; audio-visual
presentations; education facilities,
teachers' work-packs, art gallery.
G S Bk L T
On A4066, 4m SE of St Clears

Horace Walpole

Strawberry Hill, St Mary's College,
Waldegrave Road, Twickenham,
Middlesex TW1 4SX
Tel: 081–892 0051

Contact: Coralie Green
Owned by St Mary's College
Tours by prior appointment, but open
tours available Sun p.m. July–mid-Sep
Off A309/A316
BR Strawberry Hill

Izaak Walton

Izaak Walton's Cottage, Shallowford, nr
Stafford, Staffordshire ST15 0PA
Tel: (0785) 223181
Contact: Tourism Officer
Owned by Stafford Borough Council
Open Apr–Oct daily, exc. Mon; Nov–Mar,
Sat & Sun
Coach parties accepted with advance
notice
Guided tours by arrangement
P G Mu
Off A5013, 4m NW of Stafford
BR Norton Bridge, 1m N

Gilbert White

The Wakes, Selborne, nr Alton,
Hampshire GU34 3JH
Tel: (042 050) 275
Contact: Anna Jackson (Reception
Manager)
Owned by private trust
Open Mar–Oct daily, exc. Mon (unless
Bank Hol); Nov–Dec, Sat & Sun
Coach parties accepted with advance
notice
Short introductory talk to groups by prior
arrangement
G S Bk Ma Dis
On B3006, $4\frac{1}{2}$m S of Alton
BR Alton $4\frac{1}{2}$m N

Virginia Woolf

Monk's House, Rodmell, Lewes, East
Sussex BN7 3HF
Tel: (0892) 890651

Contact: Peter Battrick
  (Regional Public Affairs Manager, Kent
  and East Sussex Region)
Owned by the National Trust
Open Apr–Oct, Wed & Sat
G
Off A27, 3m S of Lewes
BR Lewes, 3m N

William Wordsworth

Wordsworth House, Main Street,
  Cockermouth, Cumbria CA13 9RX
Tel: (0900) 824805
Contact: Yvonne Osbourne (Custodian)
Owned by the National Trust
Open Apr–Oct daily, exc. Thur
Coach parties accepted with advance
  notice, but not Sun
Video display in old stables
G S L T
In town centre
BR Maryport 6½m NW

Dove Cottage, Town End, Grasmere,
  Cumbria LA22 9SH
Tel: (05394) 35547/35544/35003
Contacts: Dr Terry McCormick (Resident
  Curator)/Sylvia Wordsworth
  (Marketing Officer)
Owned by registered charity
Open all year daily (closed Christmas &
  mid Jan–mid Feb)
Coach parties accepted with advance
  notice

Regular guided tours; weekend and
  residential courses; education
  programme
P G S Bk Mu Ma Sp C L T
On A591, ½m S of Grasmere

Rydal Mount, Ambleside, Cumbria LA22
  9LU
Tel: (053 94) 33002
Contact: Mr D. Brookes (Curator)
In private ownership
Open Mar–Oct daily; Nov–Feb daily, exc.
  Tue
Closed last 3 weeks of Jan
Coach parties accepted
Introductory talk; information boards
P G S Bk Mu Ma D
Off A591, 1½m NW of Ambleside
BR Windermere, 7m SE

W. B. Yeats

Thoor Ballylee, Gort, Co. Galway
Tel: 0001-91 63081
Contact: Noel O'Rourke (Servicing
  Executive)
Owned by Ireland West Tourism
Open May–Sept daily
Coach parties accepted
Guided tours by arrangement; audio-visual
  presentations; education facilities; craft
  shop
G Bk Ma T D Dis
1m off N18 (Gort–Galway road), 1m off
  N66 (Gort–Loughrea road)

MAPS

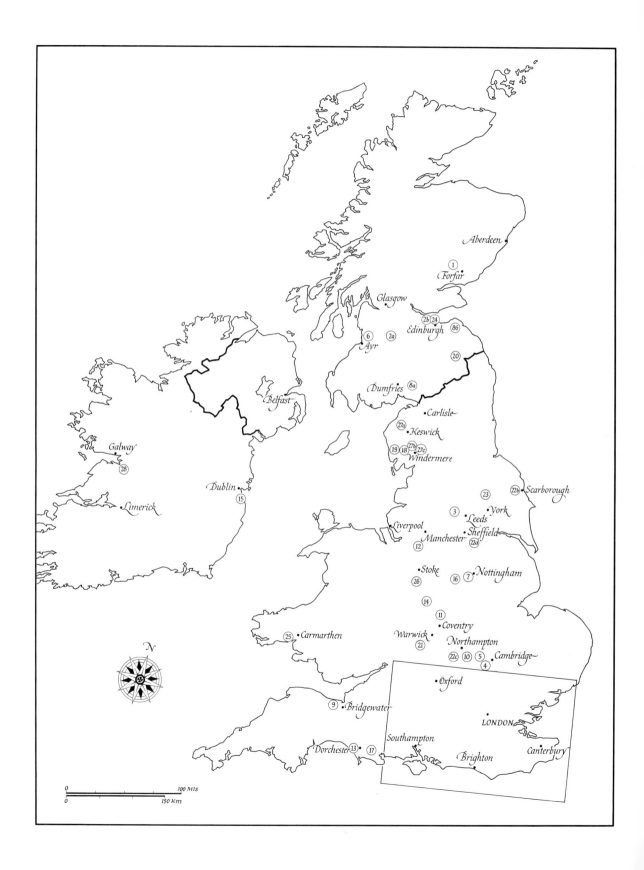

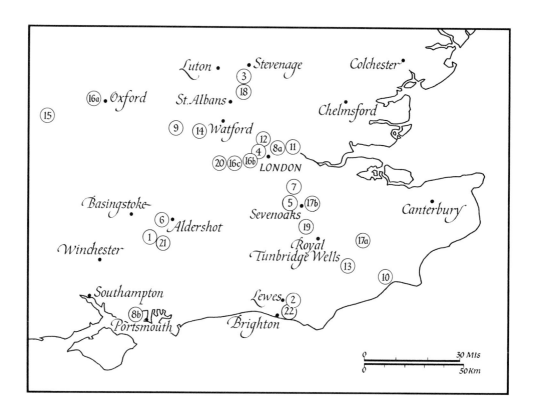

1   Jane Austen, Chawton
2   Bloomsbury Group, Charleston Farmhouse, Firle
3   Edward Bulwer Lytton, Knebworth House, nr. Stevenage
4   Thomas and Jane Carlyle, Cheyne Row, London SW3
5   Winston Churchill, Chartwell, Westerham
6   William Cobbett, Farnham
7   Charles Darwin, Down House, Downe, nr. Farnborough, Kent
8a Charles Dickens, Doughty Street, London WC1
8b Charles Dickens, Portsmouth
9   Benjamin Disraeli, Hughenden Manor, High Wycombe
10 Henry James, Lamb House, Rye
11 Samuel Johnson, Gough Square, London EC4
12 John Keats, Hampstead, London NW3
13 Rudyard Kipling, Bateman's, Burwash
14 John Milton, Chalfont St Giles
15 William Morris, Kelmscott Manor, Lechlade